The Anarchy of Naz

Out of the numerous books and articles on the Third Reich, few address its material culture, and fewer still discuss the phenomenon of Nazi memorabilia. This is all the more surprising given that Nazi symbols, so central to sustaining Hitler's movement, continue to live long after the collapse of his 12-year Reich. Neither did Nazi ideology die; far-right populists would like to see the swastika flown over the White House or Buckingham Palace. Against a backdrop of right-wing extremism, military re-enactors think nothing of dressing up in Waffen-SS uniforms and romanticising the Third Reich in the name of living history. Auctioneers are prepared to hammer down Nazi artefacts to the highest bidder, but who is buying them, and why do they do so? Should collectors be allowed to decorate their homes with Nazi flags?

The Anarchy of Nazi Memorabilia begins by examining the creation and context of Nazi artefacts and symbols during the volatile Weimar Republic to their wider distribution during the Third Reich. There were few people in Nazi Germany who did not wear a badge or uniform of some sort. Whether it be mothers, soldiers or concentration camp inmates, they were all branded. The chapter on the Second World War demonstrates that although German soldiers were cynical about being given medals in exchange for freezing in Russia. They still continued to fight, for which more decorations were awarded. A large proportion of this book is therefore given to the meaning that Nazi symbols had before Nazi Germany was eventually defeated in May 1945. Equally important, however, and one of the characteristics of this book, is the analysis of the meaning and value of Nazi material culture over time. The interpreters of Nazi symbols that this book focuses on are internationally based private collectors and traders. Sustained attention is given in a chapter outlining the development of the collectors' market for Nazi memorabilia from 1945 onwards. No matter how much collectors go out of their way to paint the hobby in a positive light, their activities do not fully escape the troubled past of the material that they desire. So contested are Nazi symbols that another chapter is devoted to the ethics and morals of destroying or preserving them. The issues surrounding private versus public custody and ownership of Nazi artefacts are also discussed. So far, in this book, the examination of Nazi artefacts has been restricted to physical objects within societies that are generally aware of the consequences of Hitlerism. As we increasingly move into the digital age, however, and there are few survivors of the Second World War left to relay their horrific experiences, the final chapter contemplates the future of Nazi symbols both digitally and physically, fake or real.

This book will appeal to all those interested in the Third Reich, Nazi ideology, Neo-Nazism, perceptions of the Nazis post-1945, modern European history and political symbolism. It will also hold particular appeal to those interested in the collecting and trading of contested and highly emotive artefacts. It considers aesthetics, authenticity, commodification, gift exchange, life histories of people and objects, materiality and value theory.

Michael Hughes obtained his Doctorate in Economic and Social History from the University of Glasgow in 2016. His life changed when he fully lost his eyesight in 1998. It gave him the opportunity, however, to change direction away from Quality Engineering and to devote more time to collecting military artefacts. He subsequently combined his academic ability and interest in the social life and function of military and political symbols to complete his doctorate and conduct further research, resulting in this book. He describes himself as a reformed collector and is doing his best to resist accumulating things.

I dedicate this book to my grandfather Adam Hughes (1922–2004), who served with the British army in North Africa and Italy during the Second World War. I would also like to mention my grandmother Catherine Rae (1926–1997), who worked in a factory that made munitions. It is because of both of them, and millions like them, most of whom regarded themselves as simply doing their bit, that we enjoy the freedoms that we have today.

Material Culture and Modern Conflict
Series editors
Nicholas J. Saunders
University of Bristol and Paul Cornish, Imperial War Museum, London

The Material Culture and Modern Conflict series adopts a genuinely interdisciplinary approach to re-appraise the material legacy of twentieth and twenty-first century conflict around the world. It offers a radical departure in the study of modern conflict, proving a truly interdisciplinary forum that draws upon archaeology, anthropology, military and cultural history, art history, cultural geography, and museum and heritage studies.

The Poetics of Conflict Experience
Materiality and Embodiment in Second World War Italy
Sarah De Nardi

Decoding a Royal Marine Commando
The Militarized Body as Artefact
Mark A. Burchell

Rediscovering the Great War
Archaeology and Enduring Legacies on the Soča and Eastern Fronts
Edited by Uroš Košir, Matija Črešnar, and Dimitrij Mlekuž

Material Cultures of Childhood in Second World War Britain
Gabriel Moshenska

Archaeologies of Hitler's Arctic War
Heritage of the Second World War German Military Presence in Finnish Lapland
Oula Seitsonen

The Anarchy of Nazi Memorabilia
From Things of Tyranny to Troubled Treasure
Michael Hughes

For more information about this series, please visit: www.routledge.com/ Material-Culture-and-Modern-Conflict/book-series/MCMC

The Anarchy of Nazi Memorabilia

From Things of Tyranny to Troubled Treasure

Michael Hughes

Routledge
Taylor & Francis Group

LONDON AND NEW YORK

First published 2022
by Routledge
2 Park Square, Milton Park, Abingdon, Oxon OX14 4RN

and by Routledge
605 Third Avenue, New York, NY 10158

Routledge is an imprint of the Taylor & Francis Group, an informa business

British Library Cataloguing-in-Publication Data
A catalogue record for this book is available from the British Library

Library of Congress Cataloging-in-Publication Data
A catalog record for this book has been requested

ISBN: 978-0-367-42200-4 (hbk)
ISBN: 978-1-032-16971-2 (pbk)
ISBN: 978-1-003-00061-7 (ebk)

DOI: 10.4324/9781003000617

Typeset in Times New Roman
by Apex CoVantage, LLC

Contents

Acknowledgements

I wish to acknowledge the assistance of those who have enabled me to complete this book, as without their time and commitment it would not have been possible to have done so. I especially thank the editors of the Routledge Series in Material Culture and Modern Conflict, namely Professor Nicholas Saunders and Paul Cornish for considering my initial proposal and for their subsequent help and sound advice. I also thank Robert Langham at Routledge for commissioning this book and for the help I received from his assistants Dana Moss and Tanushree Baijal. Louis Nicholson-Pallett, Routledge's editorial assistant for medieval and early modern history also provided assistance at the manuscript submission stage. This publication benefitted from a thorough external copy-editing process, although I am pleased to report that only light touches were required. I am grateful to the anonymous reviewers of my proposal and the timely way in which they provided valuable comments. I took them on board and this book is consequently all the better.

This publication ultimately stemmed from my doctorate awarded by the University of Glasgow in November 2016. I received expert supervision from Professor Raymond G. Stokes of the Department of Economic and Social History, and it is due to his patience and support that the Ph.D. was completed, as those with less stamina would have abandoned the arduous journey. Dr. Ben Shepherd of Glasgow Caledonian University was the external examiner, and his critique of the subject matter (particularly in the area of German military history) has also helped to shape the contents of this book. Professor Jeffrey Fear of Glasgow University was the internal examiner, and he encouraged me to stretch my interpretation of 'stuff.'

As a result of my sight loss, I have also had the assistance of German natives who read aloud inaccessible documents, which improved my German language skills. They were also able to contribute critical voices. Sophie Baumert supported me at the crucial stage of my Ph.D. submission, and as a result, the tight deadlines were met. She also assisted in proofreading this book in 2021 and offered valuable suggestions. My other assistant, Dr. Bernadette Mekker, read aloud numerous drafts of this book, and it is due in no small measure to her sharp mind that it is more focused.

Shona Robertson of the University of Glasgow's disability service ensured that my needs were met whilst I was studying at the university. Denise Curry, my liaison officer at the University of Glasgow's library, helped to facilitate interlibrary loans and continues to provide assistance. Lauren Trimble and Chris Bulin at JStor enabled me to access many inaccessible journal articles, which have informed the contents of this book. Casting further back, I would not have been ready to embark on this project had it not been for my M.Phil. at the University of Portsmouth, which was supervised by Professor Mike Kaye. It was in a statistically based subject area, and although this book does not directly relate to the qualification, its grounding in quantitative methods proved useful. The M.Phil. was a progression of my B.Sc. in Quality Engineering obtained from the University of the West of Scotland, and I am grateful to the late Professor William McEwan OBE for organising a one-year placement in Denmark as part of the qualification. Whilst I was in the country, I took the opportunity to visit military museums, as well as antiques and militaria fairs, and I am grateful for this international experience, especially at a time when I still had sight. Having said this, my subsequent sight loss meant that I was able to approach my Ph.D. by utilising my other senses. I can say that had I still had sight, I would probably not have been able to interpret the artefacts discussed in this book in such a critically detached manner. During my first meeting with Professor Stokes, he said that he did not want to end up with a 'badge book', and I can thankfully say my Doctorate was certainly not that, and neither is this publication.

I especially thank my parents, Mary Teresa and Grant, who read the numerous drafts of my manuscript aloud, and their unpaid labour is greatly appreciated, as without their assistance this book would not have been completed. I also thank the many collectors and traders who agreed to do interviews, most of whom are acknowledged throughout the text. I apologise to those whose comments are not explicitly cited, but they provided context. I am also grateful for the assistance of the Institute of Contemporary History in Munich and to my assistant at the time, Stephanie Wiche, who read aloud and translated primary documents. I also thank Richard Winkler at the Bavarian Economic Archive, who supplied scarce primary documents relating to a medal and badge firm based in Munich. Despite the contributions of others, I bear all responsibility for the contents of this book, as well as its conclusions. Due to the careful and considered way in which it was written, it should be able to withstand the passage of time.

Illustrations

Note that if the term 'replica' is not used in the following captions, the badges were acquired by the author as authentic artefacts from the collectors' market in the U.K. and Germany over the last 30 years for nominal amounts. The dates beside each of the badges indicate when they were instituted.

Chapter 4

Chapter 5

Chapter 6

Chapter 7

Series Introduction

Material Culture and Modern Conflict

Modern warfare is a unique cultural phenomenon. While many conflicts in history have produced dramatic shifts in human behaviour, the industrialised nature of modern war possesses a material and psychological intensity that embodies the extremes of our behaviours, from the total economic mobilisation of a nation-state to the unbearable pain of individual loss. Fundamentally, war is the transformation of matter through the agency of destruction, and the character of modern technological warfare is such that it simultaneously creates and destroys more than any previous kind of conflict.

The material culture of modern wars can be small (a bullet, machine-gun or gas mask), intermediate (a tank, aeroplane or war memorial) and large (a battleship, a museum or an entire contested landscape). All share one defining feature – they are artefacts, the product of human activity rather than natural processes. In this sense, for example, the First World War's Western Front is as much a cultural artefact as a Second World War V2 rocket, a cold war early-warning radar station, wartime factories and bombed buildings, as are photographs, diaries, films, war souvenirs and a host of conflict-related art forms. Similarly artefactual, though not always understood as such, are people – the war-maimed (sometimes fitted with prostheses), war refugees and their camps, collectors of memorabilia and the post-conflict 'presence of absence' in towns and cities of large numbers of missing men, women and children. Each in their own way – through objects, memories, attitudes and actions – perpetuates different engagements with conflict and its painful and enduring aftermath.

The material culture of conflict offers a field of study which is both rich and fiercely relevant to the world which we inhabit. Wars and other forms of conflict have formed that world. Today we still live in the shadow of two world wars which set new standards for extremes of violence, and violent conflicts remain in progress across the globe as this series of books is inaugurated. These events have created a truly massive volume of material culture. The ways in which people engage with it are conditioned by society's equivocal attitude to violent conflict itself. As John Keegan wrote, 'We are cultural animals and it is the richness of our culture which allows us to accept our undoubted potentiality for violence but to believe nevertheless that its expression is a cultural aberration' (Keegan 1994:4). Keegan himself knew that the reality was not so clear-cut as this reassuring vision. The relationships which people have with the material culture created in a context of violence add weight to this assessment, for they are simultaneously capable of supporting and undermining the perception of warfare as an aberration or exception.

Now as never before, we perceive unfamiliar but underlying truths in the way in which these artefacts reveal infinitely varied interactions with people: a 'social life' created by human engagement with objects. Although overwhelmingly inanimate, they are not merely passive signifiers, reifications or receptors of 'meaning', but can exercise positive agency in forming and embodying human thoughts and emotions. In short, objects make people as much as people make objects. The behaviours provoked by conflict illustrate how an individual's social being is determined by their relationship to the objects that represent them – how objects are a way of knowing oneself through things both present and absent. This is as true for First World War battlefield pilgrims (often widows), survivors of the Holocaust and Second World War civilian internees and prisoners of war as it is for uniformed service personnel who took part in both world wars, the Vietnam War, the Sarajevo militia of the Bosnian Conflict and the war-maimed from Afghanistan and Iraq, to name just a few.

A further incentive to focus on this subject lies in developments in the academic world. For decades, anthropologists and historians have devoted increasing amounts of effort to the study of conflict. Until recently their studies have followed discrete paths, but change has been afoot since the closing years of the last century. A slow-burning revolution in academic engagement with warfare (not to say a 'rebranding') relocated historians of conflict from the unfashionable suburb of 'military history' to uptown locales like 'war studies' and 'First World War studies'. Everyone now accepts that what we call 'peace' cannot be understood without knowing what happens in wars, any more than wars can be comprehended in isolation. Furthermore, ground-breaking work began to appear in which historians addressed wars from the perspective of their material and cultural milieus or manifestations.

Parallel advances have been occurring in the disciplines of archaeology and anthropology. The re-appraisal of materiality has been at the forefront of these developments. The ways in which we view and think about the things we make, their complex volatility and their elusive meanings have been brought under academic scrutiny. The transformative quality of the material culture of modern conflict, and its ability to move across disciplinary boundaries, demands a robust interdisciplinary response. Focused on material culture, such an approach offers to revitalise investigations into the physical and symbolic worlds that conflict creates and that define us as subjects through memory, imagination and technology.

Since the turn of the century the editors of this series have taken a lead in focusing the gaze of both disciplines on the material culture of conflict. Moreover, they have opened the discussion out to practitioners of the widest possible range of disciplines and vocations, including historians, anthropologists, archaeologists, museum curators and artists. For this growing international group of collaborators, the material culture of conflict represents the nodal point at which their disciplines can meet and cross over. This series of books seeks to build on this foundation and to offer a platform for those wishing to publish new research on the subject.

The series adopts a genuinely interdisciplinary approach to re-appraise the material legacy of twentieth and twenty-first century conflict around the world. By conceiving and studying the material culture of conflict, it helps to construct biographies of objects and explore their 'social lives' through the changing values and attitudes attached to them over time. The series aims to show how objects can survive as expressions of 'war beyond conflict', revitalizing meanings and creating new engagements between and understandings of people and 'war things'. It offers new perspectives on the intricate web of connections that bind and separate people and places in times of conflict and beyond.

In so doing, the series offers a radical departure in the study of modern conflict – providing a truly interdisciplinary forum that draws upon, but does not privilege, archaeology, anthropology, military and cultural history, art history, cultural geography and museum and heritage studies. The complexity of modern conflict demands a coherent, integrated and sensitised hybrid approach which calls on different disciplines where they overlap in a shared common terrain – that of the materiality of conflict and its aftermath. This approach has extraordinary potential to bring together the diverse interests and expertise of a host of disciplines to create a new intellectual engagement with the understanding of conflict.

Series Editors' Preface

On entering Germany in December 1933 at the beginning of his epic walk to Constantinople, young traveller Patrick Leigh Fermor's attention was drawn to a shop window displaying 'swastika arm-bands, daggers for the Hitler Youth, blouses for the German Maidens and brown shirts for grown-up S.A. men; swastika buttonholes were arranged in a pattern which read *Heil Hitler*' (Leigh Fermor 1979:43). At that moment Germany had been a single-party state for just five months. Nazi regalia was already proliferating even before Hitler's seizure of power could be considered complete.

It is clear that this regalia was both central to the functioning of the Nazi regime and one of the most widespread and noticeable manifestations of the Nazi state. As objects infused with ideology, the regalia exercised agency, carrying, presenting and disseminating powerful messages and preparing the physical and psychological landscapes of Germany and beyond for what was to follow; indeed, they commemorated what followed in hierarchical visual and symbolic forms. They formed a small but important building block of the Reich, a material sign of how Germans had had their social value and identity remade by the state. It is curious therefore that this material culture of totalitarianism receives so little notice from historians of the era. This is perhaps indicative of the material itself, which the vile nature of Nazism has imbued with a disreputable, almost pornographic taint.

In the spirit of material culture studies, this book does not shrink from dealing directly with this stigma and the difficult back-story of such objects, but it also reminds us of their fundamental importance in the Third Reich.

Badges and medals served a crucial purpose in securing loyalty (both civil and military) and binding Germany's citizens into the racially exclusive people's community – the *Volksgemeinschaft* – that was the basis of society under the Nazis. Existing institutions, like veterans' organisations, youth movements and even the German Red Cross, were taken over or absorbed by the Party, with their insignia accordingly Nazified. Meanwhile new enterprises, like the Labour Service (RAD), the *Winterhilfswerk* relief fund and the *Kraft durch Freude* leisure organisation spawned a completely new range of badges and emblems. The requirement for such insignia was all the more pressing because conscious efforts were made to put much of society into uniforms of one sort or another. Thus, as Adolf Hitler himself put it: 'Germans can walk together arm in arm without regard to their station in life' (Overy 2005:240).

The Army and Navy, lured into supporting the new regime by the promise of a restoration of Germany's military might, soon found themselves swearing an oath of loyalty to the person of the *Führer*.[1] Their insignia and medals were correspondingly Nazified, although the regime was quite happy to pander to military tastes by co-opting imagery and devices redolent of former manifestations of German military dominance like the Prussia of Frederick the Great or the *Kaiserreich*.

The coming of war saw a huge growth in the use of medals as a means of rewarding meritorious service and securing military loyalty. They were supplemented by an array of special badges, awarded for participation in specific types of combat. These might be seen as the bottom end of a reward pyramid that culminated at the top in secret financial payments or the award of stolen lands and property to senior officers (Mazower 2009:192; Seaton 1983:143–144). In the longer term their proliferation has created a rich field for collecting, albeit, and in keeping with their nature, a still highly contested one.

This volume explores how people have engaged with these manifestations of material culture, from the time of their creation up to their current incarnation as 'collectibles'. In the post-war era these engagements have naturally been complicated by the general abhorrence directed at the socio-political forces that created this material. On the one hand, the waters have been further muddied by the proliferation of reproductions, fakes and downright inventions purporting to be real Nazi-era memorabilia. On the other, the power and unpredictability of their social afterlives has been revealed by drawing in issues of authenticity, ethics and 'real', fabricated, fantasy or partly elaborated identities. Interestingly, this is not limited to high-value items, as the sordid products of the recent boom in Holocaust fakery makes clear (Taylor 2014:153–154; Tulkoff 2000). But as the author shows, material value is not directly related to the value accorded to an object by collectors.

At present in the UK, collecting of Nazi memorabilia is identified by counter-terrorist operatives as a potential early sign of right-wing extremism (ACT 2020:3–4). This is perhaps unsurprising as most right-wing extremists readily reveal themselves as addicts of the 'brand' created by the Nazis (or at least a garbled version of it).[2] While this certainly does not mean that all collectors of such material harbour extreme right-wing beliefs, it is indicative of the difficulties inherent in the milieu in which they have chosen to pursue their hobbies and businesses.

It is worth remembering, of course, that few collectors of any variety choose to collect 'easy' or readily obtainable items. Difficulty is part of the attraction and challenge of their hobby. While the editors of this series have met many collectors and are familiar with their mindset, the author speaks with the authority of an insider and specialist in the difficult material addressed in this volume. It is a mark of his achievement that he navigates this rich but ambiguous and challenging topic in such a sure-footed analytical fashion, confronting and disentangling complex threads, and turning a long-overdue and searching light onto such important but complex and troubling subject matter.

Series editors: Nicholas J Saunders, *University of Bristol*
Paul Cornish, *Imperial War Museum, London*

Notes

1 The air force (*Luftwaffe*) was of course a Nazi creation from the outset and more strongly identified with the Party than the other services.
2 For example, their infatuation with Germanic blackletter fonts, when in fact these were officially replaced at Hitler's behest in 1941 by more modern typefaces and approved handwriting.

References

ACT (UK Government counter-terrorism policing) (2020) www.oscb.org.uk/wp-content/uploads/2020/04/Safeguarding-from-Radicalisation-Reference-Guide.pdf
Keegan, J. (1994) *A History of Warfare*. London: Pimlico.
Leigh Fermor, P. (1979) *A Time of Gifts*. London: Penguin.
Mazower, M. (2009) *Hitler's Empire*. London: Penguin.
Overy, R. (2005) *The Dictators*. London: Penguin.
Seaton, A. (1983) *The German Army 1933–45*. London: Sphere.
Taylor, J. (2014) Concentration Camp Uniform as a Tool of Subjugation, in *Bodies in Conflict*, edited by Cornish P., Saunders, N. J. London: Routledge, 144–155.
Tulkoff, A. (2000) *Counterfeiting the Holocaust*. Atglen, PA: Schiffer Military History.

1   Introduction

Fascination

The fascination with the Third Reich and its legacy shows no sign of abating, whether among scholars or the general public. The term 'fascination' only goes so far, and any discussion of Nazi artefacts should not lose sight of the victims of Hitlerism. As I lost my eyesight as a result of a genetic condition, had I lived during the Third Reich I might have been sterilised along with thousands of other blind people (Teicher 2019). Despite sustained interest in the Nazi movement, there is a shortage of scholarly literature on the symbols and ritual objects produced and deployed by and for the Nazi Party (NSDAP), emblems created to construct a Nazi identity and ethos, first among Party members and then, after the seizure of power in 1933, for Germany as a whole. This important subject has traditionally been left for the most part to those who choose to controversially collect and trade Nazi memorabilia. It has only been in the last few years that scholars have started to investigate the meaning and value of Third Reich medals.

The study of these decorations has typically been the domain of 'dubious militaria collectors' (*zweifelhafter Militaria-Sammler*) (Römer 2012:131). Scholar Warren Gade reviewed a publication on the Nazi Close Combat Clasp in gold, but complained that it was a form of 'vanity' publishing that had no analysis and merely listed the 538 recipients of the award (Gade 1988:518). Secretly recorded conversations between German prisoners of war reveal that military decorations had a 'very significant meaning' (*besaßen militärische Auszeichnungen überragende Bedeutung*) (Römer 2012:131). In *Wages of Destruction*, Tooze (2006:595) mentioned decorations given to civilian workers who built tanks, but he did not contextualise these otherwise common medals, nor indicate what the workers thought of them.

For the postwar period, there are only a few articles and books that engage with the perplexing phenomenon of Nazi memorabilia. A classic article is Susan Sontag's 'Fascinating Fascism' (Sontag 1980), in which she offered a highly critical review of Jack Pia's *SS Regalia* (Pia 1974) (Figure 1.1). Sontag compared the allure of SS memorabilia to sadomasochism and soft pornography, and to support her claim, she observed that the SS armband on the front cover of Pia's book was obscured by a tag which read *Over 100 brilliant four-colour photographs*, which

DOI: 10.4324/9781003000617-1

Figure 1.1 Front cover of *SS Regalia*.

Source: Pia (1974) SS Regalia. New York: Ballantine. Scanned by author. Reproduced by permission of Penguin-Random House, request number 59654, 13 October, 2020.

she stated was 'exactly as a sticker with a price on it used to be affixed, part tease, part deference to censorship, on the cover of pornographic magazines over the model's genitalia' (Sontag 1980:98). Pia's book could be seen in the context of the so-called 'Hitler Wave' (*Hitler-Welle*) of the 1970s (Binion 1974; Becker 2018; Caplan 2019), a decade in which numerous books and films catered to, and arguably fuelled the public's insatiable appetite for, the Third Reich.

In the 1980s, fascination with fascism reached dizzying heights during the fake Hitler diaries affair, vividly brought to life in Robert Harris's *Selling Hitler* (Harris 1986). Although Harris focused on the fraudulent diaries, he made two points which are relevant here: firstly, the forger Konrad Kujau and the journalist Gerd Heidemann, who was duped by him, both traded in Nazi memorabilia; secondly, by the 1980s this trade had an annual turnover of USD 50 million (Harris 1986:183).[1] In other words, in spite of the significance of Nazi regalia, before and after 1945, there is a deficit of scholarship on it.

In the last few years, there are signs that scholars are beginning to have an analytical interest in Nazi memorabilia. Historian Richard Overy penned the foreword to a heavily illustrated book entitled *The Third Reich in 100 Objects* (Moorhouse 2017:xii), astutely stating that during the Third Reich, the deployment of symbolism by the Nazi movement replaced the need for people to 'think seriously about what it all meant.' Much of the research on Nazi symbols has taken place under the umbrella of material culture studies. In 'You Shall Know Them by Their Objects: Material Culture and Its Impact in Museum Displays about National Socialism,' Paver (2010:172) remarks that 'Everyday items whose National Socialist content is not apparent until it is pointed out suggest even more strongly the reach of National Socialist influence.' An influential archaeological project entitled *Dark Heritage* engaged with the remnants of Germany's military footprint in Finland (Thomas et al. 2016). There are differing attitudes in Finland to so-called German war junk. Metal detectorists consider it treasure; others find it a blight on Lapland's winter wonderland; indigenous Sami People say it evokes an aura and should be allowed to decay with age (Seitsonen 2018:62; Seitsonen 2020). Similarly, for some residents of the British Channel Islands, occupied during the Second World War, German steel helmets once regarded as hated junk became collectors' objects (Carr 2016). In addition to the forementioned authors, I also take inspiration from the anthropological material culture approach advocated by Saunders (Saunders and Cornish 2009) when asking: How did Nazi symbols facilitate the creation and maintenance of the Third Reich, then after it collapsed, how did these discredited emblems manage to be transformed into highly prized collectors' items?

Material culture

According to Appadurai, commodities 'like persons, have social lives' (Appadurai 1986:3). Kopytoff advocated a biographical approach to the study of things in which he was interested in finding out 'where does the thing come from? What has been its career so far? And what do people consider to be an ideal career for such things?' (Kopytoff 1986:66). There is 'nothing else to social life but symbolic exchanges and the joint construction and management of meaning, including the meaning of bits of stuff' (DiMaggio 2013:III). The meaning of Nazi regalia has undergone a transformation from ritual objects to trash to commodities sold to the highest bidder. As such, I 'follow the thing' from commodity production to commodity consumption (Appadurai 1986:5).

Another aspect of my approach is that although medals are inanimate objects, I assess the degree to which they can be considered alive. Material culture 'emphasises how apparently inanimate things within the environment act on people, and are acted upon by people, for the purposes of carrying out social functions' (Woodward 2007:3). Jane Bennett also sought to break down the distinction between inanimate and animate objects (Bennett 2010). Samuel Alberti acknowledged that although 'objects prompted, changed, and acted as a medium for relationships,' he contended that they were 'nonetheless inanimate' (Alberti 2005:561). In contrast, rather than 'seeing matter and thought as playing off each other, they are better thought of as entwined in complex, non-linear ways' (Richardson *et al.* 2014:17). Material culture keeps history alive, although even a lucky bullet can be buried with its wearer; thus, the social existence of an object is often more fleeting than one might think (Saunders 2014).

Interweaving the practical nature of objects with their agency,[2] one 'would die quite quickly of exposure to the elements in the absence of clothing, buildings, heating, and whatever' (Pickering 1995:6). This statement is as relevant today as it was for freezing German soldiers on the Eastern Front during the Second World War (Assmann 1950). It should also not be forgotten that in January 1942, Jews were 'compelled to surrender their winter coats, furs, muffs, boots, woollen articles and blankets for shipment to the Eastern front' (Jelenko 1943:184). Albeit less extreme than the aforementioned example, the distribution and supply of much-needed personal protection equipment (PPE) experienced delays during the COVID-19 pandemic, thus potentially exposing healthcare workers to the virus (BBC March 2020c). Military equipment is a curious form of material culture, as although it initially had a utilitarian function, collectors do not purchase respirators in order to wear them (nor are old gasmasks safe). For some collectors, war artefacts, due to their former destructive or protective capacity, may provide reassurance that although collectors are living in an unstable world, at least they do not need to charge at a German machine gunner across no man's land or hide in an air raid shelter.

The concept of objectification is also relevant to my study, as is the extent to which Wehrmacht soldiers and citizens of Hitler's Germany were objectified through medals. An objectification perspective 'attempts to overcome the dualism in modern empiricist thought in which subjects and objects are regarded as utterly different and opposed entities, respectively human and non-human, living and inert, active and passive, and so on' (Tilley 2013:61). Furthermore, the study of material culture 'challenges the assumption, perpetuated by disciplinary divisions and also philosophical trajectories, that the object and subject are separate' (Woodward 2013).[3]

Our problem with material culture studies tends to be finding a middle route into the study of artefacts which avoids either an isolation of the artefact stripped of the social relations that produce and consume it, or an isolation of the human subject denuded of the artefactual environment which creates constraints and is a primary means by which the subject has consciousness of her or himself.

(Miller 1998:491)

In his 'Biography of a medal . . .' Jody Joy asserted that the 'physical differences between humans and things become insignificant. Once an object has been socially constituted as a thing it can transcend the traditional barriers set up in our own society between people and objects' (Joy 2002:141). In this regard, 'objects make people as much as people make objects' (Saunders 2004:6).

Artefacts constitute a historical fact (Evans 1997, 2000:285–286). Jelavich (1995:78) begins 'with an artefact and looks for issues that it generates.' Carr (2018) excavated a button and a corroded lead eagle of the Organisation Todt at the former forced labour camp Lager Wick in Jersey, which provided material evidence that it was this notorious Nazi construction organisation that ran the facility. As a blind person, I especially concur with Saunders (2014) that material culture has a multi-sensorial dimension. Additionally, everything that 'we make or own has a reason, a story behind it. These stories can be told through artefacts in fascinating ways' (Pershey 1998:18).

Key questions arise from such issues: How were Nazi badges and medals designed and produced; with what materials; and by whom? What impact did they have on the people that they were directed at? How and with what effects have markets for Nazi badges and medals emerged and developed since 1945, and what are the implications of this for the construction and reinterpretation of meaning and value over time? What makes Nazi badges and medals authentic (in both a physical and social sense), and what are the implications of replicating them?

Authenticity and the aura

I adopt an anthropological approach to authenticity (Theodossopoulos 2013; Handler 1986), a concept that has many facets. Collectors tend to merely think in terms of nominal authenticity, which constitutes the 'correct identification of the origins, authorship, or provenance of an object' (Dutton 2003:259). I distance myself from the physical characteristics of artefacts, which would seem nonsensical to collectors of German steel helmets who ascertain originality based on their leather liners (Gygi 2009). It is not for the anthropologist to adjudicate but to understand the concerns of a given community (Thompson 1979, 2017:145). Prior to losing my sight, I was more preoccupied with nominal authenticity than afterwards. My enlightened approach is a consequence of not being able to assess objects visually, although this is not to neglect the perception of touch (Hetherington 2003; Karim and Likova 2018). Rather, I am more interested in the concept of the 'aura' than simply determining nominal authenticity. This also enables a better understanding of why collectors are attracted to Nazi memorabilia in the first place.

Walter Benjamin discussed authenticity and aura in his seminal essay 'The Work of Art in the Age of Mechanical Reproduction' (Benjamin 1936). Benjamin's essay has been described as the 'canonical statement on mass-culture' (Buck-Morss 1983:212). Benjamin regarded authenticity as deriving from an object's tradition through time, affirming that the 'authenticity of a thing is the essence of all that is transmissible from its beginning, ranging from its substantive duration to its testimony to the history which it has experienced' (Benjamin 1936:section II). Authenticity has an inverse relationship with replicas; indeed, authenticity 'is a late by-product of the constant activity of reproduction by every technical means that could be invented' (Latour and Hennion 2003:94). Furthermore, 'obsession for pinpointing originality increases proportionally with the availability and accessibility of more and more copies of better and better quality' (Latour and Lowe 2011:279).

Benjamin stated that 'what withers in the age of the technological reproducibility of the work of art is the latter's aura' (Benjamin 1936:section II). Many regard the aura as meta-physical in character, pertaining to the medium of perception rather than an 'inherent property of persons or objects' (Hansen 2008:342). Namely, aura 'refers to the sense of wonder, awe and reverence experienced by the onlooker or listener in the presence of a singular authentic work of art' (Gilloch 2005:1) (hereafter perceptive aura). Alternatively, another view is that aura is a quality or emanation of an object (Bolter et al. 2006:26) (hereafter inherent aura). Indeed, although Argo et al. (2006:82) stated that people would be 'reluctant and uncomfortable coming into physical contact' with a garment that Hitler had worn, for collectors, it is not polluted and therefore to be avoided, but is imbued with an aura.

A complicating factor is whether a mass-produced object can have an aura. Some have claimed that even replicas can acquire an aura (Fernandez and Lastovicka 2011:279). The 'fictions of master and copy are now so entwined with each other that it is impossible to say where one begins and the other ends' (Davis 1995:381). The aura may even be able to withstand an onslaught of replicas, as 'copies, forgeries and fakes, which have a long history, do not threaten the aura of the original, but seek to partake of it' (Appadurai 1986:45).

Replicas are not necessarily forgeries, although collectors have been deceived by both. Forgeries 'are works made intentionally to deceive, and fakes include forgeries as well as works originally made as legitimate copies but eventually presented through intentional deception as being genuine' (Casement 2020:61). The term 'reproduction' tends to be the one that is most widely used within the Nazi memorabilia collecting community, although this masks the reasons as to why these reproductions were made in the first place. German auction houses reserve the term 'constructed for collectors' (*Sammelfertigung*) for better-quality replicas. Despite being offered as reproductions, they could end up on market stalls and be passed off as original. Indeed, is there an 'aesthetic difference between a deceptive fake and a genuine, authentic, or original work of art?' (Kennick 1985:3). If no difference is perceivable, will the materiality of the Third Reich actually be impoverished? Presumably, there are some in the collecting community who are able to tell the difference between a copy and an original. Indeed, the 'perfect copy hypothesis' should be confirmed or refuted based on an assessment by both experts and casual viewers (Bass 1987:295). As I write this, some collectors are dreamily gazing at their Nazi badges and medals in the belief that they were once earned and worn by Wehrmacht soldiers, but they were actually made outside Germany decades after the end of the Second World War.

Aesthetics

Aesthetics 'became crucial in mass society and it is this aspect which might be one of the missing links in understanding Fascism and its internal logic' (Nelis 2007:415). A 'dialectical relationship existed between the art which the regimes paraded on stage as the epitome of the new age, and the mass murder off stage of those deemed to stand in its way' (Griffin 1996:124). Cultural historian George Mosse (who witnessed the rise of Nazism) acknowledged that he had initially underestimated the aesthetics of fascism (Mosse 1996:246). Fascist aesthetics 'take the form of a characteristic pageantry: the massing of groups of people; the turning of people into things; the multiplication or replication of things; and the grouping of people/things around an all-powerful, hypnotic leader-figure or force' (Sontag 1980:91). My loss of eyesight has meant that I am no longer metaphorically blinded by the visual aesthetics of fascism. I do not wish to commit sophistry, but I am of the opinion that this has enabled me to address the aesthetics of the Nazi regime in a more objective manner.[4]

A number of frameworks can assist in unravelling aesthetic value, but an appropriate one is the response-dependence account of aesthetic properties, which holds that 'aesthetic properties are powers in objects that arouse reactions in suitably positioned subjects' (Smuts 2011:42). These subjects are not only those who were awarded medals during the Third Reich, but collectors who were born after its demise. These inter-generational subjects enable the value of Nazi badges and medals to be assessed over time. Indeed, as 'people and objects gather time, movement and change, they are constantly transformed, and these transformations of person and object are tied up with each other' (Gosden and Marshall 1999:169).

Value

The noted nineteenth-century economist Samuel Bailey recognised that defining value was of 'great difficulty' (Bailey 1825:iii). The same object 'can have the highest degree of value for one soul and the lowest for the other, and vice-versa' (Simmel 1907, 1978:62). Whilst some would reduce value to monetary worth, others would recognise that value is more than that. It is, by one account, not as 'individualist theory would have it, a simple intermediary of exchange introduced as a technical refinement, for the purpose of overcoming the inconveniences of barter' (Graziani and Vale 1997:22).

Philosophically, perhaps, price 'is quantitative and temporally neutral in character, and thus irreducible to value, which is qualitative and predispositional' (Roffe 2016:3). Alternatively, 'price has become the indicator of value, as long as a good is bought and sold in the market it must have value, so rather than a theory of value determining price, it is the theory of price that determines value.'[5] Nevertheless, collectibles tend to be prized for their utility, beauty, nostalgic value or a combination of these (Stoller 1984:93). What, however, is nostalgic about a pair of Nazi jackboots?

Collectors in the Channel Islands (most of whom were born after the Second World War) claim that they are not collecting Nazi memorabilia out of sympathy for Nazism, but that German military equipment is a reminder that their home-steads were once occupied by the Wehrmacht (Carr 2016:255). Many would argue that there is nothing nostalgic about the German occupation of the Channel Islands, especially as forced labour camps operated there. Nostalgia aside, jackboots may have a partial use value for a collector striving to complete a dis-play of a German army uniform. Medals also have little functionality (other than being part of a collection). Otherwise useful objects such as LP records are even purchased by vinyl collectors and never played (Shuker 2004). The 'pure object, devoid of any function or completely abstracted from its use, takes on a strictly subjective status: it becomes part of a collection' (Baudrillard 1968, 1996:86).

Karl Marx did not assume that the 'price paid for something was an accurate reflection of its worth' (Graeber 2001:55). This is an important point to consider, as I have tracked the prices of a representative basket of medals in order to com-pare them in an objective manner. Price on its own is nevertheless unable to reflect the value (in its broadest sense) that collectors attribute to the medals that they desire or own. Price is also not the most appropriate indicator of value when examining the social significance that medals had at their time of bestowal. Fur-thermore, the price that a collector pays does not always represent the true extent to which they value an object or the degree of satisfaction or utility they gain from owning it (Mei and Moses 2002:1664). This is not to neglect the Veblen effect, which is essentially defined as conspicuous consumption (i.e., the higher the price, the more desirable the object) (Dolfsma 2000). Even in such a situation, an emo-tional attachment to artefacts is not governed by financial value (Turkle 2011). If the 'objects someone values are a window into that person's inner self' (Richins 1994:522), what does this say about people who collect Nazi memorabilia?

Gift exchange

Another way to consider value is to regard the original bestowals of Nazi decora-tions as gifts (Graeber 2001). Allied soldiers who brought home war souvenirs may also have subsequently given them to family members. The purchase of an artefact by a collector could also be considered as a form of self-gratification. Although 'most collectibles and gifts are now purchased in an anonymous market for money, the acts of collecting and giving seek to remove these objects from associations with the marketplace and monetary value' (Belk 1998:8). The 'gift can act as terrain and metaphor for analysis of social relations that differ in kind from the cash nexus at the heart of markets' (Lapavitsas 2004:40). As gifts have been described as the 'quintessential form of exchange' (Dolfsma et al. 2009:318), they offer insights into the awarding of Nazi medals.

Goda (2000) provided examples of gifts Hitler gave to his senior officers to secure their allegiance. Medals were a highly visible sign of whom he valued, consequently fostering rivalry and envy amongst those who did not receive the most prestigious decorations. These exchanges reflected Hitler's leadership style, which 'constantly fomented insecurity and mutual mistrust among his lieutenants. The ancient principle of divide and rule was an essential element in his modus operandi.'[6] Additionally, the often murky 'art collecting of the Nazis was augmented by a culture of gift-giving, in which reciprocal exchanges of art works often served to express ties and elucidate shifting power relationships' (Petropoulos 1994:119).

Theodor Adorno mourned the capacity for humans to exchange meaningful gifts in a capitalist society, stating that the 'decline of gift-giving is mirrored in the embarrassing invention of gift articles, which are based on the fact that one no longer knows what one should give, because one no longer really wants to. These goods are as relationless as their purchasers. They were shelf warmers from the first day.'[7] The concept of off-the-shelf gifts could be considered in relation to the badges and medals awarded en masse during the Third Reich. Additionally, when discussing the decorations that Hitler, his officers and political leaders bestowed, I am not espousing the values of 'heroism, ruthlessness, violence, obedience, discipline and honor' (Wunderlich 1937:348), as these tropes were used to justify the bestowal of the medals in the first place and are also the very ones that are esteemed by collectors.

It has been said that the 'spirit of reciprocity, sociability, and spontaneity in which gifts are typically exchanged, are usually starkly opposed to the profit-oriented, self-centred, and calculated spirit that fires the circulation of commodities' (Appadurai 1986:11). Commodities are 'objects produced for sale on the market; markets, again, are empirically defined as actual contacts between buyers and sellers' (Polanyi 1944:71–72). A weakness of the aforementioned definition is that it does not take into consideration secondhand objects which circulate within a market. In a strict economic sense, 'second-hand goods are inferior goods having once been bought new' (Fox 1957:99). In the case of collectibles, it is because they have been used that they are sought.

Collecting (an economic focus)

There are 'three prerequisites for an object to make its way into the possession of any person: it must be affordable, available, and desirable. Conceptualizing the acquisition of goods in this way helps combine traditional studies of economics, anthropology, history, and material culture' (Martin 1993:156). Collectibles 'fall into the category of non-productive assets; that is tangible assets that have no value as inputs in a production process' (Gilkeson and Lamb 2000:15). This contrasts to the considerable resources expended to produce medals during the Third Reich. When a collector acquires a medal it 'ceases to be a fungible commodity and becomes a singular object that is no longer freely exchangeable for something of similar economic value' (Belk 2013:534). Nevertheless, a medal still has an exchange value which may even be enhanced (albeit its financial value is a fairly illiquid one). The 'value of an illiquid asset is generally lower than the value of a similar asset that is readily marketable' (Dyl and Jiang 2008:40). Consequently, if collectors need to quickly sell their Nazi relics, they may find it difficult to do so.

Nazi medals could not be considered in the same way as paintings, but I agree with Gell's view that the 'anthropologist is not obliged to define the art object, in advance, in a way satisfactory to aestheticians, or philosophers, or art historians, or anybody else' (Gell 1998:7). Many Nazi medals were designed by artists, although they were not unique objects as such, as they were specifically designed in order to be mass-produced and replicated. Nazi medals often comprised a series, for example, the different grades of the Iron Cross. Indeed, a 'truly unique, absolute object, an object such that it has no antecedents and is in no way dispersed in some series or other-such an object is unthinkable' (Baudrillard 1968, 1996:93).

In some respects, Nazi medals are similar to other serial objects such as baseball cards, coins and postage stamps. The Penny Black was not initially intended for collectors (nor were Nazi medals), but it subsequently obtained collectible value (Gelber 1992; Golden 2011:9). Perhaps due to similarities in their materiality, coin dealers are more likely than stamp dealers to stock some medals. The market mechanisms of these three hobbies are similar: auctions, fairs, magazines, shops and societies (Case 2009). The value of collectible coins (and therefore medals) is 'wholly independent of the quantity of labour originally necessary to produce them and varies with varying wealth and inclinations of those who are desirous to possess them' (Ricardo 1951:12). Baseball cards are objects that have even less intrinsic worth than silver or gold coins, with their value being contained in the images and text, which then assist in the generation of a price. The 'hours of labour invested in production cannot distinguish why certain types of baseball cards . . . are valued and priced higher than others' (Sherlock 1997:62). Scarcity and condition are instrumental factors, which are also relevant when considering the value of Nazi memorabilia. Although most Nazi badges were made from similar metals, it is what they represent that differentiates them. In contrast to commemorative coins or stamps that are primarily made to be collected, Nazi medals had to be earned by soldiers, rather than being purchased as collectibles. They acquired their collectible status over time, hence they have more value than objects marketed as so-called instant collectibles, such as commemorative wall plates, for example.

Oral history

Much of the material for the chapters in this book is first-hand, acquired through interviewing collectors and traders. Oral history 'offers some unique opportunities. It enriches our historical imagination and answers some questions better than any other source can' (Schultz 2016:51). Oral historians 'want to know why or how it was done and how the interviewee felt about doing it' (McCarthy 2010:163). The crimes perpetrated during the Third Reich mean that collecting and trading artefacts associated with this epoch have the capacity to offend. Oliver Sears, who is the son of a Holocaust survivor, has specific concerns relating to the market in Nazi memorabilia (see Chapter 8). Collectors generally defend their interest, and one of the purposes of interviewing them was to better understand their motivations.

The ethically grounded process took more than two years to complete, and although my experience of collecting militaria gave me a head start, I approached my task as if I was a novice to the field. It would be misleading, however, not to acknowledge that my experience gave me access to collectors and traders who might not have been accommodating to outsiders. Carr (2016) established relationships with a number of collectors of Nazi memorabilia in the Channel Islands, which meant that they were more amenable. Seitsonen (2018:153) reported that a military buff took offence at his project being entitled *Dark Heritage* and would therefore not be taking part as there was nothing dark about being interested in German military aircraft. Victims of bombing would probably disagree. Similar issues in relation to sensitive oral history projects were addressed by Yow (1997) and Jeansonne (1983).

International militaria magazines provided the contact details of traders, giving a cross-cultural dimension (Arm; MT; IMM 2013). Collectors and traders tended to be more responsive to traditional means of communication such as post or telephone, although email was also effective. Private communication via social media only resulted in a few agreements. I also received refusals, especially from auction houses specialising in Nazi memorabilia. I subsequently conducted more than 20 in-depth telephone interviews with collectors and traders based in Britain, Germany and North America. The median age of the participants was 60, although I did interview a millennial (Adam Wilcock). The vast majority of participants were men, although I interviewed Melissa Greenfield, the spouse of an imperial German militaria trader. All of the collectors of Nazi memorabilia whom Carr (2016) interviewed were men over the age of 50, and she has yet to meet a female militaria collector. Susan Pearce also found that militaria collectors tended to be men (Pearce 1998:135). A survey conducted by *Military Trader* identified that only 1 percent of the 95 respondents was female, and there were no collectors under the age of 25, with 48 percent being over 71 (Adams-Graf 2020a. In my 30 years' experience of militaria, I could count on one hand the number of women I have encountered who collected Nazi medals. Gender aside, I did not explicitly inquire into the class, education, ethnic status, income, religion or sexuality of the participants, although some of these aspects did occasionally arise. It has been noted that American gun collectors tend to be 'white, married males older than forty with some college or a bachelor's degree and incomes of $40,000 or higher' (Anderson and Taylor 2010:39). The collectors and traders I interviewed tended not to depart too much from these demographics, and I am conscious that there is a lack of diversity within the Nazi memorabilia collecting scene. Nevertheless, people from groups persecuted during the Third Reich are drawn to Nazi relics (see Chapter 8).

Structure

In Chapter 2, I describe the symbols of German nationalist organisations and the Nazi Party, emblems which contributed to the destabilisation of the Weimar

Democracy. The extent to which the ancient symbol of the swastika mobilised supporters of the NSDAP cannot be statistically ascertained, although it did have a powerful pull. I trace the role that symbols had after Hitler was levered into power in 1933, in addition to outlining the laws and decrees introduced in order to secure the hegemony of the Nazi swastika. I also unravel the agency that the membership badge of the NSDAP had and investigate how collectors have reconfigured it.

Chapter 3 focuses on the iconography and materiality of the mass-produced badges which were a tangible representation of the Nazi concept of a 'People's Community' (*Volksgemeinschaft*), such as those of the Winter Help Program (WHW) and Strength through Joy (KdF). I also interpret the iconography of the metal badges made to commemorate the monumental rallies held in Nürnberg and illustrate how documentaries of these events have inordinately bewitched collectors. In Chapter 4, I assess the symbolic value of a medal instituted in 1934 to recognise service in the Great War[8] and explain why collectors have a different perception of it compared to the soldiers who were actually awarded it. I also consider the concept of gift exchange in relation to the awarding of Nazi medals to prominent American industrialists such as Henry Ford and aviator Charles Lindbergh.

Another form of gift was the Mother's Cross, discussed in Chapter 5. This decoration was awarded to mothers in exchange for having at least four children and was inextricably chained to the Nazi racial worldview. I compare the high symbolic value this award had during the Third Reich to its lower valuation by collectors and consider the influence of its strong association with the female gender. In Chapter 6, I focus on medals which were awarded during the Second World War such as the iconic Iron Cross. Despite the 1939 version being made from lesser-quality materials than its 1914 imperial predecessor, its price is higher on the collectors' market. This suggests that there is a stronger demand for Nazi medals compared to imperial ones. I also discuss the so-called Second World War weapon badges and how they have unfortunately been part of the perpetuation of the myth of the clean Wehrmacht. These decorations have been inordinately reproduced, and I examine how fakes have affected the prices of originals.

In Chapter 7, I explore and critique the publications that have been written by collectors for collectors and argue that their authors need to make more of an effort to situate Nazi medals in their historical context. I also demonstrate how these publications have fuelled the demand for particular artefacts, which has arguably increased their prices. Although I discuss the prices of individual awards in the chapters that have already been outlined, I present the results in graphical form. Nevertheless, rather than solely focusing on financial value, I examine how cultural capital and exchange networks have evolved over time.

In Chapter 8, the lengthiest chapter, I consider the life of Nazi medals after May 1945 under the dichotomy of trash or treasure. During the Third Reich, Nazi medals were inalienable symbols which served the state and military, but from D-Day onwards, if not earlier, they were acquired by Allied soldiers and then collectors, all of whom reconfigured their meaning and value. I also discuss the ethical and moral issues that collecting and trading Nazi memorabilia raises. The international market is not completely outlawed but is restricted in certain countries such as Germany, and I outline how regulations and attitudes have evolved in the western world since 1945. I also present arguments for and against the private versus public ownership of Nazi relics.

In Chapter 9, I identify some of the factors responsible for why people decided to collect Nazi memorabilia and examine why the majority of collectors are male. I also evaluate how Nazi medals have shaped an understanding of the Third Reich and consider their future materiality and aura both digitally and physically. Taken together, these chapters go a long way in untangling the contested nature of Nazi artefacts and suggest how they can be properly contextualised and managed.

Notes

1 Harris gave no source for the figure of USD 50 million.
2 Agency is a property of 'assemblages of humans and nonhumans' (Bennett 2004:360).
3 Page numbers were not available for some sources. This was often the case where the source was a website. In case of the Woodward reference, the quotation can be found in the first paragraph of her article. The full reference can be found within my Bibliography. My loss of sight also meant that I made more use of Kindle books and publications using assistive technology, although every effort was made to give location numbers or for my sighted assistants to find page numbers.
4 For articles which address aspects of how blindness impacts on aesthetics see Bolt 2013; Miyazaki 2015; Sibley and Tanner 1968.
5 Mazzucato (2018:Kindle location 4858).
6 Read (2003:Prologue). In instances where page numbers were not available, I have pointed towards the section in which the relevant quotation can be found.
7 Adorno (1951:Part 1, aphorism 21).
8 I have used the term Great War throughout this book due to my discussion of the 1920s and 1930s when the term the First World War had yet to gain widespread usage. For an article on the use of these terms see Lee (n.d.).

2 From Weimar to the Third Reich

Weimar Germany was a volcano ready to erupt. It was never able to fully recover from Germany's defeat in the Great War. Political extremists on the right sought to tear up the Treaty of Versailles and restore Germany to its pre-1914 borders. The most extreme of these groups was the Nazi party headed by Hitler. He attracted followers to his movement through his hypnotic oratory and the enigmatic swastika. His message was clear: He would be the one who would restore Germany to its former greatness. When his violent grab for power failed in 1923, he had little option but to resort to the ballot box after he was released from prison in December 1924. As unemployment soared in the late 1920s and early 1930s, Hitler proclaimed he would give Germans bread and work again. Millions flocked to the ballot box in the belief that he was their saviour. Nevertheless, the NSDAP did not receive an overall majority, and Hitler's Brownshirts were poised to take power by force. The conservative elite, more fearful of a communist uprising than a Nazi insurrection, eventually caved in and handed Hitler the chancellorship. Would he ever have reached this point without the mass deployment of symbols? After Hitler achieved power, what role did they play in sustaining his grip over Germany? Now we know the true consequences of Hitlerism, why are discredited swastika badges worth even more in financial terms than they were during the Third Reich?

Imperial legacy in Weimar

Although the Kaiserreich collapsed in November 1918, with Wilhelm II fleeing to Holland (Marks 1983), monarchical symbols still had weight. Imperial German iconography was displayed by nationalists to show opposition to the emerging republican democracy. Conservatively orientated veterans' organisations opposed 'The System' (*das System*) and favoured a return to monarchic rule, which was expressed through the display of the old Reich colours of black, white and red. Imperial symbols were volatile: For some they represented what had been lost; for others they formed the basis of new radical political movements; and for others they provided a reminder that lives and limbs were lost in exchange for them.

Artist Otto Dix, a Great War Iron Cross recipient, subsequently expressed the horror of trench warfare through his paintings of severely disabled war veterans. In 'War Cripples' (*Kriegskrüppel*) (1920), Dix depicted four amputees out for a

DOI: 10.4324/9781003000617-2

stroll (Figure 2.1).[1] The veteran at the front directs the others (one of whom is blind) by outstretching his metal hooked arm, an Iron Cross pinned to his chest. Although the Iron Cross recipient is reasonably content, Dix implied that the medal could not compensate for his life-changing injuries. Whilst the Iron Cross objectified the veteran's bravery, his disability showed the price he had paid for it. Objectification 'entails making into a thing, treating as a thing, something that is really not a thing' (Nussbaum 1995:257). No longer able to fight, injured German soldiers were given false legs and hands so they could continue to be productive in civilian life. The Great War 'did not end with the armistice of 1918, but continued in the medical clinics, rehabilitation centres, and in the factories of the Weimar Republic' (Fineman 1999:88). Ironically, as the subjects in Dix's painting exhibited 'undiminished pride, it escaped virulent protest at the time,' but was later classified in Nazi Germany as so-called degenerate art (Crockett 1992:72).

The Iron Cross was also prominent on a mutilated and facially disfigured veteran in Dix's 1920 painting 'The Card Players' (*Die Skatspieler*), which shows 'three German military officers, the shattered hulks of their bodies speaking to the devastation wreaked on Germany and on the heroic figure of the invulnerable war hero by WWI' (Figure 2.2).[2] The veteran wearing the Iron Cross pinned to his coat is missing both legs and has a metal prosthesis in place of his right arm. His

Figure 2.1 Otto Dix 'The War Cripples' (*Die Kriegskrüppel*) (1920). Licence to reproduce obtained from the Design and Artists Copyright Society (DACS). Licence Reference: LR20-140275-1. Image reproduced by permission of Bridgeman Images on behalf of Picture Alliance (reference: 10064849).

Figure 2.2 Otto Dix 'The Card Players' (*Die Skatspieler*) (1920). Licence to reproduce obtained from the Design and Artists Copyright Society (DACS). Licence Reference: LR20-140275-1. Image reproduced by permission of Bridgeman Images on behalf of Nationalgalerie, SMPK, Berlin, Germany (reference: 10064849).

jaw has been replaced by a metal plate, and his missing nose is covered by what looks like a black eye patch.

Dix was not the only German artist who made emblematic use of imperial-era medals in their work. War veteran George Grosz used them – particularly the Iron Cross – to 'badge' the people satirised in some of his pictures. Grosz's 'Germany: A Winter's Tale' (*Wintermärchen*) was named in honour of Heinrich Heine's satirical poem of 1843 (White 2007). Grosz's painting features an old-school militarist

Figure 2.3 George Grosz 'Republican Automatons' (*Republikanische Automaten*) (1920).
Licence to reproduce obtained from the Design and Artists Copyright Society
(DACS) on behalf of the estate of George Grosz, Princeton, N.J. Licence Reference: LR20-140275-1. Image reproduced by permission of Bridgeman Images
on behalf of the Museum of Modern Art, New York (reference: 10064849).

with a moustache and an Iron Cross pinned to his chest (Kranzfelder 2001:33).
The officer stands between a priest holding a Bible and a teacher holding a book
that has Goethe's name spelled incorrectly on its cover, the idea being that these
three nationalist institutions still controlled the German state.

Grosz's 'Republican Automatons' (*Republikanische Automaten*) (1920) features two faceless disabled war veterans, one of whom is wearing a formal black-tie outfit and has an Iron Cross on his chest (Figure 2.3). Cogwheels and gears are poking out from his left armpit. Phrases are floating out of his head: '1, 2, 3, hoo-ray' (Poore 2007:34). The painting gives the impression that despite their severe disabilities, the bourgeois patriots are empty-headed robots. Heinrich Zille's 1916 lithograph 'The Iron Cross' (*Das Eiserne Kreuz*) depicts a hollow-cheeked woman sheltering under her blanket from the cold and gazing down at her baby on her lap (Zille 1916). She is surrounded by her other three children, one of whom is peering at an envelope containing her husband's Iron Cross. Presumably, it had been delivered after her husband had been killed in the trenches.

In an effort to distance itself from militaristic symbols, the government during Weimar refused to sanction a campaign medal which commemorated service during the Great War. Article 109 of the Weimar Constitution prohibited the state from instituting medals, although this did not apply to decorations that were to be retrospectively awarded for service during the Great War (WC 1919). In contrast to the situation in Germany, the British introduced a trio of medals, with most participants in the war being eligible for at least two of them. Possibly due to their widespread issue, however, these decorations soon acquired flippant nicknames. The full 'set' became associated with the names of three characters from the Daily Mirror comic strip: Pip the dog, Squeak the penguin and Wilfred the rabbit (Lamb n.d.; Richardson 2009). Pip was the 1914 or 1914–1915 Star, while the British Victory medal stood in for Wilfred the rabbit. The depiction of St. George trampling a Prussian flag on the silver British War medal was symbolic of the triumph over imperial Germany rather than Squeak the penguin (Times 1919:12).

In lieu of an official medal sanctioned by the Weimar government, the conservatively oriented German veterans' society (*Deutscher Reichskriegerbund Kyffhäuser*) commissioned a medal for its members. The inscription on the reverse of the oval-shaped medal was attributed to its honorary president, the former Great War field marshal Paul von Hindenburg, and read, 'Upright and proud we walk out of the fight which we fought over four years against a world of enemies.'[3] The inscription perpetuated the 'stab-in-the-back' myth (*Dolchstoßle-gende*), which had great currency amongst nationalists. Proponents of the myth affirmed that the German army was not beaten in the trenches, but undermined by left-wing politicians on the home front, though the veracity of this has rightly been dismissed (Rurup 1968:114; for context see Diehl 1989). The medal's ribbon was invested with the former Reich colours of black, white and red, which nationalists claimed should be the flag of Germany instead of the republican colours of black, red and gold (Fritzsche 1990). The medal was not based on merit, but merely had to be purchased by the members of the association (UM November 1942:172). This contrasted to decorations such as the Iron Cross that had been awarded by the military during the Great War and meant the Kyffhäuser medal was simply a commemorative commodity. A large number of veterans did wish to mark their service, as 1,050,000 medals were purchased (about a third of the association) (Ibid.).[4]

Weimar Reichswehr soldiers were prohibited from wearing the Kyffhäuser medal as it was considered anti-republican. This small professional army was not an advocate of the Weimar democracy but was a 'state within the state' (*Staat im Staate*) (Smith 1958:351), or, to be more precise, Weimar Germany was not a state with an army, but an army with a state. In 1920, officers of the Bavarian Reichswehr refused to wear the republican eagle, which they referred to as the 'vulture of bankruptcy' (*Pleitegeier*), on their hats (Carsten 1966:127). Furthermore, rather than the eagle incorporating the Kaiserreich colours of black, white and red, it featured the 1848 anti-monarchical colours of black, red and gold (Achilles 2010). The Weimar era was a 'particularly extreme example of a society in which rival groups constructed fundamentally different images of the past with the aim of legitimising their present-day political agendas' (Gerwarth 2006:5). One of the most radical of these groups was the NSDAP, whose leaders and members sought to supplant the Weimar system by non-democratic means. To assist their goal, they had to attract followers, which they did by harnessing the symbols of Germany's imperial past as well as shaping and creating other emblems. These otherwise small items of material culture, in the form of badges and medals, therefore shine a light on the complex socioeconomic and political environment of post-1918 Germany.

The NSDAP and the deployment of symbols

The swastika, known as the hooked cross in German (*Hakenkreuz*), has been described as 'one of the most visually powerful symbols ever devised' (Heller 2000:3). It was partly for this reason that it was appropriated by the Nazi party. Before its adoption, however, the symbol had diverse and innocuous meanings throughout the world. The 'oldest swastika like patterns known to me are from objects made of mammoth-ivory which were found in the village of Mezine in Southern Russia. They belong to the culture of the Ice Age, that is to say they are about 20,000 years old' (Lowenstein 1941:49). Positive 'evidence of the origin and early migrations of the symbol is now lost in the mists of antiquity: it has been found in most parts of the world and in cultures dating back to the Bronze Age' (Balchin 1944:167).

The dentist Dr. Friedrich Krohn, a member of the antisemitic Thule Society, suggested that the Nazi party adopt the swastika, claiming that from as early as 1912 he had made it his 'scientific battle to introduce the Hakenkreuz as a national symbol' (ZS89). Hitler did not credit Krohn in *Mein Kampf*, but merely referred to a dentist from Starnberg (Hitler 1927, 1938:556). In any case, Hitler could not have been the inventor of the swastika, as not only had it been used by ancient cultures, but it was a 'widespread symbol among racists long before Hitler had been heard of' (Phelps 1963:250).

The swastika had already been deployed before the Great War by the pan-Germanic occultist Adolf Lanzis (Evans 2003:40). Nazi propaganda dating from the 1930s falsely claimed that Hitler first saw a swastika in 1897, whilst he had been a choir boy at Lambach Abbey, Austria (Bade 1933:9). For Hitler, the swastika was not only the brand sign of Nazism, but it represented his distorted worldview of racial purity (Hitler 1927, 1938:556). Despite Hitler's racial interpretation of the swastika, the 'intrinsic political meaning remained unclear,' and the appeal was to be 'mainly emotional' (Fehrenbach 1971:352).

A central component of the NSDAP's swastika was that it was meant to represent antisemitism, although nothing intrinsic to the symbol indicated this. Words 'are necessary to sustain the potency of a visual symbol' (Tuan 1980:467). Members and supporters of the NSDAP communicated that the swastika represented antisemitism through the spoken word, by violence, and in written form. An example of the latter was an article published in the *Völkischer Beobachter* in December 1920, which, according to Layton (1970), was around the time the NSDAP acquired the newspaper. The highly antisemitic article stated that the 'Jewry is Germany's deterioration, and as a sign of this awareness we want to wear the swastika visibly. It shall be the fighting sign to us, with which we are going to win' (VB Dezember 1920:3). Antisemitism was by no means the only ingredient of the NSDAP, an organisation that attracted the 'politically homeless' (Douglas 1977:72), and with the collapse of the Kaiserreich, millions were ready to blame others for their predicament.

The enigmatic nature of the swastika encapsulated the diverse emotions of 'the masses' (*die Masse*) (Jonsson 2013, 2013a). Sträter (1948:48), although acknowledging that the masses have 'always been influenced by external appearances,' attributed support for Hitler to the 'particular development of the German people' in being unable to form 'an opinion independent of their government.' This echoes the sentiment of the paintings of Dix and Grosz discussed earlier. It could be taken from Sträter's statement that he was a proponent of the 'special path' (*Sonderweg*) account of German history. According to historian Helmut Walser Smith, this included: 'The Reformation, the convulsions of the religious wars, the precarious hold of the Enlightenment, the shock of Napoleonic invasion, the failed Revolution of 1848, and the impact of Bismarck' (Smith 2008:225). Despite this rocky path, Smith added that the 'Third Reich was not predetermined by this history, but is (nevertheless) unthinkable without it' (Ibid.:225). It would also be difficult to envisage the NSDAP without its 'strong, menacing and mysterious' swastika flag (Heiden 1936:89). This flag, in the colours of black, white and red, was displayed for the first time in the summer of 1920 (Schuman 1936:24). Hitler claimed that 'we ourselves experienced an almost childlike joy when a faithful woman party comrade for the first time executed the design and delivered the flag' (Hitler 1969, 2007:452). It was stated in the critical edition of *Mein Kampf* published by the Institut für Zeitgeschichte that 'Already amongst contemporaries it was debated who was referred to here, both Friedrich Krohn and Rudolf Schüssler claimed that it was their wife who was the party comrade mentioned in *Mein Kampf*.'[5] The veneration of female patriotic sacrifice has certain similarities to the celebration of Mary Pickersgill, who stitched the American Star-Spangled Banner (Crew et al. 2000). In the earliest days of the Nazi party, female members wore swastika armbands and 'Stormtrooper' (SA) style brown shirts, but they were effectively prohibited from doing so when they were increasingly confined to their own sphere within Nazi-controlled organisations after 1933 (Koonz 1976:588).

Hitler was convicted of treason following his violent grab for power in 1923 (King 2017). At his trial in 1924, he took the opportunity to show that despite being Austrian, he was a German patriot, a claim that was supported by the medals he had been awarded during the Great War. These decorations were announced in court by the sympathetic judge Georg Neithardt (Freniere 1976:46). Hitler was awarded the Iron Cross second class on 2 December, 1914, which he described as the 'happiest day of his life' (Stern 1975:178). It was not until 4 August, 1918, that he was awarded the higher grade of the decoration in its first-class form (Weber 2010:54). An irony of Hitler's first-class award was that it was the Jewish officer Hugo Gutmann who had recommended him for the decoration (Reuth 2009:41). The first-class grade had higher semiotic properties, being a badge that could be permanently pinned to the left breast pocket, unlike the second-class medal usually confined to parades or represented by a ribbon on the military tunic. The Iron Cross was an external manifestation of Hitler's bravery, which was falsified and blown out of all proportions in Nazi propaganda (i.e., he did not earn it for storming enemy trenches and taking French prisoners but for carrying messages behind the lines). The generic nature of the Iron Cross lent itself to such distortion and romanticisation, as there was nothing on the medal itself to indicate the deeds for which it was awarded. Furthermore, its symbolic value was bolstered by the congealed courage and sacrifice of all its recipients since the decoration was instituted in 1813 during the Napoleonic wars (Heinemann 2014:9). Indeed, the Iron Cross, designed by the neo-classical architect Karl Friedrich Schinkel, is 'intimately bound up with its formation and the sacrifice of its people' (Brady 2016:10).

At his trial, Hitler also benefitted from his association with fellow antisemitic putschist and former Great War commander Erich Ludendorff, who wore his military decorations on his last day in court and protested (as he sought martyrdom) that his acquittal was an 'affront to his uniform and medals' (Jablonsky 1989:74; photo of Ludendorff and Hitler on 79). After Hitler was released from prison in December 1924, he steered the Nazi party towards a superficial course of legality, but violence was never far away (Childers and Weiss 1990). The *Berliner Tagebuch* was critical of Hitler portraying himself as a 'decorated war hero' (*dekorierter Kriegsheld*) (Plöckinger 2006:206). Whilst Hitler wore his Iron Cross to secure support from patriotic Germans, he was not a resolute monarchist, as in a secret pamphlet directed at industrialists he was critical of former imperial customs and claimed that despite their illusion of pomp and glory, they masked the era's 'inner infirmity' (Turner 1968:366).

Nevertheless, in March 1923, Hitler appointed Hermann Göring as the head of the Stormtroopers (SA) (Volz 1936:54),[6] as according to Göring (at the Nürnberg trials in 1946), Hitler was taken by the fact that he had earned one of Germany's highest military distinctions; the Pour le Mérite (originally instituted by Frederick the Great in 1740) (Kube 1987:8). Despite Göring's decorations, many 'simple party members took offence at the exaggerated and pompous way in which he performed' (Longerich 2019:109). Göring claimed that after the Great War he was attacked by members of a Socialist Soldiers' Council who tried to remove his medals (Manvell and Fraenkel 1962:24).[7]

Shirts were one of the main signifiers of fascist movements during the 1920s and 1930s, from the black shirts of Italian fascists (Paulicelli 2004; Schneider 1928:45), to their British imitators (Spurr 2003), as well as the Silver Shirt Legion of America (Toy 1989). The brown shirt of the stormtroopers identified its wearers as supporters of the Nazi party just as much as did the swastika armband (Figure 2.4). It was during a meeting in Salzburg in 1924 (when the SA was banned, and Hitler was still in prison) that a Nazi fugitive by the name of Rossbach secured a supply of desert-style shirts (Schuman 1936:22; Volz 1936). The colour was therefore a result of circumstance rather than being intentional. The power of the shirt emanated from millions of Hitler supporters wearing it, rather than its colour.

The distribution and price of brown shirts were controlled well before the NSDAP achieved power in 1933, ensuring that the members of the SA had to purchase their uniforms from authorised sources (hence raising money for the SA and Nazi party). The brown shirt was advertised in November 1925 as the 'Hitler Shirt,' by the 'Sole distributors for the new approved Hitler clothing' for RM 7.25, complete with brown tie (VB November 1925:3).[8] Hitler was therefore personified through a piece of clothing, which he also wore himself. It was not until late 1926 that the brown shirt became mandatory for SA members (Siemens 2017a:Part I, 14). The brown shirt became shorthand for the organisation, demonstrating the semiotic power of uniformity. The Stormtroopers 'have gone down in history as beefy, squat, beerhall types; mere brownshirts' (Sontag 1980:99). In contrast to Wilhelm II being 'connected to his military uniform as a marker of his

Figure 2.4 Hitler and Ernst Röhm wearing the brown shirt, Braunschweig, October 1931.

Source: Bundesarchiv. Archive number 102-02192A.

Photographer: Georg Pahl.

social significance' (Giloi 2012:423), Hitler wore a plain brown shirt to show his affinity with the common Stormtrooper, also evoking religious asceticism.

So ubiquitous did the colour brown become that the manufacture and distribution of NSDAP products was known as the so-called brown industry. An article in the *Uniformen Markt* (a trade publication for the uniform and medal industry) claimed that the sector developed from the 'National Socialist supply store' (*NS-Bedarfsgeschäft*) that operated in 1927 through the 'Economic committee in the parliamentary office' (*NS-Wirtschaftsausschuss im Büro der Abgeordneten*) (UM Mai 1935:13). A reason for storing supplies in this office was that it had parliamentary protection; hence these troublesome pieces of political identity that threatened the Weimar democracy could not be confiscated. It was not until 1 April, 1929, that the equipment supply store (*Zeugmeisterei*) was created to supply the SA with 'good and cheap equipment' (*guter und billiger Ausrüstung*) (Volz 1936:57). This organisation, which developed into the *Reichszeugmeisterei* (RZM), was effectively a 'monopoly for giving out licences to producers and retailers' (*Lizenzvergabemonopol für Hersteller und Händler*) (Liedtke 2018:188). Indeed, it has been claimed it is in the interest of those in power to introduce a rigid set of regulations to control the flow of commodities (Appadurai 1986:57). Copyright 'is never only about maximizing monetary profits. It is also about monitoring content, distribution, and end use-control that seems necessary to ensure that the artist and his/her work are not misrepresented' (Giloi 2012:411). Uniformity was key to the success of the Hitler movement.

The uniforms and insignia of the *Schutzstaffel* (SS) were more expensive than those of the SA, intentionally differentiating the SS as an elite organisation (Kater 1975:361). The SS was an extremely small band of men in the 1920s, and the black coat and the silver-coloured runes that are the postwar stereotype of Nazis in Hollywood films had yet to be introduced (Heller 2004:849). The earliest members of the SS wore the brown shirt, black trousers and a black-bordered swastika armband and had a metal skull on their hats (Volz 1936:55). The skull was not an innovation of the SS but had been the insignia of the Guard Hussar regiments of the Prussian army. Following the collapse of the Kaiserreich, it was widely deployed by the right-wing Freikorps militias. The adoption of the skull by the SS signified that the organisation was an elite outfit that did not fear death, in addition to being capable of inflicting it. Steven Helmling spoke of the Thanatos (death instinct) of the 'SS Übermenschen flouting death's-head insignia, encouraged by Himmler in explicitly Nietzschean language, self-overcoming, etc., to withstand the urgings of conscience that would impede them in their heroic task of massacring the innocents' (Helmling 2005). Thoreau pondered the extent to which 'men would retain their relative rank if they were divested of their clothes' (Thoreau 1854, 1995:14). The SS and SA adopted a bewildering array of collar patches denoting rank, a system of signs that had to be learned, supported by corresponding shoulder epaulettes. Moreover, in uniform 'a man is on his mettle and acts as a soldier. Out of uniform, he degenerates, if he takes arms, to the role of a common murderer' (Shaw 1950:215). The death's head insignia of the SS, certainly after 1933, was effectively a licence to murder and torture.

One of the badge manufacturers which supplied the SS and related Nazi organisations from an early stage was the family firm of F. W. Assmann, a company originally established in the nineteenth century in the Westphalian city of Lüdenscheid (Woods 2011:15).[9] Eberhard Assmann had the low NSDAP membership number of 16043, so either he was a committed ideologue or he joined the party so that his company would benefit (if not both). Another firm based in Lüdenscheid was Steinhauer und Lück, established in 1889, which boasted in 1935 that it was 'one of the oldest suppliers of the NSDAP' (RZM HB 1935:808). This was after Hitler had achieved power, so the company may not have been as brazen before this, although it did contribute to the NSDAP's ascension by producing badges for the organisation. Without further evidence, it cannot be assumed that all the workers who made badges at Steinhauer or Assmann were members of the NSDAP or were sympathetic to Nazism, either before or after 1933.

The Munich-based badge firm of Deschler was a major supporter of the NSDAP before 1933, as evidenced by a Deschler advert in the *Völkischer Beobachter* in March 1925, which read 'artful, association, celebration badges and medals in enamel, galvanised and compression and sports badges of all kinds' (VB März 1925). Deschler therefore supported the NSDAP at the crucial juncture when the party was being reorganised after Hitler's release from prison (if not before). In addition to making badges for the Nazi party, the company also made emblems for other groups too, and it would be interesting to see if they produced badges for the NSDAP's opponents. Deschler benefitted from being situated in Munich, the city in which the headquarters of the NSDAP was located. By 1936, Deschler was not only making the membership badge of the NSDAP (discussed shortly), but also badges and medals that commemorated the 1936 Olympic games.[10]

The efficacy of symbols

At the beginning of the 1920s, Adolf Hitler placed a modernised 'abstract and primitive' swastika at the centre of Nazi identity, a decision that played a role in turning the NSDAP, which began the decade as one of several small right-wing groups in Munich, into a modern political movement able to win 18.3 percent of the vote in the Reichstag elections of September 1930, up from 2.6 percent in May 1928 (Simmons 2000:335).

Despite the symbols worn and displayed by supporters of the NSDAP, had it not been for the Wall Street crash in October 1929 and the subsequent Depression, it is likely that the party would have remained a marginal organisation. As already noted, in the election of 1928, which was before the economic crisis, the NSDAP only polled 2.6 percent of the vote (also see O'Loughlin 2002:220). By the time of this election, the majority of highly visible symbols which may have drawn supporters to the NSDAP were already operational. Due to the small number of votes, the capacity for swastikas to achieve electoral success was negligible. This is not to say that these symbols were not further replicated, but they were not initially capable on their own of reaping millions of votes.

As a causative agent of change, the power of symbols should therefore be approached with caution. They did have an effect on impressionable youths (Abel 1938, 1986:265), but the NSDAP was far from the only political organisation which deployed symbols to attract supporters (Canning 2010). Indeed, the late 1920s have been described as the battle of the flags (Führer 2019:Chapter 7). By November 1932, the NSDAP had even lost some of the votes it had gathered in the summer of that year (O'Lessker 1968:64). Germany was experiencing a 'political, economic and social crisis' (Neumann 1942, 2012:34), so rather than the magnetism of emblems having primacy, people were especially vulnerable to a 'charismatic leader with his unshakable conviction in the truth of his message that conveys to his followers the certainty they seek' (Connor 1989:261).

George Grosz captured the threat of fascism in his 1928 painting 'The Agitator' (*Der Agitator*) (Kranzfelder 2001:52). The agitator (presumably Hitler) holds a loudhailer and a truncheon, demonstrating the power of amplified words reinforced by the threat of violence. The agitator's tie consists of a swastika; an Iron Cross dangles over his heart in the old imperial colours of black, white and red. The all-male members of the middle and working classes eagerly listen to his promises of restoring Germany's military glory and providing work and bread (Stedelijk n.d.). Hitler capitalised on the economic fallout following the Wall Street crash; indeed, constructions of 'crises and either-ors were most popular among intellectuals and politicians on both extremes of the political spectrum who were highly optimistic and confident that they would be able to realize their Utopian visions in the near future' (Graf 2010:609). It took another five years until Hitler was appointed Chancellor, after which he sought to Nazify the whole of Germany.

Co-ordination (*gleichschaltung*)

The term *Gleichschaltung* 'eventually came to refer to the Nazification of all aspects of society' (Schaarschmidt 2017:220). The Reichstag fire on 28 February, 1933, contributed to this process, as it 'allowed Adolf Hitler's government to take a major step toward dictatorial control through the Reichstag Fire Decree' (Hett 2015:200). The elections in early March (which had been planned before the fire) revealed that the majority of Germans did not vote for Hitler (Edinger 1953). As a consequence of the fire, the new Reichstag session was ceremoniously opened at the Potsdam Garrison on 21 March, where Hindenburg's handshake with Hitler symbolically transferred the Kaiserreich to the 'Bohemian Corporal' (Bessel 2004:170) (Figure 2.5).[11] Hindenburg wore his imperial uniform and medals, in contrast to Hitler, who did not wear his usual brown shirt and swastika armband, but sought to appeal to the middle class by wearing a 'frock coat and top-hat' (Horn and Gold 2011:108). Two days later, on the day of the enabling law, this political chameleon returned to his old ways, as he wore his Nazi party uniform and his tone was intimidating (Goltz 2009:175). After the required two-thirds majority was obtained by forceful manoeuvrings (Fergusson 1964), Germany was essentially governed by Hitler and his neutralised cabinet, and it only took until July 1933 until the country was declared a one-party state (DHM 2015).[12]

Figure 2.5 Hitler shaking hands with Hindenburg on 21 March, 1933, the Day of Potsdam.

Source: Bundesarchiv. Archive number 183-S38324.

Photographer: Unknown.

Nazi kitsch

German businesses selling souvenirs 'measured the so-called revolution only in terms of its potential need for relics and keepsakes' (Steinberg 1975:1). The 'National Socialists had not foreseen that their glorious symbol might be transformed into a piece of tatty merchandise, and had taken no precautions against this' (Ibid). An article in the Berliner *Illustrierte Zeitung* stated that 'this industry of tastelessness sensed a need to see and display the new colours, symbols, and national emblems of the Reich, pictures of the new statesmen and historical personalities anywhere and everywhere' (Rabinbach and Gilman 2013:79).

A law was introduced on 19 May, 1933, curtailing the production and sale of these products.[13] It was intended to ensure 'respect' for 'party symbols' and was an example of how the leaders of the NSDAP strove to make the party a para-governmental organisation (AV1). The law was a measure against so-called kitsch, although this term was not specifically used. The legislation prohibited products which did not have artistic merit; hence taste was replaced by specifications (Armstrong 1933). A governor of taste was the recently appointed Reichsminister for public enlightenment and propaganda (*Der Reichsminister für Volksaufklärung und Propaganda*), Dr. Goebbels (RGB Mai 1933). Both old and new symbols were to be controlled, with it being 'prohibited to publicly use the symbols of German history, the German state and the national uprising in Germany in a way that can hurt the sense of dignity of these symbols.'[14]

Emblems were regarded as a living expression of a nation, and only those that accorded with the new political climate were to be permitted. Inanimate objects took on agency through the meaning attributed to them. Inanimate things 'within the environment act on people, and are acted upon by people, for the purposes of carrying out social functions' (Woodward 2007:3). Objects 'have impact like falling meteorites, but in order to have agency they need to be entangled within social relations' (Geismar 2011:213). Objects 'not only mediate the self-relation of the subject, they also mediate its relation to others' (Rödig 2012:49). Flags are an 'extension of the social self, providing a series of principles and norms for living, relating to others and the past' (Tilley 1996:162). Everyday experiences in Germany contained the prerequisites for understanding the political messages of flags and symbols (Morgan 2010:60–3). Flying the imperial flag in the first few years of the Third Reich was seen as a continuation of German militarism but was later regarded as a protest sign against Nazism. Adherents 'of Nazism viewed their lives as positively transformed by the externalization and reabsorption of the performative effects of sacred symbols' (Coleman 1996:40).

So sacred were symbols such as the swastika (which remained both feared and revered) that measures were implemented to ensure that they were not com-mercialised. It was considered 'incomprehensible' that private companies were producing swastika song books merely to advertise their businesses (UM Januar 1936:13). Steinberg (1975) gave examples of prohibited objects, and although they may have been crass – for example, Hitler ashtrays – so were some of the permitted products. The 'contrasting lists of the forbidden and the permissible representations make it immediately clear that what was deemed acceptable was no less kitschy than what was forbidden' (Friedländer 1990:202). The newsletters of the RZM included the products that could be officially produced, and herein lies the crux of the matter, as although a swastika was a swastika, the primary concern was how it was deployed. If it was an official piece of political insignia which reinforced hierarchy, it was permissible. On the other hand, if it was a commercially produced commodity for private consumption, it was considered as inauthentic (both in terms of its unlicenced nature and its use value). Products were meant to boost respect for the leaders of the Nazi movement rather than undermining them.

The brooch of fear: the NSDAP membership badge

The membership badge of the NSDAP, designed by the Munich-based jeweller Joseph Füss in 1920,[15] is a cogent example of how the social life of an object can transmute over time. When the party was considered by many as a radical fringe movement, some of its members hid their badges under their lapels. Conversely, after January 1933, the badges were publicly flaunted and were sought by those wishing to jump on the Nazi bandwagon.

The badge did not acquire the name of the 'Brooch of Fear' (*Angstbrosche*) (Spiegel 1966) as a result of the terror which supporters of the Nazi party inflicted on their victims, but because opportunists were joining the organisation for personal aggrandisement rather than ideological conviction (Silverman 1988). Hundreds of thousands of 'men and women also entered the party out of fear of the party and only for the sake of being left in peace' (Sträter 1948:45). The upsurge in membership applications was so great that they were halted on 30 April, 1933, and no one was able to apply to join the party again until 1937 (Cuomo 2012). There were still opportunities to wear badges with swastikas on them, although these did not carry the same political weight as the membership badge of the NSDAP.

The Nazi party badge acquired considerable agency compared to its status before 1933. In August 1934, the deputy leader of the NSDAP, Rudolf Hess, issued a decree forbidding party members from wearing the badge whilst doing business with Jewish people.[16] The decree was not borne out of sympathy for Jewish people (i.e., avoiding offending them through wearing Nazi badges), but as a way to shame party members and change their shopping behaviour whilst financially damaging Jewish-owned businesses. The decree effectively imposed a boycott of Jewish shops by stealth, thereby avoiding a repeat of the international outcry following the public boycott of Jewish-owned stores that had taken place in April 1933 (Gottlieb 1968). Nevertheless, Hermann Göring bought carpets from a Jewish-owned business as late as 1936 (Evans 2006:383). Despite Hess introducing the decree, it has been claimed that he was one of the more 'reasonable people' within the Nazi movement (Gellermann 1936:44), which only goes to show how extreme the leaders of the NSDAP actually were.

The scapegoating of Jews was a feature of the Nazi movement from its beginnings, but after 1933 the badge decree contributed to their isolation. Jewish people were all too aware that the membership badge represented antisemitism. The reaction by a German Jew to a badge-wearing party member can be found in the case of Karl Lowith when he met his former tutor, Martin Heidegger.[17] Lowith met Heidegger in Rome in 1936 and was astonished to find that Heidegger did not think that his swastika lapel pin would offend him (Rubenstein 1989:179). In *When Hitler Stole Pink Rabbit*, a semiautobiographical children's story written by the late Judith Kerr, who had been a Jewish child during the Third Reich, a Nazi membership badge featuring the ubiquitous 'red enamel and black hooked cross' is so abhorrent that it is flushed down the 'what-not (toilet)' (Kerr 1971, 2017:11–12). There is surely symbolism in this act, which plumbs the emblem to the deepest and dirtiest of depths.

The wearing of badges acted as a sign to opponents of the Nazi regime that they had to be watchful of what they said. In his secret diary entitled *My Opposition*, Social Democrat Friedrich Kellner stated that when he began a 'conversation with a stranger, your first glance is not anywhere in the face but at the heroic breast to ascertain what kind of spiritual offspring he is' (Kellner 2018:211–212). Observing the membership badge of the NSDAP made opponents like Kellner especially wary of what they said.

The sale of the membership badge of the NSDAP generated funds for the party. A price that was regulated by the RZM in 1935 was 30 Pfennig (RZM Mai 1935). To put this price into context, a litre of milk in 1935 cost just over 16 Pfennig (Hoffman 1965:580). It is conceivable that a member owned more than one badge, thus even a small enamelled emblem presumably generated millions of marks for the Nazi Party.

In contrast to the ordinary membership badge, of which millions were produced and worn, the Golden Decoration of the NSDAP was instituted to honour those who had joined the party at an early stage (hereafter Golden Decoration or Golden Party badge) (Figure 2.6). The establishment of the badge was announced by Hitler in October 1933, in time for the tenth anniversary of the botched, albeit venerated, putsch (Doehle 1943:71). The badge was intended for the first 100,000 members who had re-joined the party after it was reconstituted in February 1925. An eligibility requirement was unbroken NSDAP membership, which meant that only just over 20,000 members qualified for the emblem (Angolia 1978:178). The low number of members who were initially entitled to it was put into context by Jürgen Falter, who stated that it was not unusual for individuals to join the NSDAP, leave the party, then join later (Falter 2013:260). Those who reluctantly joined the party after the election on 5 March, 1933, were known as those who had 'fallen in March' (*Märzgefallene*) (Falter 1998).

Figure 2.6 Replica Golden Party badge 1933.
Source: Author's collection. Photograph taken by Grant Hughes, 2020.

By this date, the opportunity to obtain a Golden Decoration based on member-ship had passed. Some women did receive the badge, but despite such a supposedly distinguished sign, they were prevented from having a leadership position except within their own sphere, such as the NS Women's Association (*Frauenschaft*). The members and leaders of this group wore a triangular badge reflecting their position within the organisation (UM August 1935:12; RZM April 1935:149). Whilst these badges symbolised and reinforced hierarchy within the NS Women's Association, they did not have much clout outside it, nor did its leader Gertrud Scholtz-Klink (Wyllie 2019).

Hitler awarded honorary versions of the Golden Decoration to commanders of the military who were not members of the Nazi party in a bid to secure their alle-giance. Political insignia was not usually worn on military uniforms, so the deco-ration was yet another way in which Nazi symbols became part of the Wehrmacht. Under the rubric of gift exchange, the bestowal of these badges was a trojan horse. Indeed, if they 'accept the award, they are to some extent bound, and other peo-ple will consider them to be supporters of the regime' (Frey 2006:382). A case in point is Grand Admiral Karl Dönitz (Hitler's eventual successor), who was given the badge late in the war by Hitler, on 30 January, 1944 (Steinert 1988:658; AV2). Ironically, although the badge was less financially valuable than gifts of paintings or money, it was far more conspicuous. In contrast to Dönitz, principled army commanders such as Werner von Fritsch rejected the 'seemingly priceless' award (Goda 2000:425), an affront that may have been in Hitler's mind when he dismissed Fritsch in February 1938 (O'Neill 1966:143).[18]

In April 1945, as the Soviets were bombarding Berlin, Goebbels's wife Magda (so-called First Lady of the Reich) received one of the last decorations awarded by Hitler, when he presented her with his own Golden Decoration as a 'token of esteem.'[19] The presentation was witnessed by the pilot Hanna Reitsch, who stated that Hitler pinned the badge to Frau Goebbels's dress and proclaimed that she was a 'staunch pillar of the "honor" upon which National Socialism was built and the German Fatherland founded' (Work 1946:571). Joseph and Magda Goebbels each wrote a letter to their son Harald Quandt (of Magda's first marriage) on 28 April, 1945, which Reitsch was to give to him. The badge was mentioned in the letters that Reitsch secretly read, and she later recalled that Joseph Goebbels stated, 'the Führer gave her the Golden Party badge which he has worn on his tunic for years and she deserved it' (Jackson 2014:198).

Although Goebbels did not use the term 'aura,' making the point that it was the badge Hitler once wore is significant. The presentation would not have had the same symbolic value had it not been Hitler's own badge. The aura and enchant-ment of the badge were also recognised by Magda Goebbels, as she stated, 'yes-terday evening the Führer took off his Golden Party badge and pinned it on me, I am happy and proud.'[20] Through the subsequent suicides of Joseph and Magda Goebbels, a 'connection can be drawn to the dangerous undercurrent of death, ruin and sacrifice which had been so masterfully constructed by their Führer' (O'Donnell 2012:237).

Even after Nazi Germany was defeated, there were still some individuals who valued the discredited symbols of National Socialism, such as Wehrmacht commander Wilhelm Keitel, who wore his honorary Golden Decoration when he signed the surrender document on 8 May, 1945, in Karlshorst (Kershaw 2011:Photograph between 278 & 279). It was Hitler who had given Keitel the badge, and by wearing it, he showed the world that there were still individuals who were not ashamed to sport badges that were strongly associated with Hitlerism.

Collectors

Despite the above, the social context and meaning of both the Golden Decoration and the standard party badge have been overlooked by collectors. Their focus is the identification of nominal authenticity and the exposure of fakes. Perhaps this is not unexpected, as it has been said that it is 'virtually impossible' for a collectible object not to 'avoid coming into contact with a system of evaluation that is external to and other than itself (such as money, social recognition, or the professional approval of the connoisseur)' (Chow 2001:298). Collectors home in on the RZM code numbers applied to these badges, rather than their social and personal meaning.

A recent publication aimed at collectors of Nazi party badges showed the emblems under 5x magnification (Rivett 2013). Ironically, by making the small gigantic, the focus on minute detail distanced the badges even further from their sociality during the Third Reich. In 'Thing Theory,' Brown (2001:8) cited Georg Simmel who stated in *The Philosophy of Money* that 'coming closer to things often only shows us how far away they still are from us' (Simmel 1907, 1978:47). Conversely, microphotography has the ability to transfix the viewer with images they would not have been able to observe with their unaided eye (Nagel 2001).

Rivett searched for micro-patina, as its existence indicates that a badge is nominally authentic. Patina is the 'worn surface acquired by goods through use and the passage of time' (Ames 1989:403). Patina exudes a strong sense of authenticity, which is why chemicals are often applied to fake badges and medals. The 'presence of the original is the prerequisite to the concept of authenticity. Chemical analysis of the patina of a bronze can help to establish this' (Benjamin 1936:Section II). Another reason for examining patina is to assist in the preservation of public statues and monuments (Bogolitsyna et al. 2009). Anthropologists tend to focus on the symbolic value of patina. Dawdy (2016) discovered that survivors of Hurricane Katrina in New Orleans preserved the patina created by the disaster rather than wiping it off their living room walls. Patina bonds the past to the present and people to objects (Holtorf 2013).

Preference for patina is very much influenced by personal taste and cultural factors. Some Westerners were astonished when the Muria Gonds of India purchased antique silver jewellery then removed the patina (Gell 1986). Patina on silver owned by old English families was material proof that their wealth was not newly acquired (McCracken 1988). It is for a similar reason that members of the Gabor Roma community in Romania in the twenty-first-century purchase patinated tankards to establish family prestige (Berta 2019). Collectors of imperial German and Nazi memorabilia do not regard patina in this way, and some have even cleaned their medals. I confess that I once cleaned layers of patina that had accumulated on the silver frame of a Great War Iron Cross, more out of curiosity than anything else. Although I experienced fleeting pleasure from the glinting frame, I felt guilty for wiping away decades of history, which only took a few seconds to accomplish. As patina transforms 'an object into something timeworn, worthy of respect' (Harvey 2011:49), I subjected the medal to physical abuse. Nevertheless, it did not have patina when it was initially awarded, so some may argue that I was simply wiping away dirt.

There 'is a tendency to draw an analogy between the ageing of human beings and artefacts' (Wagner 2019:271). Consequently, cleaning objects keeps them young, much in the same way that Laurence Binyon's poem *For the Fallen* includes the line 'Age will not weary them' (Binyon 1914, 2014). Great War widows polished pieces of Trench Art as an expression of love for their lost husbands (Saunders 2014). One must be careful, however, as too much polishing will wear down the details otherwise respected.

Both types of Nazi party badges discussed have retained their physical and symbolic patina (i.e., aura), but have lost much of their former political agency. They have been converted into collectible objects, although there is still a certain degree of stigma associated with these badges, even in collectors' circles. This has somewhat waned in recent years. In a climate where the term 'Nazi' is liberally bandied about in mainstream society (Robinson 2018), perhaps some collectors are less apprehensive about asking militaria traders for Nazi party badges.

If we accept the idea that movies could stimulate demand for particular artefacts, it is worth noting that both the standard party badge and the Golden Decoration of the NSDAP were prominently depicted in *Indiana Jones and the Last Crusade* (Spielberg 1989). Oscar Schindler wore the Golden Decoration in *Schindler's List* (Spielberg 1993), and although the real Schindler was a member of the Nazi party, he did not join until 1939, making it unlikely that he held the Golden Decoration (Marks and Torry 2000; Wildt and Selwyn 1996). Whilst the intention of these movies was not to encourage the collecting of Nazi memorabilia, they nevertheless featured Nazi regalia, which may have informed collectors' aesthetic sensibilities. The availability of these movies also means that they continue to be consumed long after they were made.

Both the ordinary party badge and the Golden Decoration have significantly increased in price in recent years. A North of England-based collector who began collecting Nazi memorabilia in the late 1960s paid just under GBP 1 for an ordinary party badge in 1971 (Czunys 2018, pers. comm.). In 2020, a trader offered similar badges ranging from GBP 95 to GBP 115 (RegPB 2020). In 1935, a party badge sold for 30 Pfennig, equivalent to about 16 pence in 1971. This represents an increase of 525 percent in real terms between 1935 and 1971. From 1935 until 2020, its price increased by over 9400 percent. The price of the badge has therefore risen more substantially from the 1970s onwards, with its meteoric price rise occurring in the last few years. Collectors' publications have influenced these recent price rises but are unlikely to be the sole factor.

The Golden Decoration has a similar trajectory, exhibiting a fairly static price during the 1980s and rising more substantially after the millennium. In contrast to the prices of the ordinary party badge taken from sporadic sources, prices of the Golden Decoration were taken from a run of German-language catalogues frequently consulted by specialist dealers in Third Reich medals. These price guides date from the late 1970s to the present (Nimmergut 1980-Nimmergut and Nimmergut 2014).[21] Similar guides did not exist when Allied soldiers acquired war booty in 1945; thus, they are emblematic of how the market in Nazi memorabilia became commodified. Out of all the main decorations that I discuss, the Golden Decoration of the NSDAP exhibited the second highest percentage increase in price in real terms (see Appendix A). The spot price of gold can be discounted, as the badge was not generally made from precious metal; hence it is the symbolic nature of the badge that appeals to collectors, namely being associated with early members of the Nazi movement. The recipient's party number on the reverse of the Golden Decoration allows for the possibility for its owner to be traced at the *Bundesarchiv* (providing it was not erased to avoid being traced). Such a reunion could be dangerous in the wrong hands.

Conclusion

Nazi symbols were a vehicle for the transmission of ideology and political demagoguery. They had a remarkable agency, destabilising the Weimar democracy, then assisting the NSDAP's consolidation of power from January 1933. For Hitler and his supporters, the swastika represented antisemitism, and as Jews were excluded from Nazi organisations, all of which had their own emblems, they were further isolated in a society where badges not only commanded power and prestige but facilitated antisemitism. Jews were also prohibited from flying swastika flags, which marked out their houses in a society where it was expected that people would do so on Hitler's birthday.

Collectors have decontextualised the meaning of Nazi symbols, which is particularly concerning in the case of the membership badge of the NSDAP, especially as it has experienced somewhat of a renaissance. As patina on Nazi artefacts contributes to their aura, some may wish to wipe it away, although if it has survived this long, it should be left alone. Abundant replicas devoid of tarnish are potentially more dangerous than scarce authentic artefacts. Much in the same way that Nazi symbols were replicated to express an affinity with Nazism in the volatile years of Weimar, societies must be on their guard against a resurgence of Nazi symbols or their derivatives being deployed by right-wing populists to destabilise or unseat democracies.

Notes

1 References for the painting 'War Cripples' by Otto Dix: Barron (1991:373); SGA (1991:110); Eberle (1985:44).
2 Reference for the painting 'The Card Players' by Otto Dix: Umland (n.d.). Full source can be found within the Bibliography.

3 German text on the reverse of the Kyffhäuser medal: *Aufrecht u stolz gehen wir aus dem Kampfe den wir über vier Jahre gegen eine Welt von Feinden bestanden.*

4 The Kyffhäuser medal was purchased between autumn of 1921 (Weimar Germany) and May 1934 (Nazi Germany), when it was prohibited, as it was not deemed an official award. It was yet another symbol that threatened the monopoly of the swastika. The Kyffhäuser association was fully co-ordinated into a Nazi-run veterans' organisation in 1938 (APKM 2011; Rossol 2014). For a history of the association see Friz (1996).

5 Hitler (2016:1252, footnote 96). Krohn was the dentist mentioned earlier, and Schüssler was the treasurer of the party at that time.

6 Hitler appointed Göring as Supreme SA leader in March 1923. Due to the failed November 1923 putsch, the SA was banned; Göring fled Germany and appointed Ernst Röhm as his deputy. Röhm then formed the Frontbann and refused Hitler's offer to become head of the SA in 1925. It was not until 1926 that Hitler appointed Franz Pfeffer von Salomon supreme commander of the SA. Hitler dismissed him in 1930 and invited Röhm back into his movement, appointing him chief of the SA in 1931, then ordered his murder in the Night of the Long Knives in 1934 (Brown 2013; Jablonsky 1988; Siemens 2017a, 2017b).

7 In relation to the phenomenon of Socialist councils which emerged after the Great War, never 'before had Germany experienced such a manifestation of popular sovereignty based on a radical form of direct democracy in the armed forces, industry, and the cities' (Bassler 1973:244).

8 RM 7.25 in 1925 is equivalent to 27 Euros (GBP 23, USD 32) in terms of spending power in 2021 (BB 2021), which does not seem expensive for a shirt and tie today. Furthermore, an original example of a Nazi brown shirt and tie would retail on the collectors' market in 2021 for well over GBP 300, which represents a considerable rise in real terms. The purpose for purchasing the garment in 1925, however, was not so it would be collectible in the future.

9 There were 18 badge-making companies in the traditional silversmith city of Pforzheim, 17 in the button city of Lüdenscheid, seven in Munich, and five in Berlin (RZM HB 1935).

10 In 1936, Deschler of Munich, one of the largest badge firms, had 72 employees, which included 50 unskilled and 15 skilled workers, as well as seven white-collar staff. The net profit for the year 1936 was RM 366,000 (which could purchase about USD 2.5 million of consumer goods in 2014) (Desch Okt37) (HSS).

11 This 'profound national feeling of the Volk was a building block of Hitler; it was a reason, why he was elevated in 1933, and the only thought that connected Hitler and Hindenburg, who despised Hitler as the "Bohemian Corporal" (*böhmischen Gefreiten*)' (Doehring 2004:659). Translated from German by Sophie Baumert. Hindenburg was fully aware that Hitler was born in the Austrian town of Braunau am Inn rather than Bohemia. Nevertheless, there was a Braunau in Bohemia, part of the Austro-Hungarian empire, now in the Czech Republic. In any case, for Hindenburg, Hitler was not Prussian. Hindenburg was born in the Duchy of Posen under Prussian control; this region was contested and is now part of Poland. It would have been more correct if Hindenburg had called Hitler the Bavarian Corporal, as he served with the Bavarian infantry during the Great War. Most standard English translations give Hitler's rank (*Gefreiter*) as a full corporal, but a lance-corporal is more accurate.

12 14 July, 1933, also marked the law authorising sterilisation of people with conditions deemed genetic, for example, blindness (Loewenstein 1936).

13 The anti-kitsch law was entitled *Gesetz zum Schutze der nationalen Symbole* (RGB Mai 1933).

14 Original German text of the law protecting national symbols: *Es ist verboten, die Symbole der deutschen Geschichte, des deutschen Staates und der nationalen Erhebung in*

Deutschland öffentlich in einer Weise zu verwenden, die geeignet ist, das Empfinden von der Würde dieser Symbole zu verletzen (RGB Mai 1933:285).

15 Rivett (2013:58). Füss also advertised badges and medals for sale in the *Völkischer Beobachter in* 1922 (VB Dezember 1922:8).

16 RZM (September 1934:1; Ley 1938:Section 8.4).

17 Martin Heidegger's party card dates his NSDAP membership to 1 May, 1933 (BA 33), hence he was more of an opportunist than a so-called old-fighter.

18 Fritsch was falsely accused of enlisting the services of a male prostitute but was subsequently cleared.

19 Kershaw (2000:Chapter 17, VI, Kindle location 18220).

20 Jackson (2014:201, Appendix 2).

21 When Nimmergut's price guides were first published, the prices were in Deutschmarks (DM), then in Euro. I therefore converted the later prices back to DM and used inflation figures in relation to Germany (WBI). I did not manage to locate the price guide for the year 1986 (although it does exist), so I replaced the missing data using the technique known as the Last Observation Carried Forward (LOCF) (Lachin 2016; Bell *et al.* 2014). Additionally, I used the geometric rather than the arithmetic mean (Coggeshall 1886; Jacquier and Marcus 2003).

3   The materiality of the people's community

The 'concept of the Volk had a particularly profound significance for National Socialism, meaning not only a "people", but also a racial entity. It was believed that a transcendental essence united the members of the Volk' (Taylor 1981:519). The 'term Gemeinschaft in the Nazi sense means the fellowship, cooperation, and solidarity of the German community' (Hess 1938:4). In light of such statements, I assess the effectiveness of badges in facilitating this community. Leni Riefenstahl depicted a sanitised version of the People's Community in her infamous documentary of the 1934 Nazi party congress in Nürnberg entitled *Triumph of the Will* (*Der Triumph des Willens*) (Riefenstahl 1935), a rally for which a metal badge was commissioned. Emblems in a multitude of materials were produced in even larger numbers to raise funds for an initiative central to the creation of the People's Community, the Winter Help Program (*Winterhilfswerk*) (WHW). This scheme was ostensibly created to reduce hunger and cold but was a vehicle for racism. I also describe and analyse the iconography of the badges produced to promote Strength through Joy (*Kraft durch Freude*) (KdF). This organisation sought to bring Germans together through subsidised vacations, of which the badges served as mementos. The KdF was under the jurisdiction of the German Labour Front (*Deutsche Arbeitsfront*, DAF), an organisation signified by a swastika within a cogwheel.

Human cogs?

The German Labour Front, established in May 1933, was headed by Dr. Robert Ley, who only renounced antisemitism in a note written before he committed suicide in October 1945 (Liskofsky 1947:458–459). The DAF's formation was a 'misshapen child of hectic improvisation,' eventually growing into a membership of approximately 20 million workers (Mason 1966:114). The DAF was pronounced as an acronym reflecting the 'worldwide linguistic trend that mirrored the technicization and bureaucratization of modern life' (Young 2005:50). In keeping with the majority of organisations associated with the NSDAP, the DAF had its own emblem consisting of a swastika within a cogwheel (Figure 3.1). The meaning of this symbol was published in an article in the *National-Zeitung* (and

DOI: 10.4324/9781003000617-3

Figure 3.1 DAF flag.

Source: Der Reichsorganisationsleiter der NSDAP (Ley 1938). Picture reproduced with permission of University of Glasgow Library, Archives & Special Collections. Matthias Nowak of the Bayrisches Staatsministerium der Finanzen und für Heimat stated that the Free State of Bavaria has no legal objections to this image being reproduced in this publication (Nowak 2020).

reproduced in the *Uniformen Markt*) entitled the 'Swastika in a Wheel' (*Haken-kreuz im Rade*), which reads:

> Every individual member of the workforce is influencing the other like a cogwheel and pushing forward work and the economy of our country as a whole. If one of the wheels stops, if it cannot be used any more, if it breaks, other wheels will stop as well, and all the work and the unified struggle and any sort of success will end.

> (UM September 1935:5)

Indeed, it has been said that the 'state instituted a politics of the body that rendered the individual body a public site whose purpose was to further the larger social organism' (Gordon 2002:164). The sacred cogwheel of the DAF was a root metaphor under which the rights of workers were obliterated (Ortner 1973). Dr. Ley and the leaders of the DAF had a difficult task in uniting workers under the DAF banner, as they were not able to totally tame class divisions, and despite the harmony which was sought, not every wheel was moving in the same direction, exacerbated by workers' opposition (Mason 1981). Labour Day, traditionally celebrated by Marxists, was therefore appropriated to acquiesce to workers (Fritzsche 2009:44–46). Despite the May Day celebrations, some workers avoided taking part in parades (Lüdtke 1992). Presumably these workers, if they were pressed into the DAF, would not have been enthusiastic about the regulation which stipulated that on 'May 1, the cogwheel and swastika badge of the DAF had to be worn.'[1] Nevertheless, far from the perception that the NSDAP was the exclusive domain of the middle class, it got support from some workers (Mühlberger 1980).

Figure 3.2 Dachau gate. Taken from a private photograph album detailing the visit of the Head of the Legal Division of the SS, Paul Scharfe (died 1942), to Dachau concentration camp. Reproduced with permission of Yad Vashem Archives, Jerusalem. Photo number 54492, album number FA1 99/5.

Photographer: SS photographer (unknown).

The metaphor of the cogwheel was also deployed by perpetrators of the Holocaust. Shortly before he was hanged, the commandant of Auschwitz, Rudolf Höss, claimed he had been a 'cog in the wheel' (Höss 1959:181). At his Israeli trial in 1961, Adolf Eichmann also claimed that he had only been a cog (Twiss 2010), but he was far from simply being a 'small cog' (Stangneth 2015). Concentration camp inmates worked and died under the perverse slogan of 'Work Sets You Free' (*Arbeit Macht Frei*) (Figure 3.2). Indeed, the sign should have been inscribed 'Annihilation by Work' (*Vernichtung durch Arbeit*) (Roth 1980:72).

Strength through Joy (*kraft durch freude*) (KdF)

The loss of liberty experienced by those branded as either political opponents or racially inferior contrasted to members of the People's Community, who went on vacations subsidised by the KdF. Nevertheless, the trips were 'not a free vacation but a temporary respite to enhance productivity and a vehicle for political manipulation' (Smelser 1990:298). The KdF was an example of the power of symbols to confirm and facilitate a culture of rewards (Lüdtke 2000:90). KdF activities were actually another way in which the Nazi regime could control workers' limited leisure time.

The badges produced to raise funds for the KdF are artefactual evidence of the companies which manufactured them, the materials used and the approved holiday destinations. Baranowski (2004:189) included a picture of two KdF emblems under the caption 'a commemorative pin and luggage label, the tangible evidence of having toured with KdF.' The badge depicted the DAF swastika within a cogwheel, in the position of the sun. According to the 'convoluted and bizarre' writings of the Nazi philosopher Alfred Rosenberg (Arnold 2006), the 'Nordic gods were light creatures with a spear and light wreath, and the cross and swastika were the symbols of the sun of the fruit bearing ascending life' (Rosenberg 1930, 1935:165; also see Mees 2004). The badges of the KdF did not always portray the swastika, suggesting that workers were being influenced in a more discreet manner. Nevertheless, the badges of the KdF still promoted the National Socialist Community, which the workers on vacation contributed to even though they were not necessarily party members.

KdF souvenirs were not exempt from the war on kitsch, as the 'type of item the tourist purchased seemed less important than how that item had been produced' (Hagen 2004:217). Nevertheless, as mass-produced KdF aluminium badges were officially approved representations of the holiday destinations, they did not constitute kitsch. Nazi propaganda 'explicitly rejected the labelling of aluminium as ersatz and instead identified aluminium as a key *Heimstoff* (home material) that would minimize German dependence on imports, even though Germany relied on Hungary and Yugoslavia for most of its bauxite' (Schatzberg 2003:239). Aluminium badges are more reflective of Nazi Germany's modernity compared to those made from traditional materials such as wood. Furthermore, aluminium emblems have survived in better condition than those made from zinc (as they have not oxidised in the same way). The decisions that were made during the Third Reich therefore affect the way in which we experience its material culture today.

Art historian Michael Tymkiw explored the 'ideological function of mass-produced housewares and decorative objects' which were part of KdF factory exhibitions (Tymkiw 2013:362). He claimed that although the cups and saucers on display were fairly innocuous, they directed workers' disposable income (which was in short supply) towards goods that aided the Nazi economy. Companies which made even more overtly Nazi symbols, such as the badge-making firm of Hermann Aurich in Dresden, also took part in KdF initiatives such as 'Beauty of Work' (*Schönheit der Arbeit*). The firm's offices were decorated with Hitler quotations, and it was even claimed that the slogans had increased the satisfaction of the workforce and were an example of how 'even smaller companies can do great things with good will and a National Socialist leadership' (UM Februar 1935:12). It was the smaller handicraft firms whose walls tended to be decorated with Hitler quotations (Rabinbach 1976:46), but despite these overt signs of enthusiasm, the workers were often unpaid and had to paint the quotations after hours (Evans 2006:475).

Further research would be required to establish the extent to which the workers and management of Hermann Aurich supported the NSDAP, although they were certainly willing to make money from badges which espoused Nazi propaganda. Aurich was founded before the Third Reich, as were the majority of the firms that made emblems for the NSDAP. In June 1945, the American military even permitted Deschler, which had produced the Golden Decoration of the NSDAP, 'to manufacture metal and enamel badges for military forces' (Desch J45). Although the company stopped making Nazi badges, it carried on in the same line of business, producing badges for organisations as long as they were able to pay for them. Whether it be the football club Bayern-München or Saddam Hussein, for the late Helmut Stillner, manager of Deschler between the 1970s and the 1990s, it was all the same (Demir 2017; Sessler 2010). No doubt he would have drawn the line had he been asked to make a key ring featuring Hitler (illegal in any case).

During the Second World War, some badge-making firms, such as Assmann and Steinhauer und Lück, resorted to using forced labour (Begler 2013). The aforementioned source, at the Lüdenscheid city archive, gave no clue as to how many individuals were forced to work (or what their tasks were), in which years they worked or the countries they were from. It is likely that badge firms in other cities also employed forced labour, for by 1944, a fifth of Germany's workforce consisted of foreigners pressed into some form of compulsory work, including outright slavery (Burleigh 2000:478–481; Mazower 2009:294–303). Consequently, Nazi badges cannot be disassociated from unethical or criminal practices (there is more on this in Chapter 6). The use of forced labour to manufacture the sanctified symbols of National Socialism exposes the distorted nature of Nazi ideology and casts a shadow over the romantic notion held by some collectors that the badges were exclusively made by traditional German craftspeople. Whether these revelations are enough to dent the rather impervious Nazi memorabilia trade is doubtful.

The Nürnberg rallies

Of 'all the aspects of Nazi Party propaganda and spectacle that fall into the realm of the theatrical, none were so visible, nor are so prominent in the public

Figure 3.3 Nürnberg Rally 1934, Luitpold arena.
Source: Bundesarchiv. Archive number 102-04064.
Photographer: Gorg Pahl.

imagination even today, as the great Party Rallies in Nuremberg' (Reed 2015:76). In his secret diary, Social Democrat Friedrich Kellner astutely remarked that the 'outward show' of the rallies, 'expressing the strengths and power of National Socialism, has to replace the internal emptiness' (Kellner 2018:408). Kellner underestimated that rally attendees turned 'themselves into iconic objects' (Coleman 1996:38). Nazi spectacle operated as a kind of 'kinetic force that sought to draw the spectator into its field of influence' (Gordon 2002:185). Furthermore, the spectacular organisation of crowds of people, in a physical space of enormous proportions, subordinated them (including Hitler) to the worship of power for its own sake (Nielsen 2020:10–12). Nevertheless, the 'Third Reich did not consist of an endless series of Nuremberg party rallies, of parades and pathos-laden speeches' (Neitzel and Welzer 2013:27). Despite much literature mentioning the rallies, little has been written about the badges produced to commemorate them.[2]

The badges which have survived are a record of which particular companies made them, the materials used, the rally they commemorated and how these events were represented through iconography. The latter is often opaque, which is one of the limitations when deciphering images without additional sources. The images also only act as an example of the final designs and do not indicate any competing versions. An examination of Nürnberg rally postcards featuring illustrations of the badges reveals that their iconography did not always correspond to the theme of each rally (Wilson 2012). Certainly, it is not possible to establish the autonomy that the designer of the badges had (based on a review of the main extant artefacts). The artist responsible for some of the designs, Richard Klein of Munich, was a 'painter of high standing in the Nazi art world' (Kasher 1992:53). More investigation is required in relation to the commissioning process, although the emblems could not be considered as examples of art for art's sake, as they were intended to commemorate highly politicised events and raise funds for the Nazi party.

The 1934 Nürnberg rally through celluloid and metal

The title of the September 1934 Nürnberg rally of 'Unity and Strength' (*Einheit und Stärke*) was meant to symbolise that the Nazi party had recovered following the purge of the SA leader Röhm in the summer of 1934 (Sennett 2014; Hancock 2011:683). It was important that Hitler was portrayed as a strong leader, already receiving a timely boost to his power following the death of President Hindenburg in August 1934. Hindenburg's 'body was scarcely cold when Hitler announced that the Presidential office would be merged in his own, thereby rounding off the dictatorship' (Binchy 1937:242). Riefenstahl enhanced Hitler's image through the manipulation of film. In her *Triumph of the Will*, she spliced together montages out of sequence, such as the large adoring crowd which greeted Hitler as he emerged from his plane taken from another scene (Kracauer 1947, 2004). The conception and nature of *Triumph of the Will* argues against Riefenstahl having an 'aesthetic conception independent of propaganda' (Sontag 1980:79). Indeed, her film did not reveal the reality of Nazism: The then-functioning Dachau concentration camp.

Riefenstahl bears some responsibility for creating the 'mystical aura that so permeates the period' (Hinton 1975:48). Her film had an impact on collector Dan Czunys, who 'saw a video of *Triumph of the Will* and was completely fascinated by the whole spectacle/pageantry' (Czunys 2018, pers. comm.). Collectors born after the Third Reich experienced this epoch through popular culture, much of which contained Nazi newsreels and footage. In contrast to moving images, rally badges give collectors the opportunity to literally hold the Third Reich in their hands.

The 1934 Nürnberg rally badge depicted a knight with a shield that contained a swastika above three oakleaves (Figure 3.4). The knight linked the new crusade of National Socialism with the city's medieval past. Oakleaves symbolised strength and were also included on a badge for German craftsmen, said to be a 'symbol of the German way and the German land, expressing the national will of the German craftsmen.'[3] Oak trees were steeped in Germanic folklore, being a symbol of German patriotism since the early nineteenth century (Hagemann 2015:222–223).

The badge depicted in Figure 3.4 was made by craftspeople from the firm of Lauer Nürnberg-Berlin, a company established in 1848 by the metalworker Ludwig Christian Lauer (Woods 2010:180; GMC 2018). A symbiotic relationship therefore existed between the Nazi party and Germany's metal badge industry. The 1934 rally badge was made from steel, which contrasted to the poorer quality materials used for later badges. By 1939, a 'drastic change' occurred, with zinc being used for all kinds of badges and medals (UM September 1940:129–130).

Figure 3.4 Nürnberg rally badge 1934, made by Lauer Nürnberg-Berlin.
Source: Author's collection. Scanned image.

Consequently, the study of the materiality of rally badges over time reflects how certain metals were being diverted towards the production of armaments.

It is somewhat ironic that the badges associated with the most spectacular event in the Nazi calendar are amongst some of the cheapest on the collectors' market, which is mainly attributable to their availability. For current-day collectors, the allegorical images on the badges do not mean much. Furthermore, an inanimate object such as a badge cannot 'recreate the grandeur, pomp, emotion, frenzy and hysteria of the Nazi rallies' (Childs 1969:291). Perhaps this is asking too much of a badge even if it does have an aura (both inherent and perceptive definitions). Nevertheless, although rally badges have been 'removed from their original context of production, they are still capable of producing powerful responses' (Coleman 1996:38). It is possible that their residual psychic power could be harnessed by neo-Nazis for destructive purposes.

The rally grounds have an even larger haunting presence. An unnamed male collector from England, bewitched by the Nürnberg rallies, decided to visit the grounds, stating, 'I can just see it all with the rallies, the crowds down there, the shouting. And Hitler just there, where I've just been standing . . . you've got to admit it, it's impressive. You can feel the power of the place. Feel the power of the buildings. Can't you?' (MacDonald 2006:121). This is surely a cogent example of how inanimate objects can possess supernatural qualities (Coleman 1996). Whilst Hitler's footprints were dissolved long ago, the rally grounds are still capable of evoking his spirit. Moreover, private collectors are effectively consuming Nazi rally regalia that absorbed Hitler's gaze.

The Winter Help Program (*winterhilfswerk*) (WHW)

An 'analysis of the NS regime cannot take place without an analysis of the integrative and legitimising effects of the WHW' (Tennstedt 1987:157). Concerning the 'social and welfare policy of the NS state, one will recurrently come across the following two organizations: The National Socialist People's Welfare (NSV) and the Winter Relief of the German People (WHW)' (Vorländer 1986:341). The WHW was a form of 'social egalitarianism' (Schoenbaum 1966, 1997:53), but this did not extend to Jews. These victims of National Socialist discrimination and persecution were only permitted to be given assistance by Jewish welfare organisations. The WHW was therefore a component of racial conditioning, which the badges of the WHW facilitated.

Background of the WHW

As with other initiatives which the leaders of the NSDAP took credit for, such as welfare to work, the WHW was not created by them, but by politicians in the last years of the Weimar Republic (Crew 1998:211). Nevertheless, in Nazi Germany it mushroomed into a gigantic programme which included the manufacture of millions of badges. The central message of the WHW (again not initially devised by NSDAP propagandists) was the 'common good over the individual need' (*Gemeinnutz geht vor Eigennutz*) (Ley 1938:282a). This is similar to the interpretation of the DAF cogwheel discussed earlier. What was best for the people was dictated by Hitler's war ambitions, as for 'the Nazis, the common good had a special twist; the communal aim was defined to be military expansion' (Temin 1990:304). The Nazi 'Brownshirts subordinated the individual to the greater collectivity of the state, thus combining the worst of capitalist economics and socialist state rule in one system' (Mitchell 1995:291). Kellner noted in his secret diary that the pressure to donate to the WHW 'might present a lesson for coming generations never to tolerate a tyranny' (Kellner 2018:480).

The common good invaded private homes through the 'one pot meal' (*Eintopf*), with people being strongly encouraged to donate the money they would have spent on their Sunday meal to the WHW and eat boiled cabbage (Fulbrook 2004:194). Moreover, the blander the meal, the greater the symbolic sacrifice. The treasurer of the Nazi party controlled the money that people had donated, fuelling suspicion that the funds were being misappropriated towards 'weapons' (*Waffen*) rather than helping the poor, symbolised by the derisory rendering of the initials WHW as *wir hungern weiter* ('we continue to be hungry') (Vorländer 1988:53). The WHW was an 'extraordinary symptom of a financially stricken party that rested on charismatic leadership' (Gerth 1940:520). Kellner added that number 15 of the 18 cardinal errors of National Socialism was begging in bulk, exemplified by party functionaries cajoling people to purchase WHW badges (Kellner 2018:76).

WHW Badges 1933–39

WHW badges were offered for sale during the numerous 'Reich street collections' (*Reichstraßensammlung*) by members of the Hitler Youth, Nazi party functionaries,

SA and SS (WHWF 1938:13). Figure 3.5 depicts a poster of an idealised, braided BDM girl holding a WHW collecting tin who informs onlookers that on 4 November, 1934, everybody will be wearing the flower of the WHW. The poster therefore insinuates that those who do not donate and wear the designated badge are not valid members of the People's Community. So incessant were the collection drives

Figure 3.5 WHW poster October 1934. The League of German Girls (BDM) in the service of the Winter Help Program 1934/35.

Source Bundesarchiv. Archive number Plak 003-016-065. Designer unknown, publisher Eisfeller, Cologne.

that 'jangling street collection tins were among the most widespread memories of the period' (Burleigh and Wippermann 1991:68). The 'issuance of badges and flags enabled collectors to home in on those not evincing the appropriate commitment' (Burleigh 2000:227). The colourful emblems particularly appealed to children and were within their reach at between 10 and 20 Pfennig each (Wirths 2009:124). As children were too young to earn military decorations, wearing WHW badges gave them a sense of identity. Children also gained a sense of achievement through selling the badges, which had the additional effect of fostering a competitive spirit (whilst raising money for the NSDAP).

The first WHW badges manufactured in Nazi Germany were for the 1933–34 WHW campaign and reflected its embryonic nature. They merely repeated the slogans of the initiative, such as the metal badge for 7–8 October, 1933, which had the message of 'we help against hunger and cold' (*Wir helfen gegen Hunger und Kälte*) (WHWHB 1939:6). As Hitler's military ambitions were growing, sufficient food supplies were essential to avoid a repeat of the turnip winter of 1916–17 (Allen 2008:180). During the 'post-1945 hunger years and still to this day, Germans recall the Third Reich, in contrast with occupation, as a time of adequate, even good, food supplies' (Weinreb 2012:51). For affluent collectors, Nazi hunger politics does not have the same resonance, although the iconography and physical materiality of these artefacts still influence their purchasing decisions. There is certainly an abundance of WHW badges available on the collectors' market, resulting from the large volume of emblems originally manufactured.

The number of badges produced for the 1933–34 campaign totalled just over a colossal 31 million, raising RM 6.2 million in sales (WHWHB 1939:7; Wulff 1940:47). By the campaign of 1938–39, the production volume increased to 169 million, raising RM 13 million in sales (Ibid.). In addition to cementing Nazi ideology through the mass sale of WHW badges, the leaders of the Nazi regime sought to make a profit, which necessitated that the badges be made from economically viable materials. Compared to other Nazi badges, the emblems of the WHW represented the most diverse range of materials, including cardboard, ceramic, leather, metal, paper, plastic, textile and wood. The badges were initially made from pressed metal, with more substitute materials being introduced over time. Despite propaganda surrounding the use of novel materials, the fact that WHW badges tended not to be made from metal reflected their lower status within the hierarchy of Nazi symbols. Nevertheless, it was the same companies which made the major Nazi party and military decorations that made badges for the WHW. It is possible that certain workers may have been responsible for producing particular emblems, especially if new skills were required to manufacture badges from novel materials. No matter their roles, all the workers in badge factories converted Nazi propaganda into a tangible form (although forced labourers could be morally excused).

Even during the Third Reich, WHW badges had a 'collectible value' (*Sammlerwert*), suggesting that there was a collector's market for them, although the source did not state how it operated (Wulff 1940). Nevertheless, the badges lost some of their sacred value and descended into the realm of a commodity. It would have been easier for people to collect WHW badges than military or Nazi party badges, as the sale of the latter emblems was restricted to those who were entitled to them.

People did not purchase all of the badges that were available in a WHW series, even in cases where the SS pressured them. The involvement of the SS with the WHW was an effort to show the SS in a more friendly light. Indeed, an article in the magazine reserved for paying supporters of the SS was entitled 'The SS helps out' (*SS Hilft Mit*) (FMZ 1937). The involvement of the SS with the WHW is further evidence that the scheme cannot be separated from antisemitism and Nazi ideology. In 1937, members of the SS took part in selling a series of 12 WHW ceramic badges featuring birth signs. Far from purchasing all of the badges, people exercised a degree of choice, as they tended to purchase the badge that represented the month in which they were born. This explains why it is not unusual for current-day traders to acquire collections of Third Reich medals that also contain a few seemingly random WHW badges. As all of the badges in a particular series would have originally cost over RM 1, it helps to explain why it is not the norm for full series to be found on the collectors' market (although they do exist; see below).

The diverse iconography of WHW badges meant that those who had not contributed to the latest campaign could be readily identified. Rather than some people avoiding the street collectors, it is conceivable that due to the public theatre of a street collection, some overly enthusiastic members of the Nazi People's Community still donated despite not taking a badge. Elfriede Müller, who was a child during the Third Reich, recalled that despite some people giving donations, the 'badges were not accepted' (*dass trotz geleisteter Spende die Abzeichen nicht angenommen werden*) (Wirths 2009:127). This was a demonstration of support for the WHW rather than a symbolic gesture against it. Nevertheless, if some individuals did not take a badge, it left them prey to other street collectors, as they had no proof that they had donated.

The badges for the 5–6 November, 1938, WHW street collection commemorated the annexation of Austria, each badge correspondingly depicting male or female Austrians in traditional costumes from regions such as the Tyrol (Figure 3.6). Each badge was made from cardboard, metal, paper and textile, thus requiring input from these respective industries. The main slogan for the 1938–39 campaign was 'the faith unites – the will succeeds' (*der Glaube eint – der Wille siegt*) (WHWHB 1939:20). Following the annexation, Austria was renamed Ostmark, but even this was too distinct for Hitler, who envisaged that the country would merely be regarded as an administrative district within Germany (Williams 1979; Wright 1944).

The Austrian-themed badges were the last ones issued before the lawless events of the November pogrom commonly euphemised as the 'night of broken glass' (*Kristallnacht*) (Mommsen et al. 1997). The quaint images on the badges starkly contrasted to the violence against Jews perpetrated by 'members of the party, SA, and SS (most of them disguised in civilian clothes)' (McKale 1973:229). Furthermore, as the Sudetenland had been annexed following the Munich agreement, Jewish shop owners were targeted even if they spoke German (Figure 3.7). Consequently, the WHW badges discussed here masked the true horror of the Nazi regime. Additionally, the false idyllic utopia they depicted obscured the everyday clothing worn in cities in an industrial society geared for war.

Figure 3.6 WHW Austrian-themed badges for street collection, November 1938.
Source: Author's collection. Scanned image.

Wartime WHW badges

Despite Germany's invasion of Poland in September 1939, a new WHW campaign was announced by Hitler in Berlin on 10 October, rebranded with the militaristic title of 'War Winter Help' (*Kriegswinterhilfswerk*) (BIN 1939:26). During the launch of the campaign, Hitler falsely stated that the 'opponents of Germany started this war for ridiculous reasons' (BIN 1939:26). As the war required munitions, WHW badges were increasingly made from substitute materials, one of which was plastic.

These badges were made from a thermal plastic branded *Trolitul* (UM mitte-September 1939:277; KM 2003). *Trolitul*, which first appeared in 1930, was produced by Dynamit Nobel AG (DAG) in the town of Troisdorf, a company which became part of IG Farben in 1926 (KMT; Haka 2011:75). *Trolitul* was one of the world's first 'thermal plastics' (*Thermoplasten*), which could be 'injection

Figure 3.7 Fabric and liquor/wine store belonging to Richard Singer, destroyed on *Kristallnacht*, November 1938. The shop was located in the 'Jewish Lane' (*Judengasse*), Karlsbad (annexed in October 1938 as part of the Sudetenland). Reproduced with permission of the photo archive at Yad Vashem. Photo number 33521. Photographer: Unknown.

moulded' (*Spritzgussverfahren*) (UM mitte-September 1939:277). Thermal plastic had the advantage over thermal setting plastic such as Bakelite, as it could be remoulded (Reinhart1967). Thermal plastic such as Polystyrene was a substitute for 'hard rubber, celluloid, ebonite, vulcanite, wood or glass' (Whelan 1941:75). Indeed, styrene had a similar appearance to glass, as it was transparent (Schild-knecht 1952:2), and in America, the polystyrene which was made by the Dow Chemical company was apparently 'so clear, people said it looked like crystal' (PT). This plastic could therefore be pigmented, thus badges did not necessarily require painting. Silver-coloured plastic badges imitated their metal counterparts, implying that metal was symbolically superior (UM mitte-September 1939:277). The quest for imitation had already been associated with plastic before this point, and some plastic products made today still attempt to mimic metal.

Styrene was 'conveniently manufactured from the aromatic hydrocarbon obtained from coal tar and ethylene, a gas which is a by-product in most petroleum refineries' (Collyer 1943:76). In contrast to America, Germany did not 'ride the 1920s and 1930s on a sea of natural petroleum' (Krammer 1981:70). By 1939, synthetic fuel was being made in Germany at 14 large hydrogenation and Fischer-Tropsch plants.[4] The German chemical industry's development of plastic was 'spurred in large measure by the desire to eliminate German reliance on imported substances such as casein' (Harrod 2008:15), which was derived from either skimmed milk or butter, and in contrast to Germany, it was available in Ireland, where religious emblems were made under the brand name of Erinoid (MacLaughlin 1944:172). The badges of the Winterhilfswerk were also referential symbols.

Plastic was particularly suitable for badges that were only intended to be worn for a short period of time,[5] hence plastic WHW badges were fit for purpose. Plastic products do not 'perish like natural rubber. They do not rust or tarnish like metals. They do not rot like wood' (MacLaughlin 1944:173).

The firm of Eckert and Ziegler in Cologne, acquired by DAG in 1934, made the machines needed to convert plastic granules into badges.[6] The company had an advert in the *Uniformen Markt* which stated that they supplied 'injection moulding machines' (*Spritzgussmaschine*) which could be used to make plaques, buttons and so on, in the form of 'thermal plastic' (*thermoplastischer*) (UM mitte-September 1939:284). The production of badges entailed the plastic granules being melted under heat, then the molten plastic being injected into the steel mould. The badges were then formed within the mould, taking a few seconds to cool before being removed.[7]

In his article 'Plastic,' Roland Barthes commented on a similar process in which the machine disguised the manufacturing process, hence it seemed to be miraculous (Barthes 1988:92). This being said, there was nothing miraculous about such a process; being the result of industrial development. It was claimed in the *Uniformen Markt* that the plastic industry had experienced a 'rapid development' (*sprunghafte Entwicklung*) (UM mitte-September 1939:277). Indeed, the sale of plastic within the former BASF plants of IG Farben, grew from 1.5 percent of their total sales in 1938 to 6.8 percent in 1942 (Stokes 2004:308–309). German plastic was said to be based on 'raw materials nearly infinitely available to us within our own country'.[8] Such optimistic statements should be regarded with caution, as few resources are infinite, and plastic production was also disrupted by bombing raids and ceased production at BASF's Ludwigshafen plant in February 1945 (Stokes 2004:319).

The 12 badges for the March 1941 'Day of the Armed Forces' campaign (*Tag der Wehrmacht*), made from Trolitul, were prominently displayed at the entrance to the Leipzig trade fair (UM mitte-März 1941) (Figure 3.8).[9] The sale of the badges raised funds for the Wehrmacht, thus most likely directing a child's pennies towards the production of armaments, although establishing such a direct connection, according to Jan Möller 'cannot be proven' (Möller 2003:22). Nevertheless, the donations would have facilitated the war effort.

The Day of the Armed Forces plastic military vehicles also acted as a substitute for toys, thus encouraging children to purchase them. Namely, in 1939, Julius Yourman stated that:

> Words and symbols appertaining to war have been endowed with a glorious sense to make war appear heroic and thrilling. Little children know and give the Hitler salute. Toy soldiers, tanks, machine guns, and simplified battle

Figure 3.8 Plastic tank from the WHW series Day of the Armed Forces March 1941.
Source: Author's collection. Scanned image.

instructions abound everywhere-symbols to transfer sanction to the later use
of real tanks and machine guns

(Yourman 1939:153)

These military themed toys were oriented towards boys, and the influence of
toys in relation to gender conditioning is addressed further in Chapter 9. Trolitul
was not entirely suitable for toys as it was 'brittle and may break, leaving sharp
edges' (Kaufman 1965:505). The tank illustrated in Figure 3.8 is indicative of
how WHW badges had deteriorated in quality, especially compared to the 1938
Austrian themed badges discussed earlier. The plastic tank and the other related
military vehicles in the 1941 series cannot even be classed as badges, as they did
not have metal pins, which would have been a measure to preserve the material,
but they could still be attached to clothing, as they had threads made from textile,
although these were very thin.

The plastic badges discussed above did not have swastikas, nor did the majority
of other WHW emblems. Consequently, people who were more lukewarm to the
NSDAP may have been more willing to wear one (hence donated). Alternatively,
the absence of a swastika was a way to differentiate WHW badges from those of
Nazi organisations that required membership. Nevertheless, by giving a donation,
people were still contributing to an initiative controlled by the NSDAP. In order

for Nazi crimes to be perpetrated, German society relied on millions of fellow travellers, many of whom bought and wore the badges of the WHW. Those who opted not to wear a WHW badge may have been giving a surreptitious sign of defiance against the Nazi regime. Consequently, WHW badges had an immaterial dimension, as people who did not wear one may have been communicating something more fundamental than those who did.

Collectors

Collectors and traders fail to recognise the important socioeconomic and political functions of WHW badges now alienated commodities thoroughly detached from their original owners. Collectors are unaware too of who once wore them, in which German city or village they were purchased, and how people reacted to seeing the badges being worn. Collectors hardly even pay much attention to the collectors who once owned them, thus their biography as a collectible object is also neglected. As WHW badges have not been replicated, they do not instil the same anxieties that other Nazi badges do, hence fail to garner much attention.

Collectors evaluate WHW badges in relation to the more substantial military or political awards, which they tend to have more understanding of and interest in. There are probably multiple reasons for their lack of enthusiasm for WHW badges, i.e., they are common, were not awarded for merit and do not generally have swastikas. In comparison to the collectors' literature on Third Reich badges, there is a lack of English language publications on WHW emblems. As the iconography of many extant WHW artefacts does not point towards the campaigns for which they were made, some collectors may be without one of the anchors that a collecting activity depends on. British-based trader Jamie Cross suggested that collectors prefer the few WHW badges that have swastikas (Cross 2017, pers. comm.), but rather than them desiring the shape as such, it is more likely that they seek it because it is emblematic of the Third Reich. Although the swastika's form does entrance collectors, their primary demand for it stems from its Nazi context.

It is still possible for collectors to purchase a complete series of WHW badges (such as the birth signs mentioned earlier), although these tend to be offered by traders based in Germany. Again, it is unknown how these series have remained intact, but it is likely that rather than a collector or trader laboriously locating single badges to make up a complete set, they remained intact or unsold before 1945, then filtered onto the collectors' market. Rather than purchasing a complete set, however, some current-day collectors may find it more satisfying to find the respective individual badges, much in the same way as completing a football sticker album (Cuttle and Law 2018). This would rely on an active network of collectors who have duplicate WHW badges to swap, or traders who have individual badges to offer for sale.

WHW badges constitute the lowest tier in terms of recognition amongst collectors, especially as they were not earned in the same way as military awards, hence fail to conjure up brave deeds. That being said, as the major military and political decorations become more expensive, perhaps more collectors will drift towards WHW emblems or tinnies, as after all, they were still produced during the Third Reich. To the best of my knowledge, WHW badges have not been replicated, hence they have not been passed off as fake in the same way as Wehrmacht badges. Although collectors can be more confident that they would be acquiring authentic relics, they have not gravitated towards WHW badges. Collectors are therefore not necessarily pursuing the auratic essence of the Third Reich, as they would experience this with a higher degree of certainty from WHW emblems. Rather, they are seeking a slightly different form of gratification, which derives from the organisation or deeds that badges signify. Indeed, as Chapters 4 and 6 show, collectors are particularly fascinated with SS badges. Whilst aesthetics have a role in shaping their interest in SS regalia, the premise that some collectors go by the motto 'the eviller the better' cannot be discounted.

Conclusion

Mass-produced badges gave material form to the intangible People's Community. An examination of these objects has shown how the Nazi worldview was embodied in these highly portable and cheaply available emblems. Although none of the badges which I examined included overtly antisemitic slogans, they were fundamental to the creation of the Nazi racial state. The swastika within a cog alluded to a performance community based on the elimination of class divisions, but did not break them. Nor did the Strength Through Joy initiative whose badges were a symbolic representation of the opportunity for workers from all classes to leave their offices and factories and holiday together in the countryside. These joyous activities contrasted to the victims of the Nazi regime who were confined and tortured in concentration camps. The Nürnberg rallies were events where antisemitism was transmitted, although the badges that were manufactured to commemorate these rallies did not advertise this fact. These stage-managed spectacles continue to bewitch collectors, although they are ironically not excited by the very badges that were purchased at the events. Collectors have decontextualised and reconfigured Nazi badges according to criteria that they have created. In this collecting environment, the romanticisation of brave deeds, rarity and dare I say, evil, are valued over the common badges that encroached even more into the daily lives of people in Hitler's Germany. If citizens of the Third Reich did not donate to the WHW, they were accused of being an enemy of the people. As such, the rather quaint badges of the WHW were even more pernicious than badges that bore the Nazi swastika. The Third Reich is a frightening example of how symbols, no matter their form, helped to prop up a totalitarian state.

Notes

1 German text referencing the wearing of the DAF badge: (*am 1. Mai trägt jedes Mitglied der DAF, als Zeichen der Verbundenheit aller schaffenden deutschen Menschen das Abzeichen der DAF, das Zahnrad mit dem Hakenkreuz*) (DAF n.d.:8).
2 As Nazi rally badges were often made from a thin sheet of stamped metal, collectors generally refer to them as tinnies. Collectors have essentially reduced the badges to their base materials, thus denigrating their original political and social purpose. The term also underestimates the strategic importance of non-ferrous metal to German re-armament and the international nature of the trade in metals (Ball 2004; Perkins 1995).

3 German text describing the meaning of oakleaves on the badge for German craftsmen: (*Sinnbild deutscher Art und deutschen Bodens, den nationalen Willen des deutschen Handwerks zum Ausdruck bringend*) (UM Juli 1935:9).

4 Influential German chemist Walter Reppe, who co-operated with the Nazi regime, developed a method to produce synthetic benzene and on January 1, 1934, he became the director of BASF's *Zwischenprodukte-Kunststoff Laboratorium* (Morris 1992:147).

5 Information on German plastic production taken from the following article: 'What is the benefit of German plastics for us?' (*Was bringen uns die deutschen Kunststoffe?*). German text on the benefits of plastic (*Abzeichen, die ihrer Bestimmung gemäß nur für kurzfristige Beanspruchung geschaffen waren*) (UM mitte-September 1939:277). Translated by Dr. Bernadette Mekker.

6 Streb (2011:189, footnote 27).

7 German text for plastic production process (*Diese beiden Kunststoffe aus Zellulosederivaten, die zu den sogenannten Thermoplasten gehören (thermoplastische Massen), werden unter Einwirkung von Wärme plastisch und können dann auf Spritzgussmaschinen unter Anwendung von Druck in die Stahlformen gespritzt werden. Nach dem Erkalten, das nur einige Sekunden in Anspruch nimmt, können die fertigen Plaketten aus der Form herausgenommen werden*) (UM mitte-September 1939:277). Translated by Dr. Bernadette Mekker.

8 German text for raw materials needed for plastic said to be available within Germany (*ihre Ausgangsstoffe stehen uns im eigenen Lande praktisch unbegrenzt zur Verfügung*) (UM mitte-September 1939:277). Translated by Dr. Bernadette Mekker.

9 Leipzig had hosted a trade fair since 1497 (Gross 2012:29), and the event continued after the Second World War to promote the East German economy (Bontje 2004).

4 Pre-war awards

More than just Eagles and swastikas

The awards instituted between 1934 and 1938 are tangible examples of the Nazi leadership's efforts to win over German society, as well as furthering militarism. The first medal discussed here exploited the memory of the Great War and is one of the few decorations instituted in Nazi Germany that Jewish war veterans were entitled to. Their oppressors in the SS were rewarded with the first medal shaped like a swastika. Another medal discussed is the Prize for Arts and Sciences, whose recipients reflected Hitler's distorted worldview, as they either disseminated racial hatred or manufactured weapons. As part of the Nazi leadership's efforts to cultivate support outside Germany, the Order of the German Eagle was presented to industrialists such as Henry Ford and aviator Charles Lindbergh. The life histories of these ideologically embedded gifts are explored, not least because they are an example of the power to construct or re-model individuals long after their demise.

The Hindenburg cross

In 1934, the twentieth anniversary of the Great War was imminent, and a state-level medal was introduced on 13 July. As stated in Chapter 2, a nationwide medal had not been introduced during the Weimar era commemorating Great War service, hence the institution of a medal was a public sign that soldiers' sacrifice was finally being recognised. A Dr. Ehmer welcomed the introduction of the medal and stated that 'only symbols that were based on older ones were capable of providing a unity that had been broken under Weimar' (UM Dezember 1934:9). The medal's title (Honour Cross) suggests that the decoration exonerated the soldiers from losing the conflict, supporting the stab-in-the-back myth. Indeed, the version with swords had a 'laurel wreath' (*Lorbeerkranz*) (Doehle 1943:14) (Figure 4.1), an evergreen more associated with victory than defeat.

The statute for the Cross of Honour stated that the medal was to be made of iron, and as this material was needed for weapons, it is evidence of the high symbolic value that the medal had. Iron has also been associated with 'males, strength, dominance and evil forces' (Haaland et al. 2002:35). During the so-called 'Iron Time' (*Eiserne Zeit*), when cash-strapped Prussia was at war with Napoleon in 1813, patriotic citizens who donated gold received bracelets and rings emblazoned with 'I Gave Gold for Iron' (*Gold gab ich für Eisen*) (Brady 2016:10; GfE 2011).

DOI: 10.4324/9781003000617-4

Figure 4.1 Cross of Honour for Front-fighters 1934.
Source: Author's collection. Photograph taken by Grant Hughes, 2020.

The Cross of Honour offered a mass opportunity to perpetuate German military tradition; a combined total of over eight million medals were awarded (Doehle 1943:14). Nevertheless, the NSDAP did not have the monopoly on the memory of the Great War, especially whilst Hindenburg was still alive, so the medal did not depict a swastika.

The most significant contribution Hindenburg made to the medal was not in the realm of its iconography, but his stipulation that there were to be no 'racial or religious requisites' (Grady 2011:132). This meant that Jewish war veterans were entitled to the decoration. The Association of Jewish Front Fighters (*Reichsbund Jüdischer Frontsoldaten*) (RJF) encouraged its 35,000 members to apply for the medal. The decoration was publicised in an article in the association's magazine, the 'Shield' (*Der Schild*).[1] The medal would be an external sign that Jewish soldiers had sacrificed for the fatherland, hence could act as a bulwark against antisemitism.[2]

The cross shape of the medal was not altered to accommodate non-Christian recipients as had been the case for the imperial Red Eagle order in the nineteenth century (Kupisch 1966:117). Eighteen percent of Jewish Great War soldiers already possessed the Iron Cross, hence a cross in itself would not have discouraged them from accepting the Cross of Honour (Wernitz and Simons 2013:409).[3]

Had the Cross of Honour depicted a swastika, Jewish war veterans would most likely have rejected it.

The Cross of Honour was an integral part of the mixed signals given to Jews during the first few years in Nazi Germany (Berger 2006:220). The medal adhered to the 'Hindenburg exemption' for Jewish war veterans, enabling them to remain in the civil service, although this was effectively revoked in September 1935.[4] Even 'in a situation gone awry, there were war veterans who refused to take their wives' warnings seriously . . . One woman, who pressed her husband to leave Germany, noted that he constantly fell back on the argument that he had been at the front in World War I' (Kaplan 1999:65–66). A ten-year-old daughter of a Jewish war veteran, who witnessed calls for boycotts of Jewish stores in 1933, was confused two years later when 'her father was still decorated for active service in the past war, receiving a citation signed by Berlin's chief of police' (Ibid.:4). By 9 September, 1937, 95 percent of RJF members who had applied for the Cross of Honour to the respective authorities had been 'positively processed' (Reichmann 1937).

In contrast to Hindenburg, Hitler's fanatical antisemitism meant that no amount of service to the fatherland could compensate for being Jewish (see rare exceptions in Chapter 6). After Hindenburg died in August 1934, Hitler gradually secured the sole right to institute awards. Jewish recipients of the Cross of Honour were not protected from persecution, especially during the Second World War. The Jewish Museum in Berlin has the Cross of Honour certificate for Jakob Schrimmer (born 1882), but his status as a veteran of the Great War did not prevent him from being sent to Sachsenhausen concentration camp in 1942, where he died (JMB). On balance, the Cross of Honour had a dangerous agency, as it gave some Jewish war veterans a false sense of security, and by the time that many realised they had to leave Germany, it was too late (Matthäus and Roseman 2010).

Collectors

During the Third Reich, a non-Jewish veteran by the name of R. Bergemann wrote to the *Deutsche Allgemeine Zeitung*, as he was concerned that the non-combatants' Cross of Honour without swords denigrated his contribution (UM Januar 1935:11). As a higher symbolic value was associated with the Cross of Honour with swords for front-line soldiers, I expected that this would be reflected in a higher price on the collectors' market, but the reverse was the case (see Appendix A). The version for non-combatants was more expensive on the collectors' market, as it was awarded in lesser numbers and is therefore scarcer. Nevertheless, collectors appreciate that both versions were made from iron, making these otherwise cheap medals 'look more expensive' (Norris 2019). Despite being made from iron, for collectors, the Cross of Honour pales into insignificance compared to the decoration made from a cheaper metal discussed below.

Rewarding sinister service

In January 1938, Hitler marked the fifth anniversary of his chancellorship by instituting a series of medals, one of which included long service decorations for members of the SS (UM Feb38). These included purely symbolic silver and gold grades which were intended for 12 or 25 years of service and were a sign of confidence that this relatively new organisation would continue to exist. They were also the first medals in the shape of a swastika (Figure 4.2), a development deemed significant, as 'the first and second class is the first honorary badge of the Third Reich where the swastika is not an emblem on another cross or a medal, but found use (*Verwendung*) as its own Order Cross' (Doehle 1943:52–53).

The SS was an 'instrument to prevent the pessimism of the High Command spreading to the population' (Reitlinger 1957:81). The iconography of the medal did not include the skull and crossbones of the SS but did depict runes.[5] The runes were not included on the police service medals instituted at the same time, even though Heinrich Himmler was also the chief of the German police, thereby obscuring his spheres of influence (Höhne 1969, 2000:198). Himmler's power base had increased following the suppression of a revolt by Berlin SA leader Walther Stennes in 1931, after which the SS motto of 'My Honour is Loyalty' (*Meine Ehre heißt Treue*) was inscribed on SS belt buckles (Padfield 1990:96). How the members of the SS were to behave was therefore depicted on what they wore and may have shaped their actions. Indeed, during his 1961 Israeli trial, Adolf Eichmann cited the SS motto as a rather weak defence (Kittrie 1964).

Figure 4.2 Replica SS medal for 25 years of service, 1938.

Source: Author's collection. Photograph taken by Grant Hughes, 2020.

One way of signifying Himmler's control of the SS would have been for his portrait to be depicted on the SS long service medals. A characteristic of Nazi decorations, however, is that they tended not to include profiles of the Nazi leadership. Had they done so, Hitler's power may have been threatened. The fractious and unstable nature of the Nazi movement would also have meant that they would have required frequent modifications (although the medal industry would have eagerly accommodated). This being said, Hitler was not depicted on coins, following the tradition of ancient Greek coinage, in which 'no mere king or tyrant, however absolute his rule may have been, ever presumed to place his own effigy on the current coin, for such a proceeding would, from old associations, have been regarded as little short of sacrilege' (Head 1883:26).[6]

Hitler was the only Nazi leader who was depicted on stamps, although it took him until 1937 to agree to this, earning him RM 50 million in one year alone from licencing fees (Evans n.d.). The lack of other Nazi leaders on postage stamps was exploited by the British when they issued a counterfeit in 1943 depicting Himmler (Lauritzen 1988:67). Nevertheless, in 1943, Germany officially issued a postage stamp marking the first anniversary of the assassination of Reinhard Heydrich, described as one of the most 'menacing designs in the history of European philately' (Ibid.:74). Presumably, it was safer for the Nazi leadership to commemorate Heydrich when he was dead than when the ambitious 'butcher' was still alive (R. J. 1944:949).

Collectors

Collectors are more concerned with the nominal authenticity of SS medals than the morality of collecting them. Scottish-based author and collector Robin Lumsden[7] was concerned that 'SS long service swastikas' were highly faked (Lumsden 1996:13). Likewise, for North of England-based collector Dan Czunys, the high price of original SS items 'has unfortunately attracted the production of countless fakes and fantasies, some of which are almost indistinguishable from the real thing. I no longer buy SS items' (Czunys 2018, pers. comm.). Consequently, fakes rather than SS ideology discourage collectors.

Fakes have most likely put downward pressure on the price of the SS medal (see Appendix A). Similarly, it is thought that returns 'are below average on fine arts, where authenticity is a concern, whereas returns are above average for graphics and silver, where authenticity is a lesser consideration' (Singer 1978:36). In contrast to British hallmarked silver, which has legal protection, the manufacture of Nazi insignia, although prohibited in Germany, can be conducted elsewhere. Indeed, the reproduction SS medal illustrated in Figure 4.2 was purchased in 2019 from a British-based retailer for GBP 24.95 (an original is well over GBP 2,300). It proved impossible to trace where these reproductions were made or to interview the supplier.

Ironically, collectors and traders have not done themselves any favours in maintaining the autobiographical and financial value of SS medals. More often than not, the medals have been thoroughly divorced from their past owners (both recipients and collectors). There are no doubt many reasons for why some SS members distanced themselves from their medals after the war. As SS long service medals were not individually named, tracing their original recipients is virtually impossible (short of accompanying documentation). Why then would a collector pay large amounts of money for a medal whose biography is tenuous? It is because they wish to possess an item that has a direct association with the SS. Collectors generally claim that their fascination for all things SS has nothing to do with the Holocaust and usually cite aesthetics when defending their interest. In the introduction to Jack Pia's *SS Regalia*, John Keegan, whilst acknowledging the allure of SS paraphernalia, reminded readers that the Nazi regime was responsible for the 'mass graves of six million innocent victims' (Pia 1974:10).

The German National Prize for Arts and Sciences

In 1937, Hitler marked the fourth anniversary of his chancellorship with a 'vendetta' towards all Nobel prizes, which he forbade German citizens from receiving (Crawford 2000:38). His reaction was a result of the decision of the Norwegian Nobel committee to award the peace activist Carl von Ossietzky, who had been interned in Nazi concentration camps and whose books had been burned, with the 1935 Nobel Peace Prize. Ossietzky's award was the only time the Nobel Peace Prize committee 'criticized and sought to effect change in a state's internal and repressive politics' (Krebs 2009:596). Ossietzky was prohibited from collecting the honour and died in May 1938 after many years of brutalisation (Brumlik 2017:18).

Hitler reinforced his contempt for the Nobel prizes by instituting the German National Prize for Arts and Sciences, thereby taking control of the awards (Doehle 1943:37). The medal was designed by the Berlin sculptor (*Bildhauer*) Hermann Müller-Erfurt and featured a profile of Athena, the Greek goddess of war and wisdom (Doehle 1943:37; Nimmergut 2001:1914) (Figure 4.3). The iconography of the award did not include any distinctive scientific symbols, being allegorical in nature. The high socioeconomic value of the decoration was reflected in its raw materials, which included diamonds, gold and platinum (Doehle 1943:37). It therefore contrasted to the majority of Third Reich medals, which were of little intrinsic worth.

The initial group of recipients was announced at the Nürnberg rally in 1937, with the first award symbolically given to Hitler's favourite architect Paul Ludwig Troost, who was posthumously honoured with the award 'from beyond the grave' (*über das Grabe hinaus*) (Doehle 1943:37). Troost had designed the House of German Art in Munich, and the project was continued by his widow Gerdy Troost (Figure 4.4). The building was a 'reductive, monumentalized neoclassicism' that concealed the underlying concrete and steel structure (Fischer 2010:122). Troost was succeeded by Albert Speer, who was not awarded the decoration but greatly coveted one (Speer 1970, 1995:466). Medals were most certainly desired during the Third Reich and acted as an objectification of an individual's worth. Indeed, by Speer not receiving the decoration, it could be said that Hitler valued a dead architect over a living one, although he did give Speer other prestigious medals. To know 'is to objectify – that is, to be able to distinguish what is inherent to the object from what belongs to the knowing subject and has been unduly (or inevitably) projected into the object' (Castro 2004:468). Embedded in the medals Hitler awarded

Figure 4.3 Decoration for Arts and Sciences 1937.

Source: Doehle (1943:35). Scanned image. Matthias Nowak of the Bayrisches Staatsministerium der Finanzen und für Heimat stated that the Free State of Bavaria has no legal objections to images from Doehle (1943) being reproduced in this publication (Nowak 2020).

Speer are the sufferings and deaths of forced and slave labourers who made munitions during the Second World War whilst Speer was the minister of armaments.

In the previous chapter, I briefly commented on the quasi-mythological-propagandistic writings of Alfred Rosenberg, and although even Hitler thought his book was too complicated for people to understand (Piper 2007:186), Rosenberg was still awarded the Arts and Sciences medal, as it was said that he had 'fought untiringly to maintain the purity of the National Socialist Worldview' (Wittman and Kinney 2016:Chapter 12). The medal was a proxy for social relations and a way for Hitler to fuel competition amongst his underlings, as evidenced by Rosenberg commenting in his diary that he was particularly pleased that Goebbels had to announce the award in view of his 'chicanery.'[8]

In contrast to the ideologically driven Rosenberg, the medal was also awarded to the German explorer Wilhelm Filchner, who had 'never concealed his anti-Nazi feelings, but the Nazis could not afford to eliminate one of the few explorers of international repute left to Germany' (Roberts 1958:145). The medal was accompanied by a substantial monetary prize of RM 100,000 (about USD 553,642 in terms of spending power in 2015) (HSS). The surgeons August Bier and Ernst Ferdinand Sauerbruch, who were also awarded the medal, had to share the cash prize (Doehle 1943:37). Conversely, Sauerbruch did not regard this as denigrating his value, stating that it was 'gratification for all German physicians' (Dewey et al. 2006:316). Not only did Sauerbruch praise Hitler during the Third Reich, but after the war he upheld the 'traditional stereotype of the omnipotent German physician' (Kater 1987:53).

The Nürnberg rally of 1938 was the backdrop for the announcement of a second set of recipients, all of whom were more reflective of Germany's military preparations. These included the automobile designer Ferdinand Porsche, but despite RM 110 million being raised by 1940 for his KdF-Wagen (better known as the People's Car) (DAF 1940:363–364), the factory was converted to the manufacture of 'aircraft parts, bombs, ovens, and a military version of the Volkswagen, with a large slave labor workforce' (König 2004:256). Hitler was the only person who received a civilian model of the car, which he gave to his mistress Eva Braun

Figure 4.4 Gerdy Troost outside the House of German Art in Munich.

Source: Bundesarchiv. Archive number 183-1992-0410-546.

Photographer: Hans Dietrich.

(Lundmark 2011:12). As she was generally unknown outside Hitler's inner circle, this was a rather conspicuous gift.

Somewhat ironically, it was only after the war that millions of what was still sometimes called 'Hitler's Car' travelled across German motorways (*Autobahnen*) (Tolliday 1995).[9] The engineer Fritz Todt was awarded the Prize for Arts and Sciences for overseeing the construction of these motorways (Doehle 1943:37). Contrary 'to the popular perception today, the military dimension of the *Autobahnen* was not the primary motivation behind their construction. It is now generally accepted in the scholarly literature that this view is one of the myths surrounding the roadways' (Zeller 2010:56). Military aircraft were far more significant. Indeed, aeroplane designers Wilhelm Emil Messerschmitt and Ernst Heinkel also received the Prize for Arts and Sciences but shared the monetary component (Doehle 1943:37). Science was deemed most efficacious when put towards the development of military equipment.

American recipients of the German Eagle Order

Nazi medals were not only awarded to Germans but to citizens of democratic countries who were deemed to be sympathetic to the Nazi regime. Awards of the German Eagle Order to Americans were especially controversial at the time and have remained so. The award to aviator Charles Lindbergh was mentioned in Philip Roth's counterfactual novel *The Plot against America* (Roth 2004a), where Roth regarded the decoration as emblematic of Lindbergh's Nazi sympathies. In the first few pages of his novel, Roth referred to Lindbergh as being 'ceremoniously decorated' with the Eagle Cross which had four swastikas, then refusing to return the medal even after the Night of Broken Glass (Roth 2004a:6–7). Roth chose Lindbergh as one of the main protagonists of his novel as 'Lindbergh as a social force was distinguished not solely by his isolationism but by his racist attitude toward Jews – an attitude that is reflected unambiguously in his speeches, diaries and letters' (Roth 2004b:10). Lindbergh's friend Henry Ford (Figure 4.5) was also awarded the German Eagle Order, as was James Mooney of General Motors and Thomas Watson of IBM (Pauwels 2003; Stern 1941:372).

A Nazi medal for IBM

Thomas Watson, the chief executive officer and chairman of International Business Machines (IBM), was the first American to be awarded the German Eagle Order, which was bestowed by the German Economic Minister Dr. Hjalmar Schacht in 1937 (TW GI 1937). Watson was in Berlin at the time, in his capacity as the president of the International Chamber of Commerce. Following the bestowal of the medal, Watson sent a telegram to Hitler in which he stated, 'before leaving Berlin I wish to express my pride in and deep gratitude for the high honor I received through the order with which you honored me. Valuing fully the spirit of friendship which underlay this honor, I assure you that in the future as in the

From the Collections of The Henry Ford (84.1.1660.P.O.114/THF125681)

Figure 4.5 Henry Ford and Charles Lindbergh shaking hands in front of the *Spirit of St. Louis*, Ford Airport, Dearborn, Michigan, 10 August, 1927. Reproduced with permission of The Henry Ford. *Photographer:* Gift of Ford Motor Company.

past I will endeavour to do all in my power to create more intimate bonds between our two great nations' (NYT July 1937:8).

Watson believed in the doctrine of 'World Peace through World Trade' (Offner 1977:376) and was 'bewitched by Germany's economic possibilities' (Cheape 1988:451). Watson and IBM were the subject of sustained criticism in Edwin Black's controversial book *IBM and the Holocaust: The Strategic Alliance Between Nazi Germany and America's Most Powerful Corporation*, in which it was claimed that IBM's tabulating machines enabled the Holocaust (Black 2001).[10]

Watson's German Eagle Order was an objectification of his relationship with Hitler and Nazi Germany, and as this changed, so did its ownership. After sustained pressure to return his medal, the German bombing of Paris in 1940 finally prompted him to post it to Hitler, as the 'present policies of your government are contrary to the causes for which I have been working and for which I received the decoration' (NYT June 1940:1). Watson was denounced in Nazi-controlled newspapers, and his portrait was immediately removed from the offices of IBM's German subsidiary (Black 2001; also see Targowski 2016). Defending Watson, IBM recently reiterated that Watson 'repudiated and returned a medal presented to him by the German government for his role in global economic relations' (IBM 2001). Nevertheless, according to McCormick and Spee (2008), there were moral and ethical deficiencies in Watson's decision to conduct business in Nazi Germany, and he was far from the only business leader whose judgement may have been clouded by a Nazi medal.

Hitler's 'great man' Henry Ford

Henry Ford had the unenviable position of being praised by Hitler in *Mein Kampf* as a 'great man' (Caspar 1958:8). In the early 1920s, Ford's newspaper the *Dearborn Independent* promulgated highly antisemitic tracts (Singerman 1981). Ford's 'campaign against the Jews, as historians have recognized, reflected the renewed racial tribalism that characterized post-World War I American society' (Woeste 2004:877). Ford's 'writings fuelled Hitler's anti-Semitism and convinced him that he had an American comrade-in-arms' (Catalano 2020:35). Ford's tracts also had an impact on Baldur von Schirach, the future leader of the Hitler Youth (Ribuffo 1980:470).

Ford was awarded the Grand Cross of the German Eagle Order on 30 July, 1938, in honour of his seventy-fifth birthday (Bosworth 2000; HF GI 1938). Americans did not normally receive medals from Nazi Germany on their birthday, and the fact that Ford received the highest grade of the order was a symbolic sign that he meant even more to the Nazi regime than Watson. In contrast to Watson, Ford was not given the medal in Germany but was awarded it by Karl Kapp, the German consul in Cleveland, Ohio, and Fritz Hailer, the German consul in Detroit. Ford's acceptance of the medal 'signified for some the corruption of all businessmen' (Shenton 1960:7), but in his biography of Ford, Simonds defended Ford by stating that he was prepared to accept medals from any country that was kind enough to bestow them, for example, Great Britain (Simonds 1946:241). Britain, in contrast to Germany, was not a fascist country, and by accepting the German Eagle Order, Ford was legitimising the Nazi regime and giving it a propaganda boost. Furthermore, his refusal to return the medal 'hinted that he was at best insensitive to the Jewish plight' (Nye 1979:91), of which his antisemitic tracts are ample evidence.

Ford's German Eagle Order is currently held at the Henry Ford Research Centre, and although the institution did not wish an image of the medal to be included here, they did provide a statement on the matter, part of which reads:

> This medal is in our collections, however it is restricted because when used out of context, it may be used to incite or promote the beliefs of Nazism or the admiration for Hitler, attitudes which, regrettably, are still held by groups in this country and abroad. We have determined that we will not display it, or make it available to view or photograph.
>
> *(HFRC 2016, pers. comm.)*

Whilst the above statement is understandable in that the museum does not wish to sacralise Ford's Nazi medal, it suggests an unwillingness to confront the 'difficult memories of the painful past' (Sodaro 2018:5). Indeed, any material that would reveal Henry Ford's unsavoury side is absent (Woeste and Gratien 2019). The mission of the museum is to provide 'unique educational experiences based on authentic objects, stories, and lives from America's traditions of ingenuity, resourcefulness, and innovation. Our purpose is to inspire people to learn from these traditions to help shape a better future' (HFM n.d.). How can a better future be realised if the past is hidden? Moreover, not displaying Ford's German Eagle

Order may inadvertently increase its aura, especially as it has been said that 'Sacred objects are not only objects at a distance from our everyday lives; by establishing that distance they also attract and intensify a desire to touch' (Schmidt 2003:85).

There is no mention of coming to terms with the past (*Vergangenheitsbewälti-gung*). This would involve pointing out that during the Second World War, the Ford plant in Cologne used Russian prisoners of war and inmates from Buchenwald concentration camp (Fings 2004:155). The use of forced labour together with Ford's antisemitic past led to the Ford company being criticised for sponsoring a television screening of *Schindler's List* (Classen and Kansteiner 2009). Although the museum is separate from the Ford Motor Company, Ford's Nazi past casts a dark shadow over both of them. Perhaps the museum should return the medal to the German government, although this would not be without its complications, i.e., would the museum publicise its return? Would the ensuing publicity affect Ford car sales? Would the German government accept the medal? If they did accept it, what would they do with it? Perhaps they would give it to a German museum, but would the museum subsequently display it? In any case, at least it is safe from private collectors.

The 'lone eagle' Charles Lindbergh

Hermann Göring adorned Lindbergh with the German Eagle Order at the American Embassy in Berlin in October 1938 (Behn 1995; Wimberly 1949). The American ambassador to Saudi Arabia, Donald Heath, was present during the impromptu presentation and recalled that Göring 'pulled out a decoration from a case and threw the ribbon around Lindbergh's neck' (Wilson 2011:72). Despite reportedly 'proudly wearing the medal for the entire night' (NYT October 1938:1), Lindbergh stated that Göring merely 'shook hands, handed me the box and papers, and spoke a few sentences in German' (Lindbergh 1970:102). His wife, Anne Morrow (who was not invited to the event on account of it being a stag do), told her husband that the medal was an 'albatross' (Cole 1974:43). Lindbergh 'thought nothing about how the world would view that gift, but Anne was shrewd enough to sense immediately that it was trouble' (Andersen 2000:290–291). The American military attaché got advance notice that Lindbergh was to be presented with the medal, but the message was only received on the day that it was due to be awarded and was not passed on to Lindbergh until the following morning (Smith 1985:132). Even if Lindbergh had received advance notice, it is unlikely that he would have refused the medal.

Lindbergh was severely criticised by American Secretary of the Interior Harold Ickes, not only for initially accepting the award, but for not returning it:

> If the fact is that while he was accepting this decoration he was serving as a superspy for his own country, then he was doing a contemptible thing. His friends are entitled to all the satisfaction that they can get out of a defence that is built on a proposition that their hero was accepting a decoration at the hands of Hitler in order to make it possible for him to spy more effectively upon Germany's air forces.
>
> (Ickes 1955:553)

It was Colonel Truman Smith, American military attaché in Berlin, who arranged for Lindbergh to visit Germany five times between July 1936 and January 1939 to gather intelligence on the strength of the Luftwaffe (Schiff 1977). Both men were blinkered by their belief that Nazi Germany was a bulwark against communism (Doenecke 1984). Lindbergh ramped up his isolationist stance by joining the America First Committee in April 1941 to publicly campaign for America to keep out of the war in Europe (Cole 1951). In the same year, entertainment impresario Billy Rose, a critic of Lindbergh, offered him a public platform in Madison Square Gardens, on the condition that the 'public melting down or hammering out of shape of your Nazi medal be made a feature of the rally' (Berg 1999:62). The location of Madison Square Garden was not inconsequential, as a 'monster' pro-Nazi rally had been held there in February 1939 (Bell 1970:592). Had Lindbergh smashed his medal, it would have been little more than low-grade silver and enamel. It was his relationship with Göring that he did not want to destroy by 'throwing it back in his face' (Whitman 1974:18). Returning the medal would also have been an 'unnecessary insult to the Nazi leadership' (Roth 2004b:10). Lindbergh was more concerned about the feelings of Göring and Hitler than their victims.

Despite her initial misgivings, his wife defended her husband's decision to accept the medal, suggesting that he was the dupe of Hugh Wilson, the American ambassador to Germany, who sought to establish stronger relations with Göring, hence refusing it would have been counter-productive (Lindbergh 1976:XXII). This contrasted to what she said to him privately, but in his memoirs, Lindbergh failed to mention that his wife had told him that the medal was an albatross, which she also omitted from her diary, hence it was left to the editor of the diary to highlight the omission (Lindbergh 1976:437).

In 1970, four years before his death in 1974, Charles Lindbergh claimed that the medal was 'relatively unimportant' (Whitman 1970:1). It was certainly significant enough for Lindbergh to initially retain the medal, then to evade its bestowal in his memoirs. The awarding of the medal was also enough to cause a furore, and stating that the medal was unimportant suggests where Lindbergh's sympathies lay. He also stated that he donated the medal to the Missouri Historical Society, but he failed to point out that this was probably not until 1951 (Smith 2016, pers. comm.). This coincided with his 1950 book *Of Flight and Life*, in which he renounced weapons of war, although he was more critical of the Soviet Union than Nazi Germany (Lindbergh 1950). In contrast to the situation regarding Henry Ford's medal, the Missouri History Museum has occasionally displayed Lindbergh's German Eagle Order (Friswold 2012; MHM 2016) (Figure 4.6). The medal physically linked Lindbergh with Nazi Germany, a connection that some visitors may not have been aware of. At least the museum did not shy away from displaying the embodiment of Lindbergh's controversial past.

During his lifetime, even more eyebrows would have been raised if Lindbergh had worn his German Eagle Order to events, especially in America, as it would have been regarded as a sign of strong Nazi sympathies. On the other hand, he may have gained additional kudos in Germany had he worn the decoration (either in Germany or in America), as it would have been a public sign that a famous

Figure 4.6 Order of the German Eagle in box, awarded to Charles Lindbergh 1938.
Copyright: The Missouri Historical Society, picture taken by staff photographer David Schultz in 1999. Reproduced with permission of the society.

American was willing to wear a medal associated with the Nazi regime. Lindbergh did not have the state at his disposal in which to reciprocate Hermann Göring with a prestigious decoration, but he rewarded Göring by arguing for America to be kept out of the war. Social interaction 'results from the fact that others control valuables or necessities and can therefore reward a person. In order to induce another to reward him, a person has to provide rewards to the other in return' (Belk and Coon 1993:396). Who benefited the most, Göring or Lindbergh? Both paid a price for supporting Nazism: Göring committed suicide shortly before he was due to be hanged in 1946, and Lindbergh's reputation was damaged from the moment he flirted with fascism and remains so long after his death.

A Nazi medal for GM

Compared to Charles Lindbergh and Henry Ford, James D. Mooney had milder Nazi sympathies, although he also harboured strong anti-communist views. Mooney was the vice president of General Motors' overseas operations, and due to his work in Germany, he was given the Eagle Order by the German consul in New York in June 1938 (Turner 2005:176; Wren 2013; NYT August 1938). The medal was therefore awarded in America, as was Ford's Eagle Order, and was surely emblematic of how Nazi tentacles were spreading abroad. A few months later, in October 1938, he gave the medal to the American navy department, primarily because he was an American naval reserve officer, and the medal was considered an unauthorised foreign award. Mooney gave the decoration to the American authorities shortly before *Kristallnacht*, helping to deflect personal criticism. Watson tried this tactic in 1940, but as he was a civilian, he was told that it was for him to decide whether or not to return the medal (Black 2001:219).

In 1940, Mooney was personally entrusted by President Roosevelt to extend peace feelers in Germany, which contrasted to Lindbergh's contentious visits (Doenecke 1984; Reich 1995). Mooney had already met Hitler in 1934 to discuss Opel's vehicles, as GM had acquired the company in 1929 (Merron 1999:Footnote 25). In 1940, Mooney visited Hitler on an unofficial peace mission armed with a letter signed by Roosevelt, but the American president's offer to act as a moderator between Germany, Britain and France has been described as 'exceptional' (Marks 1985:977), as well as 'bizarre and misguided' (Stokes 2007:708). The fruitless mission was in keeping with Mooney's naive belief in economic appeasement, which he set out in an article entitled 'American Economic Policies for the Impending World War' (Mooney 1937). He sought to distance politics from business, but such a view was not extraordinary, as for some international businessmen, 'politics was of no concern to business unless the policies of the former directly impinged on the interests of the latter' (Forbes 2007:167). Mooney was not totally apolitical, as he stated that the 'bokseviki [Bolsheviks] are to be kept out of the Baltic and the Balkans . . . only Germany can do the job' (Dunn 2013:60). The American navy returned Mooney's German Eagle Order to his widow in 1958, and it currently resides in Georgetown University (JDM), protected from being offered on the collectors' market.

The bestowals of the German Eagle Orders, certainly in relation to the above awardees, were an effective way for the Nazi regime to extend its influence abroad. Although the medals did not keep America from eventually joining the war, they had an uncanny hold over their recipients. In an entry in his secret diary on 8 December, 1941, which was only a few days before Germany declared war on America, German Social Democrat Friedrich Kellner launched a scathing attack on the 'deluded and cowardly' American isolationists and could not understand why America had not joined the war from the outset (Kellner 2018:265). Perhaps the medals did play a mild role in keeping America out of the war until December 1941; conversely, they were more likely to have fostered opposition to Nazi Germany.

Although this discussion was restricted to prominent Americans who received the German Eagle Order, further investigation would likely reveal more American awardees, as well as unearthing recipients from other countries who conducted business with Nazi Germany in the crucial lead-up to the war.

Conclusion

Whether it was the Cross of Honour awarded in its millions or the medal for Arts and Sciences only awarded to a few, these objects held great symbolic power. The former was awarded for service in the Great War, and the latter was awarded to those involved in producing weapons for the next. As the Second World War drew closer, medals presented to Hitler's shock troops of the SS were made from lesser-quality materials than the iron used for the Cross of Honour. Some collectors project themselves through elite organisations such as the SS, thereby being respected as an SS collector rather than a generalist. Even the most committed collector could not afford Henry Ford's German Eagle Order if it was ever offered for sale. They cannot even view it in the museum in which it is hidden. Nevertheless, one can still gaze at a similar German Eagle Order once held by Ford's friend Charles Lindbergh. Compared to Ford and Lindbergh, it is unlikely that Mooney's German Eagle Order would attract the same degree of interest. This is despite it being made during the Third Reich much in the same way as all the others. Watson's German Eagle Order is embedded in one of the earliest forms of tabulating technology, and it is the electronic circuitry of modern-day computers that facilitates the market in Nazi memorabilia. Underneath this industry are those who were persecuted and murdered by some of the people whose medals are traded.

Notes

1 The article in the 'Shield' was entitled the 'Honour Cross for Frontfighters, Non-Combatants, Widows, and Parents' (*Das Ehrenkreuz für Frontkämpfer, Kriegsteilnehmer, Witwen und Eltern*) (Sch 1934:2; Dunker 1977:36).

2 Antisemitism was also evident during the Great War, evidenced by the 'Jewish census' (*Judenzählung*) authorised by the war minister Adolf Wild von Hohenborn in October 1916, although the report was suppressed as it contradicted its antisemitic premise (Grady 2011:33–34). The 'census gained significance retroactively, after the Nazi accession to power in 1933, as shown in memoirs written at and after that time' (Penslar 2013:173).

3 During the Great War, 1,000 Iron Cross first classes and 17,000 second classes were awarded to soldiers of Jewish descent (Wernitz and Simons 2013:409). These relatively high numbers are testament to their sacrifice.

4 The law dated 7 April, 1933, was entitled 'Protection of the Professional Civil Service' (*Gesetz zur Wiederherstellung des Berufbeamtentums*) (RGB April 1933). On 30 September, 1935, the 'Reich Interior Ministry ordered the dismissal of all civil servants having three or four Jewish grandparents – a modification of the Civil Service Law in light of the Reich Citizenship Law that effectively suspended the Hindenburg exception' of April 1933 (Oregon n.d.:Year 1935). In September 1941, German Jewish war veterans were prohibited from wearing military decorations in public and branded with the yellow star (Oregon n.d.:Year 1941).

5 It has been claimed that the 'SS symbol was designed by illustrator Walter Heck in 1929, and was chosen less for its symbolic or magical significance than for its graphic impact' (Arnold and Hassmann 1996:78). Nevertheless, Heck's lightning or electricity bolts (initially designed for an SS badge for use in civilian wear) had a particular significance for Himmler, who believed that a long-lost mythical Aryan race derived special powers from them, hence they could also protect SS members who wore them

(Kurlander 2017). Himmler and Rosenberg were obsessed with finding evidence of so-called ancient Aryan civilisations (Mees 2004). It was not until the formation of the Leibstandarte Adolf Hitler (LAH) in 1933 that Heck's double flashes were depicted on the right-facing collar patch to denote the elite status of this regiment (Weingartner 1968). In 1906, however, Austrian occultist Guido von List had already described and illustrated a victory rune: 'Heil and Sieg!' This many-thousand-year-old Aryan greeting and fight-call, which is also found in varied forms in the extended excited greeting 'alas sal sena' (old German), is in the Sig-rune (victory rune), the 11th sign – 'The creating spirit must win' (List 1906, 1938:1:14, translated from German by Sophie Baumert). Himmler converted such ramblings into a deadly form.

6 The 'coinage of the two great Macedonian kings, Philip II and Alexander the Great, has often puzzled numismatists and historians alike' (Perlman 1965:57). Whether Alexander the Great authorised his own image to be placed on coins is contested.

'It would have been politically unwise for Alexander to be the first Greek ruler to officially place his own image on his coins in democracy-minded Greece, particularly during the early years of Alexander's reign before he established his authority. Greeks at the time abhorred the Eastern tradition of deifying kings during their lifetime and the Eastern practice of putting portraits of rulers on coins . . . On the other hand, the possibility exists that Alexander gave his tacit approval to the practice of others incorporating his features into the Herakles image of his coinage near the end of his life' (Goldsborough 2013).

7 In 2007, Lumsden, a Scottish police inspector at the time, was spotted driving his personal German-made car with a private number plate resembling the initials of the NSDAP (Nazi party) (Findlay 2007).

8 Wittman and Kinney (2016:Chapter 12, location 3095). Rosenberg and Goebbels jostled with each other over who would ultimately control the hearts and minds of the German people. From 1928–29, Rosenberg had a prominent position in the Fighting League for German Culture, but after the Nazi seizure of power, Hitler appointed Goebbels as the head of the newly created Reich Chamber of Culture (Larson 1937; MandH 2021; Steinweis 1991).

9 When I stayed in Denmark in 1995, one of my Danish friends asked one of his friends why he had bought a 'Hitler Car', i.e., the VW Beetle. Only with reluctance did he sit in it.

10 Black's claim that IBM enabled the Holocaust has been dismissed by professional historians, for example, Allen (2002); Turner (2001).

5　Medals for babies

The Honour Cross of the German Mother (*ehrenkreuz der deutschen mutter*)

The 'Nazi party was undoubtedly a dedicated opponent of female emancipation, the ultimate in male chauvinism, firmly committed to a view of women as inferior beings whose main task in life was to bear children and look after the home' (Evans 1976:123). Manliness was 'identified with the glory of the party and is used as a means of encouraging in German boys an attitude of superiority toward women and a belief in the doctrine of militarism and anti-Semitism' (Yourman 1939:153). In December 1938, the Honour Cross of the German Mother (*Ehrenkreuz der Deutschen Mutter*) (hereafter the Mother's Cross) was instituted to incentivise married couples to have more children (Mosse 1966:45–46). The Mother's Cross facilitated patriarchy, and its decree was signed by an all-male leadership headed by Hitler.[1] The Mother's Cross had considerable agency during the Third Reich, which has not been fully realised by collectors in the postwar era. They mainly regard it as a pretty medal.

A racist form of pro-natalism

Germany was said to be the 'first of the great nations to become population conscious and to develop a set of policies designed both to increase the birth rate and to improve hereditary quality' (Hankins 1937:630). The 'horrific losses at the front (Great War) and the collapse of fertility at home made it seem imperative that Germany reduce infant mortality – if for no other reason, than to ensure that the army had sufficient recruits in future' (Dickinson 1999:44). Fertility fell to '15.1 per 1000 of the total population in 1932 and 14.7 in 1933' (Glass 1940:269–270). Shortly after gaining power in 1933, Nazi officials attempted to reverse the decline in the birth rate by a series of measures that included stricter anti-abortion legislation and the introduction of marriage loans (David *et al.* 1988). Although abortion was made illegal, the perverse racist worldview of Nazism meant that Jewish women were forced to have abortions (Gordon 2002; Joshi 2011:834; Whelpton 1935).

Marriage loans were 'designed to eliminate women from the labor force during the unemployment crisis and to encourage marriage and procreation amongst racially fit couples about to marry if the woman had worked before marriage and promised not to work again until the loan was repaid' (Rupp 1977:371). Marriage

DOI: 10.4324/9781003000617-5

loans were also a way to 'stimulate consumption expenditures and, even more importantly, to spread employment among households by taking women out of the labor market' (Klein 1948:56). The loans were predicated on the newlyweds producing children, as for every 'racially acceptable' and healthy child who was born, the loan was cancelled by one quarter (Taeuber and Taeuber 1940:153). These ideologically loaded initiatives had 'little discoverable effect on population' (Staudinger 1938:146). The 'aim of the Nazi regime to restore fertility to the high levels achieved before the First World War failed since during the Third Reich it never once reached even the levels of the early 1920s' (Usborne 2011:158). Indeed, Nazi patriarchal zealots had an uphill battle in changing a society in which the 'small modern family had become the norm' (Boak 2013:234). Berlin, for example, had the lowest birth rate of any city in the world (Mason 1976:82).

By 1936, Germany's war preparations intensified, leading to full employment (Barkai 1990:225; Overy 1994:42). Consequently, women were needed to fulfil Göring's four-year economic plan, hence no longer needed to leave the labour market to be eligible for a marriage loan (Mouton 2010:950). Germany was so successful in employing women that German 'women in 1939 were already more actively engaged in the labour force than Britain's women were to be even at the end of the war' (Tooze 2006:515). This contrasted with core Nazi ideology which still espoused that the proper place for a woman was tending to the home and caring for children. In this respect, the institution of the Mother's Cross was an initiative especially intended to reward middle-class mothers for staying out of work to produce children who would grow up to be soldiers.

Children were segregated into Nazi organisations according to their gender. Boys were commandeered into the Hitler Youth (HJ) and girls into the League of German Girls (BDM). From the minute girls donned the 'BDM uniform, elaborate with emblems, letters, triangles, and swastikas, one thought governs their lives; a mature thought, nourished by biological eagerness and restlessness: What can we do, what can we learn, how can we live to prepare ourselves for our great mission? To be the mothers of Hitler's future soldiers?' (Gordon 2002:178). Girls 'were to take quiet hikes, care for wounded soldiers, prepare for raising children, and work hard in factories' (Goutam and Gautam 2014:1022). Nevertheless, the stereotype of the 'blue-eyed, naive, braided young female whose main goal in life was supposedly limited to procreation: the mothering of a goodly number of racially impeccable offspring' was not the overwhelming reality (Reese 2006:4).

Social Democrat Friedrich Kellner noted in his secret diary that that one of the 'downsides' of the Mother's Cross, and one of the reasons for introducing it, was that children would be used as 'cannon fodder' in Hitler's imperialistic campaigns (Kellner 2018:494). Hitler's thirst for war, despite his public proclamations of peace, accounted for the incompatible perceptions within NS circles, which on one hand affirmed that Germany was overpopulated, hence needed more room, whilst on the other claiming that not enough children were born (Pendleton 1978). Although these positions were contradictory, the emphasis on childbirth stemmed from the requirement to replace the losses that would ensue once Hitler embarked on his violent quest for *Lebensraum*, in which the 'borders of the German nation were not fixed by common political, social, or cultural institutions, but instead by a vague combination of pseudo-scientific and mythic notions of race' (Lower 2002:227). Only a 'world-view based on a concept of Lebensraum could fantasize and create a death world' (Neumann 2002:111, 123; also see Domansky 1992).

Iconography and symbolic value

The inscription on the front of the Mother's Cross had the designation 'For the German Mother' (*Der Deutschen Mutter*), which seems fairly innocuous until Nazi notions of race and genetics are considered. In order that a woman could be given a Mother's Cross, both parents had to be of 'German blood and genetically healthy' (*deutsch-blütig und erbtüchtig*) (Doehle 1943:63–64), discriminatory categories that excluded those with hereditary conditions. Indeed, 'every birth, even that of enthusiastic Nazi women, had a risk to reveal the mother as genetically defective by producing a disabled child and of not being an honoured German mother any-more.'[2] In keeping with Nazi racial dogma, Jews were excluded from receiving the medal. Moreover, by late 1938, when the Mother's Cross was instituted, there was an intensive 'racialization of Jewishness in the press' (Pegelow 2002:214).

Despite the NSDAP's fractious relationship with the churches, the Mother's Cross, in the form of an 'elongated cross' (*längliches Kreuz*), upheld Christian symbolism (Doehle 1943:63–64) (Figure 5.1). The inscription on the reverse of the initial design had overtones to a Christian crusade, as it read 'The 'Child Ennobles the Mother' (*Das Kind adelt die Mutter*). The leader of the Nazi Wom-en's Association, Gertrud Scholz-Klink, was inspired by the inscription, as she affirmed on Mother's Day in 1939 (despite being divorced) that the 'knightly man and the knightly woman belong together' (DNB Mai 1939).

It has been suggested that the blue and white enamel on the Mother's Cross was emblematic of the Virgin Mary (Maddox 2017). Blue was also the colour of loyalty and featured on other Nazi service-related medals (UM Juli 1935:9). The colour blue was also inspired by Queen Louisa of Prussia placing cornflowers on her eldest son's head (the future Wilhelm I) whilst fleeing Napoleon in 1806 (Hayden 1938). As the designer of the Mother's Cross, Franz Berberich, was based in Munich (Doehle 1943:64), it would not have been lost on him that blue and white were the colours of the generally anti-Nazi Bavarian royal house of Wittelsbach.

Women needed at least four children to qualify for the lowest grade of the medal. Consequently, the decoration was intended to give couples who only had two or three children a nudge to produce more. As the Mother's Cross was not awarded until 1939, couples had to produce at least four children by 1945 to earn even the lowest grade of the decoration. The population census of 1939 stated that due to the increase in fertility since 1933, there were an additional 20,000 fourth children, and 160,000 fifth and sixth children within marriages (PI 1944:31), numbers which are not extraordinarily high.

The award's grading system, comprising of bronze (four children), silver (six children) and gold (eight children) (Stephenson 2001:31), was a symbolic indica-tion that larger families were more valuable. Gold also represented completion (UM Jul35:9), thus was the ultimate representation that a woman had fulfilled her

Figure 5.1 Mother's Cross 1938 (front of gold grade).
Source: Author's collection. Photograph taken by Grant Hughes, 2020.

Nazi-prescribed role in life. The colour of gold and its sheen are also suggestive of the sun (Schoenberger 2011). Indeed, the rays of the sun emanated from the swastika positioned at the apex of the Mother's Cross. Despite the illusion of precious metal, the medals were mass-manufactured from cheap non-ferrous materials. Still, Hitler allegedly said that the Mother's Cross was the 'finest of the lot,' as it was awarded 'without regard for social position' (Cameron and Stevens 1953, 2000:119).[3] The egalitarian nature of the Mother's Cross has been questioned, instead being said to represent 'bourgeois domesticity' (Föllmer 2013:1119).

Hitler further rewarded mothers by offering to be the godfather of their ninth child or seventh son. This was yet another sign that girls were deemed less valuable. It was claimed that the 'godchild stands out from those of his age group or work mates. The government agencies that he deals with will gladly give him particular attention, since he has the Führer as godfather, which will help smooth his life's path to a considerable degree' (Bytwerk 2008:36–39). The aforementioned statement also exhibited gender bias. Not every woman welcomed Hitler as godfather. A Bavarian Catholic woman who had a large family found herself having to give her son the name of Adolf but also gave him the Catholic-inspired middle name Maria (Evans and Attar 2020). Perhaps this was overlooked because Maria was the name of Hitler's grandmother. Anti-Christian NSDAP officials ordered a family in the Austrian annexed town of Geistthal to call their fourteenth child Gerta instead of the Christian-inspired Stefanie (Schaub 2013:1).

Patriarchal propaganda

The Mother's Cross was a public sign that women who had children were valued as much as male soldiers, with the act of childbirth supposedly being equivalent to 'thunder of battles' (*Donner der Schlachten*) (VB Dezember 1938). Although women were generally excluded from combat, apart from a very limited extent at the end of the war in 1945 (Flak guns aside), their task was described as the 'birth battle' (*Geburtenschlacht*), and according to fundamental Nazi rhetoric, the cooking spoon was said to be a woman's weapon (FGFF 1981:89). It was unlikely that women would have regarded a cooking spoon and a gun, two objects that had entirely different functions, as being equivalent (for a similar line of thought see Houkes and Vermaas 2004). Whilst such overtly misogynistic language was absurd (Kudlien 1990:235), for some women, domesticity expressed Germanness (Reagin 2007).

It was expected that up to three million women would qualify for the Mother's Cross, providing Nazi officials with a mass opportunity to extract propaganda value from the bestowals of the decorations (VB Dezember 1938). The first award ceremonies took place on Mother's Day in May 1939 (Stibbe 2003:42). The medals were also awarded on Hitler's mother's birthday on the twelfth of August, further advancing the Führer cult. Hitler's connection to the Mother's Cross was materially reinforced by a facsimile of his signature on the reverse of the award. This had the potential to shape behaviour, as the Gauleiter of Berlin (presumably Goebbels) asserted that in terms of the ceremonies, it was 'obvious that the honorary cross, which bears the name of the Führer, is only to be worn with a worthy dress' (*würdigen Kleid*) (UM November 1939:314). Contrary to propaganda images of women wearing Austrian or Bavarian dirndls, there was no central policy during the Third Reich that prescribed what women should wear. Indeed, Figure 5.2 shows a Nazi official awarding a Mother's Cross to an older woman wearing a dress rather than a traditional costume.

As the medal was not awarded until 1939, there were only six years until the end of the Third Reich left to earn additional grades. It is therefore likely that the majority of women only attended one ceremony. Depending on where the ceremonies were held, they may have enhanced or detracted from the value of the award and were an opportunity for women to converse. The cult of motherhood was bolstered by the ceremonies being reported in newspapers, on the radio and in newsreels. The weekly newsreel (*Wochenschau*) was a 'sophisticated propaganda medium, remaining in the forefront of the Nazi cinematic efforts until the regime's collapse' (Chrystal 1975:31). A newsreel depicted a Mother's Cross award ceremony in Austria in 1944 (DW Mai 1944). Some of the women are greeted by their children who have returned from evacuation camps run by the Hitler Youth. Around 100 women are gathered in the town square, and the film shows three of them being presented with the Mother's Cross by Siegfried Uiberreither, the Nazi Gauleiter for the Austrian region of Steiermark. In keeping with what has been

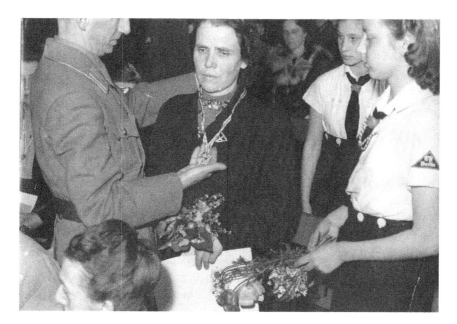

Figure 5.2 Unnamed Nazi official awarding an unnamed woman the Mother's Cross in the Litzmannschule Berlin on 17 May, 1943.

Source: Bundesarchiv, number 183-J06142.

Photographer: Unknown.

stated earlier, the women who are presented with the medals are older mothers and are wearing dresses rather than traditional costumes. The mothers are not identified (unlike the Nazi regional leader), subsumed into the wider narrative promulgating the cult of motherhood rather than honouring individuals.

From 'dearest wish' (*sehnlichster wunsch*) to rejection

A so-called 'begging letter' (*Bettelbrief*) (Schymura 2014; Hall 2014) addressed to Hitler was written by a man on behalf of his 71-year-old mother-in-law, who had expected a Mother's Cross for her Christmas in 1939, complaining 'now with the third ceremony on Christmas she had expected the mother's cross to be awarded by the Führer. Unfortunately, her greatest Christmas joy became her greatest disappointment' (Weyrather 1993:133). It is worth noting that this letter was not written by the woman herself, thus her autonomy was reduced. In her case, it appears that the woman was not refused the decoration, hence the delay was likely administrative. The contents of the letter therefore exhibited deference for Hitler and the Mother's Cross rather than being an expression of opposition.

A similar letter addressed to Hitler requesting a Mother's Cross was written by a 79-year-old woman, who politely protested:

> Since I have again not received the mother's cross on the 1st October, I want to ask you, my Führer, to award me the cross, since I have now to be ashamed of my grandchildren who are in the Hitler Youth and my daughter, who has many children herself and will probably receive the cross on Christmas. My Führer, I am so unhappy that I always have to avert my eyes when my grandchildren ask why the grandmother has not received the cross.
>
> (Weyrather 1993:134)

The grandmother's plea suggests that it was not necessarily the medal that she desired, but not being awarded one was the source of consternation within her family. The medal therefore intruded into the lives of three generations. Indeed, by 'honoring older mothers, the regime emphasized the life cycle of the maternal figure and her contribution to the continuity of the German people' (Fox 2009:25).

The letter referred to a planned bestowal on the first of October, which was of symbolic significance, as it was the Reich Harvest Festival (*Reichserntedankfest*), although large celebrations were cancelled due to the Second World War. Before the war, the largest of these harvest festivities took place near the town of Hameln, Lower Saxony. In 1935, Hitler told the assembled farmers that children 'are the most beautiful and richest crops that a people can own' (Sösemann 2000:128). The symbiosis of the land and fertility was rooted in the dogma of 'Blood and Soil' (*Blut und Boden*). The 'völkisch philosophers emphasized that the race of the future should be bred not from the unstable and degenerate inhabitants of towns but from the sessile German peasantry, rooted in the German soil' (Mazumdar 1990:194). The Minister of Food and Agriculture Walther Darre urged German women to marry 'pure-blooded men and to reproduce for the good of the race' (Lovin 1967:286). The Mother's Cross regulations were grounded in these racist notions, demonstrating that during the Third Reich, human life was unequal.

Blood and soil ideology also encroached into Christmas festivities, i.e., images of God were replaced by 'sentimental images of mothers and children' (Gershon 2015). It was the anti-clerical leaders such as Goebbels, Himmler and Rosenberg who especially attempted to distance the festival from its Christian association (Gajek 1990; Steigmann-Gall 2003). The 'remade people's Christmas (*Volksweihnachten*) celebrated the arrival of a saviour, embodied in the twinned forms of the Führer and the Son of God, who promised national resurrection rooted in the primeval Germanic forest and the blood and soil of the authentic Volk' (Perry 2005:572).

In rural Bavaria, there were public protests when the 'Nazi authorities precipitately ordered the removal of crucifixes and religious pictures from the schools' (Horn 1979:565). Crowds of 'angry women demanded the return of the crosses, with some handing back their Nazi decorations to police officials amidst shouts of if the crucifixes are removed from the schools, then we do not need any Mothers' Crosses' (Wilson 1994:318). These protests are emblematic of the difficulties that anti-clerical Nazi ideologues had in turning Germany into a secular society.

Women did not necessarily accept that they 'had to retreat into a private sphere of tending to the needs of the children, the kitchen, and the church, earning mother crosses for faithful subservience' (Johnson 1997:241). Likewise, some women did not 'equate emphasis on motherhood with the renewal of the German Volk, nor did they, after Hitler's seizure of power, thank him for giving them an important role to play as mothers in the new Germany' (Gellott and Phayer 1987:94). Indeed, a National Socialist woman named Paula Siber von Grote asserted that the 'woman's question cannot be solved today merely by the brutal slogan of procure husbands for women and put women back to the cooking pot' (Wunderlich 1935:336).

The idea that the Mother's Cross could increase the birth rate was 'ludicrous' (Kudlien 1990:235). This is supported by a postwar oral history with bronze Mother's Cross recipient Frau Ludwig, 'who remains indignant at the insinuation that her decision to have a large family was anything other than strictly personal' (Mouton 2010:966). A form of dissent was the derogatory name given to the Mother's Cross of the 'Bunny Order' (*Kaninchenorden*) (Ziegler 1986:28). A more direct form of action was fertile German women going 'on strike' (Gumpert 1940:17).

Medal as agency

Members of the Hitler Youth (HJ) and the League of German Girls (BDM) were instructed to salute women in public wearing the Mother's Cross. No doubt it was 'intended to impress on the young, that these women were living examples of what they should themselves aim to achieve, in addition to enhancing the national esteem for mothers in a demonstrable way' (Stephenson 1975:50). Minister of the Interior Wilhelm Frick explained that this instruction would create a 'deep connection between the youth and mothers. Adolescents now see that the troubles and sacrifices of mothers are not in vain. The adolescent girl sees and learns that motherhood is the highest duty to the people and that the fatherland is grateful to the mother' (DNB Mai 1939). Figure 5.3 shows a Mother's Cross ceremony attended by BDM members wearing black neckerchiefs indicating they had passed their probationary period. Nevertheless, despite being indoctrinated with Nazi propaganda, not every BDM member equated their role in life with producing children.

Some 'women were pressured to apply for [the Mother's Cross], many were not even asked first if they wanted to have it, and were regarded with mistrust and denounced if they declined the award.'[4] Consequently, even an inanimate object such as the Mother's Cross, which in its material form was little more than metal and enamel, had a powerful agency. Thing power is the 'curious ability of inanimate things to animate, to act, to produce effects dramatic and subtle' (Bennett 2004:351). Under the dictatorial system of the Third Reich, in which party functionaries became ever more radical in the belief that they were fulfilling Hitler's wishes (Kershaw 1993), the so-called Bunny Order could have negative consequences for those not deemed wholesome members of the Nazi People's Community (*Volksgemeinschaft*).

Figure 5.3 Members of the League of German Girls (BDM) attending a Mother's Cross
        ceremony.

Source: Bundesarchiv, number 146-1977-008-01A.

Photographer: Unknown.

Comparative perspective

It was not only Nazi Germany where medals were instituted (and failed) to
increase the population. The introduction of medals and other incentives as part of
the Battle for Births in fascist Italy failed to 'check the gradual decline in the fertility of Italian women' (Staudinger 1938:126). A 'social battle based on emotions,
appeals to the past greatness of ancient Rome, and bombast was ultimately insuf-
ficient to reverse the demographic trends' (Forcucci 2010:10). The Soviet Union
introduced what has been described as 'one of the most decisive pro-natalist pro-
grams ever inaugurated in any country' (PI 46:167). The Soviet initiative begun
in July 1944 included the institution of three distinctions for mothers, spurred
by a 'heavy fall in the birth rate' exacerbated by soldiers not being given leave
and heavy losses at the front (Stone 1969:394). The decorations comprised the
Motherhood medal for five children, the Order of the Glory of Motherhood for
seven children, and the title of Mother Heroine for ten children (Simpson 2004;
Tay 1972). Despite Soviet policies, the 'glorification of motherhood and birth
bonuses failed to have much effect' (Hoffmann 2000:47). Medals for motherhood,

no matter which regime bestowed them, were yet another way in which to stamp female citizens with the symbols of their respective political masters.

Despite Britain also having a low birth rate (Seccombe 1990), a medal for motherhood was not introduced. Indeed, Britain has 'always resisted the idea of population policy' (McIntosh 1986:319). In Germany, it was men who controlled marriage loans, as it was the husband who was given the benefit by the state,[5] contrasting to the arrangement in Britain: Family allowance being paid to women rather than men (Allen 2000). British family allowances aimed to 'alleviate poverty and not to raise the birth rate, as was intended in the European family allowances programmes' (Riley 1979:101).

The decline of the French population was one of the reasons which was given for France's military defeat in 1940 (Coleman and Rowthorn 2011:227). Her 'military manpower and her income-producing capacity were not quite six tenths that of Germany's. By 1939 the German margin had become appreciably greater' (Spengler 1951:411). The low French birth rate was despite a medal being instituted in 1920, the same year in which a law was passed prohibiting the promotion of abortion and contraception (Sonn 2005; Tomlinson 1985). Despite the law, abortions were performed illegally, which had also been the case since their initial prohibition in 1810 (Stetson 1986). Analysing abortion rates is not the best way to approach the issue of low birth rates, as it is already a poor state of affairs if a country's birth rate is dependent on eliminating abortions, and the promise of a medal was unlikely to have prevented a woman from having an abortion if she found herself in difficulty.

Smith et al. (1994) affirmed that Nazi policies failed to significantly increase the number of children born in Germany. In contrast, it was claimed that by 1940 the German birth rate was higher than the combined numbers in Britain and France (Proctor 1997:208). The effectiveness of National Socialist population policy was considered by Leo Martin in the *American Catholic Sociological Review*, hence his fairly positive assessment of the National Socialist anti-abortion and anti-contraception stance should not come as a surprise. He concluded that the gamut of pro-natalist policies that were introduced during the Third Reich had an effect in raising the birth rate, although he acknowledged that it was difficult to identify their respective contributions. He mentioned the Mother's Cross, although he did not elaborate on its efficacy. He conceded that 'despite the rapid increase in the birth rate in the thirties, the births in no year were sufficient to give a reproductive rate of 1.000, that is, to maintain even a stationary population' (Martin 1945:81).

Dudley Kirk, a population studies expert, acknowledged that the German birth rate had risen, but he was not convinced that it was due to pro-natalist measures and suggested that it was a result of Germany's increased rate of employment (Kirk 1942). The employed were not necessarily in a better financial position than they had been in the late 1920s, as in 1937, real wages were 'almost the same' as in 1928 (Temin 1991:584). The situation varied, as there was a 'wage spiral in the metal industries' (Mason 1966:130). As such, it is likely that a combination of family circumstances, housing, industry sector, wages and working hours, rather than a medal, influenced the decision to have children.

Efficacy

The accumulated evidence indicates that the Mother's Cross did not directly influence married couples to have more children. Rather, the value of the Mother's Cross resided in the domain of political propaganda. Indeed, some Nazi functionaries were masters of deluding themselves by their own propaganda (Bytwerk 2010). It has been said that the regime was 'more generous with cheap honors than with material assistance for mothers' (Heineman 2001:155). Whether incentives on their own were enough to have increased the birth rate could also be disputed.

In the late 1920s, a peasant wife claimed that her husband treated her like a 'dog or a baby-producing machine, and rarely appreciated her until she was dead' (Bridenthal 1973:152). This grim scenario hardly changed during the Third Reich, and it would not be too strong to suggest that women were branded by the Mother's Cross. In addition, although one of the purposes of the medal was to honour mothers, their autonomy was restricted. Mothers did not even have an inalienable right to keep the medal, as it could be taken away if the parents became 'unworthy' (RGB Dec38). In fact, the children who were drafted into the Hitler Youth had already been taken away from their parents. Frieda Wunderlich described how children were consumed by the Nazi Party and the totalitarian state from birth to death:

> Parents and children are estranged and families are dispersed by the various party organizations, which start as early as Kindergarten then school, which are supplemented by party organizations during leisure time. The young German enters the Hitler Youth at the age of ten, passes to country camps, labour camps, the boy then to storm troops, the army and veterans' organizations.
>
> (Wunderlich 1937:349)

Kellner added that parents were proud that their 'children were learning about broadcasting, flying, or riding, but at the drama's end, they are shattered by the loss on the battlefield' (Kellner 2018:258). Some teenagers rejected the discipline of the Hitler Youth and formed their own gangs, such as the working-class Edelweiss Pirates or the middle-class Swing Youth. These rebellious teens appropriated either the edelweiss (worn as a cap badge by the army's mountain light infantry) or the death's head (Horn 1973). Consequently, the meaning of insignia depended on the context in which it was worn. Furthermore, the social context of Nazi insignia was drastically altered after the Third Reich was defeated.

Collectors

When a Mother's Cross is offered on the collectors' market, its past is usually not revealed, reinforced perhaps by the tendency of collectors and traders to fetishise material artefacts rather than their social lives. Celebrating and displaying the Mother's Cross as an object are some of the ways in which collectors go about this (Dant 2009:511–512). Namely, the Mother's Cross is decontextualised, disembodied and disenfranchised. This stripping of a given Mother's Cross's past is facilitated by the certificate that accompanied the medal usually being absent. Even if it was present, the rather generic document would not reveal much about the mother awarded it. Furthermore, the ways in which a given Mother's Cross has circulated on the collectors' market are antithetical to its recipient being identifiable.

If a mother decided to sell her medal after the war, she would have been metaphorically selling her children, hence there may have been few direct sales (unless the medal was sold to benefit them). Alternatively, if a mother felt that she was pressurised into having children during the Third Reich, she may have subsequently sold or thrown out her medal in an act of deferred defiance. It is also possible that her children performed similar acts in the postwar era. Militaria traders have also played their part in merely regarding the Mother's Cross as something to be bought rather than being a window into the social history of the Third Reich. These disassociations – and by no means are these the only pathways – they help to explain how the Mother's Cross has become an anonymous artefact on the collectors' market.

Nevertheless, the Mother's Cross has been retained within some families, thereby offering opportunities to learn about its recipient. Gerta Kollmann, mentioned earlier, explained to her niece in 2013 that although Hitler was her honorary godfather, he was an 'abomination' and she switched off her television every time he appeared (Schaub 2013). She also explained that the date of 16 December, 1938, on the reverse of the Mother's Cross did not represent the day she was born but was the medal's institution date (again contributing to individuals being subsumed within the wider Nazi scheme of things). By sheer coincidence, she was born a day later, on 17 December, 1938. She observed that the date on the medal was difficult to read, thus patina was slowly exercising its agency in addition to marking the passage of time, much in the same way as her ageing body. It was the swastika, however, which signified that she was inextricably linked with the Nazi past. Although she said her parents did not talk about the Third Reich much, they did not throw away the medal they had been given for producing children (perhaps as one of their sons was killed during the war). One of Gerta's brothers gave her the medal after their mother died in 'honour' of their mother. Consequently, at least for Gerta, rather than the 'Honour Cross of the German Mother' representing Nazi ideology, it is a reminder of her mother.

For collectors, rather than a Mother's Cross representing a family's unique story, it falls into the category of the so-called 'mass-awards that have shown slight decrease in price' (Nimmergut 2010:5–6). Low financial value partially explains why collectors and traders have not given much attention to it. Although collectors find it attractive, its abundance has subdued prices, being the second lowest in terms of percentage increase (see Appendix A).

In terms of gender, it was the only medal which I monitored that was directly associated with women. By its very nature, it was not worn by men, which distanced it even further from a military environment. The alteration of an object's gender association was explored by Hermkens (2007:4) in relation to how 'maro (cloth) changed from a female-gendered object and product into a male-associated commodity,' providing similar insights into the transformation of the Mother's Cross. The medal has fallen from being a Nazi symbol of female fertility to being collected by men, who are responsible for reconfiguring its meaning and value. Male 'entrepreneurs place themselves in a complexly gendered situation, in which they take an interest in handling objects that in all other respects are the purview of women' (Addo and Besnier 2008:50). Male collectors of the Mother's Cross have relegated the medal to the bottom tier, which is in stark contrast to the social esteem that the medal had during the Third Reich. These collectors would rather collect a medal awarded for killing four soldiers than one awarded for giving birth to four children.

Conclusion

Under the National Socialist swastika, German society was geared for war, hence male children were required to become soldiers. Parents were reluctant to have large numbers of children, so to encourage childbirth the Honour Cross of the German Mother was instituted to incentivise them, but it had little effect. It would have taken more than a piece of metal (however sanctified) to reverse the trend for smaller families. The application process for the medal was yet another way in which Nazi authorities encroached into the private sphere and had negative consequences for those who were rejected. Even if the medal did not directly lead to more children, it embedded Nazi notions of race and eugenics within the German population. After 1945, the Mother's Cross was divested of the agency that it once had, and rather than being a source of public veneration, it was kept out of sight. The decoration was subsequently acquired by collectors who did not need to produce children to have one. These collectors, predominantly men, prefer medals that were awarded to soldiers rather than civilians, failing to recognise the degree to which German society was mobilised for war. These collectors tend to idealise the Wehrmacht through the acquisition of decorations such as the Iron Cross. Medals made from iron tend not to display well beside enamelled medals, leading to the further segregation of medals associated with the female gender. Both physicality and meaning therefore combine to prevent the Mother's Cross from being more integrated within collections. Whether this should be done is another matter, not least due to the sinister ideology underlying the decoration. Beneath the attractive blue and white enamel of the Mother's Cross lies the most disturbing manifestation of eugenics – turn the medal around and the signature of the man responsible for sterilising those deemed inferior is revealed.

Notes

1 The Mother's Cross decree of 16 December, 1938, was signed by Hitler, Rudolf Hess the Deputy Führer, Wilhelm Frick of the Interior Ministry and Otto Meissner, the State Minister and Chief of the Presidential Chancellery of the Führer (RGB Dezember 1938).
2 Weyrather (2015:Kindle location 3858 of 4987). Translated from German into English by Dr. Bernadette Mekker from Weyrather (1993)
3 For source criticism of Hitler's *Table Talk* see Carrier (2003).
4 Weyrather (2015:Kindle location 3858 of 4987). Translated from German into English by Dr. Bernadette Mekker.
5 Bock (1983:Footnote 54).

6 Wartime awards

All ironed out

German medals reached their zenith during the Second World War. Never had a single conflict generated so many, nor has one since. Whilst men were earning badges for commanding tanks, their wives were given medals for producing the shells they fired. Whilst male Luftwaffe crews were awarded decorations for bombing London, women received badges for shooting down Allied planes over Berlin. Despite the falling bombs, babies were born and medals awarded for producing another child for the Führer. German soldiers whose fingers fell off due to frostbite received what was nicknamed the 'frozen flesh medal.' Warm clothes would have been more beneficial. Jews were classified as partisans, and for killing them, German soldiers received Himmler's Bandit badge. Only in National Socialist Germany could the 'link between ideology and marketing of ideas through images acquire an exemplary significance' (Skradol 2011:602).

An icon of iron

Historical context

Hitler earned the Iron Cross during the Great War, and upon launching his own conflict, took the opportunity to reinstitute the decoration along his lines. Kaiser Wilhelm's monogram was erased and replaced with the swastika (Figure 6.1). There was no getting away from the origins of the Iron Cross, hence its institution date of 1813 was retained on the reverse of the medal, but the imperial crown was obliterated. The Reich colours of black, white and red replaced Prussia's black and white ribbon. For the first time, the Iron Cross symbolised the whole of Germany. Despite the iconographic changes, the preamble to the 1939 version tapped into the old trope of Germany being surrounded by enemies and affirmed that in the past, the Iron Cross had been instituted on account of Germany's 'brave sons' having to defend the 'homeland' (*Heimat*).[1] It was Hitler, of course, who was responsible for invading Poland.

Steinhauer und Lück, a company which had produced the Great War Iron Cross and was known as the Iron Cross King, was one of the manufacturers that made the decoration (Maerz and Stimson 2010:174). As stated in Chapter 3, Steinhauer was one of the badge-making firms that used forced labour during the Second World

DOI: 10.4324/9781003000617-6

Figure 6.1 Iron Cross 1914, and 1939 Second Class.

Source: Author's collection. Photograph taken by Grant Hughes, 2020.

War (Begler 2013, pers. comm.). When contacted, the still functioning Steinhauer responded that none of their wartime records were available (Blechen 2013, pers. comm.). Further research is warranted in relation to medal companies and forced labour, but the practice was widespread within the German wartime economy, especially as German workers were conscripted into the Wehrmacht. The clothing firm of Hugo Boss, for example, used forced labourers to make uniforms during the Second World War (Köster 2011). Forced labourers were essentially compelled to produce uniforms and medals so that occupying German soldiers could be clothed and rewarded for further enslaving and killing their compatriots.

Even though the core of the cross could have been made from a non-ferrous metal, the symbolic importance of iron was so great that it continued to be the material foundation of the decoration. Iron Cross recipients might have felt cheated had the medal turned out to be a piece of tin. Nevertheless, a nickname which was given to the 'Knight's Cross of the Iron Cross' (*Ritterkreuz des Eisernen Kreuzes*) (hereafter the Knight's Cross) was the 'Tin Tie' (*Blechkrawatte*) (DUZ Oktober 1943:3). This was considered as soldiers merely letting off steam, and by no means was it the only military decoration given a nickname (see below). As the Knight's Cross was worn at neck level (WHWO n.d.:15th image), those who coveted the award were said to be 'suffering from sore throats' (Grunberger 1971, 2013:189). Soldiers and officers desired the Knight's Cross so much that when, in 1943, Inspector General of Armoured Forces Heinz Guderian attempted to reorganise antitank gun crews, one of the nonsensical reasons given in opposition to his proposal was that it would prevent the gunners from earning the medal (Guderian 1952, 2009:298).

The Knight's Cross replaced the imperial Pour le Mérite (PLM), awarded 687 times during the Great War (Erinkmann 1982:1). In contrast to the PLM, the Knight's Cross was not restricted to 'high-ranking commanders' (Neitzel and Welzer 2013:40). In theory, it could be awarded irrespective of rank, thereby fostering an egalitarian community that recognised merit over Prussian aristocratic lineage, a development which the writer Eckart von Naso commended in the trade publication for the uniform industry (DUZ November 1944:1). As Naso was of Prussian aristocratic lineage, his support of privates being entitled to the Knight's Cross is symptomatic of how the war was shaking up German society.

The Knight's Cross had several grades, including Oakleaves, Swords and Diamonds. Namely, for 'all these awards existed several ranks, so that the acquisition of an award immediately motivated soldiers to acquire the next class' (Römer 2012:132). Hitler was known to use the swords to the Knight's Cross as a form of retirement gift. According to gift exchange theory, the 'gold watch presented at retirement is normally more representative of a feeling of good riddance than of recognition for achievement' (Schwartz 1967:6). Although the Oakleaves and Swords were made from real silver, as they only weighed around 9 grams, their value in scrap silver was negligible. Indeed, it would have been unlikely that such a symbolically prestigious award would have been melted down during the Third Reich (seeChapter 8). During the Second World War, the value of the Oakleaves and Swords was purely symbolic, maintained by only being awarded 160 times (Bowen 1986:232). Hitler presented Field Marshal Erich von Manstein with the Swords to his Oakleaves after dismissing him on 30 March, 1944 (Manstein 1958:614). Compared to some other army commanders who incurred Hitler's displeasure, Manstein got off lightly. After the war Manstein sought to distance himself and the German army from Hitler's more compromised henchmen who also earned the Iron Cross.

Not an ordinary piece of iron

Perpetrators of the Holocaust Adolf Eichmann, Josef Mengele, Reinhard Heydrich and Erich von dem Bach-Zelewski all earned the Iron Cross. The latter 'hardened mass-murderer' received the Knight's Cross for suppressing the Warsaw uprising in 1944 (Wistrich 2001:6). After Hitler presented him with the medal, Bach-Zelewski facilitated the deportation of Hungarian Jews to Auschwitz (Alexander 1948:317).

Before conducting gruesome and unethical medical experiments at Auschwitz, Mengele earned the Iron Cross second and first class whilst serving with the Waffen-SS on the Eastern Front. Consequently, Mengele 'was the only doctor in Auschwitz who possessed that array of medals, and he was enormously proud of them; he frequently referred to his combat experience to bolster his arguments on a variety of matters' (Lifton 1985:16). The Iron Cross had travelled from Waterloo in 1815 to the gates of Auschwitz.

Shortly after his role in deporting Hungarian Jews to Auschwitz, Eichmann earned the Iron Cross second class for facilitating the evacuation of a German military field hospital in August 1944 (Cesarani 2005:189). During Eichmann's 1961 Israeli trial, his German defence lawyer Dr. Servatius made the point that Eichmann had committed acts 'for which you are decorated if you win and go to the gallows if you lose' (Arendt 1964:15). This statement has been described as one of the 'most poignant of the century' (Bauman 1989:18). Indeed, Eichmann would probably have been honoured with more decorations had Germany won the war and the extermination of all Jews realised.

Eichmann's superior, and architect of the Holocaust, Heydrich, was not only the head of the Security Service (SD), but a volunteer Luftwaffe fighter pilot, earning the Iron Cross second class whilst in Norway, 1940. The 'real purpose of Heydrich's visit, was not to indulge his passion for flying, but to orchestrate the first wave of arrests of political opponents in Oslo and other Norwegian cities' (Gerwarth 2011:174). In July 1941, whilst his special task forces were killing Jews on the Eastern Front, he flew with the Luftwaffe, this time earning the Iron Cross first class. His respect for the award did not extend to German Jews, as on 10 October, 1941, he stated that decorated Jewish Great War veterans should not be exempt from being deported to the east (Gerlach 1998:770). They had already been prohibited from wearing their military decorations in September 1941 and branded with the yellow star.[2]

Nevertheless, decorations still held a certain resonance. On 16 December, 1941, Wilhelm Kube, the otherwise cruel Generalkommissar of Belorussia, was 'outraged' when German Jews with the Iron Cross were sent to Minsk for so-called special treatment (i.e., eventual extermination) (Arendt 1964:102; Kube 1941). Only ten German Jews sent to Minsk survived the Holocaust (Yad Vashem n.d.). The issue of German Jewish recipients of Great War medals was raised at the infamous Wannsee Conference chaired by Heydrich on 20 January, 1942, where it was proposed that holders of the imperial Iron Cross first class were not to be immediately deported to their deaths, but sent to the so-called Theresienstadt old-age ghetto (Davis 1999:27–28). Indeed, one of the most sinister aspects of Theresienstadt, apart from thousands of its inmates being sent to Auschwitz, was that it acted as a cover for the outright extermination of Jews in death camps (Dawidowicz 1975).

Jewish Iron Cross recipients

During the Second World War, 244 Iron Crosses and 18 Knight's Crosses were awarded to soldiers of Jewish descent (Rigg 2002:39). Those with Jewish heritage were able to serve in the Wehrmacht due to concessions and the difficulty of authorities applying the so-called Nürnberg race laws. Erhard Milch, a field marshal in the German air ministry, was awarded the Knight's Cross despite his

Jewish ancestry and was one of the most extreme examples of someone with Jewish heritage who became a perpetrator (Gelbin 1997:144). After the Nazis came to power, his mother, fearful of the German secret police (*Gestapo*), claimed that she had an affair with her uncle, hence Erhard's Jewish father was not his biological one (Hertz 1997:56). Only in Nazi Germany could it be more acceptable to be a child of an incestuous affair than to have Jewish ancestry. Hermann Göring supported Milch, saying that it was he who decided who was a Jew ('*wer Jude ist, bestimme ich*') (Gossman 2013:178). Milch was subsequently certified to be of 'German Blood' (*Deutschblütigkeitserklärung*). Milch was asked by Justice Robert Jackson at the Nürnberg trials about his Jewish heritage, but he replied that he was not Jewish (AV3).[3] Indeed, historian David Cesarani stated that soldiers of Jewish descent did not think they were Jewish and 'wanted to prove they weren't Jewish by fighting for the Führer' (Scheinberg 1997). Milch was sentenced to life imprisonment for his involvement in forced and slave labour (but released in 1954) (NYT January 1972:32). Milch is an example of the moral grey zone that soldiers of Jewish heritage confronted during the Second World War (Dunn 2007).

Jews who served in the Finnish army were also faced with a moral dilemma when Finland and Germany became brothers-in-arms between 1941 and 1944 (Seitsonen et al. 2017). The Finnish Jewish military doctor Skurnik was recommended for the Iron Cross second class for successfully organising the evacuation of a German military field hospital but refused the award (Rautkallio 1994:69). His rejection led to a demand by the German authorities that he be handed over, which did not appear to have happened (Ibid.:Footnote 38). The article did not state whether the person who initially recommended Skurnik for the Iron Cross knew that he was Jewish, which would likely have been an obstacle. In any case, the incident accords with gift exchange theory, as the benefactor was offended by the intended recipient refusing the gift (which is perhaps a natural reaction, although one that takes on a potentially dangerous turn during a genocidal war). Seitsonen (2018:47) mentioned another two Finnish Jewish soldiers who rejected offers of an Iron Cross. In contrast, Blood (2006) is not aware of any perpetrators of the Holocaust who rejected Nazi medals.

Iron maidens

It has been stated that 39 women earned the Iron Cross second class during the Second World War (Campbell 1993:317). The recipients were generally restricted to traditional female roles, for example, Red Cross nurse Else Grossmann (Schulze-Wegener 2012:140). Nevertheless, test pilots Hanna Reitsch and Melitta Schiller von Stauffenberg earned the decoration. Reitsch was the first woman during the war to be given the Iron Cross, presented by Hitler in March 1941 (Reitsch 1951, 2015:202). The award was a result of her friend Ernst Udet, a Great War fighter ace now in a senior position in the Luftwaffe, witnessing one of her flights. A public celebration was held in her hometown of Hirschberg to commemorate her award (Lomax 1988:Photographs between 148 & 149) (Figure 6.2). The festival was probably the 'last truly happy day of her life' (Piszkiewicz 1997:Chapter 3). As

Figure 6.2 Pilot Hanna Reitsch wearing the Iron Cross second class, Hirschberg, 5 April, 1941.

Source: Bundesarchiv. Archive number 183-B02092.

Photographer: Ernst Schwahn.

she had a 'fetish for honour,' no doubt she relished the attention (Work 1946:566). Reitsch was awarded the Iron Cross first class in 1943 after nearly being killed testing the ME163B jet aircraft, although her mother was rightfully concerned by her daughter being 'elevated to the status of a Nazi heroine' (Lomax 1988:85). Indeed, Reitsch is best known for her precarious flight to Hitler's Berlin bunker in April 1945, and she stayed loyal to Hitler's memory in the postwar era. Pilot Schiller von Stauffenberg was also awarded the Iron Cross second class, but due to her father's Jewish background, she did experience antisemitism (Zegenhagen 2007:590). Indeed, she was torn between her commitment to the Luftwaffe and knowing that she was aiding the Nazi regime, a moral dilemma facing many with Jewish ancestry during the Third Reich.

Youth

In the last years of the war, children who had been indoctrinated with Nazi propaganda eventually got the chance to prove themselves in combat as draftees of the German home guard (*Volkssturm*). Children were particularly susceptible to medals, as 'by appealing to the emotional, primary wishes of youth with symbols, martial music, the use of color, uniforms, etc., youth was fired with enthusiasm for their new leader' (Kunzer 1938:346). The presentation of the Iron Cross to young teenagers diluted the symbolic value of the decoration, as it magnified how desperate and futile the military situation had become. A small number of Hitler Youth boys were assembled for propaganda purposes in Berlin so that Hitler could present them with Iron Crosses.[4] The bestowal of the medals was recorded in a newsreel to be shown on Hitler's fifty-sixth birthday in 1945. The youngest of these boys, 12-year-old Alfred Zech, was awarded the Iron Cross second class for rescuing 12 injured soldiers under fire in his hometown of Goldenau, Upper Silesia (Figure 6.3). Zech threw his Iron Cross away before capture but purchased a replacement from a junk shop after the war (Pattrson 2011). Whilst this did not have the aura of his original Iron Cross, it absorbed his personhood.

The award ceremony did not occur on Hitler's birthday, but a month earlier. Goebbels's diary entry for 21 March, 1945, reads, 'they make an excellent impression. A people which has youngsters like this available at a time like this cannot, according to the laws of history go under' (Goebbels 1978:192; photograph on 242–243). His remarks demonstrate the fantasy world in which he was living, although the tragedy was that the death and destruction that Goebbels, Hitler and others unleashed was all too real. His diary entry should be approached with scepticism, as it was intended for posterity in the public domain, and if Germany had won the war, his comments would have been proof of his commitment to National Socialism when even hardened Nazis knew that the war had been lost.

Weighed down by iron

By 1944 over half a million first-class Iron Crosses and over three million second-class examples had been awarded (1971, 2013:185). These huge numbers, overwhelmingly awarded to men, put the few crosses given to women in perspective and reflect the gender bias of the Third Reich. No women held the Knight's Cross, of which 5,068 had been awarded by September 1944 (Doehle 1945:22), increasing to 7,300 by May 1945 (Schulze-Wegener 2012:148). This rapid escalation was a consequence of the intensive fighting in the last year of the war, although the high numbers still damaged its symbolic value. Indeed, when a 'regime fears for its survival there is a great incentive to try to forestall this collapse by using awards as incentives to supporters' (Frey 2006:385). Whilst the value of the Iron Cross second class was eroded, the first-class version was relatively robust (Römer

Figure 6.3 Twelve-year-old Alfred Zech wearing the Iron Cross, April 1945.
Source: Bundesarchiv. Archive number 183-J28836A.
Photographer: War reporter (Kriegsberichter) Koch.

2012:138). Despite a general level of award inflation, the 'accolade system' during the Second World War was more transparent than the one that was in place during the Great War (Neitzel and Welzer 2013:42), although favouritism still existed.

The Iron Cross could be awarded posthumously and was permitted to be held by a dead soldier's family as a memorial piece. Nevertheless, for some widows, the intrusion of a medal may have been alienating. Essentially, the product was not worth the price (Brandt 1994:110). A holder of the Knight's Cross who survived the war reflected on his award, and whilst showing it to a collector stated, 'to think I risked my life for this piece of tin' (Williamson 2017, pers. comm.), hence echoing the term the 'Tin Tie.' For those who earned the Iron Cross and paid the ultimate price, both were immortalised on 'death cards' (*Totenzettel*), although the tradition of distributing these at funerals pre-dated the Nazi era

Figure 6.4 Erwin Rommel's funeral procession, 1944.
Source: Bundesarchiv. Archive number 183-J30704.
Photographer: Heinrich Hoffmann.

(Berlis 2016). On a national level, it was suggested that a public memorial should be built to honour the recipients of the Iron Cross, so that after they had died, their 'grandchildren could look with reverence up to this memorial place under which their heroic victories were gained' (Reichel 1940, 2011:45). A corporal cynically stated in one of his private letters that every soldier should 'get the Iron Cross, but along with it most also get the wooden one' (Fritz 1997:99). Likewise, military leaders 'know many of the soldiers being honored at all the fronts will likely not survive the war – so the Führer patronizingly distributes the Knight's Cross and other badges as compensation and does it with much fanfare' (Kellner 2018:455).

Hero 'worship and The Cult of the Fallen Soldier represent the clearest and most affecting examples of the paradoxical nature of Hitler's dream for Germany' (O'Donnell 2012). A cynical example of a hero's funeral was that of Field Marshal Erwin Rommel, who committed suicide following accusations that he was aware of the plot to assassinate Hitler (Fuhrman et al. 2016). This was hidden from the thousands of people who lined the streets in Herrlingen, Württemberg, on 19 October, 1944, to pay their respects, although Hitler was conspicuously absent (Figure 6.4).

Golden Diamonds

It reached the stage that even the silver Oakleaves, Swords and Diamonds to the Knight's Cross could not maintain its symbolic value. A version in real gold was therefore instituted on 29 December, 1944 (RGB Januar 1945) (hereafter Golden Diamonds). It was therefore one of the few awards that actually contained precious metal, and it would not be unreasonable to question where it came from. In contrast to other decorations, only 12 awards could be bestowed, ensuring that it would not be devalued by award inflation (Schulze-Wegener 2012:154). In fact, only one Golden Diamonds was awarded, the recipient being the Luftwaffe pilot Hans-Ulrich Rudel, who received it from Hitler on 1 January, 1945. Rudel recalled the ceremony in his postwar autobiography, stating that the 'many lights in the room make the diamonds sparkle in prismatic colours' (Rudel 1952, 2012:210–211). This statement is all the more remarkable in light of the carnage inflicted during the Second World War.

In late December 1944, Hitler even considered the relatively low-ranking Rudel as his successor, demonstrating that Hitler thought his designated successor Göring was no longer suitable (although he had yet to be dismissed). Hitler told his adjutant, Nicolaus von Below, 'now there's a successor for me. Intelligent. What are his views on art and culture?' (Below 1980:223). Hitler would not have considered Rudel as his successor or awarded him the highest grade of the Knight's Cross had Rudel not been antisemitic. Another reason for Hitler awarding the Golden Diamonds to a Luftwaffe pilot was that after the failed attempt to assassinate him in July 1944, his existing suspicions of the army's officers intensified. No 'important air force officer took part in the plots against Hitler' (DeWeerd 1949:199).

Hitler's making of the sole award of the Golden Diamonds to a Luftwaffe pilot instead of a member of the army or navy was a sign that he had not altogether lost faith in the Luftwaffe of 'Herr Meyer' (Göring).[5] Nevertheless, the Luftwaffe was unable to command the skies over Germany due to mismanagement and a lack of resources. Men and planes were even squandered on the day that Rudel was awarded the Golden Diamonds, as the Luftwaffe sustained heavy losses in a futile sortie in the west (Muller 2003:55).

Rudel stayed loyal to the spirit of National Socialism after the war. Historian Omer Bartov suggested that the glorification of the Third Reich or the expression of quasi-totalitarian views by veterans after 1945 was 'much better proof of the degree of these men's conviction than expressing them when Hitler was at the height of his powers' (Bartov 2003:113). Indeed, Rudel was active within neo-Nazi circles (Jaura 1976:1922).

As Hitler was proud of and benefited from the medals he earned during the Great War, he recognised the value of awarding decorations.

> The world has learned over the centuries how to inspire soldiers. The German is unusually ambitious, sensitive to praise, and enthusiastic about special recognition. He will be more than just a little proud if he can have one little

star, one little ribbon, or one medal more than his neighbour. The Führer recognized his people's weakness and used it to the utmost.

(Kellner 2018:333–334)

Hitler despaired to von Below that despite awarding medals, he had been betrayed by the 'circles . . . who had profited the most from National Socialism. I pampered and decorated them. And that was all the thanks I got' (Below 1980:223). It is debatable whether medals were enough to have secured allegiance.

War trophy

Even before the war ended, German medals fell into enemy hands. Indeed, it has been said that Nazi symbols were 'destined to be liberated' (Skradol 2011:607). Shortly after the Allies landed in Normandy in June 1944, Captain Bill Cotton of the 4th County of London Yeomanry was photographed sporting a Nazi Iron Cross first class on 17 June, 1944 (IWM 5682) (Figure 6.5).[6] Cotton presumably wore the Iron Cross as a hunting badge of honour, which was probably also intended to unsettle his German opponents. This was a bold move on the part of Cotton, as he may have been shot if captured. When Cotton acquired his Iron Cross, Nazi medals were not regarded as collectibles in the same way that they are today.

Collectors

Collectors did not have to storm the Normandy beaches to 'liberate' an Iron Cross; they merely had to purchase one from a militaria trader. Their interest in the decoration was fuelled by both the Iron Cross first class and the Knight's Cross being prominently featured in war movies. In *The Eagle Has Landed* (Sturges 1976), Michael Caine played a highly decorated Luftwaffe Major called Steiner, who was described by Lenny Rubenstein as 'as nice a German officer as has ever crossed a studio lot. Wearing the Knight's Cross around his neck for some extraordinary paratroop feat' (Rubenstein 1977:33). The SS officer who reprimanded Steiner for attempting to save a Jewish girl also wore a Knight's Cross, but it did not have Oakleaves and Swords, consequently elevating the Luftwaffe major into a purely military hero. Rubenstein added that 'Hollywood stipulated that while all the proper Nazi scoundrels were in the SS or Gestapo and spoke with as thick a German accent as could be safely carried on a soundtrack, all the decent sorts were in the army' (Rubenstein 1977:35).

Collectors no longer solely seek a representative example of the Iron Cross but are prepared to pay high amounts of money for attributes that the collecting community deems desirable. This is characteristic of an object that has morphed into a collectible, with it no longer being appropriate to simply talk about one price, but many different prices governed by collectible scarcity (Culler 1985:6; Williamson 2017, pers. comm.). Whereas 'a collection in the past might have a couple of Iron Crosses, specialized collectors now have dozens, if not hundreds. They are able to

Figure 6.5 Captain Bill Cotton (to far left of photo) wearing a German Iron Cross 1944.
Source: Imperial War Museum London, number B_005682.

study marks, manufacturing techniques and extrapolate many details that can only be learned through studying many examples side by side' (Adams-Graf 2011).

Hamburg-based militaria trader Helmut Weitze claimed that the soldiers who earned the decoration 'didn't give a penny, to them a medal was a medal, no Knight's Cross winner was checking with his buddy if this was made by Juncker, or by Steinhauer, or by Klein and Quenzer, that's a true collector thing' (Weitze 2018, pers. comm.). This was further corroborated by author Gordon Williamson, who interviewed many veterans and stated that for the soldiers who earned medals, maker marks were 'totally irrelevant. They had no interest in who made them whatsoever' (Williamson 2017, pers. comm.). Nevertheless, it is a virtue of the Iron Cross that collectors are prepared to have more than one, which is not the case for many other Nazi decorations.

I recall purchasing a 1939 Iron Cross first class from an antiques shop around 1991 and experiencing difficulties in convincing some general militaria traders that it was authentic. Their main concern was that the cross was not maker-marked. I had just started collecting and was not even sure which kind of marks it should have. I examined the reverse of the cross with a magnifying glass under a lightbulb but could not find any marks (when I was sighted, of course). Dust had settled on the iron core, hence I was even more convinced that the badge was original; all I needed was a maker mark to prove it. I stared at the cross for so long that I thought I found one, but when I rubbed my good eye, it was gone. I subsequently learned from specialist collectors that far from my Iron Cross being a copy, it was probably made earlier in the war before licensing schemes were introduced.[7]

I recount the above tale as it highlights the obsession that collectors have for both intrinsic validating signs on artefacts and acceptance of these artefacts within the collecting community. As a partial consequence of asymmetrical knowledge, many original badges without marks have been avoided and fakes with marks purchased. Indeed, maker marks are deliberately included on fakes to fool collectors. Namely, for 'deception to occur, the victim must have expectations, the deceiver must have expectations about the victim's expectations, and the deceiver must act with those expectations in mind' (Mitchel 1996:823).

As the 1939 Iron Cross did not generally have a real silver frame and was awarded in greater numbers compared to its imperial predecessor, it would be expected that it would be less expensive on the collectors' market. A review of prices between 1980 and 2014 revealed that the reverse was the case (see Appendix A). Whilst the 1939 Iron Cross was more expensive than its 1914 predecessor, the latter exhibited the highest percentage increase in price out of all the medals that I monitored (Appendix B, Figure B.2). This was mainly due to its steeper price rise in recent years, which suggests that it was previously undervalued. The centenary of the Great War may have boosted interest, although more empirical research would need to be conducted to ascertain whether prices increased for all imperial medals. I suspect that due to the Iron Cross being such an iconic award, its demand is unique (see Chapter 7 for corroboration). Interest in the Knight's Cross was also strong, being the most expensive award, although it only had fifth position in terms of its percentage increase in price (see Appendix A). The latter result is likely to be a consequence of high-quality fakes suppressing enthusiasm for this otherwise desirable award. Aesthetically speaking, the imperial Iron Cross is more elegant than its bulkier Nazi successor and also has more to look at in the form of oakleaves and crowns. Nevertheless, it does not feature the Nazi swastika, nor was it awarded for actions during the Second World War. This is not to pit one war against another, but there is more interest in Second World War German militaria compared to that of the Great War.

Collectors are especially drawn to the mobile nature of the Second World War (although tanks and planes did exist during the Great War). Collectors are particularly enthralled by the mechanised fighting machines emblematic of Hitler's 'lightning war' (*Blitzkrieg*). Nevertheless, if there 'has been any military organization subject to myth-making, it is the German Army of the Second World War' (DiNardo 1996:384). Indeed, at least '2,000 of the German army's 2,900 tanks employed against Poland in 1939 were obsolete' (Balsamo 1991:267). Hitler's lightning attacks only achieved so much, and Germany could not outmatch the resources of America and the Soviet Union.

The weapon badges

It was the various 'combat badges' (*Sturmabzeichen*) administered by their respective high commands that symbolised a soldier had served in a plane, submarine or tank. Indeed, each of the branches of the Wehrmacht competed for recruits through distinctive decorations and uniforms (Frey 2006). Combat badges were a stylised representation of the weapons and vehicles deployed during the Second World War. A submarine badge had initially been introduced in 1918, designed by the sculptor Walter Schott (Schott 1930; Woods 2013:279). During the Third Reich, the Berlin sculptor Otto Peekhaus replaced the Hohenzollern crown with a refined eagle and swastika (Doehle 1943:94) (Figure 6.6). Indeed, the 'fascist style at its best is Art Deco, with its sharp lines and blunt massing of material, its petrified eroticism' (Sontag 1980:94).

There is nothing erotic about the destruction that the German U-Boats inflicted. Heinrich Bleichrodt, the commander of U-48, received the submarine badge after torpedoing without warning the SS *City of Benares* that was transporting child

Figure 6.6 Submarine badge 1939.

Source: Author's collection. Photograph taken by Grant Hughes, 2020.

evacuees from Liverpool to Canada on 17 September, 1940, resulting in the loss of 77 children and hundreds of adults.[8] Amongst the dead was nine-year-old Beryl Myatt, whose parents, unaware of the tragedy, wrote to their daughter on 21 September, 1940, 'we expect that you enjoyed your voyage on the boat across the wide Atlantic Ocean,' a letter which her pet dog had marked with his muddy paw (IWM BM n.d.).

German submariners also incurred heavy losses. Out of the 41,500 men (women were excluded) who served on submarines, 28,000 were killed and 5,000 were taken prisoner (Mulligan 1992:261). Despite these high losses, submarine warfare failed to starve Britain, leading to the claim that the resources spent on producing over 1,000 submarines would have been better put towards the manufacture of tanks (Weinberg 2014:89).

The 'Tank badge' (*Panzerkampfabzeichen*) was instituted on 20 December, 1939, with further grades being introduced on 22 June, 1943, to denote either 25, 50, 75 or 100 days of service (Doehle 1943:88–89) (Figure 6.7). Indeed, soldiers had little choice in the matter, as they were either injured, killed or survived to fight another day. In 1943, an attempt was made to restore Germany's declining military situation on the Eastern Front by a tank battle near Kursk, codenamed 'Citadel' (*Zitadelle*) (Mulligan 1987). The additional grades of the Tank badge

Figure 6.7 Tank badge 1939–1940.

Source: Author's collection. Photograph taken by Grant Hughes, 2020.

were introduced in advance of this attack to 'commemorate the once more proven readiness to fight in tanks' (Doehle 1945:106).

The badges were not capable of winning the Kursk battle, and despite the new Panther (Panzer) and Tiger tanks, the Soviet T-34 vastly outnumbered the German forces, thus 'quantity really does have a quality all its own' (Citino 2012:143). Although the German forces were not able to decisively break through the Russian defences, the German tank crewmen were still regarded as being an elite branch of the Wehrmacht. Collectors have not associated the Tank badge with war crimes or crimes against humanity, and the iconography of the badge concealed these acts, which is another reason why artefacts require to be contextualised. Such a contextualisation would be a reminder to collectors that in the autumn of 1941 Colonel-General Erich Hoepner's Panzer group assisted the Einsatzkommandos of the Sicherheitsdienst Task Force A in the murder of 137,567 Jews on the Eastern Front (DeGroot 1947:535).

Collectors

Fuelled by a romantic notion of tank warfare, collectors contributed to the Tank badge exhibiting the third highest percentage increase in price (see Appendix A), with the Submarine badge immediately behind it. Indeed, military awards are the most popular amongst collectors (Nimmergut and Nimmergut 2011:7). The strong demand for and prices of weapon badges have encouraged replicas and fakes, but one of the central questions is what effect do these have on prices? In the 1970s and 1980s it was thought that fakes were responsible for increasing the prices of originals, as it was claimed that the 'flood of reproductions has had the unfortunate effect of making many collectors lose confidence in Nazi military badges, automatically assuming that any reasonably priced item is faked' (Cayley et al. 1983:45). Consequently, the prices of originals may have been artificially raised to signify authenticity. Illustrating the chicken-and-egg complexity of this issue is the fact that during the early 1970s, it was claimed that the doubling in price of Third Reich medals led to a 'flood of fakes and re-strikes' (Johnson 1971:50). No doubt some collectors and traders profited from selling reproductions as originals.

In recent years, fakes have had a counter-effect on relative prices (i.e., lowering the prices of originals) as 'combat badges of the marine and air force stagnated, which can be led back to insecurities of collectors due to a flood of fakes' (Nimmergut 2010:5). If collectors were unable to distinguish a replica from an authentic artefact, then overall increase in badge supply may have suppressed prices. Namely, if there were no fakes, demand would be restricted to only authentic examples, and as these are limited in supply, an increase in demand would have increased prices (Stoller 1984:90). Collectors may be more comfortable buying an original medal when its price is low (less risk) and more comfortable purchasing a copy when an original is expensive (avoiding risk) (see Qian 2011).

A British-based retailer of replicas offered a reproduction silver Tank badge for GBP 23.95, describing it as having a 'really nice distressed aged finish. With makers mark and original style steel needle pin. This item could be original – it is so realistic'

(NMRTB). If it is so realistic there is a high chance that it could end up on a stall and be passed off as original. Indeed, rather than being a replica, as it was made to look like a medal that had accumulated patina, it is in the realm of a fake. Nevertheless, no matter how old a replica looks, it will never possess the inherent aura of an authentic badge.

When a collector is examining a Tank badge, they are not holding a piece of cheap metal, but wondering if it was worn by a tank commander defending the Normandy beaches. When they are running their fingers along the slender submarine on the U-Boat badge they are not hankering after zinc but are absorbing the spirit of the North Atlantic wolfpacks. These collectors did not experience frozen Russian winters or bombardment by depth charges. Nor do they necessarily think about nine-year-old Beryl Myatt who never got to see her parents or pet dog after being killed by U-48. Indeed, u-boats are fetishised through the rather abstract figures of tonnage sunk and whether or not their commanders earned the Knight's Cross.

Collectors' experiences of submarines and tanks have been mediated through war films (some more accurate than others) made decades after the Second World War. The quirky *Kelly's Heroes* depicted German tanks and American soldiers wearing German medals (Hutton 1970; Brownfield 2020). The German movie *Das Boot* (Petersen 1981) dramatically depicted the perilous nature of the German submarine fleet. The gritty *McKenzie Break* (Johnson 1970) highlighted the ideological nature of the Kriegsmarine. Whilst in the dock at Nürnberg, Grand Admiral Dönitz (Hitler's eventual successor after Göring was dismissed in April 1945) claimed that he was apolitical despite making highly antisemitic comments on Heroes' Memorial Day in March 1944 (Hadley 2000:13). Collectors may not be aware of this, nor associate the navy with Nazism or antisemitism. Dönitz was also anti-communist, and despite the German-Soviet pact, the 'German assault on the USSR was central to Hitler's conception of race war' (Uldricks 1999:643).

Limbs for medals

A wound badge was instituted in September 1939 to symbolically recognise the horrific injuries that soldiers would experience (Doehle 1943:17). The magnitude of injuries was reflected by either a black, silver or gold badge (made from base metal). Significant injuries hardly needed to be symbolically represented by a badge, as these were marked by eye patches and artificial arms and legs. Claus von Stauffenberg (Figure 6.8), who nearly assassinated Hitler by planting a bomb in July 1944, received the gold Wound badge in 1943 after losing an eye, his right hand and two fingers on his left hand in North Africa (Hoffmann 1970:12).

Hitler especially valued the Wound badge (Cameron and Stevens 1953, 2000:119), it being one of the few badges that he frequently wore (having been awarded the black grade in 1918). During a disagreement with the chief of the general staff of the army, Franz Halder, he said to him, 'you, who don't even wear the black insignia of the wounded?' (Kershaw 2000:228–229). As Halder had been a staff officer during the Great War, Hitler's reaction was a manifestation of only being a lance-corporal. Hitler was not the only one who valued the Wound badge, as according to Alfred Crammer von Clausbruch, a pilot in the Luftwaffe

Figure 6.8 Claus von Stauffenberg (to far left of photo) meeting Hitler at the Wolf's Lair five days before he tried to assassinate him, 15 July, 1944.

Source: Bundesarchiv. Archive number 146-1984-079-02.

Photographer: Unknown.

before being taken prisoner, the silver Wound badge was a 'nice thing, you can wear it with honour' (*ist auch ein schönes Ding, das kann man schon mit Ehren tragen*) (Römer 2012:133). In contrast, Guderian (1952, 2009:408) overheard an officer say that a 'golden decoration for wounds means absolutely nothing.' Insignia that indicated a soldier had been wounded, however, did show to others that they had most likely fought on the front line, as was the case for British soldiers awarded the Wounded Stripe during the Great War (Jeffreys 2009).

German soldiers sustained considerable injuries following the invasion of the Soviet Union in July 1941. The German 'Eastern Army' (*Ostheer*) sustained 'close to 750,000 casualties, rising to over a million, or a third of the entire army in the East, by late March 1942, of whom more than a quarter were either killed or missing' (Bartov 1992:38–39). The Russian campaign had not been won by the winter of 1941, and the freezing temperatures led to frostbite, weapons not functioning (Stolfi 1980:219), as well as horses succumbing to 'frost and famine' (Pasher 2014:40). In late 1941, Hitler took over supreme command of the army after unceremoniously dismissing the commander-in-chief, Walther von Brauchitsch, for failing to take Moscow (Mawdsley 2011:37).

In January 1942, Hitler also dismissed army commander Erich Hoepner for withdrawing troops on the Eastern Front without his permission (Figure 6.9). Hitler denied Hoepner his pension and symbolically stripped him of his medals (Gruchmann 2003:514). Consequently, Hitler introduced a decree on 3 May, 1942, permitting him, with military court approval, to remove awards, hence even the ownership of medals that had been previously earned was dependent on perpetual satisfactory conduct (Grossmann 2003).[9] As stated earlier, Hoepner was responsible for atrocities on the Eastern Front, so he should not be regarded with sympathy. He was implicated, however, in the July 1944 bomb plot against Hitler, for which he was executed, although he remained ruthlessly opposed to communism (Hürter 2018:34).

The Russian campaign was symbolically represented by the medal for the 'Winter Battle in the East' (*Winterschlacht im Osten*) (Doehle 1943:31) (Figure 6.10). Soldiers needed to have served between 15 November, 1941, and 15 April, 1942, to be eligible (Ibid.). 15 November, 1941, was the start of von Bock's army group centre's 'fresh offensive – the last gamble of Operation Barbarossa – and their forward units actually came within sight of Moscow' (Bell 2011:53). The German 'Eastern Army' (*Ostheer*) never reached the Russian capital, and thousands of ill-equipped soldiers unnecessarily froze to death or suffered from severe frostbite in one of the coldest winters in 150 years (Anon. 1942:608). The situation was reminiscent of Napoleon's ill-fated retreat from Moscow in 1812, although unlike Napoleon, Hitler never set foot in the Russian capital (Brinton 1942).

The magnitude of the Russian campaign was reflected in the 30 sardonic names German soldiers gave to the medal. They 'call the Eastern Medal, for heroes fighting in Russia, the Frost Medal (a pun on Ost Medaille? Frost-Medaille), or The Order of Frozen Feet (a pun on Eisbein), or, more grimly, Snowman in Steel Helmet' (Thompson 1944:201). Another name given to the medal was the 'Vacation Substitute' (*Urlaubsersatz*) (DUZ Oktober 1943:3). This was a cynical reflection

Figure 6.9 Erich Hoepner (sitting). Right of Hoepner is Generalmajor Franz Landgraf.
August/September 1941.

Source: Bundesarchiv. Archive number 1011-210-0142-13A.

Photographer: Artur Zell.

of the bitter conditions on the Russian Front, significantly harsher than occupied
France. A characteristic of the Russian landscape was its barrenness, rhetorically
merged with the medal to form the *Tundra-Orden* (Ibid.). Lieutenant Günter
Dewit, a combat engineer, did not think much of being awarded the Russian Front
medal, saying that he 'did not receive anything' (*bei Russland habe ich nichts
bekommen*) (Römer 2012:132). It was not exactly clear what he expected, but he
had already earned the Iron Cross both first and second class, so perhaps he was
coveting a Knight's Cross. He also had the Close Combat Clasp (a substantial decoration), so either he did not value the Russian Front medal as it was distributed
en masse, or it did not compensate for his service in such a harsh environment.

Collectors

During the Second World War, soldiers were entitled to purchase a replacement
Russian Front medal from shops specialising in medals and orders for RM 2.35
(DUZ November 1944:4), which equates to about USD 11.60 worth of consumer
goods in 2014 (HSS). The financial value of the medal has increased in real terms

Figure 6.10 Russian Front medal 1941–1942.
Source: Author's collection. Photograph taken by Grant Hughes, 2020.

by about 500 percent, and although this is substantial, it has not risen as much as other medals. On the collectors' market, the Russian Front medal exhibited a flat price (being the third lowest) and was the second least expensive (see Appendix A), its low cost being attributable to its availability. Despite the Russian Front medal being described as 'one of the most aesthetically pleasing decorations of the war' (Woods 2010:197), there are simply too many on the market. Had Germany the manpower, the Wehrmacht would have willingly awarded more.

During the Third Reich, the price of medals was governed by their production costs rather than their symbolic value, with a Russian Front medal retailing for more than a Submarine badge. Collectors, on the other hand, value scarcity and the organisation that a medal represents. Moreover, collectors are more interested in collecting the Russian Front medal according to manufacturers' stamps rather than 'what is sitting behind it' (Weitze 2018, pers. comm.). Despite Weitze's comments, which are certainly valid, American-based collector Adam Wilcock (born in 1990) was generally aware of the medal's context, as 'when it came down to it, the technical name, the crass name would be the frozen meat medal' (Wilcock 2018, pers. comm.).

Although the Russian Front medal is available on the collectors' market, reproductions do exist, shattering the myth that only rare medals are copied. Common medals were even reproduced as far back as the late seventeenth century, as it was observed that 'common medals can be faked as well as rare ones' (Jobert 1697:197). A retailer of replicas based in the U.K. offered reproduction Russian Front medals for £10.95 which were 'slightly tarnished, and the medals have a two-tone effect with a chemically blackened centre' (NMRRF). Again, adding patina makes the replica a fake rather than a reproduction. It is curious as to why replicas of the Russian Front medal would need to be manufactured, as the medal was not worn in combat, hence military re-enactors would have no need for one.

Countries (and other polities) that assisted Nazi Germany at certain points included Bulgaria, Estonia, Finland, Hungary, Latvia, Lithuania, Romania, Slovakia and Ukraine. In July 1942, Hitler instituted a medal to recognise the service of these 'Eastern Troops' (*Osttruppen*) (Doehle 1943:87). The medal was entitled the Bravery and Service Distinction for the Members of the Eastern Peoples (*Die Tapferkeits- und Verdienstauszeichnung für Angehörige der Ostvölker*) (Figure 6.11). The first-class version of the badge could be accompanied by 'money or other assets.'[10] It was not typical for relatively low-ranking medals to be formally associated with additional prizes such as cash or incentives, and it is likely that the latter would have been alcohol,

Figure 6.11 Eastern Peoples' award 1942 (Bronze without swords).

Source: Author's collection. Photograph taken by Grant Hughes, 2020.

cigarettes or foodstuffs. Alcohol has been said to be the 'easiest way to make heroes' (Fritz 1997:112), but it also dulled the senses of those who committed war crimes (Browning 1992, 2001). The inclusion of extra incentives suggests that non-German soldiers may have been less motivated by Nazi medals, although fringe benefits were sometimes given to German soldiers who were awarded decorations too.

In contrast to the majority of medals intended for German soldiers, the medal did not depict a swastika, in keeping with distorted notions of its so-called Aryan origin.[11] Moreover, the swastika's absence may have kept up the pretence that the Eastern soldiers were fighting for liberation from the Soviet Union rather than facilitating their respective countries' enslavement under Nazism. This was certainly the case for Finland, whose air force had actually incorporated the swastika before the Luftwaffe did. From the perspective of an American-based trader, the lack of the 'phallic' swastika on the Eastern Peoples' decoration makes it less desirable (Shea 2015, pers. comm.). For Hamburg-based trader Helmut Weitze, there was more to the Eastern Peoples' medal despite its lack of a swastika, as 'When you know the history, Hitler in the beginning did not allow them to wear a swastika, it took a while to find out that these were very good brave soldiers' (Weitze 2018, pers. comm.). The absence of a swastika on the medal did not make it any less ideological.

On the collectors' market, the price of the Eastern Peoples' decoration failed to increase in line with inflation, representing the poorest performance (see Appendix A). By no means was it the cheapest medal, attributable to its relative scarcity. The Eastern Peoples' decoration has also been reproduced, demonstrating that medals without swastikas are not exempt from being copied, although it is unclear why this dress decoration would need to be replicated. Perhaps the copies enable collectors who are not seeking the aura to obtain one at a cheaper price and profits made by those producing and selling them.

Himmler's Bandit badge

In June 1943, Erich von dem Bach-Zelewski became Himmler's chief of anti-bandit formations, with the war against so-called bandits being a disguise for the murder of Jews (Shepherd 2016:366). Dem Bach-Zelewski was a recipient of the 'anti-Partisan badge' (*Bandenkampfabzeichen*) (literally the gang fighting badge), a decoration instituted by Hitler on 30 January, 1944, upon the eleventh anniversary of his chancellorship (Doehle 1945:132). The name of the badge invoked the image of marauding gangs, with German soldiers acquiring their 'blueprints from antiquity' (Blood 2006:XI).[12] The iconography of the badge may have been influenced by the Greek legend of the Lernaean Hydra (Figure 6.12), and the manner in which Heracles and his nephew Iolaus killed the multi-headed snake (Feka 2014) was brutally put into action in 1941 when Germans and their Eastern European allies set Russian villages on fire and herded Jewish women and children into swamps (Breitman 1991).

When the Wehrmacht retreated from Russia in 1943, 'scorched earth contributed to a further radicalizing process, resulting in growing indiscipline, brutalization, and a sharp increase in violence and the will to destruction' (Fritz 2011:373–374).

Figure 6.12 Replica anti-Partisan badge 1944.

Source: Author's collection. Photograph taken by Grant Hughes, 2020.

The hydra was also indicative of the expansive and multi-faceted nature of the SS (Allen 1996:531). In addition to the Waffen-SS, members of the Luftwaffe were also entitled to the anti-Partisan badge (Doehle 1945:133), debunking the prevailing myth that the Luftwaffe was purely the domain of apolitical air aces. Indeed, members of a Luftwaffe security battalion in a Polish forest committed acts of 'widespread murder of Jews, partisans, and other civilians' (Blood 2010:247).

Collectors

Reference books aimed at collectors have glossed over the brutal nature of anti-partisan activities, i.e., the anti-Partisan badge is mentioned only briefly as awarded to those 'combatting partisans behind German lines' (Littlejohn and Dodkins 1968:156). Despite the nature of the badge, it was permitted to be worn in a de-Nazified form according to a regulation introduced in West Germany in 1957 (BMJG), thus contributing to its rehabilitation. Medals that were deemed to be representative of Nazi ideology, for example the Mother's Cross, were not permitted even in a so-called de-Nazified form (i.e., without the swastika). A veteran who had once killed partisans could therefore wear the anti-Partisan badge, albeit without the swastika and skull, but a mother whose children were still alive could not celebrate them through wearing a modified version of the Mother's Cross. On a practical level, the manufacture of badges in a de-Nazified form meant that veterans could wear representations of the decorations they had earned without needing to erase the swastika from their original badges (if they had managed to keep them). Indeed, collections of decorations sometimes come onto the collectors' market that include a soldier's original medals from the Second World War as well as their de-Nazified counterparts. These collections are a material representation that the soldier was proud of their military achievements despite serving in an army responsible for multiple war crimes (which they no doubt downplayed).

It was the companies which made Nazi badges during the Second World War such as Steinhauer und Lück that manufactured the so-called de-Nazified decorations. This pushes the concept of the aura to its extremes, i.e., would an anti-Partisan badge or Iron Cross made in 1957 using the same machines and labour as in 1944 have inherent aura (quality or emanation of an object) or a perceptive one (awe and reverence)? To complicate matters further, what if leftover materials from the Second World War were used to make 1957-style badges? The last scenario enables a stronger argument to be made that these badges possess inherent aura, as their raw materials were sourced during the Third Reich. Nevertheless, the social and military environments in 1957 were entirely different to those of 1944. Consequently, the 1957 versions of the anti-Partisan badge or Iron Cross do not have the same psychic energy as those worn during the Third Reich, thus their inherent aura is diminished. Nevertheless, it is veterans who are the link in the chain. It is likely, however, that many 1957-style badges directly entered the collectors' market rather than being purchased by soldiers entitled to them (especially in later years). Having said this, 1957-style decorations, even if made by Steinhauer in the 1980s, still have a reverent quality due to their association with one of the most prolific badge-making firms of the Third Reich.

On the collectors' market, the Nazi-era anti-Partisan badge was the third most expensive, although its percentage increase was only in seventh position (see Appendix A). Rather than collectors being discouraged by the dubious ethics of the badge, these results suggest there is an interaction between the price of the badge and concerns in relation to fakes. The dark aesthetics of the badge made a strong and lasting impression on collectors and traders, as it was the only one that Carlisle-based trader Malcolm Bowers mentioned when recalling a visit to Bill Tobin's London-based militaria shop in 1971 (Bowers 2017, pers. comm.). Tobin's premises made even more of a lasting impression, as it was a steel-doored cellar in a dilapidated block of houses next to Tobin's home (Ibid.).

Also noteworthy is the price increase of the anti-Partisan badge over the last 40 years. In 1971, Tobin valued the medal at GBP 50 (Ibid.), and in January 2020, a similar badge was advertised for GBP 1,995 (RegJ 2020). A Portsmouth-based trader, Nick Hall, offered valuable insights into the post-war social life of these medals, describing how collectors acquired Nazi memorabilia from the 1950s, when Bill Tobin had a 'stall on the Portobello Road, and the Black Shirts used to meet there, and apparently he used to supply them' (Hall 2017, pers. comm.). If Hall's recollections are accurate, he shines a rare light onto the underbelly of the emerging Nazi memorabilia scene. Indeed, Tobin was unlikely to have refused to sell Nazi artefacts to Nazi sympathisers. Collectors and traders during this era were aware of the hobby's more sinister side, although some traders adopted distancing strategies (see Chapter 7).

Tobin appeared in the film *It Happened Here* (Brownlow and Mollo 1964), which contains unfiltered antisemitic propaganda, as well as fascist characters promoting eugenics. A recent article on the British Film Institute's website addressed the controversial nature of the 1964 movie, not least the inclusion of real ex-fascists in its cast (Ford 2018). Mollo also authored a book on uniforms and insignia worn by concentration camp guards (Mollo 1971), but reading the publication, one gets the impression that the most serious misdemeanour that Dachau camp guards committed was not following SS clothing regulations.

Conclusion

It took 11 years from when Defence Minister Werner von Blomberg ordered in 1934 that the eagle and swastika was to be worn on the army uniform until officers were able to finally 'tear off this damned swastika thing' after Nazi Germany was defeated.[13] Millions of uniforms and badges were produced during this time, some of which were made by forced labourers. As the war dragged on, more medals were needed to motivate soldiers to keep fighting until the impossible final victory, assisted by children knocking out tanks with crude handheld grenade launchers. Germany barely had any iron left for weapons, although the Iron Cross was still awarded. The more it was appropriated by liberating Allied soldiers, the more it descended into a collectible object. Over time, these souvenirs or trophies became alienated from their wartime past the more they circulated on the collectors' market. Profit and the fear of fakes currently preoccupy collectors more than the social lives medals had during the Second World War. Wartime decorations have become entangled in issues of forgery that were insignificant when they were actually worn. Little will be learned about the Second World War through badges unless collectors re-direct their focus. This chapter has shown ways in which the imbalance can be addressed.

Notes

1 RGB (September 1939:1575–1576, part I).
2 Oregon (n.d.:Year 1941).
3 Extract from Nürnberg trials: MR. JUSTICE JACKSON: And at that time Göring had you – we will have no misunderstanding about this – Göring made you what you call a full Aryan; was that it? MILCH: I do not think he made me one; I was one. MR. JUSTICE JACKSON: Well, he had it established, let us say? MILCH: He had helped me in clearing up this question, which was not clear (AV3). It should also be acknowledged that Judaism is matrilineal i.e., one must either be born of a Jewish mother or convert to Judaism (Cohen 1987; Freistadt and Wedell 1995).
4 It was Artur Axmann, who took over from Baldur von Schirach as Hitler Youth leader in 1940, who physically presented the Hitler Youth boys with the Iron Crosses in March 1945.

5 Göring 'boasted that if British bombs ever fell on Berlin his name would be Hermann Meyer' (Caldwell 1947:77). Consequently, after Berlin was bombed, Berliners called air raid sirens 'Meyer's trumpets.'

6 Bill Cotton was subsequently awarded the Military Cross by General Bernard 'Monty' Montgomery for his 'gallantry during the Battle of Villers-Bocage' (NAM MC). The battle in this small French town was where the German Panzer ace Michael Witmann destroyed numerous British tanks. Cotton's regimental museum is unaware of what happened to Cotton's German Iron Cross (Taylor 2019, pers. comm.).

7 From 1 March, 1941, the newly established 'Association of German Order Makers' (*Leistungsgemeinschaft der Deutschen Ordenshersteller*) (LDO) stipulated that medals intended for sale in medal and order shops had to be stamped with their assigned LDO code (UM März 1941:48).

8 For references consulted on the sinking of the SS *City of Benares* see AV4; Clemenson 2018; Kershaw 2015; UBN n.d.

9 The law dated 3 May, 1942, was entitled Protection of the Combat Badges of the Armed Forces (*Verordnung über den Schutz der Waffenabzeichen der Wehrmacht*) (RGB Mai 1942).

10 Original German text detailing fringe benefits associated with the Eastern Peoples' badge: *Mit der Beleihung von der 1. Klasse können Zuwendungen in Geld oder sonstigem Besitz verbunden werden* (Doehle 1943:85).

11 In the 1870s, Heinrich Schliemann found swastikas on fragments of pottery during his excavation of what he believed to be ancient Troy, a discovery that was twisted by some as proof that the symbol was of so-called Aryan origin (Boissoneault 2017; Boxer 2000; Thomas 1880; Wilkes 2020). Also see Chapter 2 for the swastika's appropriation in 1920 by the Nazi party.

12 In his introductory chapter, Blood (2006) suggests that Himmler and the Waffen-SS took cues from Hannibal's guerrilla fighting tactics against the Roman Empire and committed acts of barbarity hardly witnessed since the Thirty Years' War between 1618 and 1648. The violence and destruction on the Eastern Front during the Second World War resembled apocalyptic scenes in the Biblical Book of Revelation. For a general reference on *Hannibal* see Hoyos (2008); for the Thirty Years' War see Wilson (2009).

13 Wheeler-Bennett (1953:312); Neitzel (2007:248).

7 Nazi objects as texts and trade

Collectors, rather than academic historians, have been primarily responsible for writing books about Nazi medals. The target readership of these publications was (and still is) other collectors. Indeed, it has been said that a fundamental part of collecting is 'accumulating a library of books to enable the collector to identify objects and illuminate their histories' (Rubel and Rosman 2001:318). The books discussed here could generally be classified as self-published, hence their contents were not subjected to academic peer review. Despite their numerous shortcomings, the books have had a profound impact on the Nazi memorabilia hobby and are cultural artefacts in their own right.

Collectors' literature as artefacts

> Before 1967, there were no definitive texts describing Third Reich militaria as a collectible. Some booklets existed which superficially described awards, uniforms and side-arms, but did not give the collector much useful information to help navigate the increasingly precarious collecting waters.
>
> (BP n.d.; Adams-Graf 2020b)

Evidence of fakes circulating in the 1960s was put forward in a book entitled *Fakes and Frauds of the Third Reich* (Mollendorf 1968), which had the effect of making some collectors even more anxious as it revealed that few items were exempt from replication (PW 1970:7). It has been said that the 'souvenir lends authenticity to the past, and the past lends authenticity to the collection' (Stewart 1984, 1993:151). Consequently, if erroneous Third Reich medals were inadvertently mistaken for originals, they may have led to collectors gaining incorrect information in respect to the materials Nazi badges were made from or the companies that manufactured them. Nevertheless, there may be little difference in the iconography of a copy compared to an original, hence historical truth is not necessarily compromised. Kennick (1985:11) contemplated whether there is 'no aesthetic difference between an original painting and an exact copy of it.' Furthermore, it is the 'passing off' which is fraudulent, not the works themselves' (Hillman-Chartrand 1990:86).

DOI: 10.4324/9781003000617-7

As fakes improved in quality, authors of collectors' books presented badges in even more detail. The physicality of artefacts specifically photographed for collectors' books therefore displaced the social lives the badges had during the Third Reich. Nazi badges were essentially re-framed as items in collections. A casualty of this metamorphosis was that much of the meaning of the badges was lost.

A fundamental weakness of collectors' publications, especially the first generation, is that they lacked citations to period sources and were too reliant on other collectors for information. These exchange networks created cultural capital, and it is likely that some collectors and traders exploited their expertise for profit, although this is not peculiar to Nazi memorabilia. In relation to the market in primitive art, it has been observed that objects 'gain pedigree, the collectors prestige, the historians jobs, and the dealers money. Collectors, experts, and dealers coexist and mutually support one another. They cannot be separated' (MacClancy 1988:163). Likewise, mutual coexistence facilitates the market in Nazi memorabilia, although the competitive nature of collecting means that community relations are more fragile than one might think. Collectors and traders have exploited the asymmetrical level of knowledge that exists in the collecting community regarding nominal authenticity. Consequently, despite the numerous books that have been written for collectors, they have not been able to dispel their anxieties, and some even contain inaccurate information.

It has been claimed that books aimed at collectors 'deal specifically with the material culture of military history – in simpler terms, books about the stuff!' (Adams-Graf 2015). Unfortunately, the ways in which authors of collectors' books have engaged with stuff is rather limited. Although collectors create themselves through the medium of stuff (Miller (2010:99), the majority of collectors' books separate collectors from the objects they collect. This is all the more surprising if we acknowledge that 'our possessions are a major contributor to and reflection of our identities' (Belk 1988:139). Furthermore, people 'buy things not only for what they can do, but also for what they mean' (Levy 1959:118). Although objects 'serve as personal storehouses of meaning' (Wallendorf and Arnould 1988:532), collectors have not generally revealed what Nazi badges mean to them, nor have the original recipients. The lack of reflexivity is not necessarily because collectors of Nazi memorabilia seek to distance themselves from these morally controversial artefacts, but it also applies to books devoted to other collectibles. Perhaps the collecting impulse did not need to be communicated, or maybe collectors found it difficult to pinpoint why they yearned to own Nazi memorabilia.

Serious leisure 'participants are often unable to explain their activities in rational language acceptable to non-participants' (Olmsted 1988:278). A trader briefly acknowledged that viewing war films in the late 1960s and being given badges by a relative who had served in Germany contributed to his interest in imperial German and Third Reich decorations (Ailsby 1987). The majority of collectors' books fail to contain even such limited information. Belk et al. (1991:181) described the difficulty they had in steering collectors away from focusing on the objects that they collected towards the 'process and meaning of collecting as a consumption activity.' Most collectors of Nazi memorabilia have been so preoccupied with collecting that they have not stopped to assess their motivations or realise they are taking part in a practice that has wider societal relevance (Isyanova 2009).

Another weakness of collectors' books is that their authors do not critically engage with the agency of Nazi badges and medals. Namely, although badges are inanimate objects, they can produce effects that were not predicted. Collectors inordinately focus on the physical characteristics of Nazi symbols rather than what they meant to the notorious individuals who wore them or those negatively impacted by them. Through the detachment of artefacts from their politics, facilitated by diverting focus onto their physical characteristics, the intention, function and agency of the symbols was, and still is, neglected. Namely, the decorations are grossly fetishised. Furthermore, collectors tend to underplay the capacity of Nazi symbols to wreak havoc within present-day democratic societies (see Chapter 8).

A characteristic of collectors' books is that the Holocaust and other Nazi atrocities are sorely neglected. Consequently, the artefacts are distanced from the nature of the regime that produced them. The key point here is that medals should not be alienated from their historical context, and authors of collectors' books need to situate the objects accordingly. By avoiding the Holocaust, some collectors may feel less guilty for desiring Nazi medals, while others may be willing to live with the troublesome ethics of these artefacts, and some may even desire these items because of their associations.

Historian Charles Sydnor criticised a series of books published in the 1960s and 1970s on Waffen-SS uniforms and insignia endorsed by former Waffen-SS officer Otto Skorzeny.[1] Sydnor claimed the books lean heavily on apologist literature, especially as the foreword to the first volume was written by Skorzeny himself, and are targeted toward the large community of Second World War 'hobbyists and souvenir collectors more susceptible to the romanticized mythology of the Waffen-SS' (Sydnor 1973:341, footnote 7). The book that Sydnor criticised was *Uniforms, Organization, and History of the Waffen-SS* (Taylor and Bender 1969), his criticism being that the authors did not discuss Skorzeny's crimes or those committed by other members of the Waffen-SS, instead stating that 'much hate propaganda has been written about the SS, but only recently has a distinction been drawn between its political and military branches.'[2] This was controversial at the time and looks still more extraordinary now that complicity in Nazi war crimes and the Holocaust has been established not only for the SS in its entirety, but also for the army, navy and Luftwaffe. Furthermore, Taylor and Bender failed to mention Skorzeny's 1947 trial or his controversial acquittal (Weingartner 1991). In the book's foreword, Skorzeny claimed that the book represented 'true history' (Taylor and Bender 1969:7), but what sort of history was it if the crimes committed by members of the Waffen-SS were not addressed?

A characteristic of many of the first tranche of collectors' publications is that they were written by Allied veterans of the Second World War, for example, Littlejohn and Dodkins (1968). American and British veterans being primarily responsible for the first generation of books aimed at collectors of Nazi badges was a symbolic mark of victory. Despite their military service, a drawback of Littlejohn and Dodkins's book was the absence of any serious historical context, merely beginning with the 'Third Reich came into being on the 30th January 1933, with Hitler's accession to power, and ended with the defeat of Germany in May 1945.' After this glaringly superficial historical context, the authors launched into their topic – the 'number of new decorations, medals and badges of honour created during those twelve years may well appear prodigious, but it must be borne in mind that in the matter of national honours, the Nazis were obliged to start virtually from scratch' (Littlejohn and Dodkins 1968:11). They failed to note that some medals and badges were made and awarded during the Weimar era, overlooked the continuity of the companies that made them, and did not consider whether the awards may have been associated with the Holocaust or crimes committed by the Wehrmacht. This was not uncharacteristic, as it has been observed that:

> The new mood of openness toward the past legitimatized interest in the careers of former Nazis, Fascists, and collaborators; sympathy, even admiration, appeared in some quarters for those who had cast their lot with the extreme Right. The public appetite for World War II memorabilia spurred a brisk trade in Nazi insignia and full-color picture books narrating Rommel's desert war in North Africa or tank battles on the Russian steppes.
>
> (Wilkinson 1985:339)

When Littlejohn and Dodkins were writing their book in the 1960s, plenty of German ex-soldiers were alive to defend the myth of the Clean Wehrmacht. The central premise of this myth is that it was only SS and police killing squads who committed atrocities, not the army or the Waffen-SS, the latter organisation falsely being said to have only consisted of 'brave fighters' (Smelser 2008:250). The success of this myth has cynically been described as the 'Wehrmacht's greatest victory' (Wette 2006:195). It was not until the *Crimes of the Wehrmacht* exhibition in Germany in the 1990s that it was fully debunked (Eley 2000; Heer and Caplan 1998; Loneragan 2016). Despite this vast body of evidence, it is still propagated in books aimed at Nazi memorabilia collectors.

A reason for the first generation of books being accommodating to former members of Hitler's armed forces is that their contents were dependent on the input from these compromised individuals. The late Dr. Klietmann of Berlin, author of a 1944 article on army and Waffen-SS badges and insignia (DUZ April 1944), supplied most of the information contained in the book written by Littlejohn and Dodkins (1968). As their publication was in English, Klietmann's material, which had previously been in German, advanced the international market in Nazi memorabilia. Klietmann therefore represented a degree of continuity in relation to NS insignia during and after the war, albeit playing down the Nazi propaganda. It would, of course, have been illegal for Klietmann, who was a West German citizen, to have glorified the Nazi regime. Klietmann traded in Nazi medals, hence financial motives cannot be removed. He was also acknowledged by John Angolia, whose books have been highly influential on the Nazi memorabilia collecting circuit.

American-based Angolia (born 1936) started to collect Nazi memorabilia in the 1940s, but it was not until he visited West Germany in the 1970s, after serving with the American military in Vietnam, that he built relationships with former members of Hitler's armed forces. He was so successful that recipients of the Knight's Cross referred to him as 'our Major' (Adams-Graf 2019). Angolia partially relied on German veterans to supply him with medals, so perhaps it is not surprising that he did not criticise them. A few artefacts were attributed to Karl Wolff, personal liaison officer between Himmler and Hitler, although his convictions for actively facilitating the Holocaust were not mentioned.[3] Angolia essentially made collecting Nazi badges more palatable by not associating their recipients with crimes against humanity. Furthermore, Himmler was portrayed in a highly sanitised manner in Angolia's 1978 *For Führer and Fatherland.* The jovial scene catered to collectors wishing to see medals presented. The portrayal of Nazi medals, both during their initial time of use and in our current age, presents many challenges.

Angolia's book hinted at the social world of collectors in the 1970s, although he did not discuss collecting culture in any great detail. He acknowledged the assistance of about 50 collectors (only one of whom was female) (Angolia 1978:Acknowledgements). The collectors who owned the rarer badges (all of whom were men) were credited as possessing these supposedly sought-after artefacts. The original recipients of many of the badges were not named, although Angolia and the collectors probably did not know who earned them. The decorations were alienated from their original owners and were given a new home within the collecting community. As German decorations were not named on the reverse, this was almost inevitable, especially if they had become separated from their award certificates. The random manner in which medals came onto the collectors' market was therefore not conducive to historical knowledge. Some collectors may even have jettisoned the genealogies of medals as a way of claiming them. Divestment 'allows the new owner to avoid contact with the meaningful properties of the previous owner and to free up the meaning properties of the possession, claiming them for him/herself' (McCracken 1986:80). It has also been said that some 'people act to appropriate the commodity, to stamp it with their identity, and so convert it into a possession' (Carrier 1990:25). Collectors may do this because they have no confidence that an object's biography, if provided, is accurate (especially if only communicated verbally, i.e., a tall tale). Indeed, a 'good Collector casts a jaded eye upon those dealers who insist that their reputation take the place of details of provenance' (McIntosh et al. 1995:60).

Angolia sold his collection of Third Reich medals in 1974, as he claimed:

He did not care for the growing lack of ethics among the collecting community, the growth of the instant experts, the pursuit of the dollar (when a collector would ask me how much is this worth? I knew he wasn't a serious collector), the impact of reproductions, the rapid escalation of prices where the dollar meant more than the history of the item.

(Adams-Graf 2019)

Even though Angolia sold his badges, he continues to have a lasting association with them through his books. Angolia did not include prices in his publications, but collectors' preoccupation with financial value led to a price guide on Third Reich medals being published in the late 1980s (Forman 1988), contributing to the further commodification of Nazi medals. One of Forman's intentions was to make Third Reich medal collecting more respectable and to distance Nazi symbols from being seen as the domain of bikers and neo-Nazis (Forman 2018, pers. comm.). Indeed, Forman sought to present the Nazi memorabilia hobby in a professional light, including wearing a tie at his indoor stall at London's Portobello market as early as 1969 (Figure 7.1). In 1978, he left the hustle and bustle of Portobello

Figure 7.1 Adrian Forman at his weekend militaria stand at Portobello market, London, 1969. A Nazi naval flag once flown on ships whilst Grand Admiral Dönitz was on board is displayed in the background. Permission granted by Adrian Forman.

Photographer: Susan Forman.

market (and fascists? see Chapter 6) and opened a shop at the more prestigious address of 92 Piccadilly, Mayfair (Forman 2021a; Forman 2021b, pers. comm.).

When Forman started trading assorted militaria and Nazi memorabilia in the 1960s, the book by Littlejohn and Dodkins (1968) had not yet been released, but a collector starting out today could fill many shelves. Whilst some may regard the professionalisation of the Nazi memorabilia hobby as a positive development, books and price guides have knocked much of the naivety and personal discovery out of it. Moreover, authors of 'price guides may, in fact, develop considerable economic power and the ability to manipulate collectible goods markets in ways that would be difficult to detect' (Stoller 1984:93). Likewise, the 'largest single force in manipulation of collectible firearms markets, as a whole, has been the presence of price guides produced with the intent of bringing order to the marketplace and attracting new investors into the marketplace' (Avery and Colonna 1987:59).

Collecting and the market

Collecting 'seems to reside only in the pores of consumer behaviour, beyond the rational and the useful, and so often prone to the passion of unrestraint and excess' (Bianchi 1997:275). Indeed, the market in Nazi memorabilia is a cogent example of this. The majority of interviewed collectors and traders are baby boomers, born between 1945 and 1965. It has been claimed that the 'baby boomers seem to have had all the luck' (Willett 2010:83). It does appear that baby boomers, or even members of Generation X (born between 1965 and 1979) who started to collect from their teens or twenties, were able to purchase Nazi memorabilia at relatively lower prices than collectors who started later. Nevertheless, life was not all plain sailing for baby boomers, as some English traders recall rationing still being in force in the early 1950s (Bowers 2017, pers. comm.; Fisher 2017, pers. comm.). Although the aforementioned traders did not live during the Second World War, they experienced it through illustrated magazines, films and toys. Some were even given German medals and badges by family members who had served in the war. A retired trader born in 1941 recalled that when he was a child in Portsmouth (a city bombed by the Luftwaffe) he played at soldiers after the war with an authentic swastika flag (Hall 2017, pers. comm.). The key thing here is that these items did not have the financial value they have today, although they are still vulnerable to being destroyed (see Chapter 8).

The general political and socioeconomic landscape has undergone significant changes since Nazi medals became an increasingly specialist collecting genre in the late 1960s. It has been contended that:

> Globalization, the accumulation of large wealth in small elites, the rise of large emerging economies such as China, India, Russia, Brazil and others, the growing use of the internet for trading, the increased orientation of artwork as an investment-class asset, are all trends that are reshaping the art market.
>
> (Solimano 2019:1)

The internet has given collectors access to a wider number of traders on an international basis. Before the internet, collectors had to subscribe to expensive printed catalogues, but they can now view offerings online without charge, widening their choice. Auctions that sold Nazi memorabilia before the internet did have a global customer base, but with fast broadband, collectors can now watch auction sales and bid in real time. Auctions are more transparent, thereby losing much of their mystique. By 'incorporating the social agency of both objects and persons into the construction of price we may view the auction as a performative tournament, with a catalogue-script, a stage, an audience, and so on' (Geismar 2001:27–28). Auctions have been referred to as a judgement device (Kharchenkova and Velthuis 2018). If particular pieces of Nazi memorabilia fail to sell, it gives a signal that collectors and traders have concerns about authenticity or that they were too expensive. If a trader did purchase an item deemed sold as seen (a hallmark of auctions), the trader presumably had confidence in its authenticity. Consequently, a collector may be willing to purchase the said item at a higher price from a retailer offering a lifetime guarantee of authenticity. Alternatively, some collectors are 'disinclined to buy pieces from dealers previously illustrated in an auction catalogue: thanks to the illustration a collector can identify the object a dealer is offering him and so assess his profit margin' (MacClancy 1988:167). A useful insight is that a 'middleman has no more bargaining power than a buyer. Thus, his only advantage over buyers is his ability to identify quality after making a large investment that a buyer would not want to incur' (Biglaiser 1993:216). Many collectors lack the knowledge that professional traders have and may lack the interest or time to acquire it.

Auctions are characterised by low starting prices, which can conversely lead to 'higher final prices: Low starting prices lower barriers to entry and increase the number of bidders' (Galinsky et al. 2009:357). Informed traders would be less likely to fall victim to a phenomenon known as the winner's curse, i.e., paying too much as a result of being the last remaining bidder (Hendricks et al. 2008). An auction sale is only one part in the consecration or destruction of an object's market value, and there are many other forms of exchange, for example, collector to collector. A collector stated that he does not purchase Third Reich badges from auctions and prefers to deal with traders that he has built close relationships with (Czunys 2018, pers. comm.). Such relationships may result in regular collectors being offered rare objects in the first instance, which is not generally the way auction houses operate.

A regular collector may also be able to negotiate better discounts with traders and obtain authentication services not generally available to others (Godfrey-Wood and Mamani-Vargas 2016). Many traders are reluctant to make negative comments about artefacts as it can damage their relationship with the trader who sold the collector the questionable object (Fisher 2017, pers. comm.). Some collectors may have more confidence in the authenticity of items offered by traders than auctions, although those with more knowledge are more comfortable purchasing from a wider range of sources. Collectors should also bear in mind that in 'cases of high-quality and credible forgeries, a dealer is likely able to convincingly assert that he, too, was deceived' (Amineddoleh 2015:428).

It was claimed in the late 1980s that America was the largest Nazi memorabilia market, followed by Germany, then Britain (Forman 1988:4). It is likely that Germany has since overtaken America, as in September 2019, uniforms and medals reputedly once worn by Hitler were auctioned for well over EUR 1 million (Crossland 2019). It is still the case that auctions held in Germany (ATAA) eclipse those held in Britain. Two representative sales held in England only totalled 156 lots hammering for GBP 65,325 (BAA 2019; CTA 2020a). In contrast to the relatively small British market in Nazi memorabilia, the British government's House of Commons Culture, Media and Sport Committee, Market for Art reported in 2005 that 'with a global share of 26%, the UK has by far the largest art and antiques market in Europe and is second only to the USA in the world' (HCC-MSC 2005). It was claimed in the 1980s that the trade in Nazi memorabilia had an annual turnover of USD 50 million (Harris 1986:183). I would suggest that it is currently between USD 30 million and USD 100 million in terms of annual sales. My lower estimate means that the annual volume has reduced by 40 percent since the 1980s, and even the higher figure of USD 100 million would not have exceeded it in real terms. It is possible that there are fewer collectors and fewer artefacts than before, thereby levelling out annual sales, the former of which could be a result of demographics.

There are likely between 10,000 and 30,000 collectors currently active internationally; and with global sales of some USD 30 million, this would mean that 30,000 collectors spent on average USD 1,000 per year, whereas, if the sales totalled USD 100 million, then each collector would be spending USD 3,300, a figure which may be too high. There are at least 20 professional militaria traders catering to these collectors in the U.K. alone, the majority of whom have been in business since the 1970s (OT 2020). The general trend has been for these dealers to start off at market stalls, attend militaria fairs, open shops, then mainly trade online. Each of these spheres of exchange has influenced the degree to which Nazi badges have become alienated from their original recipients (for this mode of thought see Carrier 1994). The impersonal nature of auctions, especially those conducted online, whereby collectors compete for anonymous artefacts, further contributes to this estrangement.

Before the internet, particularly between the 1960s and the early 1980s, there was more of an experiential element in the construction of prices, in accordance with the statement that pricing, 'like most business decisions, is an art' (Nagle 1984:3). Indeed, London-based militaria trader Malcolm Fisher recalled going down to 'Portobello Road, buying stuff there, seeing what other people were asking for stuff, you know, looking on other people's early catalogues, and you just form an opinion from that casual research' (Fisher 2017, pers. comm.). Fisher would have been aware of fellow London-based dealer Adrian Forman, who offered a flag featuring the monogram of Grand Admiral Dönitz for around GBP 500 at Portobello market in 1969 (about GBP 7,100 of spending power in 2021) (Figure 7.1).[4] Hamburg-based militaria trader Helmut Weitze formulates his prices not on the cost of running his shop, but as a result of the knowledge obtained through '30 years in the business, on the one side I started with catalogues, there are price guides existing for the German medals and orders but you also watch the auction results, and in several cases you have the customers tell you what they are willing to invest' (Weitze 2018, pers. comm.). These traders are essentially seeking opportunities for arbitrage, which can be gained through purchasing Nazi memorabilia at an auction or from collectors who wish to part with some of their items. A characteristic of collections is that they do not stay static, a consequence of fashion (Simmel 1957), changing tastes (Park 2020), financial hardship or even collectors capitalising on medals that have increased in price.

It 'will come as no surprise that many of the popular press sources of pricing information on collectibles, including the burgeoning set of price guides, tend to display some optimism about the future course of prices' (Burton and Jacobsen 1999:196). Indeed, in relation to Nazi memorabilia, it has been claimed that 'prices are only going one way, and that's upwards' (GCGM 2018:Introduction). A reason for analysing prices was to subject such optimism to empirical rigour. In terms of the 12 badges I monitored, they increased in real terms by 5.6 percent every two years. This is not spectacular and is similar to Frey and Eichenberger's (1995) analysis of the art market. My calculations did not include auction fees, insurance premiums, risk factors or storage costs, all of which can be considerable (Renneboog and Houtte 2002:331). Most of the medals I monitored, discussed in previous chapters, range in price from a few dollars to a few hundred and more. Most of the medals discussed are within the grasp of collectors, hence represent their everyday experience of handling Nazi artefacts.

The prices of medals on the collectors' market do not bear any relation to the prices they were sold for in specialist shops during the Third Reich. Nevertheless, symbolic value also tended to be independent of production costs prior to Nazi Germany's defeat. In terms of collectibles, price 'determined by cost of production is wholly inapplicable' (Knight 1921:310). Indeed, although collectors are generally cognisant of the symbolic value that medals held during the Third Reich, they have reconfigured them.

Analysis shows that the prices of most Nazi decorations moved little from c. 1980 until the millennium, when they rose steeply, then dipped slightly from 2010, although never lower than in 2002. Demand for the Iron Cross was especially strong – the 1939 Knight's Cross, the 1939 Iron Cross second class, and also the latter's predecessor, the Iron Cross 1914 (which exhibited the highest increase in price). Although the 1914 Iron Cross second class was awarded over five million times, the iconic nature of the symbol contributed to its premium price. The Iron Cross could be regarded as what Chintagunta (2002) would consider a national brand. It would therefore take less effort for traders to persuade collectors to purchase the 'most famous gallantry award in the world' (Weitze 2018, pers. comm.).

The 'price of an asset is traditionally a function of supply and demand and since demand is dictated by value, we must ask who and what dictates value' (Gamson 2017:Part 1). Anthropologist Daniel Miller (1995:153) noted that 'prices show remarkably little relation to demand when studied in detail.' Furthermore, modern 'capitalists do not conduct their affairs according to the formulations of neoclassical dogma' (Godfrey-Wood and Mamani-Vargas 2016:139). Nevertheless, the laws of supply and demand should not be dismissed out of hand. General inelasticity 'implies that consumers alter their consumption very little while elasticity implies that consumers make a relatively major change in the amount consumed' (Leuthold and Nwagbo 1977:23). Schnitzel (1979) observed that commemorative postage stamps had an inelastic supply, and it is suggested here that Nazi memorabilia shares this quality. This is because no more authentic medals can be produced, and presumably the number of originals dwindles over time. If there is more demand for them, there would be an inadequate supply; hence in theory prices would increase. This being said, price is a poor measure of the symbolic and cultural value that collectors attribute to particular Nazi artefacts. Likewise, the 'economist's confident stance on the firm ground of scarcity is shaken once he realises that his feet are actually sinking into the shifting sands of cultural values' (Thompson 1979, 2017:216).

Issues relating to nominal authenticity partially explain why the prices of some decorations have remained static. Both the SS medal and the anti-Partisan badge appear in the graph of flat prices, reflecting collectors' concerns about the faking of SS artefacts (Appendix B, Figure B.1). Despite the opportunity for collectors to consult specialist books and internet forums, reproductions are still depressing the prices of originals. Asymmetrical knowledge means that 'uninformed buyers will be unwilling to pay an above-average price, forcing sellers of superior quality either to depreciate it, to withdraw from the market, or to accept a price that does not accurately reflect their products' value' (Nagle 1984:6). This is known as adverse selection. In relation to online auctions of collectible postage stamps, it was found that 'prices would be 10–15% higher in the absence of quality uncertainty' (Dewan and Hsu 2004:514). It is also likely that adverse selection is present within the Nazi memorabilia market, putting pressure on the prices of medals that collectors have less experience of.

In a strict economic sense, Nazi medals are luxury goods, hence the ability to purchase them is presumably dependent on real disposable income (credit aside) (Jones 1954). According to the 'theory of consumer choice, income and relative prices help to explain trends in consumption per head' (Espenshade 1978:150). The 2008 financial crisis could be partially responsible for prices of Nazi medals tailing off. It has been said that the 'art market is sensitive to macroeconomic cycles of expansion and contraction' (Solimano 2019:8). Alternatively, following the 2008 financial crisis, collectibles and fine art might have been regarded by some as so-called safe havens (Graham 2014), albeit even less regulated than financial investments. Another element to consider is that the 'art market exhibits few if any of the traditional indicators of speculation or other instabilities in pricing. Unlike real estate, most art is purchased with cash in hand. There are no sub-prime mortgages propping up the purchasing of art, no unstable supports to come crashing down in periods of price correction' (Diamond 2016:30). Similarly, Nazi medals are owned by individual collectors who have generally paid in cash (part exchange aside). On a cautionary note, bubbles are 'often believed to exist in goods with positive fundamental value, such as antiques, bottles of wine, paintings, flower bulbs, rare stamps, houses, land, and so on' (Wang and Wen 2012:186). Whilst experienced collectors would be less likely to get trapped in bubbles, they may be unable to suppress their enthusiasm.

Some collectors may regard rising prices as a sign that Nazi memorabilia could provide opportunities for financial investment. Even 'if most collectors scorn the word "investment" and few like to acknowledge that it is part of the game, all collectors seem to derive greater pleasure from the contemplation of items which they know to be worth more than they gave for them' (Rogan 1998:46). The 'unorganized art market is generally classed as an inefficient market in which investors have a reasonable chance of making above normal returns' (Coffman 1991:93). By an unorganised market, Coffman was envisioning collectors discovering under-priced antiques at flea-markets, then realising a profit by selling them through an international auction house. Although experienced collectors of Nazi memorabilia are in a better position to recognise the potential for profit making, some still refrain from purchasing items that do not fit into their collection. Hoarding 'items merely for their investment value is not collecting because it invokes a utilitarian reason for the accumulation' (Belk et al. 1988a:550). Namely, 'when profit is the sole purpose for acquisition and possession, the items acquired are likely to lack the sacredness and unity found in a true collection' (Belk et al. 1991:185).

A collector who solely buys items with a view of making a profit has to think about what other collectors would like rather than buying for their own pleasure. Collectors who slide into the position of being dealers often find that the pressure to make money means that they have 'less fun' than they did when they were collectors (Dannefer 1980:405). Indeed, 'scratch a dealer and you will find a collector' (Rubel and Rosman 2001:323). Belk et al. (1991:185) found that a 'collector who is also a dealer can remain a collector if the items in the collection and those that are merchandise are kept separate. We find that this is common and that such dealers generally have firm rules that objects cannot freely pass between the collection and the saleable stock of merchandise.' Objects that a dealer keeps in their personal collection are usually imbued with a higher sacred value than those offered for sale. Alienable 'wealth is that which is not so closely linked to an individual's corporate identity and, thus, can be more easily relinquished' (Lillios 1999:240). Nevertheless, the items that a trader sells subsequently acquire special meaning for the collector who purchases them. This may be the case if the objects evoke memories of when and where they were acquired (Benjamin 1931, 1968).

A collectible medal is a status good, which Miller (1975:141) defined as 'one whose utility derives at least partially from the amount the purchaser pays for it. In most cases this is because display of the good serves to demonstrate that the user can afford it.' In contrast to jewellery, collectors do not generally purchase Nazi medals to wear them, although they have opportunities to display their medals at militaria fairs, post pictures of them on specialist internet forums and also converse with other collectors. Belk (2013:536) observed that collectors 'delighted' in showing off their acquisitions to fellow collectors. Much in the same way that an expensive bottle of vintage wine is never opened, Nazi memorabilia is consumed symbolically through gazing, dreaming, talking, photographing and handling it rather than wearing it (Featherstone 1990). Its original function pales into insignificance compared to its exchange and prestige value on the collectors' market. Even at militaria fairs, where handling is usually encouraged, field marshals' batons are so expensive that they are protected behind glass, watched over by dedicated security guards and only permitted to be handled if a collector is serious about purchasing them.

By displaying their collections at a militaria fair, collectors are taking part in 'affiliation seeking' (Klein et al 1995:328). Eagerly sought-after items such as Nazi steel helmets are displayed to attract the attention and praise of esteemed specialists within this sub-genre of the Nazi collecting hobby. Conspicuous consumption is alive and well (Veblen 1899; Mandel 2009). Indeed, when 'people shop, they tend to buy lavishly' (Levy 1959:118). A display of Nazi memorabilia on a collector's stall is a marker of collecting prowess and financial resources. The items also advertise that the stallholder specialises in a particular area, for example, Nazi daggers, hence they may be more likely to be offered these items by soldiers' descendants. A vast display of homogenous German army daggers (especially to the untrained eye) helps to drive down prices of the German army daggers that the dealer manages to buy in, as it gives the impression that they are obtainable. This does not mean that these collectors or traders will offer items at fair prices. On the contrary, they seek to capitalise on their expertise. They are able to buy cheaply and sell dearly at fairs as they often do not mark the items they offer with a price tag.

A trader who displays 30 Iron Crosses as opposed to a trader who only has one is more likely to be sought by relative novice collectors prepared to pay a premium in the belief they are obtaining an authentic example. To a layperson, all Iron Crosses look the same, but to a connoisseur, even a small difference, especially in terms of the firm that originally made it, can be a matter of hundreds of dollars. A trader complained that collectors no longer simply desire any old Iron Cross, preferring one made by a manufacturer with a higher standing within the collecting community (Cross 2017, pers. comm.). Traders and authors of collectors' books have to take responsibility for advancing this trend. As prices of Nazi artefacts have generally increased, a collector who began to accumulate items in the 1970s is more likely to own rarer relics than a collector who started today. The objects displayed on stalls graphically represent this. Nevertheless, even the largest militaria traders operating today started from small beginnings.

As with every other kind of commercial activity, collecting Nazi memorabilia was affected by the Coronavirus pandemic. Specialist militaria auction houses were forced to introduce COVID-19-related restrictions: either postponing sales or conducting auctions under lockdown conditions. The restrictions meant that bidders could not physically attend auctions on sale days, although even before the pandemic, auctions had already offered remote live online bidding. Had the pandemic occurred before auctions had invested in and embraced this technology, their businesses would have been more vulnerable. The pandemic meant that auctioneers conducted auctions in empty rooms, albeit supported by physically distanced staff taking both online and telephone bids. Absent was the interaction between bidders in the room and the auctioneer, further contributing to the anonymity of exchange. Auctions have embraced this efficiency, meaning that Nazi artefacts are only a few clicks away.

Although one would have thought that the COVID-19 crisis would have negatively affected sales, the auctions generally achieved favourable results. Collectors were able to bid live at weekday auctions from the comfort of their own homes. On the downside, remote bidding meant that inexperienced collectors were unable to follow the actions of experienced collectors or traders on the auction floor. The format of the online auctions still enabled potential bidders who were less confident in their private valuations to take cues from other bids (Simonsohn and Ariely 2008:1624). Collective behaviour is a characteristic of many auction formats, and 'with more bidders, each worries more that if the price is fair, why hasn't someone else bought it?' (Bulow and Klemperer 2002:2). Signals are especially important in a market littered with fakes.

A specialist militaria auction in November 2020 had to be conducted online due to a second lockdown imposed in England (DNW 2020). The vast majority of the 850 lots comprised British medals, although there were five lots of Third Reich badges. Despite the restricted conditions under which the auction took place, not to mention the general anxiety concerning the COVID-19 pandemic, the lots fetched favourable prices. They hammered for GBP 1,385, which was about 20 percent above their lower estimates. A Third Reich civil service medal (*Treuedienst-Ehren-zeichen)* that had a lower estimate of GBP 60 hammered for GBP 110 (lot 814). Bizarrely, a similar medal could have been purchased from a German militaria trader for the equivalent of GBP 60 (Weitze 2020). The bidder therefore paid considerably more than the medal retailed for, hence the law of one price is not a strong feature of the international market in Nazi memorabilia. This also applies to the international art market (Liu 2015:22). Perhaps the bidder was not aware that they could have purchased this relatively common medal elsewhere, or they may even have succumbed to auction fever. It is notable that the lower reserve was more in line with the retail price of the medal, which suggests that the bidder exercised a degree of irrationality by paying too much. At the time, however, it is quite possible that the bidder believed they were behaving in a rational manner.

It is the competitive nature of the auction environment that encourages bidders to get carried away. Auction fever is a strange phenomenon; as illogical 'as it may seem, experience shows repeatedly that buyers will pay prices at auction that they will refuse to pay in cold blood, so to speak, from a dealer's stock' (Reese 2000:159). Furthermore, auction fever 'lasts only during the auction process, and at the end of the auction, the bidder's value of the object is the same as before the auction' (Dodonova and Khoroshilov 2012:88). This being said, the psychology of an auction is entirely different to a retail environment. The aim of an auctioneer is to achieve the highest price by encouraging a number of bidders, whereas a collector will try to drive down the price haggling one-on-one with a trader.

An auction of Nazi cloth insignia conducted under lockdown conditions in April 2020 is also insightful and warrants close examination (CTA 2020b). The collar patches, shoulder boards and armbands offered had been accumulated by

Brian Davis, author of *German Army Uniforms and Insignia 1933–1945* (Davis 1971) and *Badges and Insignia of the Third Reich 1933–1945* (Davis 1983), thereby giving collectors more confidence in the authenticity of the sale objects. Notably, Davis had purchased the insignia from the collectors' market in much the same manner as other collectors. It was his seal of approval that subsequently made them more desirable. Belk et al. (1988:550) acknowledged that 'an item can also gain sacred significance by having been a part of a famous collector's collection.' Indeed, the high auction estimates were set with collectors in mind rather than traders, as there were few opportunities for arbitrage, providing further evidence that financial motives are not the primary reason why collectors seek Nazi memorabilia.

As the sale progressed, the auctioneer reduced prices of lots by half if they did not attract an initial bid. This is not atypical – 'an artwork is placed in an auction only if the seller's reservation price is less than the auction estimated price' (Candela et al. 2012:292). Whilst all the lots sold, 32 percent went for below their lower estimates. An auction in which all the lots sell is known as a white glove sale.[5] This is especially remarkable due to the auction taking place under lockdown conditions, suggesting that although collectors did not have the opportunity to physically inspect the material, its association with the Brian Davis collection gave them confidence to bid, supporting my contention that collectors' books help to sell Nazi memorabilia.

Specialist militaria businesses responded differently to lockdown conditions, depending on whether they were auction houses or bricks-and-mortar retail outlets. Whilst shops were forced to close their doors, some continued to offer Nazi memorabilia online. Postal services permitting, militaria traders were able to post items collectors ordered either online or over the telephone. Collectors and traders were unable to pitch stands at militaria fairs, as the vast majority of these important events for buying and selling were cancelled internationally. Collectors and traders who had already established networks were therefore in a better position to service their customer base. The niche market in Nazi memorabilia was better able to cope with the existential COVID-19 crisis than businesses dealing with perishable items, such as the horticultural sector (HTA 2020). The durable nature of Nazi memorabilia means that it is not as fragile or dependent on seasonable demand. Unlike a vendor of fruit at a market stall who reduces prices at the end of the day to shift the stock (Gordon 2010), there is no need to do this in the case of metal badges. It is the robust physical nature of militaria that permits items to be offered over an extended period of time.

The pandemic enabled some collectors to devote more time to their hobby. The editor of *Military Trader* published an article entitled '5 Tips for Collecting During the Pandemic,' stating, 'we are still collectors and our passions are very much a part of what makes us who we are' (Adams-Graf 2020c). This is the essence of what differentiates collecting from financial investment or speculation. Rogan (1998:40) found that 'few if any possessions were the object of so much concern and care, money spending and time consumption as were collectibles.' A collection may even have provided security and order amidst the uncertainties of the pandemic (Wallendorf and Arnould 1988). By 'collecting, the collector brings order to a controllable portion of the world. Collected objects form a small world where the collector rules' (Belk 2013:540). At the time of writing (March 2021), the Nazi memorabilia hobby is fairly impervious to COVID-19.

A far more damaging and indeed intriguing consequence of COVID-19 in relation to collecting Nazi relics is that collectors may reflect on their attachment to non-essential goods and stop collecting. Indeed, it has been contended that a 'significant reorientation of consumer culture could curtail collecting' (Belk et al. 1991:Conclusion). Demographics are another consideration. Baby boomers are the ones who have been the most emotionally invested in Nazi relics, and as this generation gradually departs, younger generations may have a lesser desire to own items associated with the Second World War.

Conclusion

Ever since 1945 Nazi relics have been fighting several battles, of which one has been successful: the erasure of their historical meaning. The main actors of this affront to historical context are the very people who earned the medals during the Third Reich, especially veterans of the Waffen-SS. Collectors desired to own these medals so much that they were complicit in whitewashing the Nazi past so that they could obtain them. The attention of collectors was diverted by the increasing accuracy of fakes; hence the mission of collectors' publications was to arm collectors with sufficient knowledge to ferret them out. A weakness of some of these publications is that they presented a number of fake badges as real, further muddying the waters. As prices continue to spiral the fakes got better and better. For those who continued to collect, even more of their time was spent sorting out the good from the bad. Fakes come with the territory, and for some collectors, even contribute to the dynamism of the Nazi memorabilia hobby. Nevertheless, collectors did not set out with the intention of spending most of their time collecting Nazi memorabilia identifying fakes. Novices, unless they were lucky, got stung, subsequently bailing out or switching direction. For those who remained, not even the COVID-19 crisis could dampen their enthusiasm. Indeed, a major American-based trader claimed that 2020 was his best year for sales.[6]

The market in Nazi memorabilia is in danger of bursting like a balloon. It is certainly in need of some soul searching. Whether collectors and traders are willing to reassess their attachment to Nazi badges is another matter. Indeed, the collectors who were in a position to ask veterans questions were blinded by their medals rather than the agency of the decorations. The best that can be done is to unpick the past and to encourage collectors to ask new questions and challenge traders. A sea change is required.

Notes

1 Otto Skorzeny is best known for his daring glider rescue of Mussolini in 1943, consequently earning the Knight's Cross. He was highly active within neo-Nazi circles after 1945 until his death in 1975 and has been described as a 'Nazi thug' Campbell (2012:142).
2 Taylor and Bender (1969:Introduction, unpaginated section, fourth page).

3 Whilst in his capacity as liaison officer between Himmler and Hitler, Karl Wolff witnessed a massacre of Jews in Minsk in 1941 (in the presence of Himmler) and also facilitated the deportation of Jews to Treblinka death camp in 1942. From 1943 he was the highest police chief and SS leader in Northern Italy. He arranged the surrender of German forces in Northern Italy in 1945 with the help of Allen Dulles of the Office of Strategic Services under *Operation Sunrise* (Scott 1985; Sharma 1990). This benefited Wolff at the Nürnberg trials and subsequent de-Nazification proceedings. His wartime crimes caught up with him more substantially in the 1960s, when he was sentenced by a West German court to 15 years imprisonment, although he only spent a few years in jail. Despite his foggy memory in relation to his role in the Holocaust, he was more candid when speaking to *Stern* journalist Gerd Heidemann when they both visited South America to meet Klaus Barbie, the Butcher of Lyon, and Walter Rauff, the inventor of the infamous gas vans (Lingen 2020).

4 GBP 500 for the Dönitz flag in 1969 indicates that even in the late 1960s certain pieces of militaria were expensive. It would probably not fetch the equivalent of GBP 7,100 in 2021, thus it has depreciated in financial value in real terms. This suggests that more of these flags filtered onto the market after the 1960s (Forman 2021b, pers. comm.; InfC 2021).

5 A white glove sale is one in which an auctioneer manages to sell all the lots on offer, after which they are presented with a pair of gloves as a symbolic reward (ATG 2019). Alternatively, it could refer to sales in which the goods on offer are so expensive (or susceptible to getting tarnished) that they can only be handled whilst wearing gloves, hence the reason for gloves being present in an auction environment in the first place. I was once presented with a pair of cotton gloves upon expressing an interest in handling an expensive imperial German spiked helmet at an auction house in Munich. As a blind person I found the experience most alienating, and the auction porter thankfully let me handle the helmet without me having to wear the gloves. In contrast, I have never encountered gloves being mandated whilst handling militaria in retail outlets. On the other hand, I have observed, when I was sighted, a trader specialising in silver wearing a pair of white gloves at a regular antiques fair. It was understandable that he did not want to tarnish his silver, but the impression was rather pretentious.

6 See Shea (2021a).

8   Trash or treasure

How do you solve a problem like Nazi memorabilia?

Nazi paraphernalia has a split personality, signifying trash to some and treasure to others. The meaning and value of Nazi symbols have changed over time, even in the case of the swastika, which was once an icon of Nazism but was then appropriated by motor-biking Hells Angels, rockers and nihilist punks. Many argue that the safest place for Nazi artefacts is in museums and that private collectors should be prevented from owning them. Some people are even so incensed by Nazi relics that they wish to see them destroyed. Ironically, the disposal of Nazi regalia since 1945 (either deliberately or inadvertently) has increased the prices of the authentic artefacts that have survived. This is especially the case for the iconic steel helmet (*Stahlhelm*), which is partly a result of unadulterated helmets being difficult to find. Since 1945, they have been turned into flower pots, have been modified by bikers and have had fake decals added to fool collectors. Even though Nazi artefacts command high prices on the collectors' market, they remain potentially discardable as apparently worthless family heirlooms. Nazi relics are therefore still vulnerable to being discarded, much in the same way that they were as Hitler's regime collapsed around him. Nevertheless, rather than destroying them, these inanimate objects offer insights into the material culture of the Third Reich.

To preserve or destroy

Here, I address an under-acknowledged but important issue – how Nazi material culture was perceived, destroyed or exchanged as the Third Reich was collapsing, and in the immediate aftermath of its downfall until the present. Integral to understanding this issue is to consider how and why it is possible that the same object can circulate within different regimes of value simultaneously. In *Rubbish Theory*, Thompson (1979, 2017:4) sets out a linear trajectory from transient (value decreases with time), to rubbish, then durable (value increases with time). The status of Nazi regalia has bucked this linear progression and moved in and out of these categories from the moment it was created. Indeed, an 'artefact can arouse different patterns of response according to the belief systems of the perceivers' cultural matrices' (Prown 1982:6).

The value of Nazi medals did not move automatically from production to durable (Thompson 1979, 2017:134) but travelled through a transient stage validated

DOI: 10.4324/9781003000617-8

through consumption, influenced by the number of times a particular award was bestowed and the organisation it represented. Exactly when medals moved into the rubbish category is rather nebulous, as it depended on attitudes to the Nazi regime. That being said, an appropriate juncture is the so-called zero hour, i.e., the official surrender of the Wehrmacht on 8 May, 1945. After this point, if not before, wearers of the membership badge of the NSDAP or SS insignia disposed of the emblems that once gave them licence to perform unspeakable acts. In Günter Grass's novel *The Tin Drum* (*Die Blechtrommel*), Nazi party member Alfred Matzerath swallows his membership badge to prevent Russian soldiers from finding it, but his choking aggravates them and they shoot him dead (Grass 1959, 1980:348). Either way, the badge was a liability. It arguably took a few decades until the status of Nazi medals and badges became more stable, mainly as a result of collectors. On the other hand, non-collectors who had Nazi artefacts for whatever reason, for example, relatives of war veterans, may not have realised their value. Consequently, rather than Nazi memorabilia being exclusively durable, it currently resides within the consumption category, and whilst it could return to rubbish, it is more likely that it will end up as durable (although this is by no means certain).

In 1945, an Allied soldier was more likely to have sought a Nazi medal as a souvenir than as a collectible, hence the object was in limbo until it was integrated into a purposeful collection. Objects that were once ignored, then 'rediscovered and revalued' are characteristic of collectibles (Montgomery 2004:177). The 'tipping point' for a person to start forming a collection is to have more than three items (Gao et al. 2014:144). The nature of Nazi badges means that collectors will have many different examples. In contrast to some Allied soldiers who threw away their war souvenirs, collectors treasured the items they purchased. Collectors therefore valued Nazi objects more than the soldiers who defeated Nazi Germany. Rubbish 'is undifferentiated, while the very essence of durables is their differentiation' (Culler 1985:6). For a member of the Wehrmacht or liberating Allied soldier, one Iron Cross was no different to another, but by comparing examples side by side, collectors have identified subtle manufacturing attributes, thereby increasing their financial value. Allied soldiers sought an Iron Cross for its souvenir value irrespective of the firm that made it. Whilst one Iron Cross may have been enough for an Allied soldier, current-day collectors desire many.

The act of exchange between a soldier and a collector transformed a war souvenir into a collectible commodity. As such, people 'cannot afford to throw anything away on the grounds that it is not important since the unimportant things of today can become the valuable treasures of tomorrow' (Montgomery 2004:177). Objects associated with the Great War are a case in point, as they have a curious and unique character. They exist (physically and meta-physically) in a seemingly infinite number of cultural and personal worlds simultaneously and so can appear as worthless trash, cherished heirlooms, historical artefacts, memory items or commercially valuable souvenirs depending on those who own or observe them. They can be rusting mud-covered artefacts excavated from the earth, treasured mementos in peoples' homes, captioned exhibits in museum displays, exquisitely polished objects in private collections or commodities for sale at militaria fairs and on the internet.[1] The same can be said about Nazi relics, the difference being they were an integral part of a racist and antisemitic regime.

Whilst the act of preservation could be considered as a sign of value, destroying artefacts makes surviving examples scarcer still. In this respect, the value of a thing may only be appreciated once it can no longer be obtained. Additionally, whilst precious objects are treasurable, 'those things that do bring us joy are fleeting and ultimately perish' (Belk 1998:7). Value need not wholly be governed by a limited supply – the 'supply of contemporary art is potentially indefinite while the assessment of artistic value is here marked by uncertainty' (Moulin and Vale 1995:36). The value of antiques and works of art is often transient, dictated by taste and fashion (Brown 2019a; Park 2020). Consequently, objects once common, hence susceptible to being thrown away, may subsequently become scarce. In 'The March of the Toy Soldier: The Market for a Collectible,' Wellington and Gallo (1981:72) described how after the production of lead soldiers ceased in the late 1960s, it only took a few years until they became scarce.

The interesting thing about lead soldiers is that they are not as fragile as origami, for example, nor were they manufactured to be disposed or recycled. Their scarcity is a consequence of play versus display and subsequent disposal. What we 'keep for posterity must be weighed with what we should get rid of because it's irrelevant or simply put: trash' (Brown 2019). Junk is 'stuff that is of no real value but that you are keeping around because, well, you never know, and besides, you just haven't got around to throwing it out' (Culler 1985:4). Things that did not end up in the dustbin may not necessarily have a high financial value but are still an important record of a past society's material culture. Moreover, if objects are a mirror of a given society (Scarpaci 2016), our knowledge will be skewed by those objects that were preserved. Consequently, it is everyday objects most likely discarded that had the greatest potential to show how a given society functioned. This material culture of nothingness presents challenges, especially if a historian sought to learn from the utilitarian garments or tools of a past society. Even in the case of the Third Reich, it is the seldom-worn dress jackets of the army that appear on the collectors' market rather than field uniforms.

Although collectors may not necessarily engage with the themes cogent to material culture studies, they agree with academics that 'one man's rubbish can be another man's desirable object' (Reno 2017:pXii). Indeed, the late Joe Lyndhurst, an avid collector of militaria, acknowledged that 'one collector's rubbish is another collector's treasure' (Lyndhurst 1983:10). Collectors would also agree with Susan Pearce's study on collecting which categorised militaria as an 'authentic' form of collectible as opposed to 'commercial Kitsch' (Pearce 1998:135). Despite its distasteful nature, Nazi memorabilia is not junk, although the issues it raises in relation to its preservation are just as contentious today as they were when Nazi symbols were destroyed at the end of the Second World War.

In *Battle for the Ruhr*, Derek Zumbro tells of American soldiers entering a house in Cologne and stamping on a railway official's hat which had a swastika badge (Zumbro 2006:386). In another house they found a Nazi party official's uniform and a bust of Hitler, which were both thrown out of the window (Ibid.).

Furthermore, not only was there souvenir hunting on the battlefield – taking pistols, helmets and flags from German soldiers – but also widespread looting of civilian homes. Servicemen justified their actions by claiming wartime necessity, opportunities for profit, keepsakes and revenge for Nazi atrocities (Givens 2010:3). American soldiers were permitted to bring or post home war souvenirs provided they had no intelligence potential or intrinsic value and were signed off by an officer (Johnson 1984:VI). The regulations were not always obeyed, and an 'American official was caught shipping Hitler's silverware and gold-plated pistol to his parents' home in Brooklyn, New York' (Kirkpatrick 2010:18). Members of the American 101st Airborne Division took pieces of Hermann Göring's monogrammed silverware home as souvenirs, which is somewhat ironic considering Göring was behind much of the art that was looted during the Third Reich (Alford 2013:73–74; USHMM 2020).

According to the Geneva Convention of 1929, German soldiers taken prisoner were entitled to keep and wear their decorations (GC 1929), although the rules were not always followed. After Hitler's successor, Karl Dönitz, was taken prisoner by the British on 23 May, 1945 (Padfield 1984, 1993:433), his ceremonial baton went missing (Ludde-Neurath 1950:122). Some Germans who managed to keep their decorations, but who then found themselves in a prisoner of war camp, used them as items of exchange (Givens 2010:396). The nature of these exchanges highlights the extent to which even the Iron Cross first class had lost its symbolic value for some Germans, as in one case the medal was traded with a guard for two cigarettes. Although the cigarettes would have been quickly consumed, the medal lived on. The German soldier who exchanged his Iron Cross may even have regretted it later. Similarly, many collectors regret selling certain items they once owned, going to great lengths to re-acquire them. Indeed, the physical absence of former possessions may have a haunting presence (Holmes and Ehgartner 2020). Furthermore, many collectors mourn pieces of militaria they wished they had purchased.

Nazi relics that survived the war still remain vulnerable to damage and destruction. Artist Edmund de Waal stated he would relish the opportunity to smash pieces of Nazi decorative porcelain, known in collectors' circles as Allach (BBC February 2020c). It may be difficult to see why anybody would want to smash an ornament of an innocent dachshund puppy, but such figurines exemplify the sinister interchange of art and politics during the Third Reich. The racist Nazi worldview was expressed through un-glazed white Allach porcelain that harked back to classical Greek sculpture. The porcelain factory was a pet project of Heinrich Himmler and was situated next to Dachau concentration camp (DS 2018). Some concentration camp inmates were even forced to make the porcelain. Inmate Hans Lindauer recalled how 'strange it was that this group of workers in the Allach porcelain factory, from so many different nations, were the people who had to produce the cult symbol of the party, the Julleuchter (SS candle holder), and that making this product could give him and his fellow prisoners a higher chance of surviving the camp' (de Waal 2015). Overtly SS ritual objects aside, it is the notoriety of Allach porcelain that accounts for collectors spending large amounts of money on ceramic animals (Fisher 2019). It is therefore understandable that de Waal had the urge to smash the porcelain rather than see it being fetishized by collectors, not to mention profits being made through its sale. Perhaps a safer alternative would be for Allach porcelain to be held within publicly run or charitable institutions where it can be properly contextualised.

The moral dimension

Collectors and traders of Nazi memorabilia do not generally regard their activities as immoral. Many auction houses are willing to make a profit from the sale of Nazi memorabilia, not least because, in part, 'supra-legal moral obligations in our society appear to be optional; and, it is unreasonable to expect business people to be obligated to principles which appear to be optional' (Fieser 1996:463). Nevertheless, public reaction internationally to the sale of Nazi memorabilia can be extreme even today, over 70 years after the end of the Second World War. An auction in western Australia was condemned as 'morally repugnant by Jewish group' (Lucas 2019); a British newspaper headline announced 'Fury as Nazi memorabilia is sold off at auction house on the most solemn day in the Jewish calendar' (McDermott 2012); an auction in Lincoln sparked the *Daily Mail* headline 'Fury over sale of Nazi regalia from SS Death's Head squad that massacred 100 British soldiers' (DM Jul2008); *The Economist* headlined an article with 'Is it wrong to collect Nazi memorabilia?' (Econ 2009), and the *Washington Post* ran the headline of 'Sale of Hitler's belongings and Nazi artifacts stir backlash amid rising anti-Semitism' (Shapira 2019).

Although these headlines were generally negative, they still brought the trade in Nazi memorabilia to the public's attention, hence the auction houses that were named received free publicity. The *Daily Mail*, despite publishing one of the critical articles, failed to sensitively consider Hitler's victims when publicising an auction of a Nazi-era private photograph album with the headline 'Pictures show Hitler through the eyes of his bodyguard' (Stickings 2020). A characteristic of these articles is that they tend to overestimate the historical value of the artefacts on offer. They also fall into the trap of publicising auctions of Nazi memorabilia, especially where quirky objects are concerned; for example, an auction of Nazi relics in Dublin prompted the headline 'Nazi toilet paper among Hitler-era memorabilia up for auction' (Parsons 2016; BBC March 2019). This publicity tactic is frequently used by auction houses, not only boosting interest in the headline-capturing artefact (hence its price), but the other Nazi items offered, as well as potentially attracting others for future auctions.

The collecting of Nazi memorabilia raises similar issues to the collecting of guns. In 'Morally Controversial Leisure: The Social World of Gun Collectors,' Olmsted posed the following questions: 'who wishes to make this activity illegal and why do they attack so strongly? Why and how do gun collectors resist? How can collectible guns symbolize good to one group, and evil to another?' (Olmsted 1988:280). As stated in Chapter 1, collectors of Nazi memorabilia based in the Channel Islands sought to distance the items they collected from Nazism by claiming they were collecting German military artefacts rather than Nazi things (Carr 2016:255). In terms of guns, collectors negotiated the stigma associated with collecting them by stressing that they cannot be held responsible for people who have committed crimes (Yamane 2017). Likewise, whilst a Nazi memorabilia trader conceded there is a 1 percent fringe element (Rohrer 2009), presumably the rest act responsibly. This is a moot point, as what does handling metaphysically toxic artefacts in a responsible manner entail? Additionally, is there only a 1 percent fringe element? If so, where do these right-wing fanatics obtain Nazi artefacts from, and what do they do with them?

Are the individuals who dress up in replica Waffen-SS uniforms part of this 1 percent fringe or representative of the wider Nazi memorabilia hobby? Worrying aspects of the Nazi re-enactor community were highlighted in a BBC Panorama documentary in 2007 entitled *Weekend Nazis* (Sweney and Conlan 2008). The programme was filmed at the outdoor military enthusiasts show War and Peace in Kent, England. It would have been illegal for re-enactors to have publicly paraded about in Waffen-SS uniforms in Germany and some other European countries, hence the English event attracted re-enactors from all over Europe. A re-enactor was secretly filmed expressing offensive remarks (Gallagher 2008; Ofcom 2008). The event was also attended by David Irving, recently released from an Austrian prison for trivialising, grossly playing down and denying the Holocaust (Whine 2008; Usborne 2013).

Equally concerning was a Nazi memorabilia trader who offered a trolley that he claimed was from Bergen-Belsen concentration camp. The trolley raises a number of issues, including the intention of things (Joerges 1999), and leaving aside the purpose of the trolley in Bergen-Belsen, the trader sought to make a profit from its association with the Holocaust. Perversely, this gave the object its auratic and financial value. Despite its awful association, the trader neglected to state (certainly on camera) that over 50,000 people had died in Bergen-Belsen (Bauer 1983). Presumably, he would have sold it to anybody willing to pay the money and wheel it out of the grounds.

The legalities of Nazi memorabilia

The public display, distribution and glorification of Nazi symbols and related objects has been the subject of laws and regulations in many countries since 1945, especially in Germany. The August 1945 Potsdam agreement set out to 'demilitarize, deNazify, decartelize, and democratize.'[2] Of particular relevance here is the de-Nazification process, which not only included the detention and punishment of war criminals, but the destruction of Nazi symbols. Destroying swastikas, however, did not erase the ideology underlying them; this goal was confounded by the fact that many compromised individuals made their way back into German society. Nevertheless, laws were implemented to prevent Nazi symbols from taking root again.

In September 1945, the 'use of Nazi and military uniforms and insignia, salutes, medals, anthems, and music' was made illegal under American occupation (Plischke 1947:822). Four years later, in September 1949 (which was four months after the establishment of the Federal Republic), law number seven of the Allied High Commission for Germany was introduced, prohibiting the wearing, manufacturing, buying or selling of any forbidden articles of the former German armed forces or the NSDAP (AHCG 1949). Separate regulations were introduced later in both East and West Germany to curtail the display of Nazi symbols. Even if these regulations had not been introduced, it is doubtful whether the discredited Nazi swastika would have been able to rally the masses in the same way it did in Weimar and Nazi Germany. Although there were unrepentant Nazis, the majority of German people were not ready to reinstate the Nazi party, nor would the Allies have let them. Rather than lining the streets like they had during the Third Reich, swastika flags were set on fire or taken by Allied soldiers as souvenirs. Many were even quietly hidden; after all, there was still a slight chance that the Nazis might come back and the swastika could be unfurled again. We had never stopped being Nazis, many Germans would have said, just like they denied ever being one in the first place.

In East Germany, the criminal law prohibited the use of certain extremist symbols, and individuals could be punished if they publicly 'expressed comments of a fascist, racist, militaristic or revanchist character or use, distribute[d] or put up symbols of this character' (Trips-Herbert 2014). A West German assembly law in 1953 penalised the display of symbols of former National Socialist organisations (GV 1953). Although the public display of the Nazi swastika was effectively prohibited in both East and West Germany, there was still a demand for Nazi memorabilia, leading to an under-the-counter culture.

West German-based Konrad Kujau, the forger of the Hitler diaries, acquired authentic Nazi memorabilia by placing notices in East German newspapers seeking to buy 'old toys, helmets, jugs, pipes, dolls, etc.' (Harris 1986:109). Although the advert did not specifically mention Nazi memorabilia, 'helmets' were broad enough to give readers an idea. Kujau then smuggled Nazi relics into West Germany, where he sold them at a profit to collectors, some of whom were West German policemen.

In the 1960s, the late American intelligence officer Jim Atwood, who is considered a pioneer in the world of Nazi dagger collecting, scoured antique shops in West Germany, where he managed to buy Nazi edged weapons from 'under the counter' (Alford 2018:96). There was a general lack of supply, no doubt as most of the edged weapons had either been destroyed at the end of the war or taken out of Germany by Allied soldiers. Many of the Nazi daggers found were de-Nazified, thus the swastika's absence made them less desirable. Nevertheless, in terms of material culture, the absence of the swastika is an important aspect of the dagger's social life, although few collectors view it in these terms. For collectors, the object has essentially been castrated, thus no longer represents Nazism in its heyday but after its defeat. Nevertheless, the swastika is still there in the minds of collectors staring at the space it once occupied, a clue to the metal it was made from provided by the remaining eagle that clutched it.

Whilst never mainstream, the trading of Nazi memorabilia, especially in West Germany, became more established as buying and selling Nazi relics for legitimate purposes was enshrined into law (albeit still generally taboo). In 1968, West Germany was gripped by the rise of the far-right as well as left-wing student protests (Schmidtke 1999). In order that symbols could not be used to unseat the West German democracy, article 86 was introduced to regulate the public display of unconstitutional symbols (Bleich 2011). Although this law, which is still in force, curtailed the public display and 'distribution' (*Verbreitung*) of Nazi emblems, it did not prohibit their trade in certain circumstances. The law permitted Nazi symbols to be used for 'citizen education, the defence against unconstitutional efforts, for art or science, for research or education, for news coverage of historical or current affairs, or similar purposes' (SGB 1997).[3]

German collectors and traders position themselves within this framework, consequently covering swastikas with stickers at militaria fairs or airbrushing them online. One of the questions concerning this practice is whether it heightens the mystique of the symbol, as even if the swastika is hidden, once a collector purchases a Nazi badge, they will take it home and remove the sticker. By doing so, they presumably experience pleasure from intimately viewing the emblem. The kick that collectors experience may prove transient, as 'when we do get it, we tire of it anyway' (Schwichtenberg 1981:27). Indeed, some collectors are on a quest for ever larger and bolder swastikas. American-based collector Adam Wilcock admitted being afflicted with 'swastika fever' (Wilcock 2018, pers. comm.). For collectors, owning one Nazi badge is not enough. No wonder collecting has been referred to as an unruly passion (Münsterberger 1994).

Although collecting and trading Nazi memorabilia is generally legal in Germany providing unconstitutional symbols are not publicly displayed, the existence of the market has been a source of concern, especially when right-wing politicians have offered Nazi memorabilia for sale. Rudolf Müller, a candidate for Alternative für Deutschland (AfD) in the Saarland region, was discovered selling Nazi medals and currency (the latter from Theresienstadt concentration camp) from his antique jewellery shop (Löer 2017). He was taken to court but found innocent, because he was selling to individuals rather than distributing Nazi material for propaganda purposes (Bolz and Bongen 2016). Despite Müller's insensitive attitude to profiting from Holocaust-related material,[4] it did not stop the AfD from gaining seats in the regional parliamentary elections; Müller managed to take office (Steffen and Caspari 2017). Presumably those who voted for the party were not discouraged by Nazi relics.

With right-wing politics on the rise in Germany, many traders of Nazi-related items have come under scrutiny. In order to present the hobby in a more respectable manner, Hamburg-based militaria trader Helmut Weitze stopped offering material directly associated with the Holocaust, but this does not apply to the majority of SS artefacts, as he stated that 'if I did that, where would you start it, and where would you end?' (Weitze 2018, pers. comm.). British-based traders take a similar approach regarding SS items, with one stating, 'we deal in history, not politics' (Fisher 2017, pers. comm.). The aforementioned trader had also taken this position when interviewed by BBC television, despite offering for sale identity documents once held by concentration camp guards (Fisher 2015). His main defence was that offering these items to collectors and institutions helps to ensure that the horrors of the Nazi past will not be repeated.

For some, the situation is highly personal. Oliver Sears sees no difference between a swastika and a 'can of Zyklon B' (Sears 2018, pers. comm.). Indeed, from the earliest days of the NSDAP, as we have seen, the swastika represented antisemitism. Levene (2002:286) considered whether a 'phobia-driven, redemptive, even eschatological antisemitism' led to the death camps, but he could not provide a definitive answer. Elsewhere, it was observed that while the racialisation of Jews since the late nineteenth century played a part in the Holocaust, the events of the Second World War facilitated it (Herbert 2020; JT 2020). Also uncomfortable is the view that 'without Christian, or traditional anti-Judaism, modern, nationalistic and racial antisemitism would have been impossible' (Bauer 1980:36).

In 2012 an auction of Nazi memorabilia in Bristol prompted an early day motion in the British House of Commons, which called for the 'Government to bring in immediate regulation and control of this abhorrent trade' (HC 2012). Only 22 MPs supported the proposal, including John Mann and Jeremy Corbyn of the Labour party. The auction house stated that it would cease trading Holocaust-related material such as yellow stars, but this did not seem to include general Nazi memorabilia (BBC March 2012). As the early day motion did not progress, it is presently up to individual British-based auction houses and traders whether to offer Nazi artefacts. The vast majority of relics sold end up in private hands, and whilst the historical value of many objects is negligible, for example, common Nazi daggers, businesses are making a profit through the sale of objects most people would rather see destroyed or kept in museums. Indeed, potential for profit means that it is less likely, certainly in the short term, that Nazi artefacts will be donated to institutions. Whilst plentiful mass-produced Nazi medals devoid of their biographies have little historical value, Nazi documents and literature with research potential should be publicly accessible rather than held by private collectors as fetish objects.

The display and sale of Nazi memorabilia in France, a country occupied during the Second World War, is especially contentious. Despite France also suffering during the Great War, the display of imperial German items is not prohibited. At the turn of the millennium, French anti-racist activists mounted a court action against Yahoo in North America, as it was claimed that French citizens were able to buy Nazi memorabilia from Yahoo's auction site (Leighton et al. 2013; Cohen-Almagor 2012). This pitted the restricted display of Nazi symbols in France against the right to display them in North America. Despite objections, mainly on the grounds that laws in France should not have any bearing on the free speech of companies based in North America, Yahoo eventually prohibited the sale of Nazi memorabilia on its site. In 2014, protests by anti-racist activists led to an auction house in Paris cancelling a sale of items reputedly once owned by Hitler and Göring (BBC April 2014). Despite these cases, the collecting of Nazi memorabilia is not prohibited in France, although the public display of Nazi symbols is an offence (FC 2010). Consequently, a French militaria trader stated that he obscures the swastika on the Nazi artefacts he offers for sale (Leroy 2019). The environments in France and Germany are therefore similar.

Whilst traders in the U.K. can display swastikas as long as the intention is not to incite racial hatred, swastika flags have especially caused offence at regular markets (Kitching 2018). In order to avoid causing offence, traders, especially at general antique fairs, could fold up Nazi flags and cover the swastikas on badges with stickers in a similar way to German traders. One would have thought that as London was bombed by the Luftwaffe, and Hamburg was bombed by the Royal Air Force, reminders of the Second World War in the form of Nazi memorabilia would be banished. In actual fact, London and Hamburg were the two main centres of the Nazi memorabilia trade in the postwar era. The number of dealers in these cities has diminished as shops have closed, although a major international trader still has his Hamburg shop. The trend in England is for traders who had shops in London to mainly operate online or at militaria fairs. Munich, despite trying to shake off its reputation as the birthplace of Nazism, was another trading hub (and still hosts one of the largest international auction houses). Even residents of the British Channel Islands, occupied by the German army during the Second World War, began to collect helmets and equipment left behind (Carr 2016). Likewise, so-called German war junk was sought, and still is, by hobbyists and treasure hunters in Finland (Herva et al. 2016; Seitsonen 2018, 2020). Still, no matter the location, the display of Nazi artefacts has always been a sensitive matter.

In 1995, whilst living in Denmark, I visited antiques fairs, and although there were plenty of Third Reich-era German toy soldiers, there was little in the way of distinctive Nazi insignia, for example, black, white and red swastika armbands. Perhaps this was a trait of general Danish antiques fairs, and much the same could be said about similar events in Britain (minus the abundance of German-made soldiers). I observed Nazi armbands and flags at a Danish militaria fair, but these tended to be displayed by Danish dealers rather than by those who had travelled from Germany. The German dealers could usually be identified as the badges and medals they displayed still had stickers partially covering their swastikas, even though it was not illegal to publicly display the symbol in Denmark. It was obviously more practical for German dealers just to keep the stickers on. Swastika flags are not used to decorate stalls at German militaria fairs, although German traders do discreetly stock them.

Whilst people are theoretically free to publicly display Nazi symbols in the U.S.A. (Katz 2003:312), an intriguing example reveals how the issue of selling and displaying swastika-decorated items has changed over time. An American trader displayed a large swastika battle flag on his stall at a general market when he began trading in the 1960s and 1970s but would be less likely to do so today (Shea 2017, pers. comm.). It would be incorrect to suggest that a swastika banner was not contentious then, but symbols have become increasingly divisive in recent years. At the so-called 'Unite the Right' rally in Charlottesville in 2017, Nazi and American Confederate battle flags were displayed to fuel racial division (Howard-Woods 2018:11). In an attempt to present the militaria hobby in a more acceptable manner to the general public, American militaria fair organisers have introduced regulations partially prohibiting the display of swastika flags, although they still defend the right for them to be sold on account that many were brought home by American soldiers as souvenirs or trophies (OHV).

A distinction could be made between a souvenir and a war trophy.[5] A Nazi regimental flag captured under fire could be considered as a trophy and a reward for defeating one's enemy, whereas swastika bunting taken from a German street by an Allied soldier without risk to life is more along the lines of a souvenir. Either item could subsequently be inscribed by the Allied soldier who initially acquired it, as well as the names of their comrades. Rather than inscribed flags, however, some collectors may prefer unadulterated flags that represent Nazi Germany before it was defeated. The premise that collectors are merely honouring Allied soldiers could therefore be questioned.

The issues relating to Japanese flags are somewhat different. In contrast to Nazi flags, which were often flown from military installations and were the property of the army rather than an individual soldier, Japanese soldiers carried flags inscribed by their family as a good luck charm on their person into battle. Consequently, if a soldier carrying one of these flags was killed, their talisman, stained with blood, might be taken by an Allied soldier as a grim war trophy. It has been argued that where possible these flags should be traced to the dead Japanese soldier's descendants, who can then make the decision as to whether the flag should receive a dignified burial (Harrison 2008). There is an even greater case to be made that these flags closely linked to a soldier's personhood should not be sold on the open market, or if a collector does acquire one, then they should do their utmost to repatriate it as soon as possible. In the clamour to acquire relics or profit from them, few collectors and traders have behaved ethically.

Private versus public ownership and possession of Nazi memorabilia

Nazi memorabilia is a curious form of material culture in which to explore the changing nature of private property. Collectors are only able to own Nazi memorabilia once conserved by somebody else. As noted earlier, some items might even have been taken from their original owners against their will – 'to the victor belong the spoils' (Spencer 1944:208). Some allied soldiers also acquired battlefield relics, or those who did not manage to do so may have bartered with each other so that they could take home a souvenir. Over time, these artefacts were given to relatives, kept, discarded or sold. No matter the pathways Nazi objects travelled, collectors say that they have the right to purchase them. On the other hand, some people argue that collectors should not be allowed to own Nazi relics and that the most appropriate place for them is in museums.

Notwithstanding the moral dimension of collecting Nazi artefacts, the looting of art by members of the Nazi regime was most certainly not legal, a point made by Hector Feliciano in *The Lost Museum: The Nazi Conspiracy to Steal the World's Great Works of Art* (Feliciano 1997:3). During the Third Reich, ill-gotten objects were often presented as gifts, with it being critically observed that 'soldiers who heedlessly believe they are receiving gifts will come to realize property wrongly acquired will not prosper' (Kellner 2018:484–485). Indeed, 'more than 60 years after the end of World War II, courts in the United States and elsewhere continue to struggle with questions of ownership and restitution relating to artwork and other objects of value looted during that conflict' (Chanen 2006:52).

German soldiers did not actually own their decorations, which could be taken back if they acted dishonourably. They were therefore merely holding-in-trust their decorations or honorary signs. In March 1945, Hitler ordered that tank crews of the Waffen-SS division Leibstandarte Adolf Hitler be stripped of their cuff titles for retreating from Hungary without his permission (Goebbels 1978:245;252). After the war, the once-esteemed SS cuff titles became a liability and may have been discarded by some of their wearers. In May 1945, Heinrich Himmler even took off his SS uniform and disguised himself in a military greatcoat, although his forged identity document suggesting that he was a member of the Secret Field Police raised suspicions when he was stopped at an Allied checkpoint (Padfield 1990:600). If SS collar patches were discarded at the end of the war, it may account for the inordinate amount of so-called un-issued SS cloth emblems currently available on the collectors' market. This does not explain how these items, providing they are authentic, initially arrived on the market. Moreover, as they were never applied to uniforms and worn, their aura is diminished. On the other hand, collectors who prefer items in pristine condition would rather have un-issued emblems. They were, after all, still produced during the Third Reich. Many people would regard the collecting of SS artefacts as abhorrent, but collectors defend their right to own them.

For private ownership and possession of Nazi artefacts

It has been insightfully observed that 'private property and private ownership are concepts of which many different conceptions are possible, and that in each society the detailed incidents of ownership amount to a particular concrete conception of these abstract concepts' (Waldron 1985:317). If 'early human societies instinctively accorded special privileges of possession or ownership to the person who captured, found, made, or productively used a thing, perhaps that is an inherently sensible theoretical foundation for modern property law' (Thomas 2006:29). Ownership 'is distinct from possession, for any person can own anything. Ownership per se does not make a possession of the object, does not mark the individual object with the unique person-hood of the owner' (Carrier 1990:24). Indeed, it could be said that museums own objects, but collectors possess them. Our 'fragile sense of self needs support, and this we get by having and possessing things because, to a large degree, we are what we have and possess' (Tuan 1980:472).

A vast number of Nazi objects purchased by collectors are sourced through auction houses. These businesses rely on a steady supply of material, some of which has directly come from the families of deceased soldiers, whose right to benefit financially from their Nazi heirlooms has been noted (Payne 2018, pers. comm.). Moral objections to the trading of Nazi relics aside, the collectors who purchased them became their owners, hence at liberty, within legal limits, to do as they pleased with them. Provided Nazi artefacts are not deployed to incite racial hatred, private ownership could be considered fairly innocuous. Some collectors may even have donated Nazi memorabilia to an institution, if one was willing to accept it.

The United States Holocaust Memorial Museum, for example, does not accept 'textiles which are inauthentic or without provenance information, such as Nazi uniform pieces brought back to the United States by Allied military personnel, or material purchased at auction or at flea markets' (USHMM n.d.). Perhaps they should accept it, simply for the reason that the material would then be taken out of circulation. Political philosopher Michael Buckley stated that Nazi regalia should not be sold on the open market, as a neo-Nazi could purchase it to 'promote hate or to sow the seeds of division between communities' (Conti 2018). In contrast, cultural theorist Kwame Anthony Appiah, who was given a Nazi souvenir belt buckle by his father, who had earned the American Bronze Star and Purple Heart, concluded that the 'impulse to destroy troubling historical artifacts is usually best resisted. Even if the item did end up in the wrong hands, the primary responsibility would lie with those who used this relic to celebrate Nazi ideas' (Appiah 2017).

Against private ownership and possession of Nazi artefacts

There 'is a lot of pressure from people who don't look at it as collecting history, they look at it like we are these closed-minded evil people who are trying to collect all these things, and fetishising, you know, racial purity, and all this, they look at it, it is just evil history that needs to be buried' (Wilcock 2018, pers. comm.). In a bid to ensure that a top hat supposedly worn by Hitler did not fall into the hands of 'Nazi worshipers,' Swiss-based real estate magnate Abdallah Chatila purchased it for over 50,000 euro from a Munich auction house so that he could donate it to a Jewish charity (Bershidsky 2019). Chatila effectively took the hat out of circulation, although one person on their own could not do this for every Nazi artefact offered on the open market. The historic value of the top hat is negligible, its value solely resting in the fact that it apparently once belonged to Hitler. Rather worryingly, 'collecting encompasses the combined meanings of fetishism found in the religious fetishism of anthropology, the commodity fetishism of Marx, and the sexual fetishism of Freud' (Belk 1998:17). This is a heady cocktail in itself, never mind the issue of privately owning Nazi relics. For Thomas More, the private ownership of wealth was an anathema to a utopian society:

> As long as there is any property, and while money is the standard of all other things, I cannot think that a nation can be governed either justly or happily: not justly, because the best things will fall to the share of the worst men; nor happily, because all things will be divided among a few (and even these are not in all respects happy), the rest being left to be absolutely miserable.
>
> (More 1516, 2005:30)

It has been said that More's *Utopia* remains 'astonishingly radical stuff. Not many lord chancellors of England have denounced private property' (Eagleton 2016:412). For a 'preference to be socially valid, it must utilize a good to satisfy a need that is social in nature rather than isolated to the mere preferences, or false needs, of a few or one' (Thompson 2015:259). As such, most people would argue that the most appropriate place for Nazi memorabilia is not in private hands. An American auctioneer of Nazi memorabilia acknowledged that he gets criticised for offering Nazi regalia on the open market, and that 'a lot of people tell me how can you sell that material? It should be in a museum' (Anon. 2018a: pers. comm.). Similarly, it was proposed that the best place for the statue of Edward Colston dumped into Bristol harbour by Black Lives Matter protestors in June 2020 was a museum. Indeed, the Mayor of Bristol, Marvin Rees, stated it would be placed in one (Mukena 2020). This decision is a symbolic gesture indicating that Britain's colonial past is being contextualised within an institution rather than presented as a feature of a cityscape. Indeed, it is a valid alternative to being destroyed, as 'if there is no object, there is no debate, there is no discourse, there is no learning' (D'arcy 2019). The anti-racist graffiti that the protestors sprayed on the statue will also be preserved (BBC June 2020d), providing further material evidence of the statue's contested social life.

In 1945, Nazi monuments raised similar dilemmas, often resolved by Allied soldiers blowing them up, for example, the giant swastika at the Nürnberg rally grounds (USHMM 1992). The large eagle at Tempelhof Airport in Berlin was temporarily covered by an American flag before being dismantled and sent to America (Strugalla 2014). Its dismembered head was then returned to Germany, where it now resides close to the spot where it was once perched, de-throned and no longer representing Nazi Germany's quest for global domination. It has been mutilated and put on public display, much in the same way that the genitals on pagan statues were chiselled off during the late Roman empires transition to Christianity (Jacobs 2010:278).

Although the majority of large Nazi monuments were destroyed or their swastikas removed, many small Nazi objects survived, leading to concerns that right-wing extremists could purchase them to spread hate or be so enthused by them that it could fuel or inspire their actions. These concerns are not unfounded, as Adam Thomas and Claudia Patatas, found guilty at Birmingham crown court of belonging to the terrorist organisation 'National Action,' possessed a 'pastry cutter shaped like a swastika, as well as pendants, flags and clothing emblazoned with symbols of the Nazi-era, SS and National Action' (BBC November 2018). These trashy trinkets were an overt expression of their racist views; even making biscuits was an ideologically inspired act. It is possible that the pastry cutter was not authentic, thus the availability of reproductions is dangerous. The question could also be asked as to the pastry cutter's origin, for example, was it sold as a Nazi swastika or perhaps a religious symbol? Indeed, a proposal for the swastika to be outlawed in the European Union was defeated as it is a religious sign of Hindus (BBC January 2007). If the pastry cutter was manufactured during the Nazi era, it may have been desired for the allure of its presumed 'social life' – perhaps used by a Nazi-supporting housewife in the time of the Third Reich (Wyllie 2019).

The sale of material more directly related to the Holocaust is particularly contentious. In February 2020, an auction house offered photographs in their 'Fine Militaria Sale' depicting the liberation of Bergen-Belsen concentration camp. The auctioneer defended their right to sell the photos on the grounds that they were 'offering these items as we feel they are of historical interest, we certainly do not intend to glorify the atrocities which took place in Nazi Germany during the period of the Third Reich' (CTA 2020a: Lot 575). The images were subsequently sold to an online bidder for GBP 160, again raising the question as to whether private individuals should be able to own such material.

A key issue concerns how collectors display their Nazi memorabilia. American-based trader Shea spoke about his 'inner-sanctum' (Shea 2017, pers. comm.), which houses a jacket once worn by Martin Bormann displayed on a mannequin. In an online video, another American-based trader, Thomas Wittmann, gave collectors an intimate tour of his 'collecting room,' and although Wittmann said that viewing his collection of SS daggers and other assorted imperial and Nazi memorabilia 'set him up for the day,' others would be highly disturbed by the glorification of Germany's militaristic past (Wittmann 2019). Hamburg-based Helmut Weitze, although offering Nazi items in his shop, only displays imperial-era militaria in his home, as it 'can sit in the living-room without scaring the neighbours!' (Weitze 2018, pers. comm.). In contrast, American-based collector Adam Wilcock displayed a Nazi flag on his bedroom wall but did remove it before visitors arrived, in case they got the wrong idea of him (Wilcock 2018, pers. comm.).

Private homes are probably not the safest place for such metaphysically toxic artefacts, especially as it means they can be fondled in an unsupervised manner. Indeed, some collectors may even decorate their living space with Nazi daggers and swords, hence their entire family would be exposed to them on a daily basis. Such an anarchic display may even assert itself so much that it prevents visitors being invited to the home. The collection would therefore foster social isolation and lead to resentment or family arguments. It is not unknown for military artefacts to invade the home, for example, Great War trench art (Isyanova 2009). Ironically, whilst bullets and brass shells were intended to kill before being fashioned into letter openers and vases, Nazi badges are potentially more dangerous. Whether Nazi memorabilia takes over the entire home or is compartmentalised and glorified in a dedicated room, many would argue that relics from such a haunted past should be held in public institutions.

For public ownership of Nazi artefacts

As 'spaces of political as much as scientific or aesthetic imagination, museums have always sought to articulate through both their archiving practices and their exhibition of artefacts an idea of society and of the subjects within it' (Hetherington 2011:460). By the eighteenth century 'private collections became public – most spectacularly at the Louvre – and what was perceived as the irrationality of the cabinet became rationalized' (Conn 2010:20). Many collectors of Nazi memorabilia fail to behave rationally, nor may their collections have any educational purpose. In contrast, the 'public museum's focus has long been defining and constructing particular identities through its historically defined educational mandate' (Trofanenko 2006:310). Nevertheless, there are debates within the museum and collecting communities as to whether the role of museums is to educate the public or to be the custodians of historical artefacts, although these need not be mutually exclusive.

The editor of *Military Trader*, John Adams-Graf, a former museum curator, disapproves of institutions that focus on education whilst reducing the number of artefacts on display (Adams-Graf 2015). Indeed, a critical role of museums is to preserve objects so that the material culture of a past or current society is documented. Insightful in this matter is that 'perhaps the most important and novel aspect of the fledgling museum was its determination to make its collections relevant to the individual, and to acquire items that were redolent of the involvement of the common man and woman in the war, whether at the Front or at home' (Cornish 2004:38). Museums have a crucial role in preserving and displaying mundane, everyday objects in their 'social and historical context' (Calderon 1990:139). Some militaria collectors do have an interest in acquiring utilitarian objects, although the majority probably prefer to collect more aesthetically pleasing ones, even though they fail to tell a personal story. Consequently, a private collection is less likely to possess the educational value of a museum.

So sensitive is the public display of Nazi artefacts in Germany today, even within a museum setting, that the German Historical Museum in Berlin had to carefully consider how Nazi memorabilia was to be displayed in their exhibition entitled *Hitler and the Germans* (Fischhaber and Reinbold 2010; DHM HD). A swastika flag was displayed, but one side of it was partially obscured by anti-Nazi pamphlets, which was material evidence of opposition to Hitler. The exhibition also contained a piece of furniture that Hitler apparently used, but in order that it could not be a source of veneration, it was partially hidden by netting. Conversely, this may actually have enhanced the aura of the object. Nevertheless, visitors were prevented from touching it.

Private collectors got the chance to get close to furniture Hitler sat on when a chair and desk from his Munich apartment were sold at an auction house in Ohio in 2018. Its value was grossly inflated, with the lot description stating, 'this simple piece of furniture is one of the most iconic and important items in WWII History' (MSA 2018). An article following the sale was entitled 'Adolf Hitler's desk provides an Education for Collectors' (Fraser 2018), but the furniture offered little educational value. It was purchased purely for its association with Hitler. It did provide a lesson for auctions not to overestimate historical value or auction estimates. It was expected to fetch between USD 100,000 and one million but hammered for USD 35,000 (Ibid.). Although it sold for considerably lower than its estimate, presumably the buyer would not have been interested had the furniture not been connected to Hitler.

Another case in point is a toilet seat Hitler is thought to have sat on at his mountain retreat, auctioned in North America in 2021 for USD 15,000 (HTS 2021). The wooden seat complete with lid is said to have created a frenzied bidding war (Hodge 2021), although it only reached its top estimate (estimated between USD 10,000–15,000). Nevertheless, the fact that somebody was prepared to pay so much for something they could have purchased for considerably less had it not been Hitler's leaves a bad smell. There would be nothing to stop the buyer from installing the seat in their own bathroom or using it as a source of entertainment or theatre, thus trivialising Hitler's crimes. The object may even take on religious cultic properties much in the same way as relics of saints and be chopped up and dispersed to Hitler worshipers around the world.

Against public ownership of Nazi artefacts

An 'institution cannot be defended by employing the antique distinction of public versus private. Rather, the debate should be re-articulated in the fundamental tension between the public (co-dependent with the private) and the common' (Joselit et al. 2011:98). Collectors have contributed to the democratisation of Nazi memorabilia. They also facilitate its wide geographical dispersal, providing an element of protection in times of crisis, for example, wars or environmental disasters. It can also be owned by anybody, irrespective of their disability, gender, race or sexuality, something which was not possible during the Third Reich.

The ability to get close to objects was one of the reasons why Walter Benjamin defended the right of private ownership. In his 1931 essay 'Unpacking my Library,' he stated that 'even though public collections may be less objectionable socially and more useful academically than private collections, the objects get their due only in the latter' (Benjamin 1931, 1968:67). As Benjamin was opposed to the fascist aestheticisation of politics, of which Nazi symbols were an integral part, it is worth contemplating what he would have thought of collectors possessing them. Many 'collectors like to fondle or stroke the objects they own or to look at them over and over from every angle, both up close and at a distance, activities that are impossible in a museum' (Belk 1998:14). Many collectors are concerned that art and antiques would be 'imprisoned for life by the museums' (Eccles 1968:16). Presumably, artefacts held by private collectors experience an element of respite, although in the case of Nazi relics, non-collectors would probably agree that they should be permanently confined within the walls of institutions. Moreover, it is the relatively free way in which Nazi relics are sold which is the source of consternation. Nazi relics are imbued with considerable agency and potentially anthropomorphic. Consequently, collectors are hard pushed to defend private possession.

The roundabout of private versus public ownership and possession of Nazi artefacts

Museums could inadvertently legitimise Nazi memorabilia, as they act 'as a guarantee for the aristocratic exchange . . . so the fixed reserve of the museum is necessary for the functioning of the sign exchange' (Baudrillard 1981:121). If museums refused to store or display Nazi memorabilia, it would give a signal to collectors that Nazi artefacts were not worthy of institutional backing. Their prized collectibles shunned, collectors may switch their attention to less contentious objects. Items that are accepted into a museum are no longer considered junk and are 'marked as durable' (Culler 1985:6). If one therefore wished to totally trash Nazi relics, removal from museums and destruction might be effective. One should think carefully, however, before advocating such an iconoclastic act. It would be challenging to totally erase Nazi symbols, as they exist in many forms, including digitally (see Chapter 9).

No man's land for Nazi artefacts

A number of measures could help to bridge the intractable divide of private versus public ownership. The challenges would be implementing the measures in a fair and consistent manner across the world. Auction houses and sole traders already claim to have a watchful eye (Anon. 2018a). A German auction house claimed that they vetted their bidders (DW 2019), and whilst it is not illegal to sell Nazi memorabilia in Germany, the sale of Nazi relics is highly emotive. Auction houses in the U.K. could implement vetting measures, although they may be reluctant to do so on a voluntary basis. As many transactions now take place over the internet, traders have even less intimacy with their customers than before. Nevertheless, traders could make more of an effort to get to know their customers and refuse to sell to those whose intentions they had concerns about.

Governmental regulations would help to clean up the trade but would require political commitment and enforcement. Registers of collectors and traders could be established, although qualification criteria would need formulating and licensing schemes administered. Blacklisted individuals could still attempt to view Third Reich memorabilia in a museum, although they may be discouraged by the formal setting, especially if they had to show identification (already a requirement of the Institute of Contemporary History in Munich).

Finding middle ground regarding private and public ownership might be helped by establishing an association which loans Nazi memorabilia as a library does books. For collectors who still seek to make a financial profit, a scheme could be established similar to the one that permits art investors not only to potentially reap financial returns, but to visit their holdings (Loader-Wilkinson 2010; Schindler et al. 2018). The majority of Nazi artefacts have not reached the lofty prices of fine art, so it would take socially minded individuals or institutions to operate a similar scheme (ethical considerations aside). In any case, renting Nazi medals is unlikely to provide the same 'psychic benefits' ownership offers (Frey and Eichenberger 1995:216).

Collectors and traders may be less resistant to a total prohibition of Nazi memorabilia if they were sufficiently financially compensated for their deprivation, especially if their collection was a financial investment. On the other hand, a 'good collector would seem to be someone who loves his or her collected objects and appreciates them for themselves rather than as status symbols or as a form of wealth' (Belk 1998:7). This statement raises a number of issues, especially when applied to the collecting of Nazi memorabilia, as many would consider it problematic if a collector loved their anti-Partisan badge, for example (see Chapter 6). To alleviate these concerns, the requisitioned items could be stored in military museums. Nevertheless, the cost of compensating collectors would be considerable and would surely run to hundreds of millions of U.S. dollars globally.

An alternative to banning the sale of Nazi memorabilia whilst raising money for the public good is the levying of a sales tax on such items. Proceeds could be donated to charities challenging discrimination and racism. This was suggested by Oliver Sears as 'one of the results of coming from my particular background, for me it has manifested itself in a very firm commitment to democracy and human rights' (Sears 2018, pers. comm.). Despite this suggestion, some charities may be unwilling to accept money from the sale of Nazi memorabilia (Marcus 2019). In any case, a tax would send a clear message that Third Reich relics are not ordinary collectibles.

Never mind the swastikas

The 'swastika . . . is one of the most common forms of shock graffiti in the United States, typically spray-painted by juveniles who are not actually white suprema-cists but simply want to use the image to shock and alarm people' (ADL 2021). Similarly, the 'cross and the crucifix no longer have the honoured place they used to hold in our culture; but there is no visual image that packs the same emotional punch as a swastika' (HT 2020). Consequently, various non-conformist groups and even a member of the British royal family have hijacked the swastika. Perhaps the first to do so were American renegade motorcycle gangs such as the Hell's Angels that emerged in the late 1940s. These outlaws also appropriated German steel helmets and the Iron Cross. As the bikers considered themselves social outcasts, the tainted nature of Nazi symbols suited their identity. Nazi symbols underwent a transformation, as not only were they iconic of the Wehrmacht but became associ-ated with violent bearded bikers tearing across American highways. Susan Sontag observed that 'boots, leather chains, Iron Crosses on gleaming torsos, swastikas, along with meat hooks and heavy motorcycles have become the secret and most lucrative of paraphernalia of eroticism' (Sontag 1980:102).

Hell's Angels, rock and roll, and Nazi symbols are a particularly volatile com-bination. In December 1969, a group of Hell's Angels stabbed and beat to death Meredith Hunter, an 18-year-old African American, during a Rolling Stones per-formance in Altamont, California (Austerlitz 2018; White 1992). It was a brutal end to a year in which the founder of the band, Brian Jones, was found dead in his swimming pool (Zobenica 2007). In the 1960s, Jones's lifestyle and antics were the source of many headlines. In 1966, he posed in an SS uniform, sourced from a film costume department in Munich, whilst standing on a toy doll, his sadomasochistic German/Italian girlfriend, Anita Pallenberg, kneeling at his feet (Sheffield 2017; Wells 2020).[6] Rolling Stones guitarist Keith Richards was also fond of Nazi uniforms, wearing a German army tunic on America's *The Ed Sul-livan Show* in the summer of 1965 (Evening Standard 2007).[7] He also allegedly wore a full SS uniform to Mick and Bianca Jagger's French wedding reception in 1971 (Getlen 2016; Evening Standard 2007). Jagger was also no stranger to caus-ing controversy; whilst performing 'Satisfaction' in Berlin, he 'sparked a riot by goose-stepping and giving the Nazi salute' (Brendon 2013).

English rock and blues singer Chris Farlowe (born in 1940) collaborated with the Rolling Stones and claimed that he visited Jones at his house and sold him a Nazi uniform, suggesting that Jones had a deeper interest than dressing up for publicity (Anon. 2018b; Garcia 2019). It was whilst gigging in Hamburg that Farlowe picked up his first Iron Cross, thus his tours and interest in Nazi memorabilia dovetailed neatly (Harrys n.d.). Farlowe's interest in Nazi memorabilia led to him opening the A Call to Arms militaria shop in North London. His collection was so extensive that he contributed to the first generation of collectors' books on Nazi memorabilia, supplying a kepi once worn by Hitler's Brownshirts for Jack Pia's book *Nazi Insignia* (Pia 1971:34).

The late Keith Moon, the drummer in the rock band The Who, was also fascinated with Nazi regalia. In 1970, he went on a week-long drinking spree in a Nazi uniform, hiring an open-topped Mercedes and visiting the 'heavily Jewish London neighbourhood of Golders Green' (Epstein 2020). His offensive behaviour did not cease there, as when he moved to California he had a disagreement with Steve McQueen and turned up at the Hollywood actor's attorney's office dressed as Erwin Rommel (Fletcher 2014). His behaviour cannot be attributed to his drinking binges; rather, the affinity that Moon, Farlowe, members of the Rolling Stones and others had for Nazi regalia is symptomatic of the profound impact the Second World War had on their generation.

In April 1976, a hoard of Nazi memorabilia and literature was discovered in the late glam rocker David Bowie's luggage at the Polish-Russian border (NME 2018). Shortly afterwards, he told a Swedish reporter that Britain could benefit from a fascist leader (BB 2018). In September of the same year, Bowie stated in an interview for *Playboy* magazine that Hitler was one of the first rock stars, much in the same way that Mick Jagger was for his generation (Crowe 1976, 2016; Pearce 2016). Bowie was born immediately after the Second World War in London, hence the formative years of his childhood were permeated with destroyed buildings juxtaposed with a raft of films glamourising wartime missions, not to mention his Berlin years in the 1970s.

Lemmy of Motörhead, born in 1945, was another rock star who collected Nazi memorabilia. He bemoaned that people did not 'understand' his fascination (Kilmister and Garza 2002:224), which was brought to the public's attention by his trademark Iron Cross. Nazi regalia and uniforms had an aesthetic appeal for Lemmy, as he contended that 'it's always been the bad guy who dressed the best' (Duerden 2010).[8] It could be taken from Lemmy's statement that aesthetics had primacy over politics. Indeed, he claimed he did not 'collect the ideas, just the stuff' (Adams 2015). Similarly, although journalist Mark Binelli was shocked to see swastika flags and Nazi uniforms displayed inside Lemmy's Hollywood home, he concluded that his vast collection of Nazi memorabilia was not borne out of racist motives and that Lemmy was simply a 'man who loves the transformative power of a uniform' (Binelli 2009). Uniforms might be understandable, but owning a comb and hairbrush once used by Hitler's mistress Eva Braun takes fascination to another level, especially as they were casually displayed on Lemmy's 'coffee table next to an overfull ashtray and a half-empty tumbler of whiskey' (Ibid.). Whilst staring at the mirror, did Lemmy see his own reflection or that of Braun or even Hitler? Many would rather such a highly charged object imbued with so much aura was smashed or held securely in an institution.

Taking their cues from rockers and bikers but distorting the swastika even further, punks shocked mainstream society in the 1970s with their disregard for anything that had gone before. Indeed the 'swastika was worn because it was guaranteed to shock' (Hebdige 1979:116). Siouxsie Sioux of Siouxsie and The Banshees strove to upset middle-class suburbia with her dominatrix whip, black leather, PVC and swastika armband (Ikin 2020; Cost 2007). The 'imperative to shock and disturb above all led some punks to display the Nazi swastika, not out of allegiance to fascism or the growing ranks of British fascists surrounding them, but as an irresponsible addition to their confusing montage of degeneracy and depravity' (Moore 2004:312). Sid Vicious of the Sex Pistols had a studded swastika on his leather jacket, and although his intention was not to offend Jewish people, the symbol naturally managed to do so. Viv Albertine of the female punk band the Slits recalled, 'once we hailed a cab and the driver said he wouldn't take us because he was Jewish and offended by the swastika on Sid's jacket' (Lewis 2014).

Malcolm McLaren, the manager of the Sex Pistols, the son of a Jewish mother and raised by his Jewish grandmother, encouraged his band to wear swastikas. Indeed, McLaren's 'liberationist, anarchistic politics, utilizing situationist tactics, included the swastika, and therefore the Second World War and, by association, the Judeocide in his play of signs' (Stratton 2008:217). McLaren also had original Nazi artefacts, although he apparently did not sell these (Stratton 2007), suggesting they acted as a reminder of the Jewish plight, although he was not the only Jewish person who collected Nazi objects. Chris Stein, boyfriend of Debbie Harry and co-member of the punk-inspired band Blondie (also the name of Hitler's dog), 'overcame his Holocaust paranoia by collecting Nazi artefacts' (Goldman 2014). Likewise, North American-based collector Norman Ross, whose mother was persecuted during the Nazi era, also claimed that owning an SS dagger was his way of coming to terms with the past (Adams 2000). Similarly, a few black people collect advertising items that once depicted black people in a stereotyped manner as they say these document black oppression (Baker et al. 2004).

Malcolm McLaren said that 'we wanted to have a clean slate. We decided that we liked certain icons from the past and wanted to reinvent them' (Farndale 2007). Consequently, McLaren and 'his partner at the time, Vivienne Westwood, designed bondage shirts screen printed with swastikas' (Hoare 2015). Punk swastikas had a do-it-yourself ethos in line with punk's rebellion against commodification. Although these swastikas were not authentic artefacts from the Third Reich, they became authentic expressions of punk culture much in the same way that they had been for Hell's Angels (albeit with less racist intentions). Despite the appropriation of the swastika, punks did not manage to dislodge it from being associated with Nazism. Indeed, had they done so, the symbol would have lost its power, and the punks would have needed another one capable of offending mainstream society (Gottdiener 1985:985). The racist meaning of the swastika was therefore pretty much indestructible, and it remains so to this day.

The appropriation of Nazi symbols by bikers or punks, either replicas or fantasies, threatened Nazi memorabilia as a legitimate hobby, especially within the wider antiques trade. It was partially for this reason that Adrian Forman decided to write his price guide in the 1980s (see Chapter 7). The publication was evidence that Nazi medals were not trash, but desirable collectibles potentially worth thousands of dollars. Few collectors and traders have stated that they explicitly collect Nazi memorabilia for its shock value, although for some collectors, its taboo nature is part of its appeal. In a similar way to violent video games, it is possible that frequent exposure to Nazi symbols makes collectors 'comfortably numb' (Bushman and Anderson 2009). Consequently, despite hostility, they continue to collect. Indeed, they are never satisfied.

In line with earlier punk notions of shock, Nazi symbols have been continually deployed to shock and alarm. An exhibition by the artists Jake and Dinos Chapman featured a book with a brown cover and a gold swastika that revealed their 'almost naive trust in the power of the crooked cross to cause shock and consternation' (Sutcliffe 2011). More puzzlingly, a free speech advocate in America wore a Nazi armband as a form of protest against an anti-fascist crowd at the University of Florida who tried to silence an alt-right personality (DeSouza 2017; Chuba et al. 2017).

In 2005 there was 'Royal Nazi-Prince Harry in Swastika Shock' (Soltis 2005). An article in the *Telegraph* reported the prince wore a 'crude imitation uniform including a swastika armband' (Tweedie and Kallenbach 2005). Yet again, replicas made Nazi uniforms more accessible, with the armband being worn for effect, as Rommel's Afrika Korps did not wear Nazi party insignia on their tropical uniforms. Prince Harry's decision to wear the costume was condemned by the Board of Deputies of British Jews, a spokesperson for whom said, 'it's not a joke to dress up as a Nazi, especially as we come up to the 60th anniversary of the liberation of Auschwitz. It is important that everybody remembers the evil that the Nazis were responsible for' (Jones 2005). Prince Harry wore the outfit at a friend's birthday party which had the theme of Colonials and Natives, thus his choice of costume 'suggested that although Britain and Germany were on opposite sides in World War II, there were similarities between them in their position as imperial forces' (Gilson 2006:96). It has even been claimed that as Harry took the flak, despite his older brother William being present when he chose the costume, it was the catalyst for the breakdown of their relationship (Lacey 2020). The morning after the broadcast in the U.K. of the explosive interview Prince Harry and Meghan, Duchess of Sussex, did with Oprah Winfrey, human rights lawyer Jacqueline McKenzie, whilst supportive of Meghan and Harry, stated that it was important not to forget that Harry had thought it was once acceptable for a royal to dress up in a 'Nazi costume' (BBC March 2021).

In 2015, the British royal family was embroiled in another embarrassing Nazi-related scandal when the *Sun* newspaper released footage of Queen Elizabeth and her sister Margaret as young children performing a Hitler salute around 1933. The footage 'shows the Queen playing with a dog on the lawn in the gardens of Balmoral. The Queen Mother then raises her arm in the style of a Nazi salute and, after glancing towards her mother, the Queen mimics the gesture. Prince Edward, the future Edward VIII, is also seen raising his arm' (BBC July 2015; also see Morgan et al. 2015). Whilst the Queen and her sister could be excused due to their young age (White 2015), more ominous was the presence of their quasi-fascist uncle Prince Edward (Urbach 2019). Behind gestures, at least for some, lies their worldview. Indeed, one of the most disturbing displays of Nazi-inspired insignia being used as an outward expression of antisemitism (and, very probably, Holocaust denial) was the 'Camp Auschwitz' sweatshirt worn during the assault on Capitol Hill on 6 January, 2021 (NatGeo 2021; Simon and Sidner 2021). Under no circumstances, let alone these, could such a blatantly offensive garment be excused in the name of aesthetics or shock.

Conclusion

Nazi daggers, flags, helmets and medals were generally taken home by Allied soldiers as souvenirs rather than as collectors' items. Over time, these relics drifted onto the emerging collectors' market. Regardless of their monetary worth, some argue that such objects should be destroyed, whilst others say that they should be held in public institutions. The swastika was abused by musicians in order to sell records, which on reflection was a rather crass thing to do. One of their aims was to knock Britain out of its postwar stupor, but there were other ways in which to change society rather than wearing the symbol that older generations fought and died to defeat. Some of these musicians not only wore Nazi iconography to shock but were avid collectors.

The social taboo associated with Nazi artefacts has meant that some companies have decided they cannot be involved with the trade. Specialist auction houses and sole traders, many established before the wild-west of the internet era, have filled this void. Ironically, one of the threats to the market in Nazi memorabilia comes from far-right extremists, and without background checks, it would be difficult to control their access to Nazi symbols, either fake or real. If the collecting community fails to clean up its act, then governments may force it to do so. Although specialist militaria auction houses are willing to make a profit from Nazi relics, many of them refuse to engage with academic research. These businesses are aware that Nazi memorabilia is distasteful, as are collectors, but it is not enough to prevent them from selling the swastika. Not only have many Nazi objects defied destruction, but so has the ideology underpinning them. One cannot exist without the other. As such, Nazi symbols need to be handled with extreme care and are perhaps even beyond sensitivity.

On balance, the most appropriate thing to do with Nazi artefacts is for public institutions to keep them. I realise that some museums may not wish to hold Nazi relics, nor may they have the desire to store medals or objects that are undifferentiated. Rather than solely focusing on individual items, however, the commandeered objects could be analysed in terms of how they were formed as a collection. The institutions would therefore essentially be collecting collections, each of which would act as a time capsule of Nazi memorabilia collections held in private hands before their public appropriation. Collectors would naturally disagree with this suggestion, but there is little to support their arguments for keeping Nazi artefacts. Nevertheless, as the desire for private property is strong, it would be difficult to curtail the private ownership of Nazi relics. The danger is that an underground market would develop, which could be even more problematic than the existing one. If Nazi memorabilia was safely and successfully taken into public custody (with the potential for iconoclasm mitigated), it would lose much of the financial value that is attributed to it. Nazi memorabilia would therefore no longer be a source of private veneration and profit.

Notes

1 Isyanova 2009; Fabiansson 2004:166–178; Saunders and Cornish 2009:3.
2 References consulted on the de-Nazification process: Large 1987:79; for background see Schlauch 1970; Marshall 1980.
3 English language newspaper articles often incorrectly state that Nazi memorabilia is banned in Germany (Bell 2012). It is only the public display of Nazi symbols that is prohibited. Claiming the trade is banned merely adds to its taboo and attraction.
4 Müller exhibited an insensitive attitude to profiting from Holocaust-related material when interviewed on camera (Bolz and Bongen 2016).
5 Cornish (2009) made the distinction between war trophies and souvenirs. Trophies could be considered prizes or a reward for defeating one's enemy, for example, a regimental standard that symbolically represents victory when placed in a regimental museum. Souvenirs, on the other hand, have more of an incidental character, for example, shell fragments found on a battlefield. There is no suggestion here that the soldiers financially paid for these kinds of trophies or souvenirs. If soldiers bartered with each other for souvenirs, for example, binoculars, guns and helmets, the objects acquired commodity status.
6 It is possible Anita Pallenberg said she was born in Rome instead of Hamburg to play down her connection to Nazi Germany. Additionally, she may have said she was born in 1944 instead of 1942 to make it seem she was younger on paper. Barber (2008), who met and interviewed Pallenberg, stated she was 'born 25 January 1944 in Rome to a German secretary mother and Italian artist father.' In contrast, Gates (2017) stated, 'Anita Pallenberg was born on April 6, 1942-in Rome according to most sources, in Hamburg according to her son. (Throughout her career, she was said to have been born in Rome on Jan. 25, 1944, while Italy was under Nazi occupation, but both Marlon Richards and the spokeswoman for Keith Richards confirmed that her date of birth was April 6, 1942. Her parents were German: Arnaldo Pallenberg was a sales agent and hobbyist painter; the former Paula Wiederhold worked as a secretary.'
7 Keith Richards appears to be wearing an army parade tunic (*Waffenrock*) but without the breast eagle and swastika. Perhaps he was asked to remove it before appearing on the Ed Sullivan programme. Alternatively, the eagle could have been removed as part of de-Nazification efforts in 1945.
8 For additional articles on Lemmy's Nazi memorabilia collection see BM 2008; MF n.d.

9 Collecting Nazi memorabilia in the 21st century and beyond

The research conducted for this book cannot be separated from the time and place in which it was performed, especially as war veterans and Holocaust victims were still alive at that time and still are today in much smaller numbers. As such, the Second World War continues to generate a great deal of emotional intensity. Nazi war crimes cast a dark shadow over the activities of collectors and re-enactors. Aesthetics is usually given as a reason as to why these military buffs are attracted to Nazi regalia; their attitudes also clouded by the pervasive myth of the clean Wehrmacht. Although many people would rather avoid Nazi artefacts, collectors seek them for their aura. As fakes abound, collectors can never be sure if they are holding a medal that was once pinned to a German soldier's jacket or was made recently. Some collectors have therefore switched their attention to other forms of militaria less prone to being faked. For those who are primarily attracted to the visual side of Nazi regalia, replicas should suffice, although few explicitly collect these, suggesting that most seek something more fundamental. As we increasingly move into a digital society, images of Nazi medals and iconography have become more accessible and can be instantaneously shared. Worryingly, these pictures are prone to being manipulated and transformed into graphics that not only undermine the horrific reality of the Third Reich but are created to spread racial hatred. Furthermore, Nazi memorabilia has generally been restricted by its physicality, but digital technology makes it theoretically possible to create even more profit streams.

Collecting and re-enacting the Nazi past in the present

Why do people collect? More worryingly – why do they collect objects infused with a past which embodies and symbolizes one of humanity's darkest eras? A general difficulty (Nazi memorabilia aside) is that 'even a very serious and reflective collector is hard put to offer a clear, convincing explanation of his inclination or the intense emotion that occasionally occurs in the process of obtaining an object' (Münsterberger 1994:3). Indeed, the 'urge for collecting cannot . . . be satisfactorily explained by the collectors own listings of their motives, be it an alleged interest in the past . . . in the preservation of cultural heritage and traditional technology, in economic investment, etc.' (Rogan 1998:40). It would benefit scholarship and

DOI: 10.4324/9781003000617-9

wider society if Nazi memorabilia collectors ever explained why they are emotionally attached to Nazi regalia or at least identified contributing factors.

The collecting urge often precedes specific interests. Before specialising in
Nazi militaria, Bill Shea collected coins and much more besides (Shea 2017,
pers. comm.).[1] Hamburg-based Helmut Weitze's view is that 'when you are born
a collector you have no choice, I started a collection when I was 11' (Weitze
2018, pers. comm.). The author of 'A Rationale of Collecting' stated that there are
debates as to whether collecting is 'instinctive or acquired, about whether it is a
rational activity or a mental disease (mania being one of the terms often applied
to it, sometimes with affection, sometimes not)' (Tanselle 1998:1). For some, collecting is a mild form of hoarding behaviour, perhaps exacerbated by bereavement
(Cooperman 2019).

Collecting militaria may be a way for family members to keep the memory of
their deceased relatives from fading; this could be the case when a collector gathers
Nazi relics despite their relative once having fought Hitler's Germany. Whilst medals
awarded to a deceased relative have the strongest sentimental value, they might not
have a high financial one, for example, British Second World War campaign stars
(with the exception of the Air Crew of Europe star). In his ethnography of U.S. gun
collectors, Taylor (2008:52–53) noted that some of the guns 'most highly valued in
a collection, eliciting the most emotional response will carry the lowest monetary or
trade value,' such as a sporting gun that was part of an individual's rite of passage.

Some German collectors were influenced by family members who served in
Hitler's armed forces. The late father of Helmut Weitze served in the German
navy and was released from a Russian prisoner-of-war camp after the Second
World War (Weitze 2018, pers. comm.). Weitze started collecting German militaria when he was a child, as did most of the interviewed collectors. This supports
a finding that it was not unusual for children to view German soldiers as having
'cool uniforms with eagles and stuff' (Kingsepp 2006:233). When he was a child
in the late 1950s, trader Bill Shea was fixated by a German army cap eagle, which
belonged to his friend's father, who had presumably brought it back as a war souvenir (Shea 2010).[2] English collector Ian Strachen's late father served in Bomber
Command, and although he did not care to claim the campaign medals he was
entitled to, he supported his teenage son's collecting activities in the 1960s by
buying him a Nazi naval dagger (Strachen 2018, pers. comm.). Auctioneer Ken
Payne's late father participated in the liberation of Bergen-Belsen concentration
camp, and although Payne has no strong objections to selling Nazi memorabilia,
compared to some other traders I interviewed, his tone was more subdued when
discussing Nazi artefacts (Payne 2018, pers. comm.). As there are fewer and fewer
people left who pass on their experiences of the Second World War or the Holocaust, younger generations may fail to grasp the harsh reality behind Nazi relics.

Possessing a collector's instinct together with an interest in Nazi artefacts is an
especially potent combination. Not only is the Third Reich an intense historical
epic, but there is a vast array of objects to choose from. Although the 'presence of
the final object of the collection would signify the death of the subject' (i.e., collector) (Baudrillard 1968, 1996:92), the vast number of Nazi objects circulating

makes this unlikely. Once a series of medals is acquired, another collecting goal can be set. It is perhaps the nature of Nazi memorabilia and militaria in general that it can accommodate the changing tastes of collectors throughout their lives. Even if they lose interest in the Second World War, there is always another conflict they can switch their attention to, whether it be the Napoleonic era or the American Civil War, both of which have their own particular ethical and moral issues (and demographic challenges).

Most interviewed collectors had been exposed to images of the Wehrmacht before seeing Nazi memorabilia at flea markets or similar venues. Collectors have been said to have a particular fascination for 'Stukas, bazookas, and swastikas' (Pearson 2007:2), but can their interest solely be attributed to a desire for big war toys and geometric lines? The closest the majority of collectors got to a Stuka dive-bomber was probably a plastic model kit when they were children. Such a miniature aeroplane would not have been capable of emitting the terrifying shrill of an actual Stuka and so would lack any sensorial dimension. Although Nazi iconography stimulates a collector's interest, it has been claimed that Italian fascist regalia is more aesthetically pleasing (Sears 2018, pers. comm.). Many collectors of Nazi memorabilia do have a few Italian fascist medals, as well as some from the Soviet era. Aesthetics aside, such an amalgamation could be an expression of sympathy for authoritarian or totalitarian regimes.

Collectors and traders are at pains to stress that their interest is not borne out of support for Nazi ideology, with a typical statement in this regard being, 'it's strange, but for some reason, we seem to admire the soldiers of the Third Reich. And I firmly believe it is nothing to do with political leanings' (Fisher 2017, pers. comm.). Seitsonen (2018:142) reported that 'in our over thirty interviews with different stakeholders with an interest in Lapland's WWII German heritage, ranging from militaria collectors and traders to museum people and local villagers, none has appeared as a Nazi fan or a neo-Nazi sympathizer.' Whether or not collectors are filled with Nazi ideology, the artefacts they seek most certainly have politics (Winner 1986). Fisher was blinkered by the visual aspect of Nazi regalia, claiming that the soldiers of the Third Reich were the 'best armed, they were the best uniformed, they looked good' (Fisher 2017, pers. comm.). Similarly, a re-enactor stated that one of his reasons for joining a Waffen-SS re-enacting unit was that they were the 'elite troops and they had the best kit and they had the best uniforms' (Hardman 2018). Another Waffen-SS re-enactor stated, 'people want to look at the bad guys. And the uniforms, the equipment, the insignia – it's just better. It's more interesting' (Ibid.).

Nevertheless, Waffen-SS re-enacting could be a veiled form of racism (Strauss 2001:156). Even though the uniforms worn by re-enactors are usually replicas, they still have 'enormous emotional valence and ritual potency; allowing for dynamic exchange between the present and the past, and between the living and the dead' (Auslander 2013:163). As most collectors shared the opinion that their attraction to the design of Nazi uniforms and medals was one of the reasons why they desired to own them, I ventured beyond Nazi aesthetics by interviewing collectors and traders of imperial era German militaria.

Kenneth Greenfield, a history graduate and American-based collector of and trader in imperial era German militaria, stated that 'I don't think there is any comparison, the sheer beauty of imperial items, compared to those from the Third Reich' (Greenfield and Greenfield 2018, pers. comm.). For this highly specialised trader, the decorations of the Third Reich such as the Nazi Grand Cross worn by Hermann Göring were oversized and garish (Ibid.). Indeed, it has been said that the aesthetic of 'extravagance manifests overstatement, excess, lack of restraint and exaggeration' (Young 2011:159).

For Ken's spouse, Melissa (also a history graduate), the decorations representative of the imperial states were 'so beautiful. It seems to me it is just like the architecture, a lot of what the Third Reich did, was sort of, big and clumsy. It was intimidating, it doesn't have the heart, the soul, the beauty of the earlier decorations' (Greenfield and Greenfield 2018, pers. comm.). Beauty 'is no quality in things themselves: It exists merely in the mind which contemplates them; and each mind perceives a different beauty' (Hume 1757:209). Indeed, aesthetics can be appreciated 'even when the objects exchanged are conventionally defined as symbols of violence and not beauty' (Stenross 1994:29). The longer I talked to the Greenfields, far from the imperial era being beautiful, it became apparent how violent it was – so the issue is riven with contradictions.

Much of the military equipment so emblematic of the Wehrmacht was actually introduced prior to or during the Great War.[3] Consequently, imperial-era military items offer just as much visual appeal as Third Reich objects. Indeed, some militaria traders will display imperial German military artefacts but not overtly Nazi ones. I recall visiting a Scottish-based general antiques and collectibles fair in the early 1990s, in which a militaria trader displayed a Third Reich-era Cross of Honour (see Chapter 4). As this medal did not have any overt Nazi iconography, perhaps the trader mistook it for an imperial decoration. He also had a sword of Third Reich-era manufacture, but again it did not have an eagle and swastika. Indeed, the swastika was omnipresent by its absence on his stall. The trader had served in the British navy during the Second World War, hence had more direct experience of what the swastika meant. Collectors born after the war were more likely to try to separate Nazi ideology from the objects in which it was embedded. This reconciliation helps collectors and traders in justifying their activities.

In keeping with many objects that have become collectible, Nazi regalia has lost its 'rootedness' (Abbas 1988:219). Nazi symbols have been transformed from 'cultic-religious objects into aesthetic artistic ones' (Hasty 2009:464). Commodification has eroded the sacred nature of Nazi relics, although they still have a degree of 'totemic power' (Hubbert 2006:147). Collectors and traders may find it difficult to prevent those with extremist views from acquiring these talismanic objects to incite racial hatred.

The sinister side of the Wehrmacht re-enacting community has already been noted in the previous chapter. Whilst not all re-enactors are collectors, their presence at military displays means that collectors are potentially exposed to an atmosphere of antisemitism and misogyny. Furthermore, the way in which Waffen-SS re-enactors represent the Nazi past is highly sanitised; they are not so much 'dramatizing a past that is already known' but re-shaping it (Cook 2004:487). Re-enactors and collectors are susceptible to romantic notions of the Wehrmacht and the Waffen-SS. Indeed, much of the collectors' literature has been informed by publications written by Waffen-SS veterans who sought to dispel notions that the Waffen-SS had committed atrocities or had any involvement with concentration camps. Revisionists propagate the myth that the Waffen-SS merely 'fought for freedom, for the Fatherland and against Communism' (Hurd and Werther 2016:426). By collectors and re-enactors presenting and performing a narrow interpretation of German military history, it could become the accepted view within the wider public. Indeed, it has been acknowledged that re-enactment 'performs political and cultural work that is quite distinct from more conventional forms of historiography' (Agnew 2004:328).

Popular historians have played their part in boosting the battlefield performance of the German armed forces. Hastings (2015) eulogised the Wehrmacht's performance in his book *Overlord*, although Buckley (2014) contended in *Monty's Men* that the British army was more than a match for the vaunted Nazi war machine. Indeed, far from the Wehrmacht being a mechanised juggernaut endowed with tanks and trucks, it was largely reliant on horse-drawn transport (Balsamo 1991).[4] Hitler's armed forces 'were not quite the juggernaut they must have seemed to their bedazzled opponents or as powerful or superior as the casual student of World War II often continues to assume even today' (Balsamo 1991:265).

Gender dimension

Considering gender is a 'way of referring to the exclusively social origins of the subjective identities of men and women' (Scott 1986:1056). Indeed, male collectors may be reflecting their masculinity (or lack of it) through collecting, trading or wearing combat badges. Military re-enacting can be partly a substitute activity and also the creation of an alter-ego personality. It is the elite regiments of the Waffen-SS that re-enactors are particularly attracted to, which by their very nature means that women are marginalised. A statement on a British-based Waffen-SS re-enacting group reads, 'women must dress and act as their true life counter parts and therefore are excluded from dressing as combatants' (SBG n.d.). Women re-enactors are usually confined to supportive roles such as German Red Cross nurses. On the other hand, physically weak and often grossly overweight men who would not have been accepted into the Waffen-SS are permitted to take part in Waffen-SS role-play, constructing a male fantasy world infused with an alpha male sexual dimension.

Few women collect militaria and Nazi memorabilia in particular, but as women collect other objects, collecting per se is not a male-only activity. This suggests that there is something off-putting about militaria, and Nazi relics especially. It suggests either that there is something inherent in these objects that does not appeal to women or that societal factors are responsible. As the Nazi memorabilia community is dominated by men, women may not feel comfortable in it. Helmut Weitze stated that he only knew a few female collectors, adding, 'Tell me about a woman who is interested in war artefacts?' (Weitze 2018, pers. comm.). He claimed that women who did collect German militaria tended to favour badges of the Winter Help Program (WHW) (see Chapter 3). Perhaps women are attracted to the designs of these badges, as it has been claimed that 'women prefer strong colours and evocative images' (Lakshmi et al. 2017:34). Far from being interested in WHW badges, however, a female collector and trader of Third Reich memorabilia has a large assortment of combat-related items (Burns 2019).[5]

Melissa Greenfield, who collects imperial German swords, stated that 'rather than just seeing them as items that kill people, it is looking at the craft that went into them' (Greenfield and Greenfield 2018, pers. comm.). Another woman interested in imperial-era German items is Singapore-based collector Amy Bellars, who collects spiked helmets (*Pickelhauben*); her interest sparked after she received one as a gift from her husband (Nix 2019).[6] Similarly, it was Melissa's husband, Ken, who purchased two swords for Melissa, although it was she who chose them (Greenfield and Greenfield 2018, pers. comm.). Consequently, the interplay of gender and military objects is a complex matter.

Men routinely collect toy soldiers, so it may be that men and women are simply recapturing their childhoods, most likely conditioned along gendered lines. Some girls who wish to play with soldiers could be discouraged by their parents, either because they are female or because their parents are opposed to war toys (Goossen 2013). Dolls are another case in point, especially debates surrounding G.I. Joe and Barbie. Indeed, the company that made Action Man did not use the term 'doll' in case it discouraged boys from playing with them (Davies 2015). It is not necessarily Barbies or G.I. Joes that reinforce traditional gender roles but the accessories accompanying them. These have traditionally given the message that men fight whilst women perform domestic chores. Nevertheless, boys and girls can break gender stereotypes by manipulating toys, for example, a girl might cut off Barbie's hair to make it short.

It took until 1989 before there was officially an army Barbie (Fennick 1998:93), although she did not have a gun. In 'On Barbie, Guns and Control,' Kathryn Fischer (2006:58) stated it 'seems pretty clear to me that toy guns and plastic-perfect Caucasian dolls are part of our patriarchy and materialistic culture.' Elsewhere, and from a slightly different perspective, it was acknowledged that 'by 1959, girls were ready for a break from maternal expectations – with Barbie, and this produced the same sort of rapidly changing consumer culture for girls as existed for boys since the 1930s based on peer-driven novelty and often with a tinge of rebellion' (Cross 2017a:104). A renewed emphasis for Barbie fire-fighters may inspire girls to take up traditionally male-associated employment (Foster 2018; Davies 2019).

In 2009 the British Ministry of Defence endorsed dolls in the style of G.I. Joe that promoted the modern British armed forces (Ardles 2009). The initial series of figures consisted of male soldiers (Teather 2009), although a female naval medic complete with pistol was added shortly afterwards (HM 2021). The issue of whether boys and girls would rather play with dolls of their respective gender aside, Melissa Greenfield stated that if women are seen with weapons, they may be more likely to collect militaria (Greenfield and Greenfield 2018, pers. comm.).

It took until October 2018 before the British Ministry of Defence allowed women to take part in close combat. The Defence Secretary Gavin Williamson proclaimed that 'women have led the way with exemplary service in the armed forces for over 100 years, working in a variety of specialist and vital roles. So I am delighted that from today, for the first time in its history, our armed forces will be determined by ability alone and not gender' (Gov 2018). In February 2020 it was announced that Rosie Wild was the first woman to pass the British army's 'gruelling' P Company entry test, entitling her to the 'coveted maroon beret' of the paratroopers (BBC February 2020a). These milestones should help to break down gender inequalities, which may partly account for why there are few women militaria collectors.

Collecting immortality

How have Nazi objects survived after 75 years – not only physically, but socially and culturally, when the Third Reich has been such an historical pariah for so long? Although the Nazi regime was the most horrific to date, many people do not wish to destroy the material culture of this time, either for educational reasons, collectible and financial value, or an affinity with Nazism. The cultural understanding of the Second World War is intertwined with collective memory, which consists of 'dreamy reminiscence, personal testimony, oral history, tradition, myth, style, language, art, popular culture, and the built world' (Olick 1999:336). Many of these elements are temporal, but physical remains in the form of memorabilia illustrate something more enduring – perhaps an intentional feature of Nazi material culture large and small Nazi artefacts have a curious ability to suddenly emerge from the dark places in which they were hidden, more often than not appearing on the open market. They are a ghostly reminder of a past that some would rather forget and others wish to celebrate.

Nazi artefacts 'play a central role in negotiating both individual and collective identity in a constantly shifting present' (Hubbert 2006:157).[7] As the way in which the material culture of the Third Reich is portrayed informs our understanding of the past and has implications for future generations, it has to be managed in a responsible manner, which has not always been the case. Collectors who preserve Nazi objects have not been the best at using these artefacts to learn from the past. The Nazi relics that they possess are therefore vulnerable to having their meaning distorted. Another cautionary view is that Nazi objects can be seen 'as evidence of a previous time or event, frequently [maintaining] an unquestioned neutrality that ignores the context in which they were manufactured and utilized' (Trofanenko 2006a:98–99). Many collectors are complicit in this, further contributing to the decontextualization of Nazi badges and medals.

Compressing the past and the future in terms of Nazism's durability is the notion that Hitler and Albert Speer's 'gargantuan monumental structures were to be constructed from extra-thick stone walls, according to the theory of ruin-value, which mandated that the eventual ruins of the thousand-year Nazi Reich would be as impressive as the Roman ruins that Speer and Hitler admired' (Kasher 1992:55). Likewise, our 'continued fascination with ancient Egypt, rests in no small measure upon its monumentality. These people were so successful in their obsessive concern with preserving themselves for the afterlife that their remains permeate our own lives' (Miller 2005:15). Hitler is 'probably the last of the great adventurer-conquerors in the tradition of Alexander, Caesar and Napoleon' (Shirer 1960:x).

The shortage of authentic artefacts from these epochs (Roman coins and Napoleonic militaria aside) means that mass-produced Nazi and Italian fascist emblems are the closest substitutes to relics from monumental empires. Collectors cannot purchase items once worn by Caesar, but they can own objects owned by Hitler, and to a lesser degree by Napoleon. Those interested in historical epochs can of course purchase trinkets in museum gift shops, although they will not have been produced in ancient Rome or Egypt. The ownership of authentic Nazi artefacts therefore allows a collector to experience the aura from one of the most momentous times in history. Of concern here is that this aura is saturated with crimes against humanity.

In November 2020, a popular Danish producer of toy plastic bricks released its largest set ever to date, the Roman Colosseum, with over 9,000 pieces (Julians 2020). Will those who sit down and patiently build the structure realise that the Colosseum was a monument constructed for the 'enjoyment of murder' (Hopkins and Beard 2005:21)? Will there ever be a time in which it will be acceptable to officially release a set based on a Nazi Nürnberg rally?

Even though the Third Reich only lasted for 12 years, as it occurred in a technologically advanced society, it left behind an inordinate amount of material culture. The question is whether in 2,000 years Nazi relics will be as abundant as they are today or as rare as Roman ones are now. Present-day collectors are aware that the Mother's Cross, for example, was awarded to women for having children, but this is dependent on collectors having a historical awareness of the Third Reich. In a hypothetical future in which people knew little about the past, what message would a Nazi Mother's Cross give? The shape of the medal may indicate an affinity with Christianity, although this could be misleading, given that 'National Socialism and Christendom were completely incompatible' (Kellner 2018:404). For the reader of German, the medal's inscription may point towards an association with motherhood, although it would not reveal that the medal was given in exchange for at least four children. The date of 16 December 1938 should not be mistaken for the day on which it was awarded, as this refers to the date of the medal's institution (see Chapter 5). There is also an impression of Hitler's signature, though clearly not of his oratorical skill.

During the Third Reich, the Mother's Cross was far more than its base metal. For a collector, it is an aesthetically appealing medal. In a future society that had no understanding of the Third Reich, the Mother's Cross would be stripped of its auratic value and rendered powerless. As Cameron (2007:57) puts it, if an 'object is dislocated from its systems of meaning its aura is diminished.' Similarly, the 'historicity of a thing is the present awareness of its existence in time, stretching backwards into the past and possibly forwards into the (unknown) future' (Akker 2016:46). As such, the appeal of the Mother's Cross would solely rest in its intrinsic properties. An 'ancient crown is only an important object because of the heads that it has sat upon or were associated with it, and the hands of the people who crafted it. Without these connections, it is only an interesting piece of metal' (Jeffrey 2015:147). A harsher view is that commodities, if we take the Mother's Cross as one, despite 'all their tricks, are just stuff; little combinations of plastics or metal or paper' (Stallabrass 1996:203). If the Mother's Cross lacked its former cultural meaning, it would be unable to initiate a renewed cult of motherhood, nor is it likely to do so today. Nevertheless, right-wing populists and extremists desire to resurrect one. If their aims were realised, would surviving Nazi Mother's Crosses be re-issued?

History 'gives us memory. Without it we have no recall; we are prone to reinvent the wheel, to repeat mistakes and to make rootless decisions' (Darlington 2020:10). Concern has been expressed that as the 'participant generation passes away, the current moment of Second World War cultural memory is suffused with a sense of an imminent ending and of our passing into a new phase of engagement beyond living memory, a phase which – so it is often held – will be the poorer for lacking the validating presence of first-hand witnesses; it may even constitute a kind of closure' (Finney 2017:154). Closure or even erasure may be welcomed by some, as it has been said that 'at a collective level, the risk in our attempt to never forget is that our landscape, metaphorically and literally, becomes so cluttered with our attempts to remember the past that they crowd out our capacity to imagine the future' (Conn 2010:19). Given this, the present and past are inter-related, and one cannot exist without the other. For better or for worse, wartime artefacts will increasingly become one of the only witnesses to the past.

These artefacts will also outlive the people who collect them. The idea of people in objects/objects in people is relevant to a discussion where collectors consider how they might live on through their collections. What 'man gets from objects is not a guarantee of life after death but the possibility, from the present moment onwards, of continually experiencing the unfolding of his existence in a controlled, cyclical mode, symbolically transcending a real existence the irreversibility of whose progression he is powerless to affect' (Baudrillard 1968, 1996:96). In 'Collecting Immortality: The Field Collectors Who Contributed to the Pitt Rivers Museum, Oxford,' Petch (2004:138) stated that 'field collections can be seen as a way of buying immortality. For those field collectors for whom little biographical information is available it is clear that their collections may be the only reason for which their name is now known outside their immediate descendants.'

For the majority of collectors, the best they can hope to achieve is for an artefact they once owned to be credited in collectors' publications read by future collectors. It is rare for collectors of Nazi memorabilia to be commemorated outside the tight-knit collecting community. As much of the motivation for collecting stems from the inner-authentic self, perhaps a collector does not need to be validated through their collection after they die. Indeed, even when 'a collection transforms itself into a discourse addressed to others, it continues to be first and foremost a discourse addressed to oneself' (Baudrillard 1968, 1996:103). Nevertheless, collectors still fret about what will happen to it. So emotionally painful is this topic that the collectors and traders I interviewed did not feel comfortable discussing their collections' ultimate fates.

As Belk (1998:11) observed, it is 'perhaps understandable that family members are often unwilling to preserve the collection of a family member who has died.

It may be a reminder of the deceased, but it is also a reminder of the attention the survivors perceive that it took away from them.' Indeed, 32 percent (which was the largest single group) of respondents to the recent *Military Trader* survey stated that they would 'keep buying until they were in the ground' (Adams-Graf 2020a). I had a dear collector friend subsequently diagnosed with a terminal illness who purchased a Luftwaffe officer's dagger to give his collection a sense of completion.[8] In the main, collectors could not be called field collectors in a traditionally ethnographic sense, as they mainly purchase artefacts from traders. This is not to say that browsing antique shops does not have an experiential value and, furthermore, the journey from a junk shop to an international auction house is a valid aspect of an artefact's biography. Indeed, the ultimate fate of a collection that took a lifetime to accumulate may be its sale at an auction (immortalised by a catalogue).

In the case where a collector did not dispose of their collection before they died, it will most likely be left to their family to do so. The collection could either be a kindly reminder of a lost loved one or an uncomfortable presence that is too painful to view. A widow or widower may even have an uneasy feeling when handling their late partner's collection. Alternatively, they may continue to look after it as their partner did. Uncannily, the 'presence of an absence seems to be the very definition of aura' (Sand 2005:109). In other cases, a collection will have little meaning or value for those who inherit it. An 'object that might have felt like a precious belonging to Mom or Dad might be in a trash heap today; our children will sell, donate, or discard belongings that reflect our stories but have no meaning to them' (Bell and Bell 2012:83). More broadly, such issues have lessons about how objects make family, how families make memories, and how choices about keeping or not keeping objects contribute to the production of family histories and legacies (Ibid:63).

It is likely that the artefacts that were part of both the collection and the person who collected them will be anonymised and disembodied. What remains immutable is the physical artefacts, rather than their social lives. Nevertheless, they will embark upon a new phase and enter new homes as collectors purchase them. Indeed, even though the collection will most probably be broken up, rather than its value resting in its entirety, a test of its worth, certainly as far as the market is concerned, is the ability of its constituent parts to be desired by other collectors on their own merit. It is also at this point that fakes may be discovered, thus a golden goose will turn into a hornet's nest.

Simulating and trading futures digitally and physically

Both technologically mediated and traditional environments have profound implications for the ways in which collectors experience the material culture of the Third Reich. Before the internet, collectors located military objects at dusty flea markets, often offered by casual stallholders unaware of their full market value (opportunities which have diminished over time). Lowly military cap badges snuggled amongst bric-a-brac on trestle tables were spotted by collectors and absorbed into their collections, being re-discovered and consecrated in the process. Many military artefacts (Nazi material aside) can still be found on general online auction platforms, but the items have most likely been categorised and are accessible to wider audiences (local has gone global). Collectors have increasingly turned to specialist traders and auction houses to acquire Nazi memorabilia (both offline and online). This does not preclude undervalued items from being discovered in these outlets, but it is more likely that collectors will have to pay close to the going rate, if not more.

Digital desire

Nazi symbols in digital form offer almost unlimited opportunities for consumption, distortion and replication. Some may even go as far as branding digital objects 'terrorists' (Cameron 2007:50). In contrast to digital images vulnerable to manipulation, a positive virtue of physical Nazi artefacts is that they are less likely to be altered, thus are more reliable witnesses to the past. Nevertheless, as we have already seen, collectors are capable of altering the meaning of physical artefacts.

An advantage of digital photos is that they conveniently take up less physical space than the objects they represent (Belk 2013a). Digital images also offer collectors the ability to arrange the badges in their collection according to multiple categories, much in the same way as digital music (McCourt 2005). Collectors may actually be more reluctant to delete a digital photo than sell a physical artefact. An artwork by Banksy was even deliberately destroyed, then sold as a digital piece of art, fetching just under USD 400,000, about four times more than the price of the physical work cost (i.e., value creation through destruction) (Jeffries 2021). A collector does not necessarily even need a digital photo or artefact to recall to other collectors that they once owned a particular item.

In the main, it is debatable whether collectors would value digital photos over physical objects they could hold (either replicas or originals). Due to their tactility, it could well be that even physical replicas eclipse digital photos of authentic badges. Nevertheless, neither a digital photo of an original badge nor a reproduction made from metal were worn by a German soldier during the Third Reich, hence both lack aura. As such, digital photos are unlikely to supplant the longing for authentic Nazi badges. Indeed, a digital image acts entirely in service of the authentic object it represents (Cameron 2007:59).

In March 2021 Christies auctioned a piece of digital art by Mike Winkelmann entitled 'Everydays: The First 5000 Days' for USD 69 million (Christies 2021; Guardian 2021). The key aspect of this sale, apart from the work being entirely in the digital realm, is that the buyer can claim to be the legitimate owner due to a non-fungible token linked to a computerised blockchain (Schiller and Skillicorn 2021). A 'blockchain is a decentralized network which keeps transaction records and acts as a source of trust. The data stored on the blockchain is immutable and updated by the peer-to-peer network' (Musan 2020:7). In contrast to a cryptocurrency like Bitcoin, where one Bitcoin is worth one Bitcoin (just like swapping one physical note for another), a non-fungible token is not automatically exchangeable for another. Its value is established much in the same way as a physical piece of art (Derrick 2021). As such, non-fungible tokens 'prove that an item is one of a kind and are aimed at solving a problem central to digital collectibles: how to claim ownership of something that can be easily and endlessly duplicated' (Guar 2021). Not only is this an issue for digital goods, but as we have already seen, the physical market in Nazi memorabilia lacks transparency. Nevertheless, it is also possible to link physical objects to a blockchain (Kapilkov 2020). If utilised, blockchain technology would help to alleviate collectors' concerns about authenticity.

In relation to non-fungible digital goods, they only 'have value in the context of their ecosystem. So instead of continuing to push for tokenizing anything and everything, the better path forward is working with physical objects that have existing ecosystems built around them' (Radocchia 2018). As such, the already established market for physical Nazi artefacts would be a prime candidate for conversion into the digital realm. Indeed, non-fungible tokens are potentially 'viable as an item for trade and re-trade, and for profit, much like existing art' (Owen 2021). A cynical view is that the 'digital commodity is refigured continuously, emblematic of the ability of capitalism to endlessly reinvent itself' (McCourt 2005:252).

A collector would presumably obtain social capital from owning a rare medal converted into a digital good. Symbolic 'consumption is a communication act and a tool for building social bonds and distinctions' (Animesh et al. 2011:791). Even in the 'virtual world, stuff matters' (Boss 2007). Nevertheless, whilst 'digital possessions can be objects of self extension, they may not be as effective as material possessions' (Belk 2013a:481). Digital medals, however, may give collectors the opportunity to own a medal whose physical cost is prohibitive. This could lead to the scenario of one collector owning the physical example and another collector owning it in digital form. Non-fungible tokens also introduce additional complexities for museums that hold medals imbued with the aura of controversial historical figures, for example, Henry Ford's German Eagle Order (see Chapter 4). Non-fungible tokens may be the very thing that forces it out of its box. Digital Nazi medals raise just as many ethical and moral issues as their physical display and trade.

Collectors as producers

Three-dimensional printers theoretically enable collectors to produce their own physical representations of medals. Having said this, I am not aware of any collectors of Nazi medals who are currently doing this, although it is likely it would appeal to them, especially those experienced in building model kits. For the first time, 3-d printing gives collectors the means of production, enabling them to produce tangible representations of the medals they own and those they do not (provided the necessary files are available). The question is whether these 3-d representations would possess an aura (Jeffrey 2015:148–9). It has been claimed that the 'desire for immediacy and for auratic experience has paradoxically survived in the face of increasing levels of mediation that digital technology makes possible'

(Bolter et al. 2006:34). Nevertheless, 3-d representations are unlikely to supplant original Third Reich badges.

This being said, 3-d representations have an element of inalienability and are thereby intimate extensions of a collection (Jones 2010). An advantage of 3-d printing is that it would allow collectors to simultaneously display their medals in multiple ways. Collectors could display a 3-d representation of a scarce and expensive medal such as the Knight's Cross on a uniform, whilst displaying the original alongside other Iron Crosses. These self-generated 3-d representations would not devalue the collection in the same way that introducing replicas from the open market would. Moreover, 3-d representations made from resin are unlikely to fool other collectors if they ever appear on the market. In the interest of transparency, however, they should be inscribed in such a way that indicates when they were produced.

Three-dimensional printing permits personalisation, thus collectors could inscribe their medals with their name (Anastasiadou and Bettese 2019). By a collector personalising replicas, they further contribute to Nazi badges being distanced from their 'traditional place in communal or institutional ritual' (Hasty 2009:464–5). Collectors producing for other collectors may find themselves having to inscribe the 3-d representations with the names of other collectors, and whilst this type of commodification is likely to get out of control, it does provide an element of uniqueness to each of the 3-d representations. A biography would therefore emerge of these 3-d representations and the collectors who owned them. Furthermore, if the collector who produced the 3-d representations for other collectors also inscribed them with their own initials, they would be stamping the objects with an artistic identity. This process would further distance these 3-d representations from the artists and companies who originally produced the medals during the Third Reich. The production of 3-d representations entails more responsibility than purchasing authentic medals with a view to re-sale. A collector can only sell one physical original, but they can offer many 3-d representations. If a market did emerge, profit motives would most likely take over.

Three-dimensional representations 'exist in a somewhat awkward place in the discussion of authenticity' (Garstki 2017:743). Whilst 3-d representations could not be considered as unique works of art, they theoretically provide collectors with the opportunity to scale up aspects of a badge they find particularly interesting, thereby creating a new piece of art. Three-dimensional printing allows for a 'chain of reproductions, where each reproduction is created based on a previous reproduction' (Grishko et al. 2020:454). In such a scenario, it is the initial reproduction that is closer to the authentic article than a laser scan of a copy that is then scanned, leading to another copy. The question is whether a badge produced during the Third Reich will be able to retain its authority amongst a barrage of derivatives and tributes. Far from erasing the auratic value of authentic articles, the copies would be in the shadow of their psychic power. A collector who owns an original badge would therefore command the most prestige within the collecting community. Indeed, collectors may continue to travel many miles and spend large amounts of money to handle or acquire authentic Nazi relics. Mundane replicas or 3-d representations are unlikely to attract the same degree of intense interest. In contrast to a copy, a 'visitor to the Louvre comes to see the original Venus de Milo, with its complex history of transmission from the island of Melos in the 2nd century BC to the Louvre in the present' (Bolter et al. 2006:25). Nevertheless, art enthusiasts may travel to see high-quality replicas in museums, especially if the installations enable an artist's entire body of work to be exhibited (Bohn 1999).

The question is whether a public institution should be permitted to display a replica of an original that they do not own. This has consequences if a museum wished to display replicas of rare Nazi artefacts that they would otherwise not be able to display (because they either are held in private collections or have been destroyed). Replication, whether digital or physical, prolongs the life of Nazi artefacts that some would rather see destroyed or hidden from view. Some museums do display replica artwork, although it might not be identified as such. Disclosure has implications in relation to the aura, as displaying a replica could inadvertently increase the sacred value of the original held in storage. To 'take what is remote and unapproachable, hence auratic, and to bring it near to the subject is Walter Benjamin's recipe for destroying aura' (Bolter et al. 2006:28). Given this, the responsible public display of Nazi memorabilia might be a better strategy than concealing it.

Sinking in a sea of copies

An additional consideration is whether increasing numbers of badges advertised as replicas, i.e., not fakes, would devalue authentic badges (Schweibenz 2018). Whilst replicas are competitors, copies are unlikely to displace originals for collectors seeking the aura. In 'contrast to unique works of art, reproductions, as instances of the work, do not determine their own history: their history is determined by the original artwork of which they are a reproduction' (Akker 2016:45). Whilst Nazi mass-produced badges cannot be considered as unique works of art, they are nevertheless authentic.

Replicas intended to deceive complicate the matter. Furthermore, technology 'helps the faker in ways that will become only more sophisticated, more detailed, cheaper and less easy for all but experts to distinguish' (Darlington 2020:12). In certain situations, collectors have even thought original Nazi badges were reproductions. Consequently, advanced collectors have resorted to X-ray spectroscopy to identify the constituent materials of a Nazi Knight's Cross (Maerz 2007). A cautionary view is that the 'more the object is persecuted by experimental procedures, the more it invents strategies of counterfeit, evasion, disguise, disappearance' (Baudrillard 2000:79). Nevertheless, collectors would welcome an accessible piece of portable equipment that would be able to accurately and economically reveal the age of Nazi badges and medals.

In the main, the verification of nominal authenticity rests on the knowledge of collectors who have gathered the necessary expertise. In theory, traders should already possess the relevant knowledge, although this varies. Some traders operate under the unspoken policy that if an item is generally passable, they will offer it for sale. The phrase *caveat emptor* (buyer beware), so synonymous with the antiques trade, permeates the market in Nazi memorabilia. Fakes in collections remain to be discovered by future collectors, and unless deception ceases or a method is found to ferret out the fakes, they will erode confidence in the authenticity of Nazi memorabilia in years to come.

Conclusion

The Second World War was the most cataclysmic in history, and we live in its shadow. The material culture of this conflict is a tactile representation of how the war progressed, the millions of lives lost and the battles won. We owe it to those who were killed, especially the victims of the Holocaust, to ensure that lessons are learned and mistakes not repeated. Key to the rise of Hitler and his totalitarian regime was the exploitation of a people's longing for identity and meaning, for which a few key symbols were appropriated, then replicated in their millions. Although Hitler's dream of a thousand-year Reich died in the bunker with him, many of the symbols that sustained his regime survived. So did some of the uniforms that he wore, and whether they are real or fake, the point is that collectors are prepared to pay large amounts of money for them in the belief that they touched his skin. No wonder many agree that the trade in Hitler relics and Nazi memorabilia should be prohibited. If these talismanic objects are to continue to exist, the safest place for them is museums rather than private homes. Some people also argue that by selling these relics, auction houses and traders are profiting from the victims of the Holocaust. There will always be those who are prepared to trade in contentious relics if there is a demand for them.

Fascination with fascism shows no sign of abating, assisted by the very objects that sustained it in the first place. The temperature of Nazi artefacts needs to be reduced in order that they can be properly understood. Perhaps the Second World War is too much within living memory for this to happen, but we still need to ensure that these contested artefacts are preserved and responsibly displayed (both digitally and physically) as a reminder to future generations to be on their guard against demagogues who seek to entrap nations through political iconography.

Notes

1 Shea also has a large collection of movie car props, including two time machine DeLoreans from *Back to the Future* (Shea 2021).
2 Shea did not indicate how his friend's father acquired the metal German army cap eagle. It could have been either a war trophy or a souvenir (see Chapter 8 for distinction). A German army cap eagle would have been a necessary piece of insignia on an officer's or NCO's peaked cap, so it is unlikely that its wearer would have given it up whilst still serving in the Wehrmacht. It is yet another military artefact whose life story is incomplete.
3 Much of the military equipment and symbols iconic of the Wehrmacht had been in use during the Great War, for example, bread bag, field grey uniform, *Gott mit uns* belt buckle, Iron Cross, S84/98 bayonet, leather ammunition pouches, steel helmet, stick grenade and water bottle.

4 In 1939, when Germany invaded Poland, the army had 590,000 horses; rising to 625,000 when it invaded the Soviet Union on 22 June, 1941; expanding to over one million in oil-strapped Germany in 1945 (DiNardo and Bay 1988:130–135). Over one and a half million horses were killed and also suffered greatly.
5 Despite requests for an interview, the collector did not respond.
6 The iconic German spiked helmet was a keenly sought souvenir during the Great War, becoming more difficult to find on the battlefield after the introduction of the steel helmet in 1916 (Cornish 2009; Randall *et al.* 2009, 2019).
7 Although Hubbert's research focused on Chairman Mao badges, it is relevant to collecting in general, especially badges with a contested nature.
8 At the well-attended funeral, the minister even recalled that before the collector died, he showed him the Luftwaffe second pattern dagger he had just bought. Perhaps the collector was seeking approval for his collection in the afterlife. At the funeral tea, I was seated at the same table as his widow, also testament to the importance the collector placed on his hobby. It was most certainly part of his extended self.

Appendix A

Table A.1 Price data.

Year	Anti-Partisan	Cross of Honour	SS medal	Russian Front	Mother's Cross	Eastern Peoples'
1980	1320.83276	9.172449725	2476.561426	55.03469835	91.72449725	183.4489945
1982	1419.444036	8.349670797	2096.782739	50.09802478	83.49670797	166.9934159
1984	2329.758599	7.765861996	2838.888071	46.59517197	93.19034395	155.3172399
1986	2236.802863	7.456009544	2535.043245	52.19186895	89.47211452	149.1196256
1988	1500.951141	7.147386384	2573.059098	57.17909107	71.47386384	142.9477277
1990	1120.427798	6.831876817	2213.528089	40.9912609	75.15064498	129.8056595
1992	1512.68945	6.40970106	2377.999093	38.45820636	76.91641272	134.6037223
1994	1228.137099	9.357235037	2222.343321	35.08963139	70.17926278	111.1171661
1996	950.9116613	6.712317609	2517.119104	33.56158805	78.31037211	117.4655582
1998	1496.756834	5.54354383	2827.207353	33.26126298	83.15315745	133.0450519
2000	1528.408706	5.500481085	2621.223452	38.50336759	83.06569055	137.5120271
2002	2026.149718	8.761728509	3101.119114	57.17909107	82.14120477	149.518243
2004	1922.479235	10.68044019	3951.762872	42.72176078	85.44352156	106.8044019
2006	2533.662908	14.65755401	3990.892296	52.34840719	104.6968144	146.5755401
2008	2351.204765	18.40073294	4326.72605	61.33577647	122.6715529	153.3394412
2010	2300	20	4200	60	120	160
2012	2239.206084	19.47135725	4575.768953	77.88542899	97.35678624	116.8281435
2014	2911.591238	18.7844596	4414.348006	75.1378384	93.92229799	112.7067576
Standard mean	1829.411939	10.61126702	3103.354016	50.42069307	89.02029145	139.2860398
Geometric mean	1747.544304	9.612291236	2995.319957	48.8511557	87.94583006	137.7763535
Median	1788.478121	8.967089117	2833.047712	50.25935893	86.69467581	138.5311967
Standard deviation	556.4887897	5.154513386	871.7859996	13.18959564	14.81905885	21.08660407
Coefficient of variation	30.41899848	48.57585221	28.09173543	26.1590923	16.64683255	15.13906498
Absolute percent increase	120.4360253	104.7921784	78.24504412	36.5281189	2.396089173	-38.5623465
Geometric annual rate of return (bi-annual)	4.759421727	4.306782926	3.458394155	1.848407216	0.139381365	-2.824904153
Ranked by geometric rate of return	7	8	9	10	11	12
Ranked by geometric mean	3	12	2	11	9	6

Year	Iron Cross 1914	Golden Party	Tank	Submarine	Knight's Cross	Iron Cross 1939
1980	27.51735	825.5205	73.3796	256.8286	3668.98	54.51106
1982	33.39868	851.6664	108.5457	233.7908	4425.326	58.4477
1984	54.36103	1087.221	77.65862	279.571	5436.103	62.1269
1986	52.19187	1043.841	74.5601	268.4163	5219.207	59.64808
1988	50.0317	857.6864	92.91602	221.569	4717.275	71.47386
1990	38.25851	853.9846	88.8144	198.1244	4440.72	61.48689
1992	51.27761	858.8999	96.14552	237.1589	4102.209	76.91641
1994	51.27761	783.6684	99.42062	269.0205	4912.548	76.02753
1996	39.15519	749.5421	95.09117	279.6799	4698.622	78.31037
1998	49.89189	748.3784	127.5015	399.1352	4712.012	88.6967
2000	49.50433	770.0674	126.5111	509.4696	7920.693	88.0077
2002	54.7608	1107.543	177.2068	531.6204	8761.729	98.56945
2004	74.76308	1324.375	213.6088	555.3829	9078.374	117.4848
2006	99.46197	2093.936	198.9239	743.3474	12982.4	125.6362
2008	122.6716	4089.052	214.6752	858.7009	14107.23	112.4489
2010	120	4600	320	800	14000	120
2012	97.35679	3407.488	340.7488	827.5327	11682.81	155.7709
2014	131.4912	3287.28	232.203	798.3395	10894.99	150.2757
Standard mean	66.52062	1630.008	153.2173	459.316	7542.291	91.99106
Geometric mean	59.86045	1298.38	135.2188	400.8787	6766.963	87.21505
Median	53.27645	1065.531	127.0063	400.0069	6101.533	87.61137
Standard deviation	32.80794	1284.481	83.40763	246.2132	3708.237	31.63064
Coefficient of variation	49.31995	78.80211	54.43749	53.60431	49.16593	34.38447
Absolute percent increase	377.8484	298.207	216.4409	210.8453	196.9487	175.6792
Geometric annual rate of return (bi-annual)	9.637278	8.467723	7.011136	6.898889	6.61168	6.146608
Ranked by geometric rate of return	1	2	3	4	5	6
Ranked by geometric mean	10	4	7	5	1	8

Appendix B

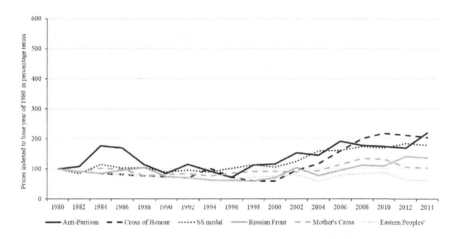

Figure B.1 Time Series of Static Medal prices.

Year	Cross of Honour	Russian Front	Mother's Cross	Eastern Peoples'	SS medal	Anti-Partisan
1980	100	100	100	100	100	100
1982	91.02989	91.02989	91.02989	91.02989	84.66508	107.4658
1984	84.66508	84.66508	101.5981	84.66508	114.6302	176.3856
1986	81.287	94.83448	97.5444	81.2867	102.3614	169.3479
1988	77.92233	103.8964	77.92233	77.92233	103.8964	113.6367
1990	74.48258	74.48258	81.93083	70.75845	89.37909	84.82738
1992	69.87993	69.87993	83.85591	73.37392	96.02019	114.5254
1994	102.0146	63.75911	76.51093	60.57115	89.73504	92.98203
1996	73.17912	60.9826	85.37564	64.03173	101.6377	71.99334
1998	60.4369	60.4369	90.65534	72.52427	114.1586	113.3192
2000	59.96742	69.96199	90.55998	74.95927	105.8412	115.7155
2002	95.52223	103.8964	89.55209	81.50399	125.2187	153.3994
2004	116.4404	77.62696	93.15235	58.22022	159.5665	145.5505
2006	159.7998	95.11891	114.1427	79.89989	161.1465	191.8231
2008	200.6087	111.4493	133.7391	83.58696	174.707	178.0093
2010	218.0443	109.0221	130.8266	87.2177	169.59	174.1326
2012	212.2809	141.5206	106.1404	63.68426	184.763	169.5299
2014	204.7922	136.5281	102.3961	61.43765	178.245	220.436

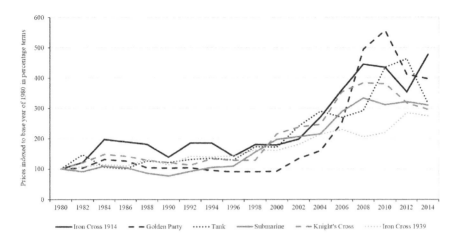

Figure B.2 Time Series of Rising Medal prices.

Year	Iron Cross 1914	Submarine	Knight's Cross	Iron Cross 1939	Tank	Golden Party
1980	100	100	100	100	100	100
1982	121.3732	91.02989	120.6146	107.2217	147.9236	103.1672
1984	197.5519	108.8551	148.1639	113.9712	105.8314	131.7012
1986	189.669	104.5119	142.2523	109.4238	101.6088	126.4465
1988	181.8188	86.27115	128.5718	131.1181	126.6238	103.8964
1990	139.0341	77.14267	121.0342	112.7971	121.0342	103.448
1992	186.3465	92.34133	111.8079	141.1024	131.0249	104.0434
1994	186.3465	104.7471	133.8941	139.4717	135.4881	94.93022
1996	142.2927	108.8975	128.0635	143.6596	129.588	90.79631
1998	181.3107	155.4092	128.4284	162.7132	173.7561	90.65534
2000	179.9022	198.3695	215.8827	161.4492	172.4063	93.28265
2002	199.0046	206.9943	238.8056	180.8247	241.4933	134.1629
2004	271.6943	216.2465	247.4359	215.5248	291.1011	160.429
2006	361.4519	289.4333	353.8424	230.4783	271.0889	253.6504
2008	445.7971	334.3478	384.5	206.2864	292.5544	495.3301
2010	436.0885	311.4918	381.5775	220.1388	436.0885	557.2242
2012	353.8015	322.2121	318.4213	285.7601	464.3644	412.7684
2014	477.8484	310.8453	296.9487	275.6792	316.4409	398.207

Bibliography

Abbas, A. (1988) Walter Benjamin's Collector: The Fate of Modern Experience. *New Literary History* 20 (1): 217–237.

Abel, T. (1938, 1986) *Why Hitler Came Into Power*. Cambridge: Harvard University Press.

Achilles, M. (2010) With a Passion for Reason: Celebrating the Constitution in Weimar Germany. *Central European History* 43 (4): 66–689.

Adams, G. (2015) Lemmy Kilmister of Motorhead made Keith Richards look like a choir boy, *Daily Mail*, December 30, 2015, www.dailymail.co.uk/news/article-3378296/Lemmy-Kilmister-Motorhead-Keith-Richards-look-like-choir-boy.html. Accessed: 04/03/2021

Adams, S. (2000) Collecting Evil, *Forbes*, December 25, 2000, www.forbes.com/forbes/2000/1225/6616164a_2.html. Accessed: 25/08/2013

Adams-Graf, J. (2011) The New Collecting Landscape, *Military Trader*, July 13, 2011. Link no longer accessible when accessed: 07/01/2020

Adams-Graf, J. (2015) JAG's Top 10 Military Collecting Books Of 2014, *Military Trader*, January 7, 2015, www.militarytrader.com/mv-101/jags-top-10-military-collecting-books-of-2014. Accessed: 24/04/2015

Adams-Graf, J. (2019) 10 Questions with LTC (Ret) John R. Angolia, *Military Trader*, November 13, 2019, https://www.militarytrader.com/militaria-collecting-101/10-questions-with-ltc-ret-john-r-angolia. Accessed: 08/10/2021

Adams-Graf, J. (2020a) A Deep Look into Militaria Collectors, *Military Trader*, February 12, 2020, www.militarytrader.com/jagfile/a-deep-look-into-militaria-collectors. Accessed: 14/02/2020

Adams-Graf, J. (2020b) Roger James Bender, *Military Trader*, January 15, 2020, www.militarytrader.com/militaria-collecting-101/roger-james-bender. Accessed: 14/02/2020

Adams-Graf, J. (2020c) 5 Tips for Collecting During the Pandemic, *Military Trader*, March 18, 2020, www.militarytrader.com/militaria-collecting-101/military-collecting-in-isolation. Accessed: 20/03/2020

Addo, P., Besnier, N. (2008) When Gifts Become Commodities: Pawnshops, Valuables, and Shame in Tonga and the Tongan Diaspora. *Journal of the Royal Anthropological Institute* 14 (1): 39–59.

ADL (2021) Swastika, Anti-Deformation League (ADL), www.adl.org/education/references/hate-symbols/swastika. Accessed: 22/11/2019

Adorno, T. (1951) *Minima Moralia*. Marxists.org, www.marxists.org/reference/archive/adorno/1951/mm/index.htm. Accessed: 03/02/2020

Agnew, V. (2004) Introduction: What Is Re-enactment? *Criticism* 46 (3): 327–339.

AHCG (1949) Law Number Seven of the Allied High Commission for Germany, www.cvce.eu/obj/laws_1_to_7_of_the_allied_high_commission_for_germany_bonn_21_september_1949en-bdd976ad-7ff0-4608-8915-14b528cadd02.html. Accessed: 01/02/2020

Ailsby, C. (1987) *Combat medals of the Third Reich*. London: Patrick Stephens, part of Thorsons Publishing Group.

Akker, C. (2016) Benjamin, the Image and the End of History. *Journal of Aesthetics and Phenomenology* 3 (1): 43–54.

Alberti, S. (2005) Objects and the Museum. *Isis* 96 (4): 559–571.

Alexander, L. (1948) War Crimes and Their Motivation: The Socio-Psychological Structure of the SS and the Criminalization of a Society. *Journal of Criminal Law and Criminology* 39 (3): 298–326.

Alford, K. (2018) *Jim Atwood: Army Officer, Charmer, Entrepreneur, Collector, Risk-Taker, Rogue, & Con-Artist*. Self-published. Kindle.

Alford, K., Johnson, T. M., Morris, M. F. (2013) *Sacking Aladdin's Cave: Plundering Herman Göring's Nazi War Trophies*. Atglen: Schiffer Publishing.

Allen, A. T. (2000) Feminism and Eugenics in Germany and Britain, 1900–1940: A Comparative Perspective. *German Studies Review* 23 (3): 477–505.

Allen, K. (2008) Food and the German Home Front: Evidence from Berlin, in *Evidence, History and the Great War: Historians and the Impact of 1914–1918*, edited by Braybon, G. Oxford: Berghahn Books, chapter 8.

Allen, M. (1996) The Puzzle of Nazi Modernism: Modern Technology and Ideological Consensus in an SS Factory at Auschwitz. *Technology and Culture* 37 (3): 527–571.

Allen, M. (2002) Review of: *IBM and the Holocaust: The Strategic Alliance between Nazi Germany and America's Most Powerful Corporation* by Edwin Black. *Technology and Culture* 43 (1): 150–154.

Ames, K. L. (1989) How Culture Shapes Consumption in the Modern World. Review of: Culture and Consumption: New Approaches to the Symbolic Character of Consumer Goods and Activities by Grant McCracken. *American Quarterly* 41 (2): 402–408.

Amineddoleh, L. (2015) Purchasing Art in a Market Full of Forgeries: Risks and Legal Remedies for Buyers. *International Journal of Cultural Property* 22: 419–435.

Anastasiadou, C., Bettese, S. (2019) From Souvenirs to 3D Printed Souvenirs. Exploring the Capabilities of Additive Manufacturing Technologies in Re-framing Tourist Souvenirs. *Tourism Management* 71: 428–442.

Andersen, E. L. (2000) *Charles A. Lindbergh, in A Man's Reach*, edited by Sturdevant, L. Minneapolis: University of Minnesota Press.

Anderson, L., Taylor, J. D. (2010) Standing Out while Fitting In: Serious Leisure Identities and Aligning Actions among Skydivers and Gun Collectors. *Journal of Contemporary Ethnography* 39 (1): 34–59.

Angolia, J. R. (1976) *For Führer and Fatherland: Military Awards of the Third Reich*. San Jose, CA: Roger James Bender.

Angolia, J. R. (1978) *For Führer and Fatherland: Political Awards of the Third Reich*. San Jose, CA: Roger James Bender.

Animesh, A., Pinsonneault, A., Yang, S., Oh, W. (2011) An Odyssey into Virtual Worlds: Exploring the Impacts of Technological and Spatial Environments on Intention to Purchase Virtual Products. *MIS Quarterly* 35 (3) (September 2011): 789–810.

Anon (1942) Policy and Strategy in the War in Russia: The Winter Interlude. *Foreign Affairs* 20 (4): 607–634.

Anon (2017) Chris Farlowe at Priory Park, as part of Festival of Chichester, *Chichester Observer*, June 26, 2017, www.chichester.co.uk/arts-and-culture/chris-farlowe-priory-park-part-festival-chichester-847732. Accessed: 07/03/2021

Anon (2018a) American Auctioneer, Interview with Michael Hughes, Transcript Held by Both Participants.

Anon (2018b) Chris Farlowe – Falling Out of Time, *Eclipsed Rock Magazin*, April 5, 2018, www.eclipsed.de/en/current/chris-farlowe-falling-out-time. Accessed: 07/03/2021

APKM (2011) War Commemorative Medal 1914/1918 of the Kyffhauser Union, *Antique Photos*, https://antique-photos.com/en/awardsdatabase/weimarawards/223-kriegsgedenkmunze.html. Accessed: 24/03/2021

Appadurai, A. (1986) Introduction: Commodities and the Politics of Value, in *The Social Life of Things: Commodities in Cultural Perspective*, edited by Appadurai, A. Cambridge: Cambridge University Press, 3–63.

Appiah, K. (2017) What Should You Do With Your Father's Nazi Keepsake? *New York Times*, March 22, 2017, www.nytimes.com/2017/03/22/magazine/what-should-you-do-with-your-fathers-nazi-keepsake.html. Accessed: 05/03/2021

Ardles, M. (2009) From Action Man to MoD action Figures, *Guardian*, May 7, 2009 www.theguardian.com/uk/gallery/2009/may/07/toys-military. Accessed: 01/03/2021

Arendt, H. (1964) *Eichmann in Jerusalem*. New York: Viking Press.

Argo, J. J., Dahl, D. W., Morales, A. C. (2006) Consumer Contamination: How Consumers React to Products Touched by Others. *Journal of Marketing* 70 (2): 81–94.

Arm. *Militaria History, The Armourer Magazine and Classic Arms & Militaria Magazine*. Bourne: Warners Group Publications, www.thearmourer.co.uk. Accessed: 28/01/2019

Armstrong, H. F. (1933) Hitler's Reich: The First Phase. *Foreign Affairs* 11 (4): 589–608.

Arnold, B. (2006) Arierdämmerung: Race and Archaeology in Nazi Germany. *World Archaeology* 38 (1): 8–31.

Arnold, B., Hassmann, H. (1996) Chapter 5 Archaeology in Nazi Germany: The Legacy of the Faustian Bargain, in *Nationalism, Politics and the Practice of Archaeology, New Directions in Archaeology*, edited by Kohl, P. L., Fawcett, C. Cambridge: Cambridge University Press, 70–81.

Ashenfelter, O., Graddy, K. (2011) Sale Rates and Price Movements in Art Auctions. *American Economic Review* 101 (3): 212–216.

Assmann, K. (1950) The Battle for Moscow, Turning Point of the War. *Foreign Affairs* 28 (2): 309–326.

ATAA. Auktionshaus Andreas Thies, Orden, Ehrenzeichen und militärhistorische Antiquitäten, www.andreas-thies.de. Accessed: 02/01/2020

ATG (2019) But why is it White Glove Sale? *Antiques Trade Gazette*, April 29, 2019, www.antiquestradegazette.com/print-edition/2019/may/2390/letters-opinion/but-why-is-it-white-glove-sale/ Accessed: 24/03/2021

Auslander, M. (2013) Touching the Past: Materializing Time in Traumatic Living History Re-enactments. *Signs and Society* 1 (1): 161–183.

Austerlitz, S. (2018) Remembering Meredith Hunter, the Fan Killed at Altamont, *Rolling Stone*, July 9, 2018, www.rollingstone.com/feature/remembering-meredith-hunter-the-fan-killed-at-altamont-630260/ Accessed: 08/03/2021

AV1. Avalon Project: Nazi Conspiracy and Aggression – Volume I Chapter VII. B. Control Acquired, https://avalon.law.yale.edu/imt/chap_07.asp. Accessed: 15/01/2020

AV2. The Avalon Project, Nuremberg Trial Proceedings Vol. 13, One Hundred and Twenty-fifth day. Thursday, May 9, 1946, morning session, https://avalon.law.yale.edu/imt/05-09-46.asp. Accessed: 15/01/2020

AV3. The Avalon Project: Nuremberg Trial Proceedings Vol. 9. Monday, March 11, 1946, https://avalon.law.yale.edu/imt/03-11-46.asp. Accessed: 31/01/2021

AV4. The Avalon Project: Nuremberg Trial Proceedings Vol. 5, Thirty-third Day. Monday, 14 January 1946, Morning Session. Accessed: 03/02/2021

Avery, A. E., Colonna, C. M. (1987) The Market for Collectible Antique and Reproduction Firearms: An Economic and Financial Analysis. *Journal of Cultural Economics* 11 (2): 49–64.

Avitabile, R. (2019) Pawn Stars' Antiques Dealer Defends Decision to Auction Uniform Worn by Hitler, *NBC 7 San Diego*, September 27, 2019, www.nbcsandiego.com/news/local/adolf-hitler-nazi-germany-uniform-auction-sale-craig-gottleib-pawn-stars-holocaust/153123/. Accessed: 15/12/2019

BA 33. Martin Heidegger. NSDAP record, Bundesarchiv.

BArch R9361-IX KARTEI 14160951. NSDAP-Gaukartei, Martin Heidegger, Eingetragen: 1. Mai 1933. Mitgl.-Nr: 3125894.

BArch R9361-VIII KARTEI 9400982. NSDAP-Zentralkartei, Martin Heidegger, Eingetragen: 1. Mai 1933. Mitgl.-Nr: 3125894.

BAA (2019) Bosleys Specialist Military and Medal Auctioneers, November 6, 2019, Militaria Auction, Third Reich items from lot 702 to 741. Marlow Buckinghamshire, England, www.bosleys.co.uk/en-GB/6th-november/auction_10021. Accessed: 02/01/2020

BAA (2020) Bosleys statement on Covid-19. March 26, 2020, www.bosleys.co.uk. Accessed: 26/03/2020

Bade, W. (Ed.) (1933) *Deutschland Erwache*. Berlin: Cigarette card album.

Bailey, S. (1825) *A Critical Dissertation on the Nature, Measures and Causes of Value*. London: R. Hunter.

Baker, S. M., Motley, C. M., Henderson, G. R. (2004) From Despicable to Collectible: The Evolution of Collective Memories for and the Value of Black Advertising Memorabilia. *Journal of Advertising* 33 (3): 37–50.

Bakker, T. (2018) *Objects in the Age of Virtual Reproduction: Aura and the Elusive Third Axis*. Master's thesis, Canada: OCAD University.

Balchin, W. G. B. (1944) The Swastika. *Folklore* 55 (4): 167–168.

Baldwin, N. (2003) *Henry Ford and the Jews: The Mass Production of Hate*. New York: Public Affairs.

Ball, S. (2004) The German Octopus: The British Metal Corporation and the Next War, 1914–1939. *Enterprise & Society* 5 (3): 451–489.

Balsamo, L. T. (1991) Germany's Armed Forces in the Second World War: Manpower, Armaments, and Supply. *History Teacher* 24 (3): 263–277.

Baranowski, S. (2004) *Strength through Joy: Consumerism and Mass Tourism in the Third Reich*. Cambridge: Cambridge University Press.

Barber, L. (2008) Lady Rolling Stone, *Guardian*, February 24, 2008, www.theguardian.com/film/2008/feb/24/1. Accessed: 07/03/2021Barkai, A. (1990) *Nazi Economics: Ideology, Theory, and Policy*. Oxford: Berg.

Barron, S. (1991) *The Fate of the Avant Garde in Nazi Germany, Los Angeles Museum of Art*. New York: H.N. Abrams.

Barthes, R. (1988) Plastic. *Perspecta* 24: 92–93.

Bartov, O. (1992) *Hitler's Army: Soldiers, Nazis, and War in the Third Reich*. Oxford: Oxford University Press. Kindle.

Bartov, O. (2003) Review of: Soldiers as Citizens: Former Wehrmacht Officers in the Federal Republic of Germany, 1945–1955 by Jay Lockenour. *German Politics & Society* 21 (2): 112–116.

Bass, W. (1987) Perfect Copies. *Journal of Aesthetics and Art Criticism* 46 (2): 293–297.

Bassler, G. (1973) The Communist Movement in the German Revolution, 1918–1919: A Problem of Historical Typology? *Central European History* 6 (3): 233–277.

Baudrillard, J. (1968, 1996) *The System of Objects*. London: Verso.

Baudrillard, J. (1981) *For a Critique of the Political Economy of the Sign*. New York: Telos Press.

Baudrillard, J. (2000) *The Vital Illusion*. New York: Columbia University Press.

Bauer, Y. (1980) Genocide: Was it the Nazis' Original Plan? *Annals of the American Academy of Political and Social Science* 450: 35–45.

Bauer, Y. (1983) The Death-Marches, January-May, 1945. *Modern Judaism* 3 (1): 1–21.

Bauman, Z. (1989) *Modernity and the Holocaust*. New York: Ithaca, Cornell University Press. Kindle.

BB (2018) David Bowie: Britain Could Benefit from a Fascist Leader, *Bowie Bible*, Original Interview April 26, 1976, date of online Article March 8, 2018, www.bowie bible.com/1976/04/26/david-bowie-britain-could-benefit-from-a-fascist-leader/ Accessed: 07/12/2020

BB (2021) Kaufkraftäquivalente historischer Beträge in deutschen Währungen. www.bundes bank.de/resource/blob/615162/d55a20f8a4ecedd6d1b53e01b89f11c4/mL/kaufkrataequiv alente-historischer-betraege-in-deutschen-waehrungen-data.pdf. Accessed: 15/06/2021

BBC (January 2007) Hindus Opposing EU Swastika Ban, *BBC News*, January 17, 2007, http://news.bbc.co.uk/1/hi/6269627.stm. Accessed: 22/11/2019

BBC (March 2012) Dreweatts in Bristol Stops Selling Holocaust-related Items, *BBC News*, March 21, 2012, www.bbc.co.uk/news/uk-england-bristol-17446565. Accessed: 09/10/2019

BBC (April 2014) France Auction House Cancels Nazi Memorabilia Sale, *BBC News*, April 14, 2014, www.bbc.co.uk/news/world-africa-27028990. Accessed: 28/07/2014

BBC (July 2015) Queen Nazi Salute Film: Palace 'Disappointed' at Use, *BBC News* online, July 18, 2015, www.bbc.co.uk/news/uk-33578174. Accessed: 12/06/2021

BBC (November 2018) National Action Trial: Three Guilty of Neo-Nazi Group Membership, *BBC News*, November 12, 2018, www.bbc.co.uk/news/uk-england-oxford-shire-46151838. Accessed: 22/11/2019

BBC (March 2019) Fury at 'Sick' Hitler Tablecloth Sale in Belfast, *BBC News*, March 11, 2019, www.bbc.co.uk/news/uk-northern-ireland-47523018. Accessed: 27/05/2019

BBC (February 2020a) Start the Week, Dresden 75 Years On, Tom Sutcliffe Discusses the Bombing of Dresden and its Aftermath with Sinclair McKay, Edmund de Waal, Stefanie Bolzen, and Sasha Havlicek, *BBC Radio 4*, Broadcast February 10, 2020, 9am, www. bbc.co.uk/programmes/m000f6sm. Accessed: 11/02/2020

BBC (February 2020b) British Army Officer Becomes First Woman to Pass Brutal Para Course, by Jonathan Beale, *BBC News*, February 18, 2020, www.bbc.co.uk/news/ uk-51553815. Accessed: 19/02/2020

BBC (March 2020c) Coronavirus: Continuing Issues with Protective Kit for NHS, says Minister, *BBC News*, March 25, 2020, www.bbc.com/news/uk-wales-politics-52035545. Accessed: 04/04/2020

BBC (June 2020d) Edward Colston Statue Graffiti will be Preserved, *BBC News*, June 17, 2020, www.bbc.co.uk/news/uk-england-bristol-53083939. Accessed: 03/03/2021

BBC (March 2021) *Today* Programme, *BBC Radio 4*, March 9, 2021, 08:14 hours, Jacqueline McKenzie as guest. Subject: Meghan Markle and Prince Harry Interview with Oprah Winfrey.

Beadle, A. (2004) *German Combat Awards 1939–1945*. Self-published: Printed by Pims Print, England.

Becker, T. (2018) Nazi-Nostalgia? Looking Back on the 1970s Hitler Wave. Lecture delivered at University College London, Institute of Advanced Studies, March 21, 2018. Text of talk kindly supplied by Tobias Becker to Michael Hughes.

Begler, T. (2013) Electronic Communication from Tim Begler, Archivleiter at the City Archive in Lüdenscheid, to Michael Hughes, April 23, 2013.

Behn, N. (1995) *Lindbergh: The Crime*. London: Penguin.

Belk, R. W. (1988) Possessions and the Extended Self. *Journal of Consumer Research* 15 (2): 139–168.

Belk, R. W. (1998) The Double Nature of Collecting: Materialism and Anti-Materialism. *Etnofoor* 11 (1): 7–20.

Belk, R. W. (2013a) Collectors and Collecting, in *Handbook of Material Culture*, edited by Tilley, C., Keane, W., Kuechler, S., Rowlands, M., Spyer, P. London: SAGE Publications, 534–545.

Belk, R. W. (2013b) Extended Self in a Digital World. *Journal of Consumer Research* 40 (3): 477–500.

Belk, R. W., Coon, G. S. (1993) Gift Giving as Agapic Love: An Alternative to the Exchange Paradigm Based on Dating Experiences. *Journal of Consumer Research* 20 (3): 393–417.

Belk, R. W., Wallendorf, M., Sherry, J. F. (1988) Collectors and Collecting. *Advances in Consumer Research* 15: 448–553.

Belk, R. W., Wallendorf, M., Sherry, J. F., Holbrook, M. B. (1991) Collecting in a Consumer Culture, in *Highways and Buyways: Naturalistic Research from the Consumer Behavior Odyssey*, edited by Belk, R. W. UT, P: Association for Consumer Research, 178–215.

Bell, L. V. (1970) The Failure of Nazism in America: The German American Bund, 1936–1941. *Political Science Quarterly* 85 (4): 585–599.

Bell, M. (2012) In Search of the Nazi Memorabilia Collectors, *Independent*, March 11, 2012, www.independent.co.uk/news/uk/home-news/in-search-of-the-nazi-memorabilia-collectors-7555059.html. Accessed: 06/08/2013

Bell, M. E., Bell, S. E. (2012) What to Do with All this Stuff? Memory, Family, and Material Objects. *Storytelling, Self, Society* 8 (2): 63–84.

Bell, M. L., Fiero, M., Horton, N. J., Hsu, C. H. (2014) Handling Missing Data in RCTs: A Review of the Top Medical Journals. *BMC Medical Research Methodology* 14: 118.

Bell, P. M. H. (2011) *Twelve Turning Points of the Second World War*. New Haven: Yale University Press.

Below, N. von (1980) *At Hitler's Side*. Barnsley: Frontline Books (an imprint of Pen and Sword).

Benjamin, W. (1931, 1968) Unpacking My Library, in *Illuminations*, translated by Zohn, H., edited by Arendt, H. New York: Schocken.

Benjamin, W. (1936) The Work of Art in the Age of Mechanical Reproduction. Philosophy Archive at marxists.org, www.marxists.org/reference/subject/philosophy/works/ge/benjamin.htm. Accessed: 02/11/2019

Bennett, J. (2004) The Force of Things: Steps Toward an Ecology of Matter. *Political Theory* 32 (3): 347–372.

Bennett, J. (2010) *Vibrant Matter*. Durham: Duke University Press.

Berg, S. (1999) *Lindbergh*. New York: Berkley Books.

Berger, M. (2006) *Eisernes Kreuz und Davidstern*. Berlin: Trafo Verlag.

Berlis, A. (2016) Conference Paper Delivered by Angela Berlis Entitled Death on the Battlefield-mourning Cards as Memorials, Faith in the First World War. Conference, University of Glasgow, July 23, 2016.

Bershidsky, L. (2019) Nazi Memorabilia Is Selling, But Who Is Buying? *Bloomberg*, November 21, 2019, www.bloomberg.com/opinion/articles/2019-11-21/who-bought-hitler-s-top-hat-the-public-has-a-right-to-know. Accessed: 11/03/2021

Berta, P. (2019) *Materializing Difference: Consumer Culture, Politics, and Ethnicity among Romanian Roma*. Toronto: University of Toronto Press.

Bessel, R. (2004) The Nazi Capture of Power. *Journal of Contemporary History* 39 (2): 169–188.

Bianchi, M. (1997) Collecting as a Paradigm of Consumption. *Journal of Cultural Economics* 21 (4): 275–289.

Biglaiser, G. (1993) Middlemen as Experts. *RAND Journal of Economics* 24 (2): 212–223.

BIN (1939) Herr Hitler's Speech on October 10, *Bulletin of International News* 16 (21) (October 21, 1939): 25–26.

Binchy, D. A. (1937) Paul Von Hindenburg 1847–1934. *Studies: An Irish Quarterly Review* 26 (102): 223–242.

Binelli, M. (2009) Lemmy Kilmister: Vampire of the Sunset Strip, *Rolling Stone*, October 29, 2009, www.rollingstone.com/music/music-news/lemmy-kilmister-vampire-of-the-sunset-strip-181614/ Accessed: 09/10/2020

Binion, R. (1974) Foam on the Hitler Wave. *Journal of Modern History* 46 (3): 522–528.

Binyon, L. (1914, 2014) For the Fallen by Laurence Binyon, *Poetry Foundation*, www.poetryfoundation.org/poems/57322/for-the-fallen. Accessed: 08/02/2021

Black, E. (2001) *IBM and the Holocaust: The Strategic Alliance Between Nazi Germany and America's Most Powerful Corporation.* New York: Crown.

Blechen, S. (2013) Electronic Communication from Simone Blechen, Steinhauer und Lück Lüdenscheid, to Michael Hughes, December 12, 2013.

Blee, K. M. (1993) Evidence, Empathy, and Ethics: Lessons from Oral Histories of the Klan. *Journal of American History* 80 (2): 596–606.

Bleich, E. (2011) The Rise of Hate Speech and Hate Crime Laws in Liberal Democracies. *Journal of Ethnic and Migration Studies* 37 (6): 917–934.

Blood, P. W. (2006) *Hitler's Bandit Hunters: The SS and the Nazi Occupation of Europe.* Sterling: Potomac Books (acquired by University of Nebraska Press in 2013). Kindle.

Blood, P. W. (2010) Securing Hitler's Lebensraum: The Luftwaffe and Bialowieza Forest, 1942–1944. *Holocaust and Genocide Studies* 24: 247–272.

BM (2008) Motörhead's Lemmy Under Investigation for Displaying Nazi Insignia, *Blabbermouth.Net*, July 9, 2008, www.blabbermouth.net/news/mot-rhead-s-lemmy-under-investigation-for-displaying-nazi-insignia/ Accessed: 04/10/2014

BMJG. Gesetz über Titel, Orden und Ehrenzeichen, Bundesministerium der Justiz, www.gesetze-im-internet.de/ordeng/index.html. Accessed: 07/01/2020

Boak, H. (2013) *Women in Weimar Germany.* Manchester: Manchester University Press.

Bock, G. (1983) Racism and Sexism in Nazi Germany: Motherhood, Compulsory Sterilization, and the State. *Signs* 8 (3): 400–421.

Bogolitsyna, A., Pichler, B., Vendl, A., Mikhailov, A. (2009) Investigation of the Brass Monument to Minin and Pozharsky, Red Square, Moscow. *Studies in Conservation* 54 (1): 12–22.

Bohn, J. W. (1999) Museums and the Culture of Autography. *Journal of Aesthetics and Art Criticism* 57 (1): 55–65.

Boissoneault, L. (2017) The Man Who Brought the Swastika to Germany, and How the Nazis Stole It, *Smithsonian Magazine*, April 6, 2017, www.smithsonianmag.com/history/man-who-brought-swastika-germany-and-how-nazis-stole-it-180962812/ Accessed: 25/03/2021

Bolt, D. (2013) Aesthetic Blindness: Symbolism, Realism, and Reality. *Mosaic: A Journal for the Interdisciplinary Study of Literature* 46 (3): 93–108.

Bolter, J. D., MacIntyre, C., Gandy, M., Schweitzer, P. (2006) New Media and the Permanent Crisis of Aura. *Convergence* 12 (1): 21–39.

Bolz, B., Bongen, R. (2016) *AfD-Spitzenkandidat handelt mit Hakenkreuzen, Das Erste – Panorama – Sendungsarchiv*, September 22, 2016, https://daserste.ndr.de/panorama/

archiv/2016/AfD-Spitzenkandidat-handelt-mit-Hakenkreuzen,afdsaarbruecken100.
html. Accessed: 08/10/2021

Bontje, M. (2004) Facing the Challenge of Shrinking Cities in East Germany: The Case of Leipzig. *Geo Journal* 61 (1): 13–21.

Boss, S. (2007) Even in a Virtual World, Stuff Matters, *New York Times*, September 9, 2007, www.nytimes.com/2007/09/09/business/yourmoney/09second.html. Accessed: 04/01/2021

Bosworth, D. (2000) Idiot Savant: Henry Ford as Proto-Postmodern Man. *Georgia Review* 54 (1): 11–39.

Bowen, D. E. (1986) *The Prussian and German Iron Cross 1813, 1870, 1914, 1939 and 1957 (addenda to first edition)*. Iron Cross Research Publications.

Bowers, M. (2017) Telephone Interview between Malcolm Bowers and Michael Hughes, transcript held by both participants. Permission granted.

Boxer, S. (2000) Think Tank; A Symbol of Hatred Pleads Not Guilty, *New York Times*, July 29, 2000, www.nytimes.com/2000/07/29/arts/think-tank-a-symbol-of-hatred-pleads-not-guilty.html. Accessed: 19/12/2020

BP. (n.d.) Bender Publishing, About Us, www.bender-publishing.com/AboutUs.html. Accessed: 08/10/2015

Brady, N. (2016) Iron in the Soul. *Building Material* (20): 151–169.

Brandt, S. (1994) The Memory Makers: Museums and Exhibitions of the First World War. *History and Memory* 6 (1): 95–122.

Breitman, R. (1991) Himmler and the 'Terrible Secret' Among the Executioners. *Journal of Contemporary History* 26 (3/4): 431–451.

Brendon, P. (2013) Mick Jagger at 70: A Rock God? No, a Silly Old Phoney! As Rolling Stones Frontman Turns 70, Still Basking in Adulation from Sell-out Concerts, a Top Historian has a Provocative View, *Daily Mail*, July 27, 2013, www.dailymail.co.uk/news/article-2379658/Mick-Jagger-70-A-rock-god-No-silly-old-phoney-As-Rolling-Stones-frontman-turns-70-basking-adulation-sell-concerts-historian-provocative-view.html. Accessed: 07/03/2021

Bridenthal, R. (1973) Beyond Kinder, Küche, Kirche: Weimar Women at Work. *Central European History* 6 (2): 148–166.

Brinton, C. (1942) Napoleon and Hitler. *Foreign Affairs* 20 (2): 213–225.

Brooke, S. (2001) A New World for Women? Abortion Law Reform in Britain during the 1930s. *American Historical Review* 106 (2): 431–459.

Brown, B. (2001) Thing Theory. *Critical Inquiry* 28 (1): 1–22.

Brown, J. (2019) Trading in Nazi Artifacts, Historical or Immoral? *Times of Israel*, January 13, 2019, https://blogs.timesofisrael.com/trading-in-nazi-artifacts-historical-or-immoral/. Accessed: 26/05/2019

Brown, K. (2019a) View of Private Influence, Public Goods, and the Future of Art History. *Journal for Art Market Studies*, ISSN: 2511–7602, www.fokum-jams.org/index.php/jams/article/view/86/157. Accessed: 08/03/2021

Brown, T. S. (2013) The SA in the Radical Imagination of the Long Weimar Republic. *Central European History* 46 (2): 238–274.

Brownfield, T. (2020) The True Story of Kelly's Heroes, *Saturday Evening Post*, June 23, 2020, www.saturdayeveningpost.com/2020/06/the-true-story-of-kellys-heroes/. Accessed: 26/02/2021

Browning, C. (1992, 2001) *Ordinary Men: Reserve Police Battalion 101 and the Final Solution in Poland*. London: Penguin Books.

Brownlow, K., Mollo, A. (1964) *It Happened Here*. United Artists.

Brumlik, M. (2017) Resistance Carl von Ossietzky, Albert Leo Schlageter, and Mahatma Gandhi, in *Resistance: Subjects, Representations, Contexts*, edited by Butler, M., Mecheril, P., Brenningmeyer, L. Bielefeld and London: Transcript Verlag.

Buckley, J. (2014) *Monty's Men: The British Army and the Liberation of Europe*. New Haven: Yale University Press.

Buck-Morss, S. (1983) Benjamin's Passagen-Werk: Redeeming Mass Culture for the Revolution. *New German Critique* 29 (Spring/Summer): 211–240.

Bulow, J., Klemperer, P. (2002) Prices and the Winner's Curse. *RAND Journal of Economics* 33 (1): 1–21.

Burden, T. (1967) *The Nuremberg Party Rallies: 1923–1939*. London: Pall Mall.

Burleigh, M. (2000) *The Third Reich: A New History*. London: Macmillan.

Burleigh, M., Wippermann, W. (1991) *The Racial State: Germany 1933–1945*. Cambridge: Cambridge University Press.

Burns, E. (2019) Not Just an Old Boy's Club, *Military Trader*, November 13, 2019, www.militarytrader.com/militaria-collecting-101/not-just-an-old-boys-club. Accessed: 14/02/2020

Burton, B. J., Jacobsen, J. P. (1999) Measuring Returns on Investments in Collectibles. *Journal of Economic Perspectives* 13 (4): 193–212.

Bushman, B. J., Anderson, C. A. (2009) Comfortably Numb: Desensitizing Effects of Violent Media on Helping Others. *Psychological Science* 20 (3): 273–277.

Bytwerk, R. L. (2008) The Führer as Godfather. *German Propaganda Archive*, www.bytwerk.com/gpa/nv35-04a.htm. Accessed: 30/10/2020

Bytwerk, R. L. (2010) Grassroots Propaganda in the Third Reich: The Reich Ring for National Socialist Propaganda and Public Enlightenment. *German Studies Review* 33 (1): 93–118.

Calderon, M. J. (1990) Museums and Communication. *Philippine Quarterly of Culture and Society* 18 (2): 137–140.

Caldwell, N. W. (1947) Political Commissars in the Luftwaffe. *Journal of Politics* 9 (1): 59–79.

Cameron, F. (2007) Beyond the Cult of the Replicant: Museums and Historical Digital Objects-Traditional Concerns, New Discourses, in *Theorizing Digital Cultural Heritage*, edited by Cameron, F., Kenderdine, S. Cambridge: MIT Press, 49–75. https://doi.org/10.7551/mitpress/9780262033534.003.0004

Cameron, N., Stevens, R. H. (Trans.) (1953, 2000) *Hitler's Table Talk 1941–1944 His Private Conversations, Introduced and with a New Preface by Trevor-Roper, H.* New York City: Enigma books.

Campbell, D. (1993) Women in Combat: The World War II Experience in the United States, Great Britain, Germany, and the Soviet Union. *Journal of Military History* 57 (2): 301–323.

Campbell, K. J. (2012) Otto Skorzeny: The Most Dangerous Man in Europe. *American Intelligence Journal* 30 (1): 142–150.

Candela, G., Castellani, M., Pattitoni, P. (2012) Tribal Art Market: Signs and Signals. *Journal of Cultural Economics* 36 (4): 289–308.

Canning, K. (2010) The Politics of Symbols, Semantics, and Sentiments in the Weimar Republic. *Central European History* 43 (4): 567–580.

Caplan, J. (2019) Hitler Waves: Biographical Approaches to the Nazi leader, *Times Literary Supplement*, November 29, 2021, www.the-tls.co.uk/articles/hitler-waves/. Accessed: 10/02/2021

Carr, G. (2016) Illicit Antiquities? The Collection of Nazi Militaria in the Channel Islands. *World Archaeology* 48 (2): 254–266.

Carr, G. (2018) The Small Things of Life and Death: An Exploration of Value and Meaning in the Material Culture of Nazi Camps. *International Journal of Historical Archaeology* 22: 531–552.

Carrier, J. G. (1990) Gifts in a World of Commodities: The Ideology of the Perfect Gift in American Society. *Social Analysis: International Journal of Anthropology* 29: 19–37.

Carrier, J. G. (1994) Alienating Objects: The Emergence of Alienation in Retail Trade. *Man* 29 (2): 359–380.

Carrier, R. C. (2003) Hitler's Table Talk: Troubling Minds. *German Studies Review* 26 (3): 561–576.

Carsten, F. L. (1966) *The Reichswehr in Politics 1918–1933*. Oxford: University of Oxford Press, Clarendon Press.

Case, D. (2009) Serial Collecting as Leisure, and Coin Collecting in Particular. *Library Trends* 57 (4): 729–752.

Casement, W. (2020) Is It a Forgery? Ask a Semanticist. *Journal of Aesthetic Education* 54 (1): 51–68.

Caspar, C. (1958) Mein Kampf: A Best Seller. *Jewish Social Studies* 20 (1): 3–16.

Castro, E. (2004) Exchanging Perspectives: The Transformation of Objects into Subjects in Amerindian Ontologies. *Common Knowledge* 10 (3): 463–484.

Catalano, S. (2020) When It Happened Here: Michigan and the Transnational Development of American Fascism, 1920–1945. *Michigan Historical Review* 46 (1): 29–67.

Cayley, B., Walker, T. Wilkinson-Latham, R. (1983) Metal Insignia, in *Military Collecting*, edited by Lyndhurst, J. London: Salamander Publishing, 42–67.

Cesarani, D. (2005) *Eichmann: His Life and Crimes*. London: Vintage (an imprint of Penguin-Random House).

Chanen, J. S. (2006) Art Attack: Ownership of Paintings and Other Objects of Value Is Being Challenged on a Number of Legal Fronts. *ABA Journal* 92 (12): 50–56.

Cheape, C. (1988) Not Politicians but Sound Businessmen: Norton Company and the Third Reich. *Business History Review* 62 (3): 444–466.

Childers, T., Weiss, E. (1990) Voters and Violence: Political Violence and the Limits of National Socialist Mass Mobilization. *German Studies Review* 13 (3): 481–498.

Childs, D. (1969) Review of: The Nuremberg Party Rallies: 1923–1939, by Hamilton T. Burden. *International Affairs* 2: 291–292.

Chintagunta, P. K. (2002) Investigating Category Pricing Behavior at a Retail Chain. *Journal of Marketing Research* 39 (2): 141–154.

Chow, R. (2001) Fateful Attachments: On Collecting, Fidelity, and Lao She. *Critical Inquiry* 28 (1): 286–304.

Christies (2021) Beeple: A Visionary Digital Artist at the Forefront of NFTs Christies, March 2021, www.christies.com/features/Monumental-collage-by-Beeple-is-first-purely-digital-artwork-NFT-to-come-to-auction-11510-7.aspx. Accessed: 18/03/2021

Chrystal, W. G. (1975) Nazi Party Election Films, 1927–1938. *Cinema Journal* 15 (1): 29–47.

Chuba, K., Humphries, M., Pyche, T. J., Milian, J. (2017) Man Wearing Swastika Explains Why He Came to Turlington Plaza, *WUFT News*, January 26, 2017, www.wuft.org/news/2017/01/26/man-wearing-swastika-at-uf-draws-200-plus-protestors/. Accessed: 03/02/2019

Citino, R. (2012) *The Wehrmacht Retreats*. Lawrence: University Press of Kansas.

Classen, C., Kansteiner, W. (2009) Truth and Authenticity in Contemporary Historical Culture: An Introduction to Historical Representation and Historical Truth. *History and Theory* 48 (2): 77–102.

Clemenson, S. (2018) LR True Stories – City of Benares, January 12, 2018, https://hec.lrfoundation.org.uk/whats-on/blogs/lr-true-stories-city-of-benares-16. Accessed: 03/02/2021

Cobain, I. (2016) Jo Cox Murder Suspect Collected Far-Right Books, Court Hears, *Guardian*, November 21, 2016, www.theguardian.com/uk-news/2016/nov/21/jo-cox-suspect-collected-far-right-books-court-hears. Accessed: 22/11/2019

Coffman, R. B. (1991) Art Investment and Asymmetrical Information. *Journal of Cultural Economics* 15 (2): 83–94.

Coggeshall, F. (1886) The Arithmetic, Geometric, and Harmonic Means. *Quarterly Journal of Economics* 1 (1): 83–86.

Cohen, J. (1987) The Conversion of Children Born to Gentile Mothers and Jewish Fathers. *Tradition: A Journal of Orthodox Jewish Thought* 22 (4): 1–17.

Cohen-Almagor, R. (2012) Freedom of Expression, Internet Responsibility, and Business Ethics: The Yahoo! Saga and its Implications. *Journal of Business Ethics* 106 (3): 353–365.

Cole, W. S. (1951) The America First Committee. *Journal of the Illinois State Historical Society* 44 (4): 305–322.

Cole, W. S. (1974) *Charles A Lindbergh and the Battle Against American Intervention in World War II*. New York and London: Harcourt Brace Jovanovich.

Coleman, D., Rowthorn, R. (2011) Who's Afraid of Population Decline? A Critical Examination of its Consequences. *Population and Development Review* 37: 217–248.

Coleman, S. (1996) All-Consuming Faith: Language, Material Culture and World-Transformation Among Protestant Evangelicals. *Etnofoor* 9 (1): 29–47.

Collyer, J. L. (1943) Crisis in Rubber. *Proceedings of the Academy of Political Science* 20 (2): 71–80.

Conn, S. (2010) *Do Museums Still Need Objects?* Philadelphia: University of Pennsylvania Press.

Connor, J. W. (1989) From Ghost Dance to Death Camps: Nazi Germany as a Crisis Cult. *Ethos* 17 (3): 259–288.

Conti, A. (2018) Getting Rid of Nazi Memorabilia Is Harder Than It Sounds, *Vice*, April 5, 2018, www.vice.com/en_uk/article/zmwqj9/getting-rid-of-nazi-memorabilia-is-harder-than-it-sounds. Accessed: 02/01/2019

Conway, J. S. (1985) History, Hitler, and the Holocaust. Review of: Hitler in History by Eberhard Jackel; Hitler and the Final Solution by Gerald Fleming; The Blood of His Servants by Malcolm C. Macpherson; Fragments of Isabella: A Memoir of Auschwitz by Isabella Leitner; Martin Niemöller 1891–1984 by James Bentley; The Oberammergau Passion Play: A Lance against Civilization by Saul S. Friedman; The Abandonment of the Jews: America and the Holocaust 1941–1945 by David S. Wyman; The Dissolution of Eastern European Jewry by Walter N. Sanning. *International History Review* 7 (3): 441–451.

Cook, A. (2004) The Use and Abuse of Historical Re-enactment: Thoughts on Recent Trends in Public History. *Criticism* 46 (3): 487–496.

Cook, S. (2018) People no Longer Go into Antiques Shops, *BBC News*, August 19, 2018, www.bbc.co.uk/news/business-45186811. Accessed: 06/01/2020

Cooperman, J. (2019) What's Causing the Rise of Hoarding Disorder? *Jstor*, January 16, 2019, https://daily.jstor.org/whats-causing-the-rise-of-hoarding-disorder/ Accessed: 06/02/2019

Cornish, P. (2004) Sacred Relics: Objects in the Imperial War Museum 1917–1939, in *Matters of Conflict: Material Culture, Memory and the First World War*, edited by Saunders, N. J. Abingdon: Routledge, 35–50.

Cornish, P. (2009) Just a Boyish Habit, in *Contested Objects: Material Memories of the Great War*, edited by Saunders, N. J., Cornish, P. Abingdon: Routledge, chapter 1.

Cost, J. (2007) Q&A With Siouxsie Sioux, *Magnet Magazine*, October 6, 2007, http://magnetmagazine.com/2007/10/06/qa-with-siouxsie-sioux/. Accessed: 29/11/2020

Crawford, E. (2000) German Scientists and Hitler's Vendetta Against the Nobel Prizes. *Historical Studies in the Physical and Biological Sciences* 31 (1): 37–53.

Crew, D. F. (1998) *Germans on Welfare: From Weimar to Hitler*. Oxford: Oxford University Press.

Crew, S. R., Becker, R. E., Thomassen-Krauss, S., Frost, C. (2000) The Star-Spangled Banner Preservation Project at The National Museum of American History. Smithsonian Institution. *History News* 55 (1): 14–17.

Crockett, D. (1992) The Most Famous Painting of the Golden Twenties? Otto Dix and the Trench Affair. *Art Journal* 51 (1): 72–80.

Cross, G. (2017) Nostalgic Collections. *Consumption Markets & Culture* 20 (2): 101–106.

Cross, J. (2017) Telephone Interview between Jamie Cross and Michael Hughes, transcript held by both participants. Permission granted.

Crossland, D. (2019) Boomtime for Hitler memorabilia, *Times*, October 5, 2019, www.thetimes.co.uk/article/boomtime-for-hitler-memorabilia-fm2dft0pj. Accessed: 02/01/2020

Crowe, C. (1976, 2016) David Bowie's September 1976 *Playboy* Interview, *Playboy*, January 11, 2016, www.playboy.com/read/playboy-interview-david-bowie. Accessed: 07/12/2020

CTA (2020a) Fine Militaria Sale, Third Reich Lots 415–578, C and T Auctioneers, February 4, 2020, Kenardington, Kent, England, www.candtauctions.co.uk www.the-saleroom.com. Accessed: 04/02/2020

CTA (2020b) C & T Auctioneers, The Brian L Davis Collection of Third Reich Insignia, April 22, 2020, The Saleroom, www.the-saleroom.com/en-gb/auction-catalogues/candt-auctioneers/catalogue-id-srct10128. Accessed: 22/04/2020

Culler, J. (1985) Junk and Rubbish: A Semiotic Approach. Review of: Rubbish Theory: The Creation and Destruction of Value by Michael Thompson. *Diacritics* 15 (3): 2–12.

Cuomo, G. R. (2012) The NSDAP's Enduring Shadow: Putting in Perspective the Recent Outing of Brown Octogenarians. *German Studies Review* 35 (2): 265–288.

Curasi, C. F., Price, L. L., Arnould, E. J. (2004) How Individuals' Cherished Possessions Become Families' Inalienable Wealth. *Journal of Consumer Research* 31 (3): 609–622.

Cuttle, C., Law, S. (2018) Got. Got. Need! The economics of Panini World Cup Football Stickers, *Frontier Economics*, www.frontier-economics.com/media/1497/201805_got-got-need-_frontier.pdf. Accessed: 12/11/2019

Czunys, D. (2018) Typed Questionnaire. Questions Set by Michael Hughes. Copies held by Dan Czunys and Michael Hughes. Permission granted.

DAF (n.d.) *Organisation der deutschen Arbeitsfront und der NS Gemeinschaft Kraft durch Freude*. No publisher noted, but booklet produced during the Third Reich.

DAF (1940) *Fundamente des Sieges – die Gesamtarbeit der Deutschen Arbeitsfront von 1933 bis 1940*. Berlin: Verlag der Deutschen Arbeitsfront.

Dannefer, D. (1980) Rationality and Passion in Private Experience: Modern Consciousness and the Social World of Old-Car Collectors. *Social Problems* 27: 392–412.

Dant, T. (2009) Fetishism and the Social Value of Objects. *Sociological Review* 44 (3): 495–516.

D'Arcy, D. (2019) As Nazi objects and Fakes Enter Collectors' Market, Should Museums Show Them? *Art Newspaper*, December 26, 2019, quote attributed to Christian Fuhrmeister of the Central Institute for Art History (ZIKG) in Munich, https://www.theartnewspaper.com/2019/12/26/as-nazi-objects-and-fakes-enter-collectors-market-should-museums-show-them. Accessed: 05/03/2021

Darlington, J. (2020) *Fake Heritage: Why We Rebuild Monuments*. New Haven: Yale University Press.

David, H. P., Fleischhacker, J., Hohn, C. (1988) Abortion and Eugenics in Nazi Germany. *Population and Development Review* 14 (1): 81–112.

Davies, C. (2015) Action Man and Star Wars figurines sell for £180,000 at auction, *Guardian*, May 27, 2015, www.theguardian.com/lifeandstyle/2015/may/27/action-man-star-wars-figures-sell-auction. Accessed: 01/03/2021

Davies, G. (2019) Fireman Sam Axed as Fire Service Mascot Because he is not Inclusive Enough, *Telegraph*, September 11, 2019, www.telegraph.co.uk/news/2019/09/11/fireman-sam-axed-fire-service-mascot-not-inclusive-enough/. Accessed: 02/11/2019

Davis, B. L. (1971) *German Army Uniforms and Insignia 1933–1945*. London: Arms and Armour Press.

Davis, B. L. (1983) *Badges and Insignia of the Third Reich 1933–1945*. Poole: Blandford Press.

Davis, D. (1995) The Work of Art in the Age of Digital Reproduction (An Evolving Thesis: 1991–1995). *Leonardo* 28 (5): 381–386.

Davis, H. (1999) What was the Role of the Wannsee Conference in the Final Solution? *European Judaism: A Journal for the New Europe* 32 (2): 26–36.

Dawdy, S. L. (2016) *Patina: A Profane Archaeology*. Chicago: University of Chicago Press.

Dawidowicz, L. S. (1975) Bleaching the Black Lie: The Case of Theresienstadt. *Salmagundi* 29: 125–140.

DeGroot, E. (1947) The Twilight of National Socialism in Germany, 1943–1945. *International Affairs* 23 (4): 531–545.

Demir (2017) TWM made by Deschler & Sohn, Turkey, Gentleman's Military Interest Club, March, 20, 2017, post by Demir mentions Deschler manager Helmut Stillner, https://gmic.co.uk/topic/70610-twm-made-by-deschler-sohn/. Accessed: 27/03/2021

Derrick, J. (2021) 4 NFT Stocks Moving on the Blockchain-Based Investment Trend, *Yahoo Finance*, March 16, 2021, www.yahoo.com/now/4-nft-stocks-moving-blockchain-193704563.html. Accessed: 18/03/2021

Desch (October 37) Deschler. BWA K1, XXI5, 48, Akt, Fall13. Letter dated October 6, 1937. Firmenauskunft Von Deschler an Wirtschaftsgruppe Eisen-, Blech und Metallwarenindunstrie, Berlin W62, Kielgan-Strasse 7. Supplied by Richard Winkler of the Bavarian Economic Archive (Bayerisches Wirtschaftsarchiv).

Desch J45. BWA, K1.1., NR. 1348, Reichsbetriebsnummer 0/0850/0416/3 (hand written) Military Government Munich, 9th June 1945. To whom it may concern, the firm of Deschler and Son, Wirtstrasse 9, Munich, is authorised to manufacture metal and enamel badges for military forces by order of the military government. Alex B. McDonell Major, Cavalry Trade and Industry. Supplied by Richard Winkler of the Bavarian Economic Archive (Bayerisches Wirtschaftsarchiv).

DeSouza, C. (2017) Swastika-wearing Man at UF, *Heritage Florida Jewish News*, February 3, 2017, www.heritagefl.com/story/2017/02/03/news/swastika-wearing-man-at-uf/7470.html. Accessed: 06/12/2018

de Waal, E. (2015) Figurines in Dachau – Edmund de Waal on the Nazis' Love of Porcelain, *Guardian*, September 18, 2015, www.theguardian.com/books/2015/sep/18/figurines-dachau-nazis-love-porcelain – porzellan-manufaktur-allach-himmler-hitler. Accessed: 05/03/2021

Dewan, S., Hsu, V. (2004) Adverse Selection in Electronic Markets: Evidence from Online Stamp Auctions. *Journal of Industrial Economics* 52 (4): 497–516.

DeWeerd, H. A. (1949) The German Officer Corps Versus Hitler. *Military Affairs* 13 (4): 199–208.

Dewey, M., Schagen, U., Eckart, W. U., Schönenberger, E. (2006) Ernst Ferdinand Sauerbruch and his Ambiguous Role in the Period of National Socialism. *Annals of Surgery* 244 (2): 315–321.

DHM (2015) Die Errichtung des Einparteienstaates 1933, Deutsches Historisches Museum, June 22, 2015, www.dhm.de/lemo/kapitel/ns-regime/etablierung-der-ns-herrschaft/ein-parteienstaat.html. Accessed: 09/02/2019

DHM HD. Deutsches Historisches Museum. Hitler und die Deutschen. Volksgemeinschaft und Verbrechen, www.dhm.de/archiv/ausstellungen/hitler-und-die-deutschen/. Accessed: 20/12/2019

Diamond, E. (2016) *A New Era: An Analysis of the Contemporary Art Market Bubble.* M.A., Harvard Extension School.

Dickinson, E. R. (1999) Welfare, Democracy, and Fascism: The Political Crises in German Child Welfare, 1922–1933. *German Studies Review* 22 (1): 43–66.

Diehl, J. M. (1989) Germany in Defeat, 1918 and 1945: Some Comparisons and Contrasts. *History Teacher* 22 (4): 397–409.

DiMaggio, Sol (2013) *The Positioning of the Coach and the Transformative Agency of Teachers: The Problem of Constituting Joint Meaning in an Underperforming Secondary Mathematics Department.* Doctor of Education, University of Melbourne.

DiNardo, R. L. (1996) German Armour Doctrine: Correcting the Myths. *War in History* 3 (4): 384–397.

DiNardo, R. L., Bay, A. (1988) Horse-Drawn Transport in the German Army. *Journal of Contemporary History* 23 (1): 129–142.

Dixon, M. (2007) The Horror of Disconnection: The Auratic in Technological Malfunction Walter Benjamin and the Virtual: Politics, Art, and Mediation in the Age of Global Culture. *Transformations* 15: 1–9.

Dixon, P. (n.d.) Charles Lindbergh – Germany and the America First Movement, *Britannica*, www.britannica.com/biography/Charles-Lindbergh/Germany-and-the-America-First-movement. Accessed: 27/05/2021

DM (July 2008) Fury Over Sale of Nazi Regalia from SS 'Death's Head' Squad that Massacred 100 British Soldiers, *Daily Mail*, July 3, 2008, www.dailymail.co.uk/news/article-1031504/Fury-sale-Nazi-regalia-SS-Deaths-Head-squad-massacred-British-soldiers.html. Accessed: 03/02/2020

DNB (Mai 1939) Dank der Deutschen Mutter, *Deutsches Nachrichtenbüro* (DNB), May 21, 1939, http://zefys.staatsbibliothek-berlin.de/index.php?id=dfg-viewer&set%5Bmets%5D=http%3A%2F%2Fcontent.staatsbibliothek-berlin.de%2Fzefys%2FSNP27058621-19390522-1-0-0-0.xml). Accessed: 19/02/2021

DNW (2020) Orders, Decorations, Medals and Militaria, *Dix Noonan Webb*, November 12, 2020, www.dnw.co.uk/auction-archive/past-catalogues/results.php?auction_id=566. Accessed: 12/11/2020

Dodonova, A., Khoroshilov, Y. (2012) Anticipation of Auction Fever: Entry Decision, Reserve Price and the Choice of Auction Design. *Managerial and Decision Economics* 33 (2): 87–98.

Doehle, H. (1943) *Die Auszeichnungen des Großdeutschen Reiches Orden, Ehrenzeichen, Abzeichen.* Berlin: Berliner Buch- und Zeitschriftenverlag.

Doehle, H. (1945) *Die Auszeichnungen des Großdeutschen Reiches Orden, Ehrenzeichen, Abzeichen.* Berlin: Berliner Buch- und Zeitschriftenverlag. Reprinted by Norderstedt: Verlag K. D. Patzwall (2000).

Doehring, K. (2004) Der Mensch in einer veränderten Staatenwelt. *Zeitschrift für ausländisches öffentliches Recht und Völkerrecht (ZaöRV)* 64: 659–664.

Doenecke, J. D. (1984) A Military Observer in Hitler's Reich. Review of: Berlin Alert: The Memoirs and Reports of Truman Smith by Robert Hessen. *Reviews in American History* 12 (4): 583–588.

Dolfsma, W. (2000) Life and Times of the Veblen Effect. *History of Economic Ideas* 8 (3):61–82.

Dolfsma, W., Eijk, R., Jolink, A. (2009) On a Source of Social Capital: Gift Exchange. *Journal of Business Ethics* 89 (3): 315–329.

Domansky, E. (1992) Kristallnacht, the Holocaust and German Unity: The Meaning of November 9 as an Anniversary in Germany. *History and Memory* 4 (1): 60–94.

Douglas, D. M. (1977) The Parent Cell: Some Computer Notes on the Composition of the First Nazi Party Group in Munich, 1919–1921. *Central European History* 10 (1): 55–72.

DS (2018) Nazi Porcelain made by Dachau Inmates Draws Unscrupulous Collectors, *Daily Sabah*, August 11, 2018, www.dailysabah.com/history/2018/08/11/nazi-porcelain-made-by-dachau-inmates-draws-unscrupulous-collectors. Accessed: 11/02/2020

Duerden, N. (2010) Lemmy Interview: The Motörhead Frontman on Heartbreak, Ageing and his Penchant for Nazi Memorabilia, *Independent*, November 28, 2010, www.independent.co.uk/news/people/profiles/growing-old-disgracefully-lemmy-on-heartbreak-ageing-and-his-penchant-for-nazi-memorabilia-2142747.html. Accessed: 21/06/2018

Dunker, U. (1977) *Der Reichsbund Jüdischer Frontsoldaten 1919–1938. Geschichte eines jüdischen Abwehrvereins*. Düsseldorf: Droste Verlag.

Dunn, J. (2007) Hitler's Jewish Soldier. *History Today* 57 (11).

Dunn, K. C. (2008) Never Mind the Bollocks: The Punk Rock Politics of Global Communication. *Review of International Studies* 34: 193–210.

Dunn, S. (2013) *1940. FDR, Wilky, Lindbergh, Hitler-the Election Amid the Storm*. New Haven: Yale University Press.

Dutton, D. (2003) Authenticity in Art, in *The Oxford Handbook of Aesthetics*, edited by Levinson, J. Oxford: Oxford University Press, www.denisdutton.com/authenticity.htm.

DUZ (Oktober 1943) *Deutsche Uniformen-Zeitschrift*, Ausgabe 7, Oktober 15, 1943.

DUZ (April 1944) Die Abzeichen und Feldzeichen der Freiwilligen-Verbände des Heeres und der Waffen-SS im Kriege, von K. Klietmann, *Deutsche Uniformen-Zeitschrift*, Ausgabe 4, April 20, 1944.

DUZ (November 1944) *Deutsche Uniformen-Zeitschrift*, Ausgabe 11, November 1944.

DW (Mai 1944) *Die-Deutsche-Wochenschau*-Nr.717, Mai 31, 1944, https://archive.org/details/1944-05-31-Die-Deutsche-Wochenschau-Nr.717. Accessed: 27/02/2021

DW (2019) Nazi Memorabilia Sold at Controversial Auction in Germany, *Deutsche Welle*, November 20, 2019, www.dw.com/en/nazi-memorabilia-sold-at-controversial-auction-in-germany/a-51336705. Accessed: 23/02/2020

Dyl, E. A., Jiang, G. J. (2008) Valuing Illiquid Common Stock. *Financial Analysts Journal* 64 (4): 40–47.

Eagleton, T. (2016) Utopias, Past and Present: Why Thomas More Remains Astonishingly Radical. *Utopian Studies* 27 (3): 412–417.

Eberle, M. (1985) *World War I and the Weimar Artists-Dix, Grosz, Beckmann, Schlemmer*. New Haven and London: Yale University Press.

Eccles, D. (1968) *On Collecting*. Harlow: Longmans.

Econ (2009) Is it Wrong to Collect Nazi Memorabilia? *Economist* (New York), September 15, 2009, www.economist.com/democracy-in-america/2009/09/15/is-it-wrong-to-collect-nazi-memorabilia. Accessed: 06/08/2013

Edinger, L. J. (1953) German Social Democracy and Hitler's National Revolution of 1933: A Study in Democratic Leadership. *World Politics* 5 (3): 330–367.

Eley, G. (2000) Historical Accountability and the Contest of Memory: Nazism and Business History. Review of: Das Volkswagenwerk und seine Arbeiter im Dritten Reich by Hans Mommsen and Manfred Grieger. *Public Historian* 22 (3): 139–145.

Elsthain, J. B. (2012) Just War and an Ethics of Responsibility, in *Ethics Beyond War's End*, edited by Patterson, E. Washington, DC: Georgetown University Press, 123–144.

Epstein, D. (2020) Keith Moon's 10 Wildest Pranks, *Rolling Stone*, September 2020, www.rollingstone.com/music/music-lists/keith-moons-10-wildest-pranks-13041/the-kidnapped-vicar-29990/. Accessed: 06/12/2020

Erinkmann, J. (1982) *Die Ritter des Orderns Pour le Mérite 1914–1918*. Hannover: Th. Schäfer Druckerei GmbH.

Espenshade, T. J. (1978) How a Trend Towards a Stationary Population Affects Consumer Demand. *Population Studies* 32 (1): 147–158.

Evans, R. (1976) German Women and the Triumph of Hitler. *Journal of Modern History* 48 (1): 123–175.

Evans, R. (1997, 2000) *In Defence of History*. London: Granta Books.

Evans, R. (2003) *The Coming of the Third Reich*. London: Penguin.

Evans, R. (2006) *The Third Reich in Power 1933–1939*. London: Penguin.

Evans, R. (n.d.) Corruption and Plunder in the Third Reich, official website of Richard J. Evans, www.richardjevans.com/lectures/corruption-plunder-third-reich/. Accessed: 16/03/2021

Evans, R., Attar, R. (2020) Nazi Germany: Everything You Wanted to Know, with Richard J Evans, *History Extra* Podcast, June 7, 2020, www.historyextra.com/period/20th-century/everything-you-wanted-to-know-about-nazi-germany-hitler-ww2-richard-j-evans-podcast/. Accessed: 19/02/2021

Evening Standard (2007) Sex, Drugs and Guns: As Rocker Keith Richards Releases his Memoirs, how much can the Hellraiser Really Remember? *London Evening Standard*, July 28, 2007, www.standard.co.uk/showbiz/sex-drugs-and-guns-as-rocker-keith-richards-releases-his-memoirs-how-much-can-the-hellraiser-really-remember-7241554.html. Accessed: 11/03/2021

Falter, J. W. (1998) Die Märzgefallenen von 1933. Neue Forschungsergebnisse zum sozialen Wandel innerhalb der NSDAP-Mitgliedschaft während der Machtergreifungsphase. *Geschichte und Gesellschaft* 24 (4): 595–616.

Falter, J. W. (2013) The Young Membership of the NSDAP between 1925 and 1933. A Demographic and Social Profile. *Historical Social Research/Historische Sozialforschung* Supplement 25: 260–279.

Farndale, N. (2007) Malcolm McLaren: Punk? It made my day, *Telegraph*, September 30, 2007, www.telegraph.co.uk/culture/3668263/Malcolm-McLaren-Punk-it-made-my-day.html. Accessed: 03/01/2020

FB MCN. Militaria Collectors Network. Closed Facebook group. Accessed: 27/12/2019

FC (2010) Article R645–1, Code pénal, www.legifrance.gouv.fr/affichCodeArticle.do?id Article=LEGIARTI000006419560&cidTexte=LEGITEXT000006070719. Accessed: 20/12/2019

Featherstone, M. (1990) Perspectives on Consumer Culture. *Sociology* 24 (1): 005–022.

Fehrenbach, E. (1971) Über die Bedeutung der Politischen Symbole in Nationalstaat. *Historische Zeitschrift* 213 (2): 296–357.

Feka, E. (2014) *The Hydra* (*The Legend of Herakles Book 3*). Reluctant Geek. Kindle.

Feliciano, H. (1997) *The Lost Museum: The Nazi Conspiracy to Steal the World's Great Works of Art*. New York: Basic Books.

Fennick, J. (1998) *The Collectible Barbie Doll: An Illustrated Guide to Her Dreamy World*. Godalming Surrey: Colour Library Direct.

Fergusson, G. (1964) A Blueprint for Dictatorship. Hitler's Enabling Law of March 1933. *International Affairs* 40 (2): 245–261.

Fernandez, K. V., Lastovicka, J. L. (2011) Making Magic: Fetishes in Contemporary Consumption. *Journal of Consumer Research* 38 (2): 278–299.

FGFF (1981) *Frauengruppe Faschismusforschung Mutterkreuz und Arbeitsbuch. Zur Geschichte der Frauen in der Weimarer Republik und im Nationalsozialismus.* Frankfurt am Main: Fischer.

Fieser, J. (1996) Do Businesses Have Moral Obligations beyond What the Law Requires? *Journal of Business Ethics* 15 (4): 457–468.

Findlay, R. (2007) Who Do you think you are kidding Mr Lumsden, *Sunday Mail*, February 11, 2007, www.thefreelibrary.com/Who+do+you+think+you+are+kidding+Mr+Lumsden%3F+EXCLUSIVE+COP+FLAUNTS . . . -a0159137388. Accessed: 25/07/2013

Fineman, M. (1999) Ecce Homo Prostheticus. *New German Critique* 76: 85–114.

Fings, K. (2004) Forced Labor at Ford Werke in Cologne, in *Working for the Enemy: Ford, General Motors, and Forced Labor in Germany during the Second World War*, contributions by Billstein, R. et. al. New York City: Berghahn Books, 135–162.

Finney, P. (2017) Politics and Technologies of Authenticity: The Second World War at the Close of Living Memory: Rethinking History. *Journal of Theory and Practice* 21 (2): 154–170.

Fischer, K. (2006) On Barbie, Guns and Control. *Off Our Backs* 36 (2): 58–61.

Fischer, O. W. (2010) In the Shadow of Monumentality. *Log* 20: 117–123.

Fischhaber, A., Reinbold, F. (2010) Hitler Ausstellung in Berlin: Sein starrer Blick ist einschüchternd, *Spiegel Online*, October 15, 2010, www.spiegel.de/fotostrecke/hitler-ausstellung-alle-sind-ein-bisschen-nervoes-fotostrecke-60571-7.html. Accessed: 12/12/2019

Fisher, D. (2019) Introduction to Third Reich Allach Porcelain for Beginners, Regimentals YouTube Channel, February 4, 2019, www.youtube.com/watch?v=1NcyrWo1BTo. Accessed: 12/02/2020

Fisher, M. (2015) Interview for *BBC Sunday Live*, Series 6, episode 4, July 12, 2015, Now live: Is it wrong to collect Nazi memorabilia? www.bbc.co.uk/iplayer/episode/b062sfg3/sunday-morning-live-series-6-episode-4. Accessed: 01/03/2021

Fisher, M. (2017) Telephone Interview between Malcolm Fisher and Michael Hughes, transcript held by both participants. Permission granted.

Fletcher, T. (2014) The Day Steve McQueen Met His New Nazi Neighbor, Keith Moon, *Newsweek*, February 20, 2014, www.newsweek.com/day-steve-mcqueen-met-his-new-nazi-neighbor-keith-moon-229741. Accessed: 07/12/2020

FMZ (1937) SS Hilf Mit, *FM-Zeitschrift* (Berlin), *Monatsschrift der Reichsführung SS für fördende Mitglieder*, Jahrgang 4, Folge 12, Dezember 1, 1937.

Föllmer, M. (2013) The Subjective Dimension of Nazism. *Historical Journal* 56 (4): 1107–1132.

Forbes, N. (2007) Multinational Enterprise, Corporate Responsibility and the Nazi Dictatorship: The Case of Unilever and Germany in the 1930s. *Contemporary European History* 16 (2): 149–167.

Forcucci, L. (2010) Battle for Births: The Fascist Pronatalist Campaign in Italy 1925 to 1938. *Journal of the Society for the Anthropology of Europe*, https://anthrosource.onlinelibrary.wiley.com/doi/pdf/10.1111/j.1556-5823.2010.00002.x#pane-pcw-details-con. Accessed: 06/10/2020

Ford, L. (2018) How we made It Happened Here, the film that imagined England under the Nazis. The story of a twentysomething director and his controversial vision of an alternative history in which Hitler successfully invaded Britain, BFI, July 30, 2018, www.bfi.org.uk/news-opinion/news-bfi/interviews/it-happened-here-kevin-brownlow. Accessed: 10/02/2019

Forman, A. (1988) *Forman's Guide to Third Reich German Awards and their Values*. San Jose, CA: Roger James Bender.

Forman, A. (2018) Telephone Interview between Adrian Forman and Michael Hughes, transcript held by both participants. Permission granted.

Forman, A. (2021a) About Adrian Forman, Adrian Forman's official website, www.adrian-forman.com/about.php. Accessed: 16/03/2021

Forman, A. (2021b) Electronic Communication from Adrian Forman to Michael Hughes, January 8, 2021.

Foster, K. (2018) As a Female Firefighter, I Tackle Fires – and Sexism, *Guardian*, February 24, 2018, www.theguardian.com/public-leaders-network/2018/feb/24/female-fire-fighter-tackle-sexism-fires-london-fire-brigade. Accessed: 07/12/2019

Fox, A. H. (1957) A Theory of Second-Hand Markets. *Economica* 24 (94): 99–115.

Fox, J. (2009) Everyday Heroines: Nazi Visions of Motherhood in Mutterliebe (1939) and Annelie (1941) *Historical Reflections/Réflexions Historiques* 35 (2): 21–39.

Fraser, P. (2018) Adolf Hitler's desk provides an education for collectors, *Paul Fraser Collectibles*, January 29, 2018, www.paulfrasercollectibles.com/blogs/memorabilia/adolf-hitler-s-desk-sold-for-well-below-estimate. Accessed: 11/03/2021

Freistadt, B., Wedell, R. (1995) Histories of Estrangement – Motherless Jews. *Bridges* 5 (1): 17–26.

Freniere, H. F. (1976) *The Hitler Trial before the People's Court in Munich*, Vol. 1, translated by Karcic, L., Fandek, P. Arlington: University Publications of America.

Frey, B. S. (2006) Giving and Receiving Awards. *Perspectives on Psychological Science* 1 (4): 377–388.

Frey, B. S., Eichenberger, R. (1995) On the Return of Art Investment Return Analyses. *Journal of Cultural Economics* 19 (3): 207–220.

Friedländer, S. (1990) Preface to A Symposium: Kitsch and the Apocalyptic Imagination. *Salmagundi* 85/86: 201–206.

Friswold, P. (2012) Last Chance to See Charles Lindbergh's Nazi Medal, *Riverfront Times*, January 17, 2012, www.riverfronttimes.com/artsblog/2012/01/17/last-chance-to-see-charles-lindberghs-nazi-medal. Accessed: 06/12/2019

Fritz, S. G. (1997) *Frontsoldaten: The German Soldier in World War II*. Lexington: University Press of Kentucky.

Fritz, S. G. (2011) *Ostkrieg: Hitler's War of Extermination in the East*. Lexington: University Press of Kentucky.

Fritzsche, P. (1990) Presidential Victory and Popular Festivity in Weimar Germany: Hindenburg's 1925 Election. *Central European History* 23 (2/3): 205–224.

Fritzsche, P. (2009) *Life and Death in the Third Reich*. Cambridge: Harvard University Press.

Friz, D. M. (1996) *Kyffhäuserbund und Kyffhäuserdenkmal*. Self-published.

Führer, K. C. (2019) Hoist the Flag! in *The Private in the Volksgemeinschaft*, edited by Harvey, E., Hürter, J., Umbach, M., Wirsching, A. Cambridge: Cambridge University Press, 156–181.

Fuhrman, H. A., Mullin, J. E., Sloffer, C. A. (2016) Field Marshal Erwin Rommel: The Head Injury that may have Prolonged the Second World War. *Neurosurgical Focus* 41 (1), https://thejns.org/focus/view/journals/neurosurg-focus/41/1/article-pE8.xml#affiliation3. Accessed: 27/02/2021

Fulbrook, M. (2004) *A Concise History of Germany*, Second edition. Cambridge: Cambridge University press. Kindle.

Gade, W. E. (1988) Review of: Die Träger der Nahkampfspange in Gold: Heer, Luftwaffe, Waffen SS, 1943–1945 by Manfred Dörr; Franz Thomas. *German Studies Review* 11 (3): 518.

Gajek, E. (1990) Christmas Under the Third Reich. *Anthropology Today* 6 (4): 3–9.

Galinsky, A. D., Ku, G., Mussweiler, T. (2009) To Start Low or To Start High? The Case of Auctions Versus Negotiations. *Current Directions in Psychological Science* 18 (6): 357–361.

Gallagher, R. (2008) Ofcom: BBC was Unfair to Couple in 'Nazi' Documentary, *Press Gazette*, November 10, 2008, www.pressgazette.co.uk/ofcom-bbc-was-unfair-to-couple-in-nazi-documentary/. Accessed: 07/12/2020

Gamson, C. (2017) Constructing the Valuation of Art as Economic & Social/Cultural. *Art and Media Interfaced, CCTP* 802, https://blogs.commons.georgetown.edu/cctp-802-spring2017/constructing-the-valuation-of-art-as-economic-socialcultural/. Accessed: 03/04/2020

Gao, L., Huang, Y., Simonson, I. (2014) The Influence of Initial Possession Level on Consumers' Adoption of a Collection Goal: A Tipping Point Effect. *Journal of Marketing* 78 (6): 143–156.

Garcia, D. (2019) *Rolling Stone: Life and Death of Brian Jones.* Chip Baker Films.

Garstki, K. (2017) Virtual Representation: The Production of 3D Digital Artifacts. *Journal of Archaeological Method and Theory* 24 (3): 726–750.

Gates, A. (2017) Anita Pallenberg, Actress and Muse of Rolling Stones, Dies at 75, *New York Times*, June 14, 2017, www.nytimes.com/2017/06/14/arts/music/anita-pallenberg-dead-actress-rolling-stones-figure.html. Accessed: 11/03/2021

GC (1929) *Convention Relative to the Treatment of Prisoners of War*, Geneva, 27 July 1929, Article 2: Their identity tokens, badges of rank, decorations and articles of value may not be taken from prisoners. Article 19: The wearing of badges of rank and decorations shall be permitted. http://hrlibrary.umn.edu/instree/1929c.htm. Accessed: 11/11/2019

GCGM (2018) *A Guide to Collecting German Militaria*, 2018. Bourne: Warners Group Publications.

Geismar, H. (2001) What's in a Price? An Ethnography of Tribal Art at Auction. *Journal of Material Culture* 6 (1): 25–47.

Geismar, H. (2011) Material Culture Studies and Other Ways to Theorize Objects: A Primer to a Regional Debate. Review of: Thinking through Things: Theorising Artefacts Ethnographically by Amiria Henare, Martin Holbraad, Sari Wastell; Stuff by Daniel Miller. *Comparative Studies in Society and History* 53 (1): 210–218.

Gelber, S. (1992) Free Market Metaphor: The Historical Dynamics of Stamp Collecting. *Comparative Studies in Society and History* 34 (4): 742–769.

Gelbin, C. (1997) The Quest for a Unified Self: Race, Hybridity, and Identity in Elisabeth Langgässer's Der Gang durch das Ried. *New German Critique* 70: 141–160.

Gell, A. (1986) Newcomers to the World of Goods: Consumption Among the Muria Gonds, in *The Social Life of Things: Commodities in Cultural Perspective*, edited by Appadurai, A. Cambridge: Cambridge University Press, 110–138.

Gell, A. (1998) *Art and Agency: An Anthropological Theory*. Oxford: Oxford University Press.

Gellermann, J. E. (1936) Rudolph Hess, Second to the Leader of Germany. *Social Science* 11 (1): 41–45.

Gellott, L., Phayer, M. (1987) Dissenting Voices: Catholic Women in Opposition to Fascism. *Journal of Contemporary History* 22 (1): 91–114.

Gerlach, C. (1998) The Wannsee Conference, the Fate of German Jews, and Hitler's Decision in Principle to Exterminate all European Jews. *Journal of Modern History* 70 (4): 759–812.

Gershon, L. (2015) What Christmas Meant to the Nazis. *Jstor* Daily Blog, December 3, 2015, https://daily.jstor.org/christmas-meant-nazis/. Accessed: 14/10/2021

Gerth, H. (1940) The Nazi Party: Its Leadership and Composition. *American Journal of Sociology* 45 (4): 517–541.

Gerwarth, R. (2006) The Past in Weimar History. *Contemporary European History* 15 (1): 1–22.

Gerwarth, R. (2011) *Hitler's Hangman: The Life of Heydrich*. New Haven: Yale University Press.

Getlen, L. (2016) Mick Jagger's 1971 Wedding was Skin-Crawlingly Embarrassing, *New York Post*, June 11, 2016, https://nypost.com/2016/06/11/mick-jaggers-1971-wedding-was-the-shabbiest-free-for-all-in-history/. Accessed: 11/03/2021

GfE (2011) Gold gab ich für Eisen, I gave Gold for Iron, review of iron jewellery, https://textilegeschichten.net/2011/05/09/im-markischen-museum/. Accessed: 10/02/2021

Gilkeson, J. H., Lamb, R. P. (2000) From Beanie Babies to Baseball Cards: A Financial Application of Collectibles Markets. *Journal of Financial Education* 26: 14–21.

Gilloch, G. (2005) Fabricating Aura: The Face in Film, in *Actualities of Aura: Twelve Studies of Walter Benjamin*, edited by Petersson, Steinskog, E. Svanesund: Nordic Summer University Press, 1–25.

Giloi, E. (2011) *Monarchy, Myth, and Material Culture*. Cambridge: Cambridge University Press.

Giloi, E. (2012) Copyrighting the Kaiser: Publicity, Piracy, and the Right to Wilhelm II's Image. *Central European History* 45 (3): 407–451.

Gilson, A. (2006) Recovering Empire's Critics. Review of: Colonial Strangers: Women Writing the End of the British Empire by Phyllis Lassner. *Twentieth Century Literature* 52 (1): 96–105.

Givens, S. (2010) *Bringing Back Memories: GIs, Souvenir Hunting, and Looting in Germany, 1945*. M.A., Ohio University.

Glass, D. (1940) *Population Policies and Movements in Europe*. Oxford: University of Oxford Press, Clarendon Press.

GMC (2018) Ludwig Christian Lauer, Glasgow Museums Collections Online, http://collections.glasgowmuseums.com/mwebcgi/mweb?request=record;id=73442;type=701. Accessed: 21/05/2021

Goda, N. (2000) Black Marks: Hitler's Bribery of His Senior Officers During World War II. *Journal of Modern History* 72 (2): 413–452.

Godfrey-Wood, R., Mamani-Vargas, G. (2016) Are Markets Moral? Understanding the Roles of Fairness and Power Relations in Rural Trade in the Bolivian Altipiano. *Latin American Research Review* 51 (3): 123–141.

Goebbels, J. (1978) *The Goebbels Diaries: The Last Days*, translated by Barry, R., edited by Trevor-Roper, H. London: Secker & Warburg.

Golden, C. J. (2011) Rowland Hill (1795–1879). *Victorian Review* 37 (1): 9–13.

Goldman, V. (2014) Never Mind the Swastikas: The Secret History of the UK's Punky Jews, February 27, 2014, www.theguardian.com/music/2014/feb/27/never-mind-swastikas-secret-history-punky-jews. Accessed: 21/06/2019

Goldsborough, R. (2013) Alexander the Great Numismatic Portrait, http://rg.ancients.info/alexander/portrait.html. Accessed: 28/03/2021

Gole, H. G. (2013) *Exposing the Third Reich: Colonel Truman Smith in Hitler's Germany*. Lexington: University Press of Kentucky.

Goltz, A. (2009) *Hindenburg: Power Myth and the Rise of the Nazis*. Oxford: Oxford University Press.

Gompert, D. C., Binnendijk, H., Lin, B. (2014) Hitler's Decision to Invade the USSR, 1941, in *Blinders, Blunders, and Wars: What America and China Can Learn*. Santa Monica, CA: RAND Corporation.

Goossen, R. W. (2013) Disarming the Toy Store and Reloading the Shopping Cart: Resistance to Violent Consumer Culture. *Peace and Change* 38 (3): 330–354.

Gordon, K. E. (2010) The Market Sets the Price: Determining Prices in a Bolivian Marketplace. *Journal of the Royal Anthropological Institute* 16 (4): 853–873.

Gordon, T. J. (2002) Fascism and the Female Form: Performance Art in the Third Reich. *Journal of the History of Sexuality* 11 (1/2): 164–200.

Gosden, C., Marshall, Y. (1999) The Cultural Biography of Objects. *World Archaeology* 31 (2): 169–178.

Gossman, L. (2013) *The Passion of Max Von Oppenheim: Archaeology and Intrigue in the Middle East from Wilhelm II to Hitler*. Cambridge: Open Book Publishers.

Gottdiener, M. (1985) Hegemony and Mass Culture: A Semiotic Approach. *American Journal of Sociology* 90 (5): 979–1001.

Gottlieb, M. (1968) The First of April Boycott and the Reaction of the American Jewish Community. *American Jewish Historical Quarterly* 57 (4): 516–517, and 519–556.

Goutam, U., Gautam, U. (2014) Pedagogical Nazi Propaganda 1939–1945. *Proceedings of the Indian History Congress* 75: 1018–1026.

GOV (2018) Historic day for the Military as all Roles are Opened to Women. gov.uk, October 25, 2018, www.gov.uk/government/news/historic-day-for-the-military-as-all-roles-are-opened-to-women. Accessed: 05/02/2019

Graddy, K., Ashenfelter, O. (2002) Auctions and the Price of Art. Department of Economics Discussion Paper Series 131.

Grady, T. (2011) *The German-Jewish Soldiers of the First World War in History and Memory*. Liverpool: Liverpool University Press.

Graeber, D. (2001) *Toward an Anthropological Theory of Value: The False Coin of Our Own Dreams*. Basingstoke: Palgrave Macmillan.

Graf, R. (2010) Either-Or: The Narrative of Crisis in Weimar Germany and in Historiography. *Central European History* 43 (4): 592–615.

Graham, J. L. (2014) Art Exchange? How the International Art Market Lacks a Clear Regulatory Framework, in *Art, Cultural Heritage and the Market*, edited by Vadi, V., Schneider, H. E. G. S. Berlin: Springer Verlag.

Grass, G. (1959, 1980) *Die Blechtrommel*. Darmstadt: Hermann Luchterhand Verlag.

Graziani, A., Vale, M. (1997) Let's Rehabilitate the Theory of Value. *International Journal of Political Economy* 27 (2): 21–25.

Greenfield, K., Greenfield, M. (2018) Telephone Interview with Kenneth and Melissa Greenfield, and Michael Hughes. Transcript held by participants. Permission granted.

Griffin, R. (1996) Review of: Totalitarian Art and the Nemesis of Modernity Art and Power: Europe Under the Dictators by David Britt. *Oxford Art Journal* 19 (2): 122–124.

Grishko, A., Eel, H., Wald, I. Y., Zuckerman, O. (2020) Embracing Imperfection in the Age of Digital Reproduction. *Conference: DIS'20: Designing Interactive Systems Conference 2020*. https://doi.org/10.1145/3393914.3395838

Gross, S. (2012) Selling Germany in South-Eastern Europe: Economic Uncertainty, Commercial Information and the Leipzig Trade Fair 1920–1940. *Contemporary European History* 21 (1): 19–39.

Grossmann, L. (2003) Generalangriff gegen die Justiz? Der Reichstagsbeschluss vom 26. April 1942 und seine Bedeutung für die Massregelung der deutschen Richter durch Hitler. *Institut für Zeitgeschichte*, www.ifz-muenchen.de/heftarchiv/2003_4_2_gruchmann. pdf. Accessed: 17/03/2021

Gruchmann, L. (2003) Bedeutung für die Massregelung der deutschen Richter durch Hitler. *Vierteljahrshefte für Zeitgeschichte* 51 (4): 509–520.

Grunberger, R. (1971, 2013) *A Social History of the Third Reich*. London: Weidenfeld & Nicholson. Kindle.

Guardian (2021) Christie's Auctions 'First Digital-only Artwork' for $70m, Art and Design, *Guardian*, March 12, 2021, www.theguardian.com/artanddesign/2021/mar/11/christies-first-digital-only-artwork-70m-nft-beeple. Accessed: 18/03/2021

Guderian, H. (1952, 2009) *Panzer Leader*. London: Penguin. Kindle.

Guenther, I. (1997) Nazi Chic? German Politics and Women's Fashions, 1915–1945. *Journal of Dress, Body, and Culture. Fashion Theory* 1 (1): 29–58.

Gumpert, M. (1940) *Heil Hunger! Health Under Hitler*, translated by Samuel, M. New York and Toronto: Alliance Book Corporation, Longmans, Green & Company.

GV (1953) Gesetz Über Versammlungen und Aufzüge (Versammlungsgesetz), Paragraph 4, Juli 24 1953, aph 4 i.V.m. Section 28. Es ist verboten, öffentlich oder in einer Versammlung Kennzeichen ehemaliger nationalsozialistischer Organisationen zu verwenden. www. bgbl.de/xaver/bgbl/start.xav?start=%2F%2F*%5B%40attr_id%3D%27bl153s0684. pdf%27%5D#__bgbl__%2F%2F*%5B%40attr_id%3D%27bgbl153s0684. pdf%27%5D__1574512485320. Accessed: 14/12/2019

Gygi, F. (2009) Shaping Matter, Memories and Mentalities: The German Steel Helmet from Artefact to Afterlife, in *Contested Objects: Material Memories of the Great War*, edited by Saunders, N. J., Cornish, P. Abingdon: Routledge, 27–44.

Haaland, G., Haaland, R., Rijal, S. (2002) The Social Life of Iron. A Cross-Cultural Study of Technological, Symbolic, and Social Aspects of Iron Making. *Anthropos* 97 (1): 35–54.

Hadley, M. L. (2000) Grand Admiral Dönitz (1891–1980): A Dramatic Key to the Man behind the Mask. *Northern Mariner/Le Marin du Nord* X 2: 1–21.

Hagemann, K. (2015) *Revisiting Prussia's Wars Against Napoleon: History, Culture, and Memory*. Cambridge: Cambridge University Press. Kindle.

Hagen, J. (2004) The Most German of Towns: Creating an Ideal Nazi Community in Rothenburg ob der Tauber. *Annals of the Association of American Geographers* 94 (1): 207–227.

Haka, A. (2011) Flügel aus Schwarzem Gold. Zur Geschichte der Faserverbundwerkstoffe. *NTM Zeitschrift für Geschichte der Wissenschaften, Technik und Medizin* 19 (11): 69–105.

Hall, A. (2014) Revealed: Begging Letters for Nazi Mother Cross, *Scotsman*, May 13, 2014, www.scotsman.com/news/world/revealed-begging-letters-nazi-mother-cross-1537155. Accessed: 21/02/2021

Hall, N. (2017) Telephone Interview between Nick Hall and Michael Hughes, transcript held by both participants. Permission granted.

Hancock, E. (2011) The Purge of the SA Reconsidered: An Old Putschist Trick? *Central European History* 44 (4): 669–683.

Handler, R. (1986) Authenticity. *Anthropology Today* 2 (1): 2–4.

Hankins, F. H. (1937) German Policies for Increasing Births. *American Journal of Sociology* 42 (5): 630–652.

Hansen, M. B. (2008) Benjamin's Aura. *Critical Inquiry* 34 (2): 336–375.

Hardman, R. (2018) So what DOES Make a Grown Man want to Dress up as a Nazi at Weekends? *Daily Mail*, August 24, 2020, www.dailymail.co.uk/news/article-6096177/ So-DOES-make-grown-man-want-dress-Nazi-weekends.html. Accessed: 07/12/2020

Harris, R. (1986) *Selling Hitler*. London and Boston: Faber and Faber.

Harrison, S. (2008) War Mementos and the Souls of Missing Soldiers: Returning Effects of the Battlefield Dead. *Journal of the Royal Anthropological Institute* 14 (4): 774–790.

Harrod, W. O. (2008) Unfamiliar Precedents: Plywood Furniture in Weimar Germany. *Studies in the Decorative Arts* 15 (2): 2–35.

Harrys, B. (n.d.) Sixties City – Bill Harry's Sixties – Articles from the Creator of Iconic 60s Music Paper Mersey Beat, https://sixtiescity.net/Mbeat/mbfilms200.htm. Accessed: 07/03/2021

Hartmann, C. (2004) Verbrecherischer Krieg – verbrecherische Wehrmacht? Überlegungen zur Struktur des deutschen Ostheeres 1941–1944. *Vierteljahrshefte für Zeitgeschichte* 52 (1): 1–75.

Harvey, M. (2011) The Master of Patina. *Agni* 73: 39–58.

Haskell, F. (1985) Museums and Their Enemies. The Journal of Aesthetic Education 19 (2): 13–22.

Hastings, M. (2015) *Overlord: D-Day and the Battle for Normandy 1944*. London: Pan MacMillan.

Hasty, W. (2009) The Singularity of Aura and the Artistry of Translation: Martin Luther's Bible as Artwork. *Monatshefte* 101 (4): 457–468.

Hayden, R. J. (1938) National Flowers. *Bulletin of Popular Information* 6 (1): 1–6.

HC (2012) Sale of Nazi Memorabilia-Early Day Motions, UK Parliament, EDM #2870, amended March 22, 2012, https://edm.parliament.uk/early-day-motion/43974. Accessed: 01/11/2019

HCCMSC (2005) The Market for Art, The House of Commons Culture, Media and Sport Committee, Sixth Report of Session, March 23, 2005, https://publications.parliament. uk/pa/cm200405/cmselect/cmcumeds/414/41405.htm. Accessed: 05/03/2020

Head, B. V. (1883) Ancient Greek Coins. *American Journal of Numismatics, and Bulletin of the American Numismatic and Archaeological Society* 18 (2): 25–30.

Hebdige, D. (1979) *Subculture: The Meaning of Style*. London: New Accents. Kindle.

Heer, H., Caplan, J. (1998) The Difficulty of Ending a War: Reactions to the Exhibition War of Extermination: Crimes of the Wehrmacht 1941 to 1944. *History Workshop Journal* (46): 187–203.

Heiden, K. (1936) *Hitler: A Biography*. Canada: MacMillan.

Heineman, E. D. (2001) Whose Mothers? Generational Difference, War, and the Nazi Cult of Motherhood. *Journal of Women's History* 12 (4): 139–164.

Heinemann, W. (2014) *Das Eisernes Kreuz die Geschichte Eines Symbols im Wandel der Zeit*. Potsdam: Zentrum für Militärgeschichte und Sozialwissenschaften der Bundeswehr.

Heller, S. (2000, 2008) *The Swastika: Symbol Beyond Redemption?* New York: Allworth Press.

Heller, S. (2004) The Ministry of Fear: Its Political Uses and Abuses. *Social Research* 71 (4): 849–862.

Helmling, S. (2005) During Auschwitz: Adorno, Hegel, and the Unhappy Consciousness of Critique. *PMC* 15 (2): N/A. http://pmc.iath.virginia.edu/issue.105/15.2helmling.html. Accessed: 15/02/2020

Hendricks, K., Porter, R., Tan, G. (2008) Bidding Rings and the Winner's Curse. *RAND Journal of Economics* 39 (4): 1018–1041.

Herbert, U. (2020) The Final Solution- New Answers to Old Questions, 20th Holocaust Memorial Lecture, delivered by Professor Ulrich Herbert in Bute Hall, University of Glasgow, January 21, 2020.

Hermkens, A. (2007) Gendered Objects: Embodiments of Colonial Collecting in Dutch New Guinea. *Journal of Pacific History* 42 (1): 1–20.

Hertz, D. (1997) The Genealogy Bureaucracy in the Third Reich. *Jewish History* 1 (2): 53–78.

Herva, V.-P., Anna-Maria Koskinen-Koivisto, E., Seitsonen, O., Thomas, S. (2016) I have Better Stuff at Home: Treasure Hunting and Private Collecting of World War II Artefacts in Finnish Lapland. *World Archaeology* 48 (2): 1–15.

Hess, H. (1974) *George Grosz*. London and New Haven: Yale University Press.

Hess, J. A. (1938) Volk und Führer. *German Quarterly* 11 (1): 4–7.

Hetherington, K. (2003) Accountability and Disposal: Visual Impairment and the Museum. *Museum and Society* 1, https://doi.org/10.29311/mas.v1i2.18

Hetherington, K. (2011) Foucault, the Museum and the Diagram. *Sociological Review* 59 (3): 457–475.

Hett, B. C. (2015) This Story is about Something Fundamental: Nazi Criminals, History, Memory, and the Reichstag Fire. *Central European History* 48 (2): 199–224.

HF GI (1938) Henry Ford Receiving German Award, Celebrating his 75th Birthday, Henry Ford Receives the Grand Cross of the German Eagle (Highest Nazi Award to a Foreigner) for Industrial Accomplishments. Image held by Getty Images, www.gettyimages.co.uk/detail/news-photo/celebrating-his-75th-birthday-henry-ford-receives-the-grand-news-photo/515306154. Accessed: 12/02/2021

HFM (n.d.) History & Mission, Henry Ford Museum, www.thehenryford.org/history-and-mission/. Accessed: 12/02/2021

HFRC (2016) Electronic Communication from Kathy M at the Henry Ford Research Centre, to Michael Hughes, July 15, 2016. Permission granted to include statement.

Hillman-Chartrand, H. (1990) Investment Protection: Reducing Financial Loss from Fraudulent Art. *Journal of Cultural Economics* 14 (1): 83–93.

Hinton, D. B. (1975) Triumph of the Will: Document or Artifice? *Cinema Journal* 15 (1): 48–57.

Hitler, A. (1927, 1938) *Mein Kampf*. München: Franz Eher Nachf. GmbH.

Hitler, A. (1969, 2007) *Mein Kampf*, translated by Mainheim, R. London: Pimlico.

Hitler, A. (2016) *Mein Kampf, eine kritische Edition Band II*, edited by Hartmann, C., Vordermayer, T., Plöckinger, O., Töppel, R. Berlin und München: Institut für Zeitgeschichte.

HM (2021) HM Armed Forces Toys & HM Armed Forces Action Figures, www.hmarmedforces.com/. Accessed: 01/03/2020

Hoare, P. (2015) It wasn't Just the Queen – Pop Music Borrowed Nazi Symbols Too, *Guardian*, July 23, 2015, www.theguardian.com/commentisfree/2015/jul/23/pop-music-nazi-symbols-art-queen-fascist. Accessed: 07/02/2019

Hodge, M. (2021) Hitler's Toilet Seat Sells for £14,000 After Being Looted by US Soldiers from his Bavarian Retreat in WWII, *Sun*, February 10, 2021, www.thesun.co.uk/news/13994757/hitler-toilet-auction/. Accessed: 11/03/2021

Hoffman, W. (1965) *Das Wachstum der deutschen Wirtschaft seit Mitte des 19. Jahrhunderts*. Berlin: Springer Verlag.

Hoffmann, D. L. (2000) Mothers in the Motherland: Stalinist Pronatalism in Its Pan-European Context. *Journal of Social History* 34 (1): 35–54.

Hoffmann, P. (1970) Opposition Annihilated: Punishing the 1944 Plot Against Hitler. *North American Review* 255 (3): 11–36.

Hoffmann, P. (1996) *Top-Level Crisis: History of the German Resistance, 1933–1945*. Montreal: McGill-Queen's University Press.

Höhne, H. (1969, 2000) *The Order of the Death's Head: The Story of Hitler's SS*. London: Penguin Classic Military History.

Holmes, H., Ehgartner, U. (2020) Lost Property and the Materiality of Absence, *Cultural Sociology*, December 2020, https://doi.org/10.1177/1749975520969007. Accessed: 04/03/2021

Holtorf, C. (2013) On Pastness: A Reconsideration of Materiality in Archaeological Object Authenticity. *Anthropological Quarterly* 86 (2): 427–443.

Hopkins, K., Beard, M. (2005) *The Colosseum*. Cambridge: Harvard University Press.

Horn, D. (1973) Youth Resistance in the Third Reich: A Social Portrait. *Journal of Social History* 7 (1): 26–50.

Horn, D. (1979) The Struggle for Catholic Youth in Hitler's Germany: An Assessment. *Catholic Historical Review* 65 (4): 561–582.

Horn, E., Gold, J. (2011) Work on Charisma: Writing Hitler's Biography. *New German Critique* 114 (Fall): 95–114.

Horrigan, B. (2002) My Own Mind and Pen: Charles Lindbergh, Autobiography, and Memory. *Minnesota History* 58 (1): 2–15.

Höss, R. (1959) *The Commandant of Auschwitz*. London: Phoenix Press (Orion).

Houkes, W., Vermaas, P. (2004) Actions Versus Functions: A Plea for an Alternative Metaphysics of Artifacts. *Monist* 87 (1): 52–71.

Howard-Woods, C. (2018) Introduction, in *Charlottesville White Supremacy, Populism, and Resistance*, edited by Howard-Woods, C., Laidley, C., Omidi, M. New York: OR Books (orbooks.com).

Hoyos, D. (2008) *Hannibal: Rome's Greatest Enemy*. Liverpool: Liverpool University Press.

HSS. Historical Currency Converter, www.historicalstatistics.org/Currencyconverter.html. Accessed: 24/02/2020

HT (2020) Why is the Public so Obsessed with the Nazis? *History Today* 70 (3), March 2020, quote attributed to Alec Ryrie, Professor of the History of Christianity at Durham University, www.historytoday.com/print/pdf/node/54391/debug. Accessed: 05/03/2021

HTA (2020) Horticultural Sector Worth £1.4 Billion Could be Wiped out by Coronavirus Shut Down in Just Weeks, *Horticultural Trades Association*, March 27, 2020, https://hta.org.uk/news/horticultural-sector-wiped-out-by-coronavirus.html. Accessed: 31/03/2020

HTS (2021) Adolf Hitler's Toilet Seat Captured at the Berghof, lot 512, estimate USD 10,000 to 15,000, sold for USD 15,000, February 8, 2021, www.alexautographs.com/auction-lot/adolf-hitlers-toilet-seat-captured-at-the-berghof_41F439F9EA/. Accessed: 11/03/2021

Hubbert, J. (2006) Collecting Mao: Memory and Fetish in Contemporary China. *American Ethnologist* 33 (2): 145–161.

Hume, D. (1757) *Of the Standard of Taste, in Four Dissertations*. London: A Millar, https://data.historicaltexts.jisc.ac.uk/view?pageTerms=mind%20which%20contempl&pubId=ecco-0113100700&pageId=ecco-0113100700-10. Accessed: 08/03/2021

Hurd, M., Werther, S. (2016) Retelling the Past, Inspiring the Future: Waffen-SS Commemorations and the Creation of a European Far-right Counter-narrative. *Patterns of Prejudice* 50 (4–5): 420–444.

Hürter, J. (2018) Hitler's Generals in the East and the Holocaust, in *Mass Violence in Nazi-Occupied Europe*, edited by Kay, A. J., Stahel, D. Bloomington: Indiana University Press, part I, chapter 1.

Huston, J. H., Spencer, R. W. (2002) Quality, Uncertainty and the Internet: The Market for Cyber Lemons. *American Economist* 46 (1): 50–60.

Hutton, B. G. (1970) *Kelly's Heroes*. Metro-Goldwyn-Mayer.

IBM (2001) IBM Statement on Nazi-era Book and Lawsuit, IBM press release, March 5, 2001, https://web.archive.org/web/20010305225955/www.ibm.com/Press/prnews.nsf/jan/E761868F46444B06852569F20064F555. Accessed: 28/10/2019

Ickes, H. L. (1955) *The Secret Diary of Harold L Ickes Volume II: The Inside Struggle 1936–1939*. New York: Simon and Schuster.

Ikin, A. L. (2020) *Following the Footsteps of a Rag Doll Dance: The Subversive Femininity of Siouxsie Sioux*. M.A.: California State University.

IMM (2013) *Internationales Militaria-Magazin*, Nr. 162, July-August 2013, Zweibrücken: Heinz Nickel Buchvertrieb.

InfC (2021) Value of 1969 British Pounds today, Inflation calculator, £500 in 1969 £7,102.88 in 2021. The inflation rate in United Kingdom between 1969 and today has been 1,320.58%, which translates into a total increase of £6,602.88. This means that 500 pounds in 1969 are equivalent to 7,102.88 pounds in 2021. The average annual inflation rate has been 5.13%. www.in2013dollars.com/uk/inflation/1969. Accessed: 17/03/2021

Isyanova, G. (2009) The Consumer Sphinx: From French Trench to Parisian Market, in *Contested Objects: Material Memories of the Great War*, edited by Saunders, N. J., Cornish, P. Abingdon: Routledge, 130–143.

IWM 5682. IWM. British Army Normandy Campaign 1944 (B 5682) Catalogue number B IWM 5682. Captain L Cotton MM (left, wearing a 'liberated' German Iron Cross!) with his Cromwell VI tank, 'Old Bill', and crew of 4th County of London Yeomanry, 7th Armoured Division, 17 June 1944. Cotton had been promoted to captain following the regiment's action at Villers Bocage. www.iwm.org.uk/collections/item/object/205202020. Accessed: 01/02/2020

IWM BM (n.d.) The Story of Child Evacuee Beryl Myatt and The Sinking of The SS City of Benares, Imperial War Museums, www.iwm.org.uk/history/the-story-of-child-evacuee-beryl-myatt-and-the-sinking-of-the-ss-city-of-benares. Accessed: 03/02/2021

Jablonsky, D. (1988) Röhm and Hitler: The Continuity of Political-Military Discord. *Journal of Contemporary History* 23 (3): 367–386.

Jablonsky, D. (1989) *The Nazi Party in Dissolution: Hitler and the Verbotzeit 1923–1925*. London: Frank Cass and Company Ltd.

Jackson, S. (2014) *Hitler's Heroine: Hanna Reitsch*. Cheltenham: The History Press.

Jacobs, I. (2010) Production to Destruction? Pagan and Mythological Statuary in Asia Minor. *American Journal of Archaeology* 114 (2): 267–303.

Jacquier, E., Kane, A., Marcus, A. J. (2003) Geometric or Arithmetic Mean: A Reconsideration. *Financial Analysts Journal* 59 (6): 46–53.

Jaura, R. (1976) Generals' Affair. *Economic and Political Weekly* 11 (50): 1922–1923.

Jay, M. (2010) Taking on the Stigma of Inauthenticity: Adorno's Critique of Genuineness, in *Language Without Soil: Adorno and Late Philosophical Modernity*, edited by Richtered G. Lincoln: Fordham University Press, 17–29.

JCRF. code: N1095, Russian Front Medal, early plated type GBP 40, Jamie Cross, www.thirdreichmedals.com. Accessed: 10/10/2015

JDM. The James D. Mooney Papers: Folder Listing Continued, Georgetown State University Library, www.library.georgetown.edu/dept/speccoll/fl/f98%7D4.htm. Accessed: 13/03/2014

Jeansonne, G. (1983) Oral History, Biography, and Political Demagoguery: The Case of Gerald L. K. Smith. *Oral History Review* 11: 87–102.

Jeffrey, S. (2015) Challenging Heritage Visualisation: Beauty, Aura and Democratisation. *Open Archaeology* (1): 144–152.

Jeffreys, A. (2009) Distinguishing the Uniform: Military Heraldry and the British Army During the First World War, in *Contested Objects: Material Memories of the Great War*, edited by Saunders, N. J., Cornish, P. Abingdon: Routledge, chapter 8.

Jeffries, S. (2021) Flying cats and a burning Banksy: why are digital art prices suddenly rocketing? *Guardian*, March 9, 2021, https://www.theguardian.com/artanddesign/2021/mar/09/nfts-flying-cats-burning-banksy-digital-art-crypto-art-bitcoin-rocketing. Accessed: 08/10/2021

Jelavich, P. (1995) Method? What Method? Confessions of a Failed Structuralist. *New German Critique* 65: 75–86.

Jelenko, M. (1943) Germany. *American Jewish Year Book* 44: 183–191.

Jennings, M. (Ed.) (2003, 2006) *Walter Benjamin Selected Writings*. Cambridge: Harvard University Press.

JMB. Verleihungsurkunde Ehrenkreuz für Kriegsteilnehmer für Jakob Schrimmer (1882–1942). Jüdisches Museum Berlin, http://objekte.jmberlin.de/object/jmb-obj-237308. Accessed: 24/02/2020

Jobert, L. (1697) *The Knowledge of Medals: Or, Instruction for those who Apply Themselves to the Study of Medals Both Ancient and Modern*. London: Printed for William Rogers. Available at the University of Glasgow special collections.

Joerges, B. (1999) Do Politics have Artefacts? *Social Studies of Science* 29 (3): 411–431.

Johnson, D. E. (1971) *War Medals*. London and Prescott: Barker, C. Tinling & Co Ltd.

Johnson, E. A. (1997) Gender, Race and the Gestapo. *Historical Social Research*/Historische Sozialforschung 22 (3/4): 240–253.

Johnson, E. L. (1970) *McKenzie Break*. United Artists.

Johnson, T. (1984) *World War II German War Booty Volume II*. Virginia: self-published.

Jones, H. (1954) Some Aspects of Demand for Consumer Durable Goods. *Journal of Finance* 9 (2): 93–110.

Jones, S. (2005) Royal Family Caught up in Nazi row, *Guardian*, January 13, 2005, www.theguardian.com/media/2005/jan/13/royalsandthemedia.pressandpublishing. Accessed: 07/12/2020

Jones, S. (2010) Negotiating Authentic Objects and Authentic Selves: Beyond the Deconstruction of Authenticity. *Journal of Material Culture* 15: 181–203.

Jonsson, S. (2013a) After Individuality: Freud's Mass Psychology and Weimar Politics. *New German Critique* 119: 53–75.

Jonsson, S. (2013b) *Crowds and Democracy: The Idea and Image of the Masses from Revolution to Fascism*. New York: Columbia University Press.

Joselit, D., Bois, Y. A., Foster, H., Witt, A., Nathancrompton, Schillinger, J. (2011) Recessional Aesthetics: An Exchange. October 135: 93–116.

Joshi, V. (2011) Maternalism, Race, Class and Citizenship: Aspects of Illegitimate Motherhood in Nazi Germany. *Journal of Contemporary History* 46 (4): 832–853.

Joy, J. (2002) Biography of a Medal: People and the Things they Value, in *Material Culture: The Archaeology of Twentieth-Century Conflict*, edited by Schofield, J. Abingdon: Routledge, 132–144.

JT (2020) Idea of Ridding World of Jews Began Before War, *Jewish Telegraph Online*, January 2020, www.jewishtelegraph.com/glas_1.html. Accessed: 26/01/2020

Julians, J. (2020) Lego Largest Set Ever Launches: Colosseum Set on Sale for Black Friday, *Radio Times*, November 13, 2020, www.radiotimes.com/technology/lego-colosseum-set-largest-ever-set/. Accessed: 01/03/2021

Kapilkov, M. (2020) Collectible William Shatner Figurines Have Now Been Authenticated on Ethereum, *Telegraph*, February 18, 2020, https://cointelegraph.com/news/collectible-william-shatner-figurines-have-now-been-authenticated-on-ethereum. Accessed: 18/03/2021

Kansteiner, W. (2002) Finding Meaning in Memory: A Methodological Critique of Collective Memory Studies. *History and Theory* 41 (2): 179–197.

Kaplan, M. A. (1999) *Between Dignity and Despair: Jewish Life in Nazi Germany*. Oxford: Oxford University Press.

Karim, A. K. M. R., Likova, L. T. (2018) Haptic Aesthetics in the Blind: A Behavioral and fMRI. *PMID* 31497677, https://doi.org/10.2352/ISSN.2470-1173.2018.14.HVEI-532

Kasher, S. (1992) The Art of Hitler. *October* 59: 48–85.

Kater, M. (1975) Zum gegenseitigen Verhältnis von SA and SS in der Sozialgeschichte des Nationalsozialismus von 1925 bis 1939. *VSWG: Vierteljahresheft für Sozial- und Wirtschaftsgeschichte* 62 (3): 339–379.

Kater, M. H. (1987) The Burden of the Past: Problems of a Modern Historiography of Physicians and Medicine in Nazi Germany. *German Studies Review* 10 (1): 31–56.

Katz, R. S. (2003) Internet Speech and the Limits of Jurisdiction. *Proceedings of the Annual Meeting of the American Society of International Law* 97: 312–313.

Kaufman, M. (1965) New Plastics and Their Application. *Journal of the Royal Society of Arts* 113 (5107): 501–513.

Kellner, F. (2018) *My Opposition: The Diary of Friedrich Kellner – A German Against the Third Reich*, translated and edited by Kellner, R. S. Cambridge: Cambridge University Press.

Kennick, W. E. (1985) Art and Inauthenticity. *Journal of Aesthetics and Art Criticism* 44 (1): 3–12.

Kerr, J. (1971, 2017) *When Hitler Stole Pink Rabbit*. London: William Collins and Sons, London: Harper Collins Children's Books (2017 edition). Kindle.

Kershaw, I. (1993) Working Towards the Führer: Reflections on the Nature of the Hitler Dictatorship. *Contemporary European History* 2 (2): 103–118.

Kershaw, I. (2000) *Hitler 1936–1945: Nemesis*. London: Penguin. Paper and Kindle editions.

Kershaw, I. (2011) *The End: Hitler's Germany, 1944–1945*. London: Penguin.

Kershaw, R. (2015) Remembering the City of Benares Tragedy, National Archives, September 17, 2015, https://blog.nationalarchives.gov.uk/remembering-city-benares-tragedy/. Accessed: 03/02/2021

Kharchenkova, S. Velthuis, O. (2018) How to Become a Judgment Device: Valuation Practices and the Role of Auctions in the Emerging Chinese Art Market. *Socio-Economic Review* 16 (3): 459–477.

Kilmister, L., Garza, J. (2002) *White Line Fever*. The autobiography. London: Simon and Schuster.

King, D. (2017) *The Trial of Adolf Hitler: The Beer Hall Putsch and the Rise of Nazi Germany*. London: Penguin-Random House.

Kingsepp, E. (2006) Nazi Fans but not Neo-Nazis: The Cultural Community of WWII Fanatics, in *Returning (to) Communities*, edited by Herbrechter, S. Leiden and Boston: Brill, 223–240.

Kirk, D. (1942) The Relation of Employment Levels to Births in Germany. *Milbank Memorial Fund Quarterly* 20 (2): 126–138.

Kirkpatrick, S. (2010) *Hitler's Holy Relics*. London: Simon and Schuster.

Kitching, C. (2018) Nazi Memorabilia at Market Leaves Shoppers Horrified as Man in German Army Uniform Sells Swastika Flags, *Daily Mirror*, August 13, 2018, www.mirror.co.uk/news/uk-news/nazi-memorabilia-market-leaves-shoppers-13074513. Accessed: 22/11/2019

Kittrie, N. N. (1964) A Post Mortem of the Eichmann Case. The Lessons for International Law. *Journal of Criminal Law, Criminology, and Police Science* 55 (1): 16–28.

Klein, B. (1948) Germany's Preparation for War: A Re-examination. *American Economic Review* 38 (1): 56–77.

Klein, S. S., Klein, R. E., Allen, C. T. (1995) How Is a Possession Me or Not Me? Characterizing Types and an Antecedent of Material Possession Attachment. *Journal of Consumer Research* 22 (3): 327–343.

KM (2003) KM Kunststoff-Magazin, März 19, 2003.

KMT. Kunststoff Museum Troisdorf, DAG, www.kunststoff-museum-troisdorf.de/geschichte/chronik/. Accessed: 02/02/2020

Knight, F. H. (1921) Cost of Production and Price over Long and Short Periods. *Journal of Political Economy* 29 (4): 304–335.

König, W. (2004) Adolf Hitler vs. Henry Ford: The Volkswagen, the Role of America as a Model, and the Failure of a Nazi Consumer Society. *German Studies Review* 27 (2): 249–268.

Koonz, C. (1976) Nazi Women Before 1933: Rebels Against Emancipation. *Social Science Quarterly* 56 (4): 553–563.

Kopytoff, I. (1986) The Cultural Biography of Things: Commoditization as Process, in *The Social Life of Things: Commodities in Cultural Perspective*, edited by Appadurai, A. Cambridge: Cambridge University Press, 64–94.

Köster, R. (2011) *Hugo Boss, 1924–1945 Die Geschichte einer Kleiderfabrik zwischen Weimarer Republik und Drittem Reich*. München: C.H. Beck Verlag.

Kracauer, S. (1947, 2004) *From Caligari to Hitler: A Psychological History of the German Film*. Princeton, NJ: Princeton University Press.

Kragen, P. (2014) Local Dealer Selling Hitler's Clothing, Items, *San Diego Union Tribune*, March 29, 2014, www.sandiegouniontribune.com/lifestyle/people/sdut-craig-gottlieb-sells-hitler-artifacts-2014mar29-htmlstory.html. Accessed: 27/12/2019

Kragen, P. (2019) Local Collector's Hitler Artefacts Could Fetch Millions at German Auction, *San Diego Union Tribune*, September 25, 2019, www.sandiegouniontribune.com/communities/north-county/story/2019-09-25/local-collectors-hitler-artifacts-could-fetch-millions-at-german-auction. Accessed: 27/12/2019

Krammer, A. (1981) Technology Transfer as War Booty: The U.S. Technical Oil Mission to Europe, 1945. *Technology and Culture* 22 (1): 68–103.

Kranzfelder, I. (2001) *Grosz 1893–1959*. Cologne: Taschen.

Krebs, R. R. (2009) The False Promise of the Nobel Peace Prize. *Political Science Quarterly* 124 (4): 593–625.

Kube, A. (1987) *Hermann Göring im Dritten Reich: Pour le Merite und Hakenkreuz*. München: Oldenbourg.

Kube, W. (1941) Application by Kube, Generalkommissar of Belorussia, to Lohse Concerning the Condition of German Jews in Minsk. From Generalkommissar for Belorussia to Reichskommissar for Ostland Gauleiter Hinrich Lohse, Riga, December 16, 1941, www.jewishvirtuallibrary.org/application-by-kube-generalkommissar-of-belorussia-to-lohse-concerning-the-condition-of-german-jews-in-minsk. Accessed: 26/02/2021

Kudlien, F. (1990) The German Response to the Birth-rate Problem During the Third Reich. *Continuity and Change* 5 (2): 225–247.

Kunzer, E. J. (1938) The Youth of Nazi Germany. *Journal of Educational Sociology* 11 (6): 342–350.

Kupisch, K. (1966) *Europa und Deutschland: Protestantische Gedanken Abseits von Konvention und Taktik*. Berlin: Käthe Vogt Verlag.

Kurlander, E. (2017) *Hitler's Monsters: A Supernatural History of the Third Reich*. New Haven: Yale University Press.

Lacey, R. (2020) Prince Harry and Prince William's Feud Began Long Before Meghan came on the Scene, New Book Reveals, *Daily Mail*, October 5, 2020, www.dailymail.co.uk/news/article-8808003/Prince-Harry-Prince-Williams-feud-began-long-Meghan-came-scene-new-book-reveals.html. Accessed: 11/03/2021

Lachin, J. M. (2016) Fallacies of Last Observation Carried Forward Analyses. *Clinical Trials* 13 (2): 161–168.

Lakshmi, V. V., Niharika, D. A., Lahari, G. (2017) Impact of Gender on Consumer Purchasing Behaviour. *IOSR Journal of Business and Management* 19 (8): 33–36.

Lamb, B. J. (Uncle Dick) (n.d.) *Pip, Squeak, and Wilfred, their Luvly adventures*. New York: E. P.

Lapavitsas, C. (2004) Commodities and Gifts: Why Commodities Represent More than Market Relations. *Science & Society* 68 (1): 33–56.

Large, D. C. (1987) Reckoning without the Past: The HIAG of the Waffen-SS and the Politics of Rehabilitation in the Bonn Republic, 1950–1961. *Journal of Modern History* 59 (1): 79–113.

Larson, C. (1937) The German Press Chamber. *Public Opinion Quarterly* 1 (4): 53–70.

Latour, B. (2002) Morality and Technology: The End of the Means. *Theory, Culture, & Society* 19 (5/6): 247–260.

Latour, B., Hennion, A. (2003) How to Make Mistakes on So Many Things at Once-and Become Famous for it, in *Mapping Benjamin: The Work of Art in the Digital Age*, edited by Gumbrecht, H. U., Marrinan, M. Redwood City, CA: Stanford University Press, 91–97.

Latour, B., Lowe, A. (2011) The Migration of the Aura or How to Explore the Original through its Facsimiles, in *Switching Codes-Thinking through Digital Technology in the Humanities and the Arts*, edited by Bartscherer, T., Coover, R. Chicago: University of Chicago Press, 275–297.

Lauritzen, F. (1988) Propaganda Art in the Postage Stamps of the Third Reich. *Journal of Decorative and Propaganda Arts* 10: 62–79.

Layton, R. V. Jr. (1970) The Völkischer Beobachter, 1920–1933: The Nazi Party Newspaper in the Weimar Era. *Central European History* 3 (4): 353–382.

Lee, S. (n.d.) The War, the Great War, the First World War, World War I Centenary, http://ww1centenary.oucs.ox.ac.uk/memoryofwar/the-war-the-great-war-the-first-world-war/. Accessed: 24/05/2021

Lehmann, G. (1913) *Die Ritter des Ordens Pour le Mérite: Auf Allerhöchsten Befehl Seiner Majestät des Kaisers und Königs bearbeitet im Kgl. Kriegsministerium.*

Leighton, T., Berners-Lee, T., Clark, D. D. (2013) The Evolution of the Internet: Emerging Challenges and Opportunities. *Bulletin of the American Academy of Arts and Sciences* 66 (3): 17–25.

Lenz, C., Heinsohn, K. (2008) De-coding the Gendered Order of Memory in Hitlers Frauen. *German Politics & Society* 26 (4): 134–149.

Leroy, J. (2019) Electronic Communication from Jean-Charles Leroy of La Tommy Militaria, to Michael Hughes, June 16, 2019.

Leuthold, R. M., Nwagbo, E. (1977) Changes in the Retail Elasticities of Demand for Beef, Pork, and Broilers. *Illinois Agricultural Economics* 17 (2): 22–27.

Levene, M. (2002) Illumination and Opacity in Recent Holocaust Scholarship. Review of: Final Solution, Nazi Population Policy and the Murder of the European Jews by Gotz Aly; The Holocaust, Origins, Implementations, Aftermath by Omer Bartov; In Perfect Formation. SS Ideology and the SS-Junkerschule-Tolz by Jay Hatheway; National Socialist Extermination Policies, Contemporary German Perspectives and Controversies by Ulrich Herbert; The Nazi Terror. Gestapo, Jews and Ordinary Germans by Eric Johnson; The Language of the Third Reich: LTI, Lingua Tertii Imperii: A Philologist's Notebook by Victor Klemperer and Martin Brady; The Nazi Persecution of the Gypsies by Günter Lewy; Understanding Nazi Genocide. Marxism after Auschwitz by Enzo Traverso and Peter Drucker. *Journal of Contemporary History* 37 (2): 275–292.

Levy, S. J. (1959) Symbols for Sale. *Harvard Business Review* 37: 117–124.

Lewis, A. (2014) First Look: Viv Albertine's New Memoir Recalls Birth of Punk Music and Fashion, *Hollywood Reporter*, www.hollywoodreporter.com/news/viv-albertine-slits-book-clothes-751933. Accessed: 29/11/2020

Ley, R. (Ed.) (1938) *Organisationsbuch der NSDAP*. München: Franz Eher Nachf. GmbH.

Liedtke, R. (2018) *111 Orte in München auf den Spuren der Nazi-Zeit*. Dortmund: Emons.

Lifton, R. J. (1985) What made this Man? Mengele, *New York Times*, July 21, 1985, www.nytimes.com/1985/07/21/magazine/what-made-this-man-mengele.html. Accessed: 05/02/2021

Lillios, K. T. (1999) Objects of Memory: The Ethnography and Archaeology of Heirlooms. *Journal of Archaeological Method and Theory* 6 (3): 235–262.

Lindbergh, A. M. (1976) *The Flower and the Nettle*. London and New York: Helen and Kurt Wolff, Harcourt Brace Jovanovich.

Lindbergh, A. M. (1979) The Changing Concept of Heroes. Talk delivered at the 130th Minnesota Historical Society meeting, October 27, 1979.

Lindbergh, C. A. (1950) *Of Flight and Life*. New York: Charles Scribner's Sons.

Lindbergh, C. A. (1970) *The Wartime Journals of Charles A. Lindbergh*. London and New York: Harcourt Brace Jovanovich.

Lingen, K. (2020) Chapter 4 A Morality of Evil: Nazi Ethics and the Defense Strategies of German Perpetrators, in *Rethinking Holocaust Justice: Essays across Disciplines*, edited by Goda, N. J. W. Oxford: Berghahn Books, 100–126.

Liskofsky, S. (1947) War Crimes Trials. *American Jewish Year Book* 48: 453–465.

List, G. (1906, 1938) *Das Geheimnis der Runen. Mit einer Galen und mehreren Textabbildungen*. Fifth edition. Guido-List Bücherei, https://kupdf.net/download/guido-von-list-das-geheimnis-der-runen_58a0afac6454a7d733b1eeaa_pdf

Littlejohn, D., Dodkins, C. M. (1968) *Orders, Decorations, Medals, and Badges of the Third Reich*. San Jose, CA: Roger James Bender.

Liu, A. (2015) Art Arbitrage – Violations of the Law of One Price Created by Fine Art Auctions. *Undergraduate Economic Review* 12 (1): 1:34, http://digitalcommons.iwu.edu/uer/vol12/iss1/5. Accessed: 15/03/2020

Loader-Wilkinson, T. (2010) The Pros and Cons of Passion Investments, *Wall Street Journal*, September 20, 2010, www.wsj.com/articles/SB10001424052748703467004575463112027277830. Accessed: 08/02/2020

Lockwood, J. (2008) Shopping for the Nation: Women's China Collecting in Late-Nineteenth-Century New England. *New England Quarterly* 81 (1): 63–90.

Löer, W. (2017) Er bekommt nun ein Landtagsmandat – und verkauft KZ-Geld und Hakenkreuz-Orden, *Der Stern*, March 27, 2017, www.stern.de/politik/deutschland/rudolf-mueller-im-saarland – afd-spitzenkandidat-verkauft-kz-geld-und-hakenkreuz-orden-7062136.html. Accessed: 02/02/2020

Loewenstein, J. P. (1941) The Swastika; Its History and Meaning. *Man* 41: 49–55.

Loewenstein, K. (1936) Law in the Third Reich. Yale *Law Journal* 45 (5): 779–815.

Lomax, J. (1988) *Hanna Reitsch: Flying for the Fatherland*. London: John Murray Publishers.

Loneragan, D. (2016) The Wehrmacht and its Involvement in War Crimes on the Eastern Front. *MHIS* 321: 41–52.

Longerich, P. (2019) *Hitler: A Life*. Oxford: Oxford University Press.

Lovin, C. R. (1967) Blut Und Boden: The Ideological Basis of the Nazi Agricultural Program. *Journal of the History of Ideas* 28 (2): 279–288.

Lower, W. (2002) A New Ordering of Space and Race: Nazi Colonial Dreams in Zhytomyr, Ukraine, 1941–1944. *German Studies Review* 25 (2): 227–254.

Lucas, J. (2019) Nazi Memorabilia Auction in Western Australian City Condemned as Morally Repugnant by Jewish Group, *ABC News* (Australian Broadcasting Corporation), June 24, 2019, www.abc.net.au/news/2019-06-24/jewish-group-calls-kalgoorlie-nazi-memorabilia-auction-repugnant/11239134. Accessed: 03/01/2020

Ludde-Neurath, W. (1950) *Regierung Dönitz. Die Letzten Tage des Dritten Reiches.* Göttingen: Musterschmidt Wissenschaftlicher Verlag.

Lüdtke, A. (1992) The Appeal of Exterminating Others: German Workers and the Limits of Resistance. *Journal of Modern History* 64: 46–67.

Lüdtke, A. (2000) People Working: Everyday Life and German Fascism. *History Workshop Journal* 50 (1): 74–92.

Lumsden, R. (1996) Beware the Super-Fakes, *Armourer*, July-August 1996, Macclesfield: Beaumont Publishing, 13.

Lundmark, T. (2011) *The Untold Story of Eva Braun: Her Life beyond Hitler.* Lexington: Self-published. Kindle.

Lyndhurst, J. (Ed.) (1983) *Military Collecting.* London: Salamander Publishing.

MacClancy, J. (1988) A Natural Curiosity: The British Market in Primitive Art. *RES: Anthropology and Aesthetics* 15: 163–176.

Macdonald, S. (2006) Words in Stone? Agency and Identity in a Nazi Landscape. *Journal of Material Culture* 11 (1/2): 105–126.

MacLaughlin, P. J. (1944) Plastics for Eire. *Studies: An Irish Quarterly Review* 33 (130): 169–178.

Maddox, R. (2017) The German Cross of Honour for the German Mother Award, 1938–1944. *IWM volunteer London blog*, November 30, 2017, https://iwmvolun teerlondon.wordpress.com/2017/11/30/the-german-cross-of-honour-for-the-german-mother-award-1938–1944/. Accessed: 07/10/2020

Maerz, D. (2007) *The Knights Cross of the Iron Cross.* Richmond: B&D Publishing.

Maerz, D., Stimson, G. (2010) *The Iron Cross 1. class.* Richmond: B&D Publishing.

Mandel, B. R. (2009) Art as an Investment and Conspicuous Consumption Good. *American Economic Review* 99 (4): 1653–1663.

MandH (2021) Kampfbund für deutsche Kultur, Music and the Holocaust, https://holo caustmusic.ort.org/politics-and-propaganda/third-reich/kampfbund-fur-deutsch-kultur/. Accessed: 24/03/2021

Manstein, E. von (1958) *Lost Victories.* London: Methuen and Company.

Manvell, R., Fraenkel, H. (1962) *Göring.* London: New English Library.

Marcus, R. (2019) UK Holocaust Charity Rejects Donation Offer from Auction House that Sold off Nazi Memorabilia, *Times of Israel*, September 28, 2019, www.timesofis rael.com/uk-holocaust-charity-rejects-donation-offer-from-auction-house-that-sold-off-nazi-memorabilia/. Accessed: 22/11/2019

Marks, C. J., Torry, R. (2000) Herr Direktor: Biography and Autobiography in Schindler's LIST. *Biography* 23 (1): 49–70.

Marks, F. W. (1985) Six between Roosevelt and Hitler: America's Role in the Appeasement of Nazi Germany. *Historical Journal* 28 (4): 969–982.

Marks, S. (1983) My Name is Ozymandias: The Kaiser in Exile. *Central European History* 16 (2): 122–170.

Marshall, B. (1980) German Attitudes to British Military Government 1945–1947. *Journal of Contemporary History* 15 (4): 655–684.

Martin, A. S. (1993) Makers, Buyers, and Users: Consumerism as a Material Culture Framework. *Winterthur Portfolio* 28 (2/3): 141–157.

Martin, L. J. (1945) Population Policies Under National Socialism. *American Catholic Sociological Review* 6 (2): 67–82.

Mason, T. W. (1966) Labour in the Third Reich, 1933–1939. *Past & Present* 33 (April): 112–141.

Mason, T. W. (1976) Women in Germany, 1925–1940: Family, Welfare and Work. Part I. *History Workshop* (1): 74–113.

Mason, T. W. (1981) The Workers' Opposition in Nazi Germany. *History Workshop* 11: 120–137.

Matthäus, J., Roseman, M. (Eds.) (2010) *Jewish Responses to Persecution, 1933–1938* (*Documenting Life and Destruction: Holocaust Sources in Context, vol. 1*). Lanham: AltaMira Press in association with the United States Holocaust Memorial Museum.

Mawdsley, E. (2011) *December 1941: Twelve Days that Began a World War*. New Haven: Yale University Press.

Mazumdar, P. (1990) Blood and Soil: The Serology of the Aryan Racial State. *Bulletin of the History of Medicine* 64 (2): 187–219.

Mazzucato, M. (2018) *The Value of Everything: Making and Taking in a Global Economy*. London: Penguin-Random House. Kindle.

MBRF. No: C55, Russian Front medal GBP 45. M and T Militaria, Carlisle, England, www.mandtmilitaria.com. Accessed: 10/10/2015

McCarthy, E. (2010) Is Oral History Good for You: Taking Oral History beyond Documentation and into a Clinical Setting: First Steps. *The Oral History Review* 37 (2): 159–169.

McCormick, D. W., Spee, J. C. (2008) IBM and Germany 1922–1941. *Organization Management Journal* 5 (4): 214–223.

McCourt, T. (2005) Collecting Music in the Digital Realm. *Popular Music and Society* 28 (2): 249–252.

McCracken, G. (1986) Culture and Consumption: A Theoretical Account of the Structure and Movement of the Cultural Meaning of Consumer Goods. *Journal of Consumer Research* 13 (1): 71–84.

McCracken, G. (1988) *Culture and Consumption: New Approaches to the Symbolic Character of Consumer Goods and Activities*. Bloomington: Indiana University Press.

McDermott, K. (2012) Fury as Nazi Memorabilia is Sold off at Auction House on the Most Solemn Day in the Jewish Calendar, *Daily Mail*, October 6, 2012, www.dailymail.co.uk/news/article-2213696/Fury-Nazi-memorabilia-sold-auction-house-solemn-day-Jewish-calendar.html. Accessed: 26/07/2019

McIntosh, A. C. (1986) Recent Pronatalist Policies in Western Europe. *Population and Development Review* 12 (Supplement): 318–334.

McIntosh, R. J., Togola, T., McIntosh, S. K. (1995) The Good Collector and the Premise of Mutual Respect Among Nations. *African Arts* 28 (4): 60–69, and 110–112.

McKale, D. (1973) A Case of Nazi Justice: The Punishment of Party Members Involved in the Kristallnacht, 1938. *Jewish Social Studies* 35 (3/4): 228–238.

Mees, B. (2004) Hitler and Germanentum. *Journal of Contemporary History* 39 (2): 255–270.

Mei, J., Moses, M. (2002) Art as an Investment and the Underperformance of Masterpieces. *American Economic Review* 92 (5): 1656–1668.

Merron, J. (1999) Putting Foreign Consumers on the Map: J. Walter Thompson's Struggle with General Motors' International Advertising Account in the 1920s. *Business History Review* 73 (3): 465–504.

MF (n.d.) World War 2 / Lemmy's War Memorabilia, Official Motörhead Forums, http://imotorhead.com/forums/ubbthreads.php?ubb=showflat&Number=709. Accessed: 25/07/2013. Link not accessible on 08/02/2020

MHM (2016) Electronic Communication from the Curator of the Civic and Personal Identity Missouri History Museum Library and Research Centre, to Michael Hughes, May 12, 2016.

Miller, D. (1995) Consumption and Commodities. *Annual Review of Anthropology* 24: 141–161.

Miller, D. (1998) Material Culture: The Social Life of External Objects. *British Journal of Psychotherapy* 14 (4): 483–492.

Miller, D. (2005) Materiality: An Introduction, in *Materiality*, edited by Miller, D. Durham: Duke University Press, 1–50.

Miller, D. (2010) *Stuff*. Cambridge: Polity press.

Miller, E. (1975) Status Goods and Luxury Taxes. *American Journal of Economics and Sociology* 34 (2): 141–154.

Mitchel, R. W. (1996) The Psychology of Human Deception. *Social Research* 63 (3): 819–861.

Mitchell, M. (1995) Materialism and Secularism: CDU Politicians and National Socialism, 1945–1949. *Journal of Modern History* 67 (2): 278–308.

Mitgang, H. (1980) Lindbergh Said to Regret Misperceptions Over Jews, *New York Times*, April 20, 1980, www.nytimes.com/1980/04/20/archives/lindbergh-said-to-regret-misper ceptions-over-jews-hindsight-and.html. Accessed: 06/12/2018

Miyazaki, S. (2015) Going Beyond the Visible: New Aesthetic as an Aesthetic of Blindness? in *Postdigital Aesthetics*, edited by Berry, D. M., Dieter, M. London: Palgrave Macmillan, 219–231.

Möller, J. (2003) *Das Winterhilfswerk. Erscheinungsbild und Bedeutung im Sozialsystem des Dritten Reichs*. München: GRIN, self-published.

Mollendorf, F. von (1968) *Fakes and Frauds of the Third Reich*. Self-published.

Mollo, A. (1971) *Uniforms of the SS Volume 4 SS-Totenkopfverbande 1933–1945*. London: A Historical Research Unit Publication.

Mommsen, H., Gordon, A., Reich, M., Goldberg, A. (1997) An Interview with Prof. Hans Mommsen. *Yad Vashem*, www.yadvashem.org/odot_pdf/Microsoft%20Word%20-%20 3850.pdf. Accessed: 07/11/2018

Montgomery, E. (2004) Recognizing Value in African American Heritage Objects. *Journal of African American History* 89 (2): 177–182.

Mooney, J. D. (1937) American Economic Policies for the Impending World War. *Annals of the American Academy of Political and Social Science* 192: 89–92.

Moore, R. (2004) Postmodernism and Punk Subculture: Cultures of Authenticity and Deconstruction. *Communication Review* 7 (3): 305–327.

Moorhouse, R. (2017) *The Third Reich in 100 Objects*. Barnsley: Pen and Sword.

More, T. (1516, 2005) *Utopia*. Stilwell: Digireads.com Publishing.

Morgan, B. (2010) Understanding the Cultural Impact of Popular Film, in *Cultural Impact in the German Context: Studies in Transmission, Reception, and Influence*, edited by Braun, R., Marven, L. Rochester, New York: Boydell & Brewer Camden House, 58–77.

Morgan, T., Reilly, J., Pisa, N., Ridley, M. (2015) Open the Archives, *Sun*, July 18, 2015, www.thesun.co.uk/archives/news/62362/open-the-archives-2/. Accessed: 07/12/2020

Morris, P. J. T. (1992) The Technology: Science Interaction: Walter Reppe and Cycloocta-tetraene Chemistry. *British Journal for the History of Science* 25 (1): 145–167.

Mosse, G. (1966) *Nazi Culture*. London: WH Allen.

Mosse, G. (1996) Fascist Aesthetics and Society: Some Considerations. *Journal of Contemporary History* 31 (2): 245–252.

Moulin, R., Vale, M. (1995) The Museum and the Marketplace: The Constitution of Value in Contemporary Art. *International Journal of Political Economy* 25 (2): 33–62.

Mouton, M. (2010) From Adventure and Advancement to Derailment and Demotion: Effects of Nazi Gender Policy On Women's Careers and Lives. *Journal of Social History* 43 (4): 945–971.

MSA (2018) 1929 Adolf Hitler's Personal Desk & Chair, Milestone Auctions, Lot 326, price realised USD 34,800.00, date sold 27/01/2018, https://milestoneauctions.hibid. com/lot/72898-120228-53778/1929-adolf-hitlers-personal-desk-and-chair/. Accessed: 11/03/2021

MT. *Military Trader Magazine*, Florida, Active Interest Media, www.militarytrader.com. Accessed: 05/01/2020

Mühlberger, D. (1980) The Sociology of the NSDAP: The Question of Working-Class Membership. *Journal of Contemporary History* 15 (3): 493–511.

Mukena, R. (2020) Edward Colston Statue to Appear in Bristol Museum Early Next Year, *Bristol Live*, November 2, 2020, www.bristolpost.co.uk/news/bristol-news/edward-colston-statue-appear-bristol-4661193. Accessed: 03/03/2021

Muller, R. R. (2003) Losing Air Superiority: A Case Study from the Second World War. *Air and Space Power Journal* 17 (4): 55–66.

Mulligan, T. P. (1987) Spies, Ciphers and Zitadelle: Intelligence and the Battle of Kursk, 1943. *Journal of Contemporary History* 22: 235–260.

Mulligan, T. P. (1992) German U-boat Crews in World War II: Sociology of an Elite. *Journal of Military History* 56 (2): 261–282.

Münsterberger, W. (1994) *Collecting: An Unruly Passion: Psychological Perspectives.* Princeton, NJ: Princeton University Press.

Musan, K. D. I. (2020) *NFT Finance Leveraging Non-Fungible Tokens.* Individual Project, Imperial College London.

Nagel, S. R. (2001) Shadows and Ephemera. *Critical Inquiry* 28 (1): 23–39.

Nagle, T. (1984) Economic Foundations for Pricing. *Journal of Business* 57 (1): 3–26.

NAM MC. General Montgomery awarding Captain Bill Cotton with the Military Cross, 1944, Online Collection, National Army Museum, London, NAM. 1975-03-63-20-46, https://collection.nam.ac.uk/detail.php?acc=1975-03-63-20-46. Accessed: 01/01/2020

NatGeo (2021) Decoding the Hate Symbols seen at the Capitol Insurrection, *National Geographic*, January 12, 2021, www.nationalgeographic.com/history/article/decoding-hate-symbols-seen-at-capitol-insurrection. Accessed: 10/03/2021

Neitzel, S. (2007) *Tapping Hitler's Generals: Transcripts of Secret Conversations 1942–1945.* Barnsley: Frontline Books (an imprint of Pen and Sword).

Neitzel, S., Welzer, H. (2013) *Soldaten – On Fighting, Killing and Dying: The Secret Second World War Tapes of German POWs.* London: Simon and Schuster.

Nelis, J. (2007) Constructing Fascist Identity: Benito Mussolini and the Myth of Romanità. *Classical World* 100 (4): 391–415.

Neumann, B. (2002) The National Socialist Politics of Life. *New German Critique* 85 (Special Issue on Intellectuals): 107–130.

Neumann, F. (1942, 2012) *Behemoth: The Structure and Practice of National Socialism.* Chicago: Ivan R. Dee (Roman and Littlefield).

Nielsen, H. K. (2020) *Aesthetics and Political Culture in Modern Society.* Abingdon: Routledge.

Nim. Price guides consulted:

Nimmergut, J. (1980) *Orden und Ehrenzeichen von 1800–1945.* Self-published.

Nimmergut, J. (1982) *Orden und Ehrenzeichen von 1800–1945.* Self-published.

Nimmergut, J. (1984) *Orden und Ehrenzeichen von 1800–1945.* Self-published.

Nimmergut, J. (1988) *Orden und Ehrenzeichen von 1800–1945.* Self-published.

Nimmergut, J. (1990) *Orden und Ehrenzeichen von 1800–1945.* Self-published.

Nimmergut, J. (1992) *Orden und Ehrenzeichen von 1800–1945.* Self-published.

Nimmergut, J. (1994) *Orden und Ehrenzeichen von 1800–1945.* Self-published.

Nimmergut, J. (1996) *Orden und Ehrenzeichen von 1800–1945.* Self-published.

Nimmergut, J. (1998) *Orden und Ehrenzeichen von 1800–1945.* Self-published.

Nimmergut, J. (2000) *Orden und Ehrenzeichen von 1800–1945.* Self-published.

Nimmergut, J. (2001) *Deutsche Orden und Ehrenzeichen bis 1945*, Band 4. Munich: Zentralstelle für wissenschaftliche Ordenskunde.

Nimmergut, J. (2002) *Orden und Ehrenzeichen von 1800–1945.* Self-published.

Nimmergut, J. (2004) *Orden und Ehrenzeichen von 1800–1945.* Self-published.

Nimmergut, J. (2008) *Deutsche Orden und Ehrenzeichen 1800–1945*. Regenstauf: Battenberg.

Nimmergut, J. (2010) *Deutsche Orden und Ehrenzeichen 1800–1945*. Regenstauf: Battenberg.

Nimmergut, J., Feder, H. (2006) *Deutsche Orden und Ehrenzeichen: Deutsches Reich, Weimarer Republik, Drittes Reich, DDR und Bundesrepublik 1871 bis Heute*. Regenstauf: Battenberg.

Nimmergut, J., Nimmergut, A. (2011) *Deutsche Orden und Ehrenzeichen 1800–1945*. Regenstauf: Battenberg.

Nimmergut, J., Nimmergut, A. (2012) *Deutsche Orden und Ehrenzeichen 1800–1945*. Regenstauf: Battenberg.

Nimmergut, J., Nimmergut, A. (2014) *Deutsche Orden und Ehrenzeichen 1800–1945*. Regenstauf: Battenberg.

Nix, A. (2019) Bidding Wars! *Military Trader*, November 12, 2019, www.militarytrader. com/militaria-collecting-101/bidding-wars. Accessed: 03/01/2020

NME (2018) Aliens, Nazis and Cocaine: Six 70s Myths about David Bowie, *NME Blog*, January 10, 2018, www.nme.com/blogs/nme-blogs/six-70s-myths-about-david-bowie-761066. Accessed: 07/12/2020

NMRRF. Nicholas Morigi Regalia Specialist, W2881 Russian Front Medal GBP 10.95, Offering the Best Selection of Fine Quality Replica Awards & Insignia Since 1975, 71a Eastbourne Rd. Lower. Willingdon, Eastbourne, East Sussex, www.nicholasmorigi.com. Accessed: 27/06/2014

NMRTB. Nicholas Morigi Regalia Specialist, NM SP068 Tank badge GBP 23.95, www. nicholasmorigi.com. Accessed: 27/06/2014

Norris, J. (2019) The German Cross of Honour, *Military Trader*, November 12, 2019, originally published January 14, 2010, www.militarytrader.com/militaria-collectibles/ german-cross-of-honor. Accessed: 11/02/2020

Nowak, M. (2020) Electronic Communication from Matthias Nowak of the Bayerisches Staatsministerium der Finanzen und für Heimat, to Michael Hughes, January 7, 2020.

Nussbaum, M. C. (1995) Objectification. *Philosophy & Public Affairs* 24 (4): 249–291.

Nye, D. (1979) *Henry Ford: Ignorant Idealist*. London: National University Publications.

NYT (July 1937) Thomas J. Watson is Decorated by Hitler for Work in Bettering Economic Relations, *New York Times*, July 2, 1937, www.nytimes.com/1937/07/02/archives/thomas-j-watson-is-decorated-by-hitler-for-work-in-bettering.html. Accessed: 12/11/2019

NYT (August 1938) General Motors Man Wins German Award; J. D. Mooney, Head of Overseas Division, Gets Order of Merit, *New York Times*, August 11, 1938, www. nytimes.com/1938/08/11/archives/general-motors-man-wins-german-award-j-d-mooney-head-of-overseas.html. Accessed: 13/11/2019

NYT (October 1938) Hitler Grants Lindbergh High Decoration After Bitter Attacks on Flier by Russians, *New York Times*, October 20, 1938, Accessed: 10/10/2021

NYT (June 1940) 1937 Hitler Decoration is Returned by Watson, *New York Times*, June 7, 1940.

NYT (January 1972) Erhard Milch, 79, Luftwaffe Chief, *New York Times*, January 29, 1972, 32, www.nytimes.com/1972/01/29/archives/erhaltd-milch-9-luftwrffe-chief-goering-protege-convicted-of-war.html. Accessed: 27/02/2021

O'Donnell, M. (2012) Dangerous Undercurrent: Death, Sacrifice and Ruin in Third Reich Germany. *International Journal of Humanities & Social Science* 2 (9): 231–239.

Ofcom (2008) Ofcom Broadcast Bulletin, issue number 121, November 10, 2008, Accessed: 07/12/2020

Offner, A. A. (1977) Appeasement Revisited: The United States, Great Britain, and Germany, 1933–1940. *Journal of American History* 64 (2): 373–393.

OHV. Captured Memorabilia, Ohio Valley Military Society, www.sosovms.com/Captured-Memorabilia/ Accessed: 01/01/2020

O'Lessker, K. (1968) Who Voted for Hitler? A New Look at the Class Basis of Nazism. *American Journal of Sociology* 74 (1): 63–69.

Olick, J. K. (1999) Collective Memory: The Two Cultures. *Sociological Theory* 17 (3): 333–348.

Olmsted, A. D. (1988) Morally Controversial Leisure: The Social World of Gun Collectors. *Symbolic Interaction* 11 (2): 277–287.

O'Loughlin, J. (2002) The Electoral Geography of Weimar Germany: Exploratory Spatial Data Analyses (ESDA) of Protestant Support for the Nazi Party. *Political Analysis* 10 (3): 217–243.

O'Neill, R. (1966) *The German Army and the Nazi Party*. London: Cassell and Co Ltd.

Oregon (n.d.) Judenpolitik. Principal Acts of Anti-Jewish Legislation in Germany, 1933–1943, University of Oregon, https://pages.uoregon.edu/dluebke/Holocaust444-544/Judenpolitik.html. Accessed: 28/03/2021

Ortner, S. B. (1973) On Key Symbols. *American Anthropologist* 75 (5): 1338–1346.

OT (2020) Online Traders, *Militaria History*, website of the *Armourer*, www.militaria-history.co.uk/dealers/online-trader/?CurrentPage=4&Sort=None&Seed=8d531156-721f-4e49-99f9-d16345a9e8c6. Accessed: 30/03/2020

Overy, R. (1994) *War and Economy in the Third Reich*. Oxford: University of Oxford Press, Clarendon Press.

Owen, M. (2021) NFT – Everything you Need to Know About Non-fungible Tokens, *Apple Insider*, March 14, 2021, https://appleinsider.com/articles/21/03/14/nft – everything-you-need-to-know-about-non-fungible-tokens. Accessed: 19/03/2021

Padfield, P. (1984, 1993) *Dönitz: The Last Führer*. London: Thistle Publishing.

Padfield, P. (1990) *Himmler Reichsführer SS*. London: MacMillan.

Park, W. (2020) The Fate of Antiques and Heirlooms in a Disposable Age, *BBC online*, August 24, 2020, www.bbc.com/future/article/20200824-the-decline-of-antiques-and-objects-that-last-for-generation. Accessed: 05/03/2021

Parsons, M. (2016) Nazi Toilet Paper Among Hitler-era Memorabilia Up for Auction, *Irish Times*, September 5, 2016, www.irishtimes.com/life-and-style/homes-and-property/fine-art-antiques/nazi-toilet-paper-among-hitler-era-memorabilia-up-for-auction-1.2779429. Accessed: 16/07/2019

Pasher, Y. (2014) *Holocaust versus Wehrmacht: How Hitler's Final Solution Undermined the German War Effort*. Lawrence: University Press of Kansas.

Pattrson, T. (2011) Downfall: The Story of a Nazi Boy Hero, *Independent*, November 16, 2011, www.independent.co.uk/news/world/europe/downfall-the-story-of-a-nazi-boy-hero-520880.html. Accessed: 26/02/2021

Paulicelli, E. (2004) *Fashion Under Fascism: Beyond the Black Shirt*. Oxford: Berg Publishers.

Pauwels, J. R. (2003) Profits Über Alles! American Corporations and Hitler, review of: IBM and the Holocaust: The Strategic Alliance between Nazi Germany and America's Most Powerful Corporation by Edwin Black; Hitler, der Westen und die Schweiz 1936–1945 by Walter Hofer and Herbert R. Reginbogin; Working for the Enemy: Ford, General Motors, and Forced Labor during the Second World War by Reinhold Billstein, Karola Fings, Anita Kugler and Nicholas Levis; Research Findings about Ford-Werke under the Nazi Regime. *Labour/Le Travail* 51 (Spring): 223–249.

Paver, C. (2010) You Shall Know Them by Their Objects: Material Culture and Its Impact in Museum Displays about National Socialism, in *Cultural Impacts in the German*

Context: Studies in Transmission, Reception, and Influence, edited by: Braun, R., Marven, L. New York: Camden House, 169–187.

Payne, K. (2018) Telephone Interview between Ken Payne and Michael Hughes, transcript held by both participants. Permission granted.

Pearce, J. (2016) Nazism & Narcissism: David Bowie's Flirtation with Fascism, *Imaginative Conservative*, February 19, 2016, https://theimaginativeconservative.org/2016/02/nazism-and-narcissism-david-bowie-flirtation-with-fascism.html. Accessed: 07/1/2021

Pearce, S. (1998) *Collecting in Contemporary Practice*. London: Sage Publications.

Pearson, H. (2007) *Achtung Schweinehund!: A Boy's Own Story of Imaginary Combat*. London: Abacus (an imprint of Little Brown).

Pegelow, T. (2002) German Jews, National Jews, Jewish Volk or Racial Jews? The Constitution and Contestation of Jewishness in Newspapers of Nazi Germany, 1933–1938. *Central European History* 35 (2): 195–221.

Pendleton, B. F. (1978) An Historical Description and Analysis of Pronatalist Policies in Italy, Germany and Sweden. *Policy Sciences* 9 (1): 45–70.

Pennock, J. R. (1980) Thoughts on the Right to Private Property. *Nomos* 22: 171–186.

Penslar, D. J. (2013) *Jews and the Military: A History*. Princeton, NJ: Princeton University Press.

Perkins, J. (1995) Coins for Conflict: Nickel and the Axis, 1933–1945. *Historian* 55 (1): 85–100.

Perlman, S. (1965) The Coins of Philip II and Alexander the Great and their Pan-hellenic Propaganda. *Numismatic Chronicle and Journal of the Royal Numismatic Society* 5: 57–67.

Perry, J. (2005) Nazifying Christmas: Political Culture and Popular Celebration in the Third Reich. *Central European History* 38 (4): 572–605.

Pershey, E. J. (1998) Handling History: Using Material Culture to Create New Perspectives on the Role of Technology in Society. *OAH Magazine of History* 12 (2): 18–24.

Pesando, J. E., Shum, P. M. (2007) The Law of One Price, Noise and Irrational Exuberance: The Auction Market for Picasso Prints. *Journal of Cultural Economics* 31 (4): 263–277.

Petch, A. (2004) Collecting Immortality: The Field Collectors who Contributed to the Pitt Rivers Museum, Oxford. *Journal of Museum Ethnography*, 16, Papers Originating from MEG Conference 2003: Developing Audiences – Developing Collections, University of Leicester (March 2004): 127–139.

Petersen, W. (1981) *Das Boot*. Neue Constantin Film.

Petropoulos, J. (1994) Not a Case of Art for Art's Sake: The Collecting Practices of the Nazi Elite. *German Politics & Society* 32: 107–124.

Phelps, R. H. (1963) Before Hitler Came: Thule Society and Germanen Orden. *Journal of Modern History* 35 (3): 245–261.

PI (1944) Untitled. *Population Index* 10 (1): 31–32.

PI (1946) The Population of the Soviet Union: History and Prospects. *Population Index* 12 (3): 163–167.

Pia, J. (1971) *Nazi Insignia*. New York: Ballantine.

Pia, J. (1974) *SS Regalia*. New York: Ballantine.

Pickering, A. (1995) *The Mangle of Practice: Time, Agency and Science*. Chicago and London: University of Chicago Press.

Piper, E. (2007) *Alfred Rosenberg: Hitlers Chefideologe*. München: Pantheon.

Piszkiewicz, D. (1997) *From Nazi Test Pilot to Hitler's Bunker: The Fantastic Flights of Hanna Reitsch*. Westport, CT: Praeger (an imprint of Greenwood Publishing).

Plischke, E. (1947) Denazification Law and Procedure. *American Journal of International Law* 41 (4): 807–827.

Plöckinger, O. (2006) *Geschichte eines Buches: Adolf Hitler's Mein Kampf.* München: Oldenburg Wissenschaftsverlag.

Polanyi, K. (1944) *The Great Transformation.* New York: Farrar and Rinehart.

Poore, C. (2007) *Disability in Twentieth-Century German Culture.* Ann Arbor: University of Michigan Press.

Proctor, R. N. (1997) Letters to the Editor. Cigarette Smoking and Health Promotion in Nazi Germany. *Journal of Epidemiology and Community Health* 51 (2): 208–212.

Prown, J. D. (1982) Mind in Matter: An Introduction to Material Culture Theory and Method. *Winterthur Portfolio* 17 (1): 1–19.

PT. Polystyrene Timeline, www.trinseo.com/company/history/polystyrene.htm. Accessed: 02/10/2015

PW (1970) Review of Fakes and Frauds of the Third Reich by Freiherr von Mollendorf, reviewed by Jay, R. M (Ed.). *Photo War*, vol. 1, issue 3, 1970. England.

Qian, Y. (2011) Counterfeiters: Foes or Friends? How do Counterfeits Affect Different Product Quality Tiers? Working Paper 16785, National Bureau of Economic Research, www.nber.org/papers/w16785. Accessed: 18/04/2020

Rabinbach, A. G. (1976) The Aesthetics of Production in the Third Reich. *Journal of Contemporary History* 11 (4): 43–74.

Rabinbach, A. G., Gilman, S. L. (Eds.) (2013) This Is National Kitsch!: What the Ban on Führer Kitsch is Supposed to Protect Us From (1933), in *The Third Reich Sourcebook*. Berkeley: University of California Press, chapter 37, 79–80.

Radocchia, S. (2018) How Non-Fungible Tokens from Physical Collectibles are Strengthening Asset-Backed Securities, *Forbes*, July 5, 2018, www.forbes.com/sites/ samantharadocchia/2018/07/05/how-non-fungible-tokens-from-physical-collectibles-are-strengthening-asset-backed-securities/. Accessed: 18/03/2021

Randall Trawnik, W. M., Schaal, R., Hartmann, W. (2009, 2019) Pickelhaube: The story of the German spiked helmet, *Military Trader*, June 18, 2009, updated November 6, 2019, www.militarytrader.com/militaria-collecting-101/pickelhaube-german-spiked-helmet. Accessed: 27/03/2021

Rautkallio, H. (1994) Cast into the Lion's Den – Finnish Jewish Soldiers in the Second World War. *Journal of Contemporary History* 29 (1): 53–94.

Rawson, A. (2012) *Showcasing the Third Reich: The Nuremberg Rallies.* Cheltenham: Spellmount (an imprint of The History Press).

Read, A. (2003) *The Devil's Disciples.* London: Jonathan Cape.

Reagin, N. R. (2007) *Sweeping the German Nation: Domesticity and National Identity in Germany, 1870–1945.* New York: Cambridge University Press.

Reed, S. (2015) *The Nuremberg Party Rallies, Wagner and the Theatricality of Hitler and the Nazi Party.* University of Hawaii 13: 74–80, https://hilo.hawaii.edu/campus center/hohonu/volumes/documents/CathedralofLight-TheNurembergPartyRalliesWag nerandTheTheatricalityofHitlerandtheNaziPartyStaceyReed.pdf. Accessed: 24/02/2020

Reese, D. (2006) *Growing Up Female in Nazi Germany*, translated by Templer, W., series editor Eley, G. Ann Arbor: University of Michigan Press.

Reese, W. S. (2000) The Rare Book Market Today. *Yale University Library Gazette* 74 (3/4): 146–165.

RegJ (2020) Anti-Partisan badge in bronze, GBP 1,995, code 74727, update January 24, 2020, Regimentals, www.regimentals.co.uk. Accessed: 29/01/2020

RegPB (2020) German WWII NSDAP party badges. Marked RZM M1/148, GBP 115, Code: 74401; marked RZM M1/34, GBP 95, Code: 72832. Regimentals, www.regimentals.co.uk. Accessed: 08/01/2020

Reich, L. S. (1995) From the Spirit of St. Louis to the SST: Charles Lindbergh, Technology, and Environment. *Technology and Culture* 36 (2): 351–393.

Reichel, A. (1940, 2011) *127 Jahre Eisernes Kreuz. 1813/14, 1870/71, 1914/18, 1939/40: Eine kurzgefasste Zusammenstellung über Entstehung, Verleihung, Symbolik.* Dresden: M. Dittert und Co., reprinted by Verlag Weber.

Reichmann, H. (1937) Letter. Hans Reichmann to CV Landesverband Mitteldeutschland, September 9, 1937, Wiener Library London, CV 1937. Copy supplied to Michael Hughes by Professor Tim Grady.

Reinhart, F. W. (1967) Engineering Properties of Plastics Applicable to Water Piping. *Journal of the American Water Works Association* 59 (4): 447–456.

Reitlinger, G. (1957) *The SS: Alibi of a Nation, 1922–1945.* New York: Da Capo Press.

Reitsch, H. (1951, 2015) *The Sky My Kingdom: Memoirs of the Famous German World War II Test Pilot.* Barnsley: Greenhill Books (an imprint of Pen and Sword).

Renneboog, L., Houtte, T. (2002) The Monetary Appreciation of Paintings: From Realism to Magritte. *Cambridge Journal of Economics* 26 (3): 331–357.

Reno, J. O. (2017) *Foreword to Revised Edition of Rubbish Theory: The Creation and Destruction of Value.* London: Pluto Press.

Reuth, R. G. (2009) *Hitlers Judenhass: Klischee und Wirklichkeit.* München: Piper Verlag.

RGB (April 1933) Reichsgesetzblatt, Gesetz zur Wiederherstellung des Berufbeamtentums, April 7, 1933, http://alex.onb.ac.at/cgi-content/alex?aid=dra&datum=1933&size=45&page=300

RGB (Mai 1933) Reichsgesetzblatt, Gesetz zum Schutze der nationalen Symbole vom Mai 19, 1933, http://alex.onb.ac.at/cgi-content/alex?aid=dra&datum=1933&page=410&size=45

RGB (Dezember 1938) Reichsgesetzblatt, Verordnung des Führers und Reichskanzlers über die Stiftung des Ehrenkreuzes der Deutschen Mutter Vom Dezember 16, 1938, http://alex.onb.ac.at/cgi-content/alex?aid=dra&datum=1938&page=2101&size=45

RGB (September 1939) Reichsgesetzblatt, Verordnung über die Erneuerung des Eisernen Kreuzes, September 2, 1939, I, Nr. 159, http://alex.onb.ac.at/cgi-content/alex?aid=dra&datum=1939&page=230&size=45.

RGB (Mai 1942) Reichsgesetzblatt, Verordnung über den Schutz der Waffenabzeichen der Wehrmacht, Mai 3, 1942, http://alex.onb.ac.at/cgi-content/alex?aid=dra&datum=1942&size=45&page=380

RGB (Januar 1945) Reichsgesetzblatt, Erlass des Führers über die Stiftung des Ritterkreuzes des Eisernes Kreuzes mit dem Goldenen Eichenlaub mit Schwertern und Brillanten, Dezember 29, 1944. Veröffentlicht Januar 22, 1945, I, Nr. 3, http://alex.onb.ac.at/cgi-content/alex?aid=dra&datum=1945&page=11&size=45

Ribuffo, L. P. (1980) Henry Ford and the International Jew. *American Jewish History* 69 (4): 437–477.

Ricardo, D. (1951) *The Works and Correspondence of David Ricardo, Volume 1 On the Principles of Political Economy and Taxation,* edited by Sraffa, P. London: Cambridge University Press.

Richardson, M. (2009) Medals, Memory and Meaning: Symbolism and Cultural Significance of Great War Medals, in *Contested Objects: Material Memories of the Great War,* edited by Saunders, N. J., Cornish, P. Abingdon: Routledge, chapter 7.

Richardson, T., Laurier, W., Weszkalnys, G. (2014) Introduction: Resource Materialities. *Anthropological Quarterly* 87 (1): 5–30.

Richins, M. L. (1994) Special Possessions and the Expression of Material Values. *Journal of Consumer Research* 21 (3): 522–533.

Riefenstahl, L. (1935) *Der Triumph des Willens* (Triumph of the Will). UFA.

Rigg, B. M. (2002) *Hitler's Jewish Soldiers: The Untold Story of Nazi Racial Laws and Men of Jewish Descent in the German Military*. Lawrence: University Press of Kansas.

Riley, D. (1979) War in the Nursery. *Feminist Review* 2: 82–108.

Rivett, J. (2013) *The Party Badge, an Advanced Study of the NSDAP Membership Badge*. Michigan: B&D Publishing.

R. J. (1944) Czechoslovakia During the War: II- Bohemia and Moravia. *Bulletin of International News* 21 (23): 943–950.

Roberts, B. (1958) Obituary: Dr. Wilhelm Filchner. *Geographical Journal* 124 (1): 144–145.

Robinson, M. (2018) Opinion: Stop Using the Word Nazi, Unless You Really Mean it, *Collegian*, October 21, 2018, www.thecollegianur.com/article/2018/09/opinion-stop-using-the-word-nazi-unless-you-really-mean-it. Accessed: 24/11/2019

Rödig, A. (2012) Interview with Daniel Miller. *Krisis, Journal for Contemporary Philosophy* (1): 49–52.

Roffe, J. (November 2016) Introduction to Abstract Market Theory in Five Propositions (2016), www.academia.edu/30469851/Introduction_to_Abstract_Market_Theory_in_Five_Propositions?auto=download. Accessed: 19/10/2019

Rogan, B. (1998) On Collecting as Play, Creativity and Aesthetic Practice. *Etnofoor* 11 (1): 40–54.

Rohrer, F. (2009) Is it OK to Collect Nazi Memorabilia? *BBC Magazine Online*, September 17, 2009, http://news.bbc.co.uk/1/hi/8261002.stm. Accessed: 06/08/2013

Römer, F. (2012) *Kameraden: Die Wehrmacht von innen*. München: Piper Verlag.

Rosenberg, A. (1930, 1935) *Der Mythos des 20. Jahrhunderts, Eine Wertung der seelisch-geistigen Gestaltenkämpfe unserer Zeit*. München: Hoheneichen-Verlag.

Rossol, N. (2014) Veterans' Organisations, Germany, International Encyclopedia of the First World War, October 8, 2014, https://encyclopedia.1914-1918-online.net/article/veterans_organisations_germany. Accessed: 25/03/2021

Roth, J. K. (1980) Holocaust Business: Some Reflections on Arbeit Macht Frei. *Annals of the American Academy of Political and Social Science* 450: 68–82.

Roth, P. (2004a) *The Plot Against America*. Boston: Houghton Mifflin Harcourt.

Roth, P. (2004b) The Story Behind the Plot Against America, *New York Times*, September 19, 2004, www.nytimes.com/2004/09/19/books/review/the-story-behind-the-plot-against-america.html. Accessed: 03/12/2018

Rubel, P., Rosman, A. (2001) The Collecting Passion in America. *Zeitschrift für Ethnologie* 126 (2): 313–330.

Rubenstein, L. (1977) Where Have All the Nazis Gone? *Cinéaste* 8 (2): 32–35.

Rubenstein, R. L. (1989) The Philosopher and the Jews: The Case of Martin Heidegger. *Modern Judaism* 9 (2): 179–196.

Rudel, H.-U. (1952, 2012) *Stuka Pilot*. London: Black House Publishing.

Rupp, L. J. (1977) Mother of the Volk: The Image of Women in Nazi Ideology. *Signs* 3 (2): 362–379.

Rurup, R. (1968) Problems of the German Revolution 1918–1919. *Contemporary History* 3 (4): 109–135.

RZM (September 1934) *Mitteilungsblatt der Reichszeugmeisterei der NSDAP*, Ausgabe 15, September 8, 1934.

RZM (April 1935) *Mitteilungsblatt der Reichszeugmeisterei der NSDAP*, Ausgabe 15, April 27, 1935.

RZM (Mai 1935) *Mitteilungsblatt der Reichszeugmeisterei der NSDAP*, Ausgabe 3, Mai 1935.

RZM HB (1935) *Handbuch der Reichszeugmeisterei* (1935). München: Franz Eher Nachf. GmbH.

Salter, M. (2007) *Nazi War Crimes, US Intelligence and Selective Prosecution at Nuremberg: Controversies Regarding the Role of the Office of Strategic Services.* Abingdon: Routledge-Cavendish.

Sanchez, T. (2010) *Up and Down with The Rolling Stones – My Rollercoaster Ride with Keith Richards.* London: John Blake.

Sand, C. K. (2005) Ruinous Aura: From Sunset Boulevard to Mulholland Drive, in *Actualities of Aura: Twelve Studies of Walter Benjamin*, edited by Petersson, Steinskog, E. Svanesund: Nordic Summer University Press.

Saunders, N. J. (2004) Material Culture and Conflict: The Great War, 1914–2003, in *Matters of Conflict. Material Culture, Memory and the First World War*, edited by Saunders, N. J. Abingdon: Routledge, 5–25.

Saunders, N. J. (2014) Nicholas Saunders – Trapped in Shells: Mindset and Materiality in First World War Trench Art, Paper Presented at the Design History Society's 2014 conference, www.youtube.com/watch?v=rEK78hZHHBw. Accessed: 11/03/2021

Saunders, N. J., Cornish, P. (Eds.) (2009) Introduction, in *Contested Objects: Material Memories of the Great War.* Abingdon: Routledge, 1–10.

SBG (n.d.) Women in the SBG, Waffen-SS re-enacting group, www.sbg1.mistral.co.uk/framesetwith%20scroll.htm. Accessed: 15/12/2020

Scarpaci, J. L. (2016) Material Culture and the Meaning of Objects. *Material Culture* 48 (1): 1–9.

Sch (1934) *Der Schild*, Juli 20, 1934, Nr 27.

Schaarschmidt, T. (2017) Multi-Level Governance in Hitler's Germany: Reassessing the Political Structure of the National Socialist State. *Historical Social Research/Historische Sozialforschung* 42 (2): 218–242.

Schatzberg, E. (2003) Symbolic Culture and Technological Change: The Cultural History of Aluminium as an Industrial Material. *Enterprise & Society* 4 (2): 226–271.

Schaub, S. (2013) Dadurch wurde Adolf Hitler automatisch mein zweiter Patenonkel. *Aargauer Zeitung*, December 28, 2013, www.tagblatt.ch/leben/dadurch-wurde-adolf-hitler-automatisch-mein-zweiter-patenonkel-ld.1810579. Accessed: 28/02/2021

Scheinberg, R. (1997) Grad Student Uncovers Jews who Fought for Adolf Hitler, *Jewish Telegraphic Agency*, June 5, 1997, www.jta.org/1997/06/05/lifestyle/grad-student-uncovers-jews-who-fought-for-adolf-hitler. Accessed: 01/02/2021

Schiff, J. (1977) The Life and Letters of Charles A. Lindbergh: A Commemorative View. *Yale University Library Gazette* 51 (4): 173–189.

Schildknecht, C. E. (1952) *Vinyl and Related Polymers.* New York: John Wiley.

Schiller, D., Skillicorn, C. (2021) Non-Fungible Tokens: Why Digital Collectibles Have Real Value, *Enjin* Blog, February 24, 2021, https://enjin.io/blog/why-nfts-have-real-value. Accessed: 18/03/2021

Schindler, S., Wilson-Milne, K., Hofman, P. (2018) The Financialization of Art with Philip Hoffman, *Art Law Podcast*, December 3, 2018, http://artlawpodcast.com/2018/12/03/the-financialization-of-art-with-philip-hoffman/. Accessed: 09/08/2019

Schlauch, W. (1970) American Policy Towards Germany, 1945. *Journal of Contemporary History* 5 (4): 113–128.

Schmidt, S. J. (2003) From Aura-loss to Cyberspace: Further Thoughts on Walter Benjamin, in *Mapping Benjamin: The Work of Art in the Digital Age*, edited by Gumbrecht, H. U., Marrinan, M. Redwood City, CA: Stanford University Press, 79–90.

Schmidtke, M. A. (1999) Cultural Revolution or Cultural Shock? Student Radicalism and 1968 in Germany. *South Central Review* 16/17 (4/1): 77–89.

Schneider, H. W. (1928) *Making the Fascist State.* New York: Oxford University Press.

Schnitzel, P. (1979) A Note on the Philatelic Demand for Postage Stamps. *Southern Economic Journal* 45 (4): 1261–1265.

Schoenbaum, D. (1966, 1997) *Hitler's Social Revolution: Class and Status in Nazi Germany, 1933–1939*. New York: Norton Paperback. Reprinted by New York: Doubleday.

Schoenberger, E. (2011) Why is Gold Valuable? Nature, Social Power and the Value of Things. *Cultural Geographies* 18 (1): 3–24.

Schott, W. (1930) *Ein Künstlerleben und gesellschaftliche Erinnerungen aus kaiserlicher Zeit*. Dresden: Carl Reissner Verlag.

Schultz, M. R. (2016) Conversations with Farmers: Oral History for Agricultural Historians. *Agricultural History* 90 (1): 51–69.

Schulze-Wegener, G. (2012) *Das Eiserne Kreuz in der Deutschen Geschichte*. Graz: Ares Verlag GmbH.

Schuman, F. L. (1936) *The Nazi Dictatorship*. London: Robert Hale & Company.

Schwartz, B. (1967) The Social Psychology of the Gift. *American Journal of Sociology* 73 (1): 1–11.

Schweibenz, W. (2018) The Work of Art in the Age of Digital Reproduction. *Museum International*, https://onlinelibrary.wiley.com/doi/abs/10.1111/muse.12189. Accessed: 19/03/2021

Schwichtenberg, C. (1981) Erotica: The Semey Side of Semiotics. *SubStance* 10 (32): 26–38.

Schymura, Y. (2014) Mutterkreuze unter Hitler: Mutterkult im Nationalsozialismus, *Der Spiegel*, May 11, 2014, http://www.spiegel.de/einestages/mutterkreuze-unter-hitler-mutterkult-im-nationalsozialismus-a-967822.html. Accessed: 05/08/2015

Scott, D. A. (2016) *Art: Authenticity, Restoration, Forgery*. Cotsen Institute of Archaeology Press at UCLA, https://doi.org/10.2307/j.ctvdmwx02

Scott, J. W. (1986) Gender: A Useful Category of Historical Analysis. *American Historical Review* 91 (5): 1053–1075.

Scott, P. D. (1985) Why No One Could Find Mengele: Allen Dulles and the German SS. *Threepenny Review* (23): 16–18.

Sears, O. (2018) Telephone Interview between Oliver Sears and Michael Hughes, transcript held by both participants. Permission granted.

Seccombe, W. (1990) Starting to Stop: Working-Class Fertility Decline in Britain. *Past & Present* 126: 151–188.

Seitsonen, O. (2018) *Archaeologies and Heritage of the Second World War German Military Presence in Finnish Lapland*. Ph.D., University of Helsinki. Helsinki: Finland.

Seitsonen, O. (2020) *Archaeologies of Hitler's Arctic War: Heritage of the Second World War German Military Presence in Finnish Lapland*. Abingdon: Routledge.

Seitsonen, O., Herva, V.-P., Nordqvist, K., Herva, A., Seitsonen, S. (2017) A Military Camp in the Middle of Nowhere: Mobilities, Dislocation and the Archaeology of a Second World War German Military Base in Finnish Lapland. *Journal of Conflict Archaeology* 12 (1): 3–28.

Sennett, A. (2014) Film Propaganda: Triumph of the Will as a Case Study. *Framework: The Journal of Cinema and Media* 55 (1): 45–65.

Sessler, S. (2010) Der Orden-Macher (The Order Maker), *TZ*, September 13, 2010, article supplied to Michael Hughes by Dr. Martin Pichl of Pichl Medaillen GmbH, the firm that recently acquired Deschler.

SGA (1991) *Otto Dix-zum 100*. Geburtstag, Städtische Galerie Abstadt. Reutlingen: Oertel Spörer Verlage.

SGB (1997) Strafgesetzbuch für das Deutsche Reich vom Mai 15, 1871, August 1, 1997, https://lexetius.com/StGB/86. Accessed: 07/12/2019

Shapira, I. (2019) History or Hatred? Selling Hitler's Belongings and Nazi Artefacts Stirs a Backlash. Sale of Hitler's Belongings and Nazi Artefacts Stir Backlash Amid Rising Anti-Semitism, *Washington Post*, January 1, 2019, www.washingtonpost.com/gdpr-consent/?destination=%2flocal%2fhistory-or-hatred-selling-hitlers-belongings-and-nazi-artifacts-stirs-a-backlash%2f2018%2f12%2f26%2fb0c21932-f27d-11e8-aeea-b85fd44449f5_story.html%3f. Accessed: 26/05/2019

Sharma, D. C. (1990) The Berne Incident. *Proceedings of the Indian History Congress* 51: 730–737.

Shaw, R. (1950) Mars in Full Dress. *Military Engineer* 42 (287): 213–215.

Shea, B. (2010) The Need for the Stahlhelm Part 1 of 8, The Wilson History & Research Center, July 27, 2010, www.youtube.com/watch?v=npxamdiKkTI. Accessed: 12/02/2020

Shea, B. (2015) Electronic Communication from Bill Shea, to Michael Hughes, May 3, 2015.

Shea, B. (2017) Telephone Interview between Bill Shea and Michael Hughes, transcript held by both participants. Permission granted.

Shea, B. (2021a) Electronic Communication from Bill Shea, to Michael Hughes, January 14, 2021.

Shea, B. (2021b) 88 MPH Time Machine, Bill Shea's Website Featuring his Collection of Movie Car Props, including those from *Ghostbusters* and *Back to the Future*, www.88mphtimemachine.com/. Accessed: 27/03/2021

Sheffield, R. (2017) Why Anita Pallenberg, Rolling Stones Muse, Was Queen of the Underground, *Rolling Stone*, June 14, 2017, www.rollingstone.com/music/music-news/why-anita-pallenberg-rolling-stones-muse-was-queen-of-the-underground-204744/. Accessed: 08/03/2021

Shenton, J. D. (1960) Fascism and Father Coughlin. *Magazine of History* 44 (1): 6–11.

Shepherd, B. (2016) *Hitler's Soldiers: The German Army in the Third Reich*. New Haven: Yale University Press.

Sherlock, S. (1997) The Future of Commodity Fetishism. *Sociological Focus* 30 (1): 61–78.

Shirer, W. (1941) *Berlin Diary: The Journal of a Foreign Correspondent 1934–1941*. London: Hamish Hamilton.

Shirer, W. (1960) *The Rise and Fall of the Third Reich*. London: Secker and Warburg.

Showalter, D. E. (1983) Letters to Der Stürmer: The Mobilization of Hostility in the Weimar Republic. *Modern Judaism* 3 (2): 173–187.

Shuker, R. (2004) Beyond the 'High Fidelity' Stereotype: Defining the (Contemporary) Record Collector. *Popular Music* 23 (3): 331–330.

Sibley, F. N., Tanner, M. (1968) Symposium: Objectivity and Aesthetics. *Proceedings of the Aristotelian Society* 42: 31–72.

Siemens, D. (2017a) *Stormtroopers: A New History of Hitler's Brownshirts*. New Haven: Yale University Press.

Siemens, D. (2017b) Franz Pfeffer von Salomon: Hitlers vergessener Oberster SA-Fuehrer. *German History* 35 (3): 468–470.

Silverman, D. P. (1988) Nazification of the German Bureaucracy Reconsidered: A Case Study. *Journal of Modern History* 60 (3): 496–539.

Simmel, G. (1907, 1978) *The Philosophy of Money*. Abingdon: Routledge and Kegan Paul.

Simmel, G. (1957) Fashion. *American Journal of Sociology* 62 (6): 541–558.

Simmons, S. (2000) Hand to the Friend, Fist to the Foe: The Struggle of Signs in the Weimar Republic. *Journal of Design History* 13 (4): 319–339.

Simon, M., Sidner, S. (2021) Capitol Hill Insurrection: Decoding the Extremist Symbols and Groups, *CNN*, January 11, 2021, https://edition.cnn.com/2021/01/09/us/capitol-hill-insurrection-extremist-flags-soh/index.html. Accessed: 11/03/2021

Simonds, W. A. (1946) *Henry Ford: A Biography*. London: Michael Joseph Ltd (now an imprint of Penguin-Random House).

Simonsohn, U., Ariely, D. (2008) When Rational Sellers Face Nonrational Buyers: Evidence from Herding on eBay. *Management Science* 54 (9): 1624–1637.

Simpson, P. (2004) Parading Myths: Imaging New Soviet Woman on Fizkul'turnik's Day, July 1944. *Russian Review* 63 (2): 187–211.

Singer, L. (1978) Microeconomics of the Art Market. *Journal of Cultural Economics* 2 (1): 21–40.

Singerman, R. (1981) The American Career of the Protocols of the Elders of Zion. *American Jewish History* 71 (1): 48–78.

Skradol, N. (2011) Fascism and Kitsch: The Nazi Campaign Against Kitsch. *German Studies Review* 34 (3): 595–612.

Smelser, R. (1990) How Modern Were the Nazis? DAF Social Planning and the Modernization Question. *German Studies Review* 13 (2): 285–302.

Smelser, R. (2008) The Myth of the Clean Wehrmacht in Cold War America, in *Lessons and Legacies VIII: From Generation to Generation*, edited by Bergen, D. L. Illinois: Northwestern University Press, 247–268.

Smith, A. L. Jr. (1958) General Von Seeckt and the Weimar Republic. *Review of Politics* 20 (3): 347–357.

Smith, G. A., Strobele, S. A., Egger, M. (1994) Smoking and Health Promotion in Nazi Germany. *Journal of Epidemiology and Community Health* 48: 220–223.

Smith, H. W. (2008) When the Sonderweg Debate Left Us. *German Studies Review* 31 (2): 225–240.

Smith, S. (2016) Electronic Communication from Sharon Smith of the Missouri Historical Society, to Michael Hughes, May 5, 2016.

Smith, T. (1985) *Berlin Alert: The Memoirs and Reports of Truman Smith*, edited by Hessen, R. Stanford, CA: Hoover Archival Documentaries.

Smuts, A. (2011) Grounding Moralism: Moral Flaws and Aesthetic Properties. *Journal of Aesthetic Education* 45 (4): 34–53.

Snyder, T. (2012) The Causes of the Holocaust. *Contemporary European History* 21 (2): 149–168.

Sodaro, A. (2018) *Exhibiting Atrocity: Memorial Museums and the Politics of Past Violence*. New Brunswick, Camden, Newark, NJ; London: Rutgers University Press.

Solimano, A. (2019) The Art Market at Times of Economic Turbulence and High Inequality. Paper to be Presented at the Investment Migration Council Academic Day 2019, (Geneva, June 3, 2019) and the Inequality Seminar Series at the European Investment Bank, Luxembourg (June 6, 2019).

Soltis, A. (2005) Royal Nazi-Prince Harry in Swastika Shock, *New York Post*, January 13, 2005, https://nypost.com/2005/01/13/royal-nazi-prince-harry-in-swastika-shock/. Accessed: 14/11/2018

Sonn, R. (2005) Your Body is Yours: Anarchism, Birth Control, and Eugenics in Interwar France. *Journal of the History of Sexuality* 14 (4): 415–432.

Sontag, S. (1980) Fascinating Fascism, in *Under the Sign of Saturn*. London: Writers and Readers, 73–108.

Sösemann, B. (2000) Appell unter der Erntekrone: Das Reichserntedankfest in der nationalsozialistischen Diktatur. *Jahrbuch für Kommunikationsgeschichte* 2: 113–156.

Speer, A. (1970, 1995) *Inside the Third Reich*. London: Phoenix (a division of Orion Books).

Spencer, I. D. (1944) William L. Marcy Goes Conservative. *Mississippi Valley Historical Review* 31 (2): 205–224.

Spengler, J. J. (1951) Population: Notes on France's Response to her Declining Rate of Demographic Growth. *Journal of Economic History* 11 (4): 403–416.

Spiegel (1966) Angst-Brosche bis Zuwachs-Arier, *Spiegel*, Juni 20, 1966, www.spiegel.de/spiegel/print/d-46407774.html. Accessed: 24/02/2020

Spielberg, S. (1989) *Indiana Jones and the Last Crusade*. Paramount Pictures.

Spielberg, S. (1993) *Schindler's List*. Universal Pictures.

Spurr, M. A. (2003) Living the Blackshirt Life: Culture, Community and the British Union of Fascists, 1932–1940. *Contemporary European History* 12 (3): 305–322.

Stallabrass, J. (1996) *Gargantua: Manufactured Mass Culture*. London: Verso.

Stangneth, B. (2015) *Eichmann before Jerusalem: The Unexamined Life of a Mass Murderer*. London: Bodley Head (an imprint of Penguin-Random House).

Staudinger, H. (1938) Germany's Population Miracle. *Social Research* 5 (2): 125–148.

Stedelijk (n.d.) Der Agitator – George Grosz, The Rabble Rouser, Stedelijk Museum Netherlands, www.stedelijk.nl/en/collection/3560-george-grosz-der-agitator. Accessed: 08/02/2021

Steffen, T., Caspari, L. (2017) Die von ganz rechts aussen, *Die Zeit*, Marz 24, 2017, www.zeit.de/politik/deutschland/2017-03/afd-saarland-landtagswahl-wahlkampf-rechtsextremismus. Accessed: 08/10/2021

Steigmann-Gall, R. (2003) Rethinking Nazism and Religion: How Anti-Christian Were the Pagans? *Central European History* 36 (1): 75–105.

Steinberg, R. (1975) *Nazi Kitsch*, translated by Morgan, S. Darmstadt: Melzer Verlag.

Steinert, M. G. (1988) The Allied Decision to Arrest the Dönitz Government. *Historical Journal* 31 (3): 651–663.

Steinweis, A. E. (1991) Weimar Culture and the Rise of National Socialism: The Kampfbund für deutsche Kultur. *Central European History* 24 (4): 402–423.

Stenross, B. (1994) Aesthetes in the Marketplace: Collectors in the Gun Business. *Qualitative Sociology* 17 (1): 29–42.

Stephenson, J. (1975) *Women in Nazi Society*. London: Croom Helm.

Stephenson, J. (2001) *Women in Nazi Germany*. Abingdon: Routledge. Kindle.

Stern, B. J. (1941) Alternative Proposals to Democracy: The Pattern of Fascism. *Journal of Negro Education* 10 (3): 368–379.

Stern, J. E. (1975) *Hitler: The Führer and the People*. Hassocks: The Harvester Press.

Stetson, D. M. (1986) Abortion Law Reform in France. *Journal of Comparative Family Studies* 17 (3): 277–290.

Stewart, S. (1984, 1993) *On Longing: Narratives of the Miniature, the Gigantic, the Souvenir, the Collection*. Durham: Duke University Press.

Stibbe, M. (2003) *Women in the Third Reich*. London: Hodder Education.

Stickings, T. (2020) Pictures Show Hitler through the Eyes of his Bodyguard, *Daily Mail*, February 11, 2020, www.dailymail.co.uk/news/article-7990797/Pictures-Hitler-eyes-bodyguard.html. Accessed: 17/02/2020

Stokes, R. G. (2004) From the IG Farben Fusion to the Establishment of BASF AG (1925–1952), in *German Industry and Global Enterprise BASF: The History of a Company*, edited by Abelshauser, W. Cambridge: Cambridge University Press, 206–357.

Stokes, R. G. (2007) Review of: Unternehmensstrategien zwischen Weltwirtschaftskrise und Kriegswirtschaft: Chemnitzer Maschinenbauindustrie in der NS-Zeit, 1933–1945 by Michael C. Schneider; General Motors and the Nazis: The Struggle for Control of Opel, Europe's Biggest Carmaker by Henry Ashby Turner Jr. *Journal of Modern History* 79 (3): 706–709.

Stolfi, R. H. S. (1980) Chance in History: The Russian Winter of 1941–1942. *History* 65 (214): 214–228.

Stolfi, R. H. S. (1982) Barbarossa Revisited: A Critical Reappraisal of the Opening Stages of the Russo-German Campaign (June-December 1941). *Journal of Modern History* 54 (1): 27–46.

Stoller, M. A. (1984) The Economics of Collectible Goods. *Journal of Cultural Economics* 8 (1): 91–104.

Stone, O. M. (1969) The New Fundamental Principles of Soviet Family Law and Their Social Background. *International and Comparative Law Quarterly* 18 (2): 392–423.

Strachen, I. (2018) Telephone Interview between Ian Strachen and Michael Hughes, transcript held by both participants. Permission granted.

Sträter, A. (1948) Denazification. *Annals of the American Academy of Political and Social Science* 260: 43–52.

Stratton, J. (2007) Punk, Jews, and the Holocaust -The English Story. *Shofar* 25 (4): 124–149.

Stratton, J. (2008) *Jewish Identity in Western Pop Culture: The Holocaust and Trauma through Modernity*. New York: Palgrave Macmillan.

Strauss, M. D. (2001) A Framework for Assessing Military Dress Authenticity in Civil War Re-enacting. *Clothing and Textiles Research Journal* 19 (4): 145–157.

Streb, J. (2011) Inter Industry Knowledge Transfer in the German plastics Industry, in *German Industry in the Nazi Period*, edited by Buchheim, C. Stuttgart: Steiner.

Strugalla, A. E. (2014) Flughafen Tempelhof: Pragmatismus machte das NS-Wappen zum US-Adler, *Welt*, July 10, 2014, www.welt.de/geschichte/article130006945/Pragmatismus-machte-das-NS-Wappen-zum-US-Adler.html. Accessed: 09/03/2021

Sturges, J. (1976) *The Eagle has Landed*. Columbia Pictures.

Sutcliffe, T. (2011) When Shock Value is the Soft Option, *Independent*, July 22, 2011, www.independent.co.uk/voices/columnists/thomas-sutcliffe/tom-sutcliffe-when-shock-value-is-the-soft-option-2318125.html. Accessed: 26/07/2019

Sweney, M., Conlan, T. (2008) BBC Faces Ofcom Criticism Over Handling of Weekend Nazis Documentary, *Guardian*, September 15, 2008, www.guardian.co.uk/media/2008/sep/15/bbc.ofcom. Accessed: 25/07/2013

Sydnor, C. W. Jr. (1973) The History of the SS Totenkopfdivision and the Postwar Mythology of the Waffen SS. *Central European History* 6 (4): 339–362.

Taeuber, C., Taeuber, I. B. (1940) German Fertility Trends, 1933–1939. *American Journal of Sociology* 46 (2): 150–167.

Tanselle, G. T. (1998) A Rationale of Collecting. *Studies in Bibliography* 51: 1–25.

Targowski, A. (2016) *The Deadly Effect of Informatics on the Holocaust*. Oklahoma: Tate Publishing & Enterprises.

Tay, A. (1972) The Status of Women in the Soviet Union. *American Journal of Comparative Law* 20 (4): 662–692.

Taylor, D. (2019) Electronic Communication from Dan Taylor, the Curator of the Kent & Sharpshooters Yeomanry Museum, to Michael Hughes, June 11, 2019.

Taylor, H. P., Bender, R. J. (1969) *Uniforms, Organization, and History of the Waffen-SS*. San Jose, CA: Roger James Bender Publishing.

Taylor, J. D. (2008) *Gun Shows, Gun Collectors and the Story of the Gun: An Ethnographic Approach to U.S. Gun Culture*. Ph.D., Ohio State University.

Taylor, S. (1981) Symbol and Ritual Under National Socialism. *British Journal of Sociology* 32 (4): 504–520.

Teather, D. (2009) Ministry of Defence Hopes New Toy Action Figures will Help Image, *Guardian*, May 6, 2009, www.theguardian.com/lifeandstyle/2009/may/07/british-armed-forces-action-man. Accessed: 01/03/2021

Teicher, A. (2019) Why Did the Nazis Sterilize the Blind? Genetics and the Shaping of the Sterilization Law of 1933. *Central European History* 52 (2): 289–309.

Temin, P. (1990) Socialism and Wages in the Recovery from the Great Depression in the United States and Germany. *Journal of Economic History* 50 (2): 297–307.

Temin, P. (1991) Soviet and Nazi Economic Planning in the 1930s. *Economic History Review* 44 (4): 573–593.

Tennstedt, F. (1987) Wohltat und Interesse. Das Winterhilfswerk des Deutschen Volkes: Die Weimarer Vorgeschichte und ihre Instrumentalisierung durch das NS-Regime. *Geschichte und Gesellschaft* 13 (2): 157–180.

Theodossopoulos, D. (2013) Introduction: Laying Claim to Authenticity: Five Anthropological Dilemmas. *Anthropological Quarterly* 86 (2): 337–360.

Thomas, D. A. (2006) Why the Public Plundering of Private Property Rights is Still a Very Bad Idea. *Real Property, Probate and Trust Journal* 41 (1): 25–71.

Thomas, E. (1880) The Indian Swastika and its Western Counterparts. *Numismatic Chronicle and Journal of the Numismatic Society* 20: 18–48.

Thomas, S., Seitsonen, O., Herva, V. (2016) Nazi Memorabilia, Dark Heritage and Treasure Hunting as Alternative Tourism: Understanding the Fascination with the Material Remains of World War II in Northern Finland. *Journal of Field Archaeology* 41 (3): 331–343.

Thompson, D. (1944) Signals from Germany. *Foreign Affairs* 22 (2): 189–208.

Thompson, D. G. (1993) Villains, Victims, and Veterans: Buchheim's Das Boot and the Problem of the Hybrid Novel-Memoir as History. *Twentieth Century Literature* 39 (1): 59–78.

Thompson, M. (1979, 2017) *Rubbish Theory: The Creation and Destruction of Value*. London: Pluto Press.

Thompson, M. (2015) On the Ethical Dimensions of Waste. *ARSP: Archiv für Rechts- und Sozialphilosophie/Archives for Philosophy of Law and Social Philosophy* 101 (2): 252–269.

Thoreau, H. D. (1854, 1995) *Walden; Or, Life in the Woods*. New York City: Dover Publications.

Tilley, C. (1996) The Powers of Rocks: Topography and Monument Construction on Bodmin Moor. *World Archaeology* 28 (2): 161–176.

Tilley, C. (2013) Objectification, in *Handbook of Material Culture*, edited by Tilley, C., Keane, W., Kuechler, S., Rowlands, M., Spyer, P. London: SAGE Publications Ltd, 60–73.

Times (1919) Design of the British War Medal, Times, May 12, 1919, www.thetimes.co.uk/archive/article/1919-05-12/12/14.html#start%3D1918-01-01%26end%3D1921-01-01%26terms%3Dwar%20medal%20by%20William%20McMillan%2C%20%26back%3D/tto/archive/find/war+medal+by+William+McMillan%25252C+/w:1918-01-01%7E1921-01-01/1%26next%3D/tto/archive/frame/goto/war+medal+by+William+McMillan%25252C+/w:1918-01-01%7E1921-01-01/2. Accessed: 07/02/2020

Tolliday, S. (1995) Enterprise and State in the West German Wirtschaftswunder: Volkswagen and the Automobile Industry, 1939–1962. *Business History Review* 69 (3): 273–350.

Tomlinson, R. (1985) The 'Disappearance' of France, 1896–1940: French Politics and the Birth Rate. *Historical Journal* 28 (2): 405–415.

Tooze, A. (2006) *The Wages of Destruction: The Making and Breaking of the Nazi Economy*. London: Penguin.

Toy, E. V. (1989) Silver Shirts in the Northwest: Politics, Prophecies, and Personalities in the 1930s. *Pacific Northwest Quarterly* 80 (4): 139–146.

Trips-Herbert, R. (2014) Das strafbare Verwenden von Kennzeichen verfassungswidriger Organisationen, Wissenschaftliche Dienste des Deutschen Bundestages, 2014, www.google.com/url?sa=t&rct=j&q=&esrc=s&source=web&cd=1&ved=2ahUKEwiV4br-z6PmAhVPThUIHat_DzMQFjAAegQIAhAC&url=https%3A%2F%2Fwww.bundestag.de%2Fresource%2Fblob%2F195550%2F2Fdb1151061f691ac9a8be2d9b60210ac%2Fdas_strafbare_verwenden_von_kennzeichen_verfassungswidriger_organisationen-data.pdf&usg=AOvVaw0_Hmj7MA2TcuP4UiVHqmLt. Accessed: 14/12/2019

Trofanenko, B. (2006a) Displayed Objects, Indigenous Identities, and Public Pedagogy. *Anthropology & Education Quarterly* 37 (4): 309–327.

Trofanenko, B. (2006b) The Public Museum and Identify: Or, the Question of Belonging. *Counterpoints* 272: 95–109.

Tuan, Y.-F. (1980) The Significance of the Artefact. *Geographical Review* 70 (4): 462–472.

Turkle, S. (Ed.) (2011) *Evocative Objects: Things We Think With*. Cambridge: MIT Press.

Turner, H. A. Jr. (1968) Hitler's Secret Pamphlet for Industrialists, 1927. *Journal of Modern History* 40 (3): 348–374.

Turner, H. A. Jr. (2001) Review of: IBM and the Holocaust: The Strategic Alliance between Nazi Germany and America's Most Powerful Corporation by Edwin Black. *Business History Review* 75 (3): 636–639.

Turner, H. A. Jr. (2005) *General Motors and the Nazis: The Struggle for Control of Opel, Europe's Biggest Car Maker*. New Haven: Yale University Press.

Tweedie, N., Kallenbach, M. (2005) Prince Harry Faces Outcry at Nazi Outfit, *Telegraph*, January 14, 2005, www.telegraph.co.uk/news/uknews/1481148/Prince-Harry-faces-out cry-at-Nazi-outfit.html. Accessed: 01/01/2020

TW GI (1937) Thomas Watson receives German Eagle Order from Hjalmar Schacht, picture of award held by Getty Images, www.gettyimages.co.uk/detail/news-photo/watson-thomas-j-businessman-usa17-02-1874-receives-from-news-photo/541795345. Accessed: 10/02/2021

Twiss, S. B. (2010) Can a Perpetrator Write a Testimonial? Moral Lessons from the Dark Side. *Journal of Religious Ethics* 38 (1): 5–42.

Tymkiw, M. (2013) Art to the Worker! National Socialist Fabrikausstellungen, Slippery Household Goods and Volksgemeinschaft. *Journal of Design History* 26 (4): 362–380.

UBN (n.d.) Korvettenkapitän Heinrich Bleichrodt – German U-boat Commanders of WWII, The Men of the Kriegsmarine, uboat.net, https://uboat.net/men/bleichrodt.htm. Accessed: 03/02/2021

Uldrıcks, T. J. (1999) The Icebreaker Controversy: Did Stalin Plan to Attack Hitler? *Slavic Review* 58 (3): 626–643.

UM (Dezember 1934) *Uniformen Markt*, Dezember 1934.

UM (Januar 1935) Zivilist oder Soldat? *Uniformen Markt*, Ausgabe 1, Januar 1935.

UM (Februar 1935) Chronik, *Uniformen Markt*, Februar 1935.

UM (Mai 1935) *Uniformen Markt*, Ausgabe 5, Mai 1, 1935.

UM (Juli 1935) Orden, Abzeichen, Plaketten, *Uniformen Markt*, Ausgabe 7, Juli 1935.

UM (August 1935) *Uniformen Markt*, Ausgabe 8, August 1935.

UM (September 1935) Fahnen und Standarten, *Uniformen Markt*, Ausgabe 9, September 1935.

UM (Januar 1936) *Uniformen Markt*, Jahrgang 1, Januar 1, 1936.

UM (Februar 1938) *Uniformen Markt*, Ausgabe 4, Jahrgang 5, Februar 15, 1938.

UM (mitte-September 1939) Was bringen uns die deutschen Kunststoffe? *Uniformen Markt*, Ausgabe 18, September 15, 1939.

UM (September 1939) Der Kurs der Uniformeneffekten, *Uniformen Markt*, Ausgabe 17, September 1939.

UM (November 1939) *Uniformen Markt*, Ausgabe 22, November 1939.

UM (September 1940) *Uniformen Markt*, Ausgabe 17, Jahrgang 7, September 1, 1940.

UM (mitte-März 1941) *Uniformen Markt*, Ausgabe 6, Jahrgang 8, Mitte März 1941.

UM (März 1941) Ab 1. März einheitliche Ordenverpackung Kennzeichen der Fabrikanten, *Uniformen Markt*, Ausgabe 6, Jahrgang 8, März 1, 1941.

UM (November 1942) *Uniformen Markt*, Ausgabe 22, November 15, 1942.

Umland, A. (n.d.) Otto Dix. Skat Players (Die Skatspieler) (later titled Card-Playing War Cripples [Kartenspielende Kriegskrüppel]). 1920 MoMA, www.moma.org/audio/playlist/198/2632. Accessed: 08/02/2021

Urbach, K. (2019) What is the Evidence that King Edward VIII was a Nazi Sympathiser? Open University Open Learn blog, August 30, 2019, www.open.edu/openlearn/history-the-arts/history/world-history/former-king-wanted-england-bombed-and-anglo-german-alliance-archives-reveal?active-tab=review-tab&all-comment=1. Accessed: 07/12/2020

Usborne, C. (2011) Social Body, Racial Body, Woman's Body. Discourses, Policies, Practices from Wilhelmine to Nazi Germany, 1912–1945. *Historical Social Research/Historische Sozialforschung* 36 (2): 140–161.

Usborne, S. (2013) Exclusive: David Irving – The Hate that Dare not Speak its Name, *Independent*, August 30, 2013, www.independent.co.uk/news/uk/home-news/exclusive-david-irving-hate-dare-not-speak-its-name-8792411.html? Accessed: 05/12/2020

USHMM (n.d.) Donate to the Collections, United States Holocaust Memorial Museum, https://www.ushmm.org/collections/the-museums-collections/donate-to-the-collections. Accessed: 09/10/2021

USHMM (1992) Nuremberg stadium, swastika blown up by US troops, United States Holocaust Memorial Museum, Accession Number: 1992.259.1, RG Number: RG-60.0465, Film ID: 406, 'US and Russian troops meet at the Elbe. Shows General Emil Reinhardt. Shows scenes of Nazi headquarters in Nuremberg. Huge US flag is raised over the giant swastika atop the Nuremberg stadium. Swastika is later blown up – the actual explosion and flying debris.' https://collections.ushmm.org/search/catalog/irn1001506. Accessed: 09/03/2021

USHMM (2020) Berchtesgaden at liberation – 101st Airborne Division; Goering's art collection moved, https://collections.ushmm.org/search/catalog/irn1001777. Accessed: 24/03/2021

VB (Dezember 1920) *Völkischer Beobachter* (Munich), Dezember 19, 1920, Ed.109, Jahrgang 34. All editions viewed on location at the Institut für Zeitgeschichte in Munich, available on microfilm.

VB (Dezember 1922) *Völkischer Beobachter* (Munich), Dezember 23, 1922, Ed102/3, Jahrgang 36.

VB (März 1925) *Völkischer Beobachter* (Munich), März 6, 1925, Ed1, Jahrgang 38.

VB (November 1925) *Völkischer Beobachter* (Munich), November 29–30, 1925, Ed.207, Jahrgang 38.

VB (Dezember 1938) *Völkischer Beobachter* (Munich), Dezember 25, 1938.3 million mothers qualify for medal.

Veblen, T. (1899) *The Theory of the Leisure Class*. New York City: Dover Publications.

Volz, H. (1936) *Daten der Geschichte der NSDAP*. Berlin: Verlag A.G. Plötz.

Vorländer, H. (1986) NS-Volkswohlfahrt und Winterhilfswerk des deutschen Volkes. *Vierteljahrshefte für Zeitgeschichte* 34 (3): 341–380.

Vorländer, H. (1988) *Die NSV; Darstellung und Dokumentation einer Nationalsozialistischen Organisation*. Boppard am Rhein: Oldenbourg Verlag.

Wachsmann, N. (1999) After Goldhagen. Recent Work on the Genesis of Nazi Genocide. *Journal of Contemporary History* 34 (3): 477–487.

Wagner, K. (2019) In Good Condition: The Discourse of Patina as seen in Interactions between Experts and Laymen in the Antiques Trade. *Culture Unbound Journal of Current Cultural Research* 11 (2): 252–274.

Waldron, J. (1985) What is Private Property? *Oxford Journal of Legal Studies* 5 (3): 313–349.

Wallendorf, M., Arnould, E. G. (1988) My Favorite Things: A Cross-Cultural Inquiry into Object Attachment, Possessiveness, and Social Linkage. *Journal of Consumer Research* 14 (4): 531–547.

Wang, P., Wen, Y. (2012) Speculative Bubbles and Financial Crises. *American Economic Journal: Macroeconomics* 4 (3): 184–221.

Ward, J. W. (1958) The Meaning of Lindbergh's Flight. *American Quarterly* 10 (1): 3–16.

Weber, T. (2010) *Hitler's First War: Adolf Hitler, the Men of the List Regiment, and the First World War.* Oxford: Oxford University Press.

Weinberg, G. L. (2014) *World War II: A Very Short Introduction.* Oxford: Oxford University Press. Kindle.

Weingartner, J. J. (1968) Sepp Dietrich, Heinrich Himmler, and the Leibstandarte SS Adolf Hitler, 1933–1938. *Central European History* 1 (3): 264–284.

Weingartner, J. J. (1991) Otto Skorzeny and the Laws of War. *Journal of Military History* 55 (2): 207–224.

Weinreb, A. (2012) For the Hungry have No Past nor Do they Belong to a Political Party: Debates Over German Hunger after World War II. *Central European History* 45 (1): 50–78.

Weitze, H. (2018) Telephone Interview between Helmut Weitze and Michael Hughes, transcript held by both participants. Permission granted.

Weitze, H. (2020) Treuedienst-Ehrenzeichen. Six medals in total listed, all in their box, prices: Two at 55 Euro, 1 at 65, 1 at 70 and two at 80, www.weitze.net/militaria/94/Treudienst_Ehrenzeichen_2_Stufe_fuer_25_Jahre__375694.html. Accessed: 14/11/2020

Wellington, D. C., Gallo, J. C. (1981) The March of the Toy Soldier: The Market for a Collectible. *Journal of Cultural Economics* 5 (1): 69–75.

Wells, A. (2020) *She's a Rainbow: The Extraordinary Life of Anita Pallenberg.* London: Omnibus Press.

Wernitz, F., Simons, V. (2013) *Das Eiserne Kreuz 1813–1870–1914: Geschichte und Bedeutung einer Auszeichnung.* Vienna: Verlag Militaria GmbH.

Wette, W. (2006) *The Wehrmacht: History, Myth, Reality.* Cambridge: Harvard University Press. Kindle.

Weyrather, I. (1993) *Muttertag und Mutterkreuz. Der Kult um die deutsche Mutter im Nationalsozialismus.* Frankfurt: Fischer.

Wheeler-Bennett, J. W. (1953) *The Nemesis of Power: The German Army in Politics 1918–1945.* New York: St. Martin's Press.

Whelan, D. B. (1941) The Role of Plastics in the Field of Entomology. *Journal of the Kansas Entomological Society* 14 (3): 73–84.

Whelpton, P. K. (1935) Why the Large Rise in the German Birth-Rate? *American Journal of Sociology* 41 (3): 299–313.

Whine, M. (2008) Expanding Holocaust Denial and Legislation Against it. *Jewish Political Studies Review* 20 (1/2): 57–77.

White, M. (2007) The Grosz Case: Paranoia, Self-Hatred and Anti-Semitism. *Oxford Art Journal* 30 (3): 431–453.

White, M. (2015) Queen's Nazi Salute a Sign of Ignorance Shared by Many in Scary Times, *Guardian,* July 20, 2015, www.theguardian.com/uk-news/2015/jul/20/queens-nazi-salute-a-sign-of-ignorance-shared-by-many-in-scary-times. Accessed: 07/12/2020

White, R. B. (1992) Crowds, Audiences, and the Liturgy of Irreverence: Rethinking the Altamont Concert as Participatory Theatre. *Studies in Popular Culture* 14 (2): 37–49.

Whiteley, C. H. (1960) On Defining Moral. *Analysis* 20 (6): 141–144.

Whitman, A. (1970) Lindbergh Says U. S. Lost' World War II, *New York Times,* August 30, 1970, www.nytimes.com/1970/08/30/archives/lindbergh-says-us-lost-world-war-ii-lindbergh-contending-that-he.html. Accessed: 10/08/2018

Whitman, A. (1974) Daring Lindbergh Attained the Unattainable with Historic Flight Across Atlantic, *New York Times*, August 27, 1974, www.nytimes.com/1974/08/27/archives/daring-lindbergh-attained-the-unattainable-with-historic-flight.html. Accessed: 10/08/2018

WHWF (1938) *Der Führer und das Winterhilfswerk. Bild und Dokumente.* Photos by Heinrich Hoffmann, 1938. Booklet produced to raise funds for the WHW.

WHWHB (1939) *Handbuch der WHW Abzeichen, 1939.* München: Carl Gerber Verlag.

WHWO (n.d.) *Des Führers Kampf im Osten* 1 (*Winterhilfswerk*). Wartime booklet produced to raise funds for the WHW.

Wilcock, A. (2018) Telephone Interview between Adam Wilcock and Michael Hughes, transcript held by both participants. Permission granted.

Wildt, M., Selwyn, P. (1996) The Invented and the Real: Historiographical Notes on Schindler's List. *History Workshop Journal* 41: 240–249.

Wilkes, J. (2020) The Swastika: Why was a Sanskrit Symbol Used by Hitler and the Nazis? *History Extra*, June 1, 2020, www.historyextra.com/period/second-world-war/how-why-sanskrit-symbol-become-nazi-swastika-svastika/. Accessed: 24/03/2021

Wilkinson, J. D. (1985) Remembering World War II: The Perspective of the Losers. *American Scholar* 54 (3): 329–343.

Willett, D. (2010) *The Pinch: How the Baby Boomers Took their Children's Future – And Why They Should Give it Back.* London: Atlantic Books.

Williams, M. (1979) German Imperialism and Austria, 1938. *Journal of Contemporary History* 14 (1): 139–153.

Williamson, G. (2017) Telephone Interview between Gordon Williamson and Michael Hughes, transcript held by both participants. Permission granted.

Wilson, H. R. Jr. (2011) *A Career Diplomat: The Third Chapter, the Third Reich.* Montana: Literary Licensing LLC.

Wilson, J. (2012) *The Nazis' Nuremberg Rallies.* Barnsley: Pen and Sword.

Wilson, P. H. (2009) *Europe's Tragedy: A New History of the Thirty Years War.* London: Penguin.

Wilson, W. J. (1994) *Festivals and the Third Reich.* Ph.D., McMaster University, Ontario, Canada.

Wimberly, L. C. (1949) Lindbergh: Shamefully Treated Man. *Prairie Schooner* 23 (4): 408–411.

Winner, L. (1986) Do Artefacts Have Politics? *Daedalus* 109 (1): 121–136.

Wirths, U. (2009) *Das Winterhilfswerk im Gau Mainfranken: Ein Instrument des NS-Regimes.* Saarbrücken: VDM Verlag, Dr. Müller.

Wistrich, R. (2001) *Who's Who in Nazi Germany,* Third Edition. Abingdon: Routledge.

Wittman, R. K., Kinney, D. (2016) *The Devil's Diary: Alfred Rosenberg and the Stolen Secrets of the Third Reich.* London: Harper Collins.

Wittmann, T. (2019) Thomas Wittmann. WAM Special Presentation #1, Thomas Wittmann Militaria, YouTube channel, www.youtube.com/user/WittmannMilitaria/videos. Accessed: 12/02/2020

Woeste, V. S. (2004) Insecure Equality: Louis Marshall, Henry Ford, and the Problem of Defamatory Antisemitism, 1920–1929. *Journal of American History* 91 (3): 877–905.

Woeste, V. S., Gratien, C. (2019) Henry Ford's War on Jews, *OTTOMAN History Podcast*, May 24, 2019, www.ottomanhistorypodcast.com/2019/05/ford.html. Accessed: 12/02/2021

Woods, M. (2010) *German Medal Makers and their Marks 1813–1957, Second Edition.* Self-published.

Woods, M. (2011) *German Medal Makers Volume II.* Self-published.

Woods, M. (2013) *German Maker Marks, combined edition.* Self-published.

Woodward, I. (2007) *Understanding Material Culture.* London: Sage.

Woodward, S. (2013) *Material Culture: Anthropology.* Oxford University Press, https://doi.org/10.1093/OBO/9780199766567-0085

Work, R. E. (1946) Last Days in Hitler's Air Raid Shelter. *Public Opinion Quarterly* 10 (4): 565–581.

WPI. World Bank GDP deflator (base year varies by country), Data, https://data.world-bank.org/indicator/NY.GDP.DEFL.ZS. Accessed: 08/01/2020

Wren, D. A. (2013) James D. Mooney and General Motors' Multinational Operations, 1922–1940. *Business History Review* 87 (3): 515–543.

Wright, H. (1944) The Legality of the Annexation of Austria by Germany. *American Journal of International Law* 38 (4): 621–635.

Wulff, E. (1940) *Das Winterhilfswerk des deutschen Volkes*. Berlin: Franz Eher Nachf. GmbH.

Wunderlich, F. (1935) Women's Work in Germany. *Social Research* 2 (3): 310–336.

Wunderlich, F. (1937) Education in Nazi Germany. *Social Research* 4 (3): 347–360.

Wyllie, J. (2019) *Nazi Wives: The Women at the Top of Hitler's Germany*. Cheltenham: History Press.

Yad Vashem (n.d.) Jewish Forced Laborers in the Minsk Ghetto, January 1943, *Yad Vashem*, www.yadvashem.org/holocaust/this-month/january/1943.html. Accessed: 26/02/2021

Yamane, D. (2017) The Sociology of U.S. Gun Culture. *Sociology Compass* 11, https://doi.org/10.1111/soc4.12497

Young, J. W. (2005) From LTI to LQI: Victor Klemperer on Totalitarian Language. *German Studies Review* 28 (1): 45–64.

Young, K. (2011) The Aesthetics of Elegance and Extravagance in Science and Art. *Narrative* 19 (2): 149–170.

Yourman, J. (1939) Propaganda Techniques within Nazi Germany. *Journal of Educational Sociology* 13 (3): 148–163.

Yow, V. R. (1997) Do I like Them Too Much? Effects of the Oral History Interview on the Interviewer and Vice-Versa. *Oral History Review* 24 (1): 55–79.

Zegenhagen, E. (2007) The Holy Desire to Serve the Poor and Tortured Fatherland: German Women Motor Pilots of the Inter-War Era and their Political Mission. *German Studies Review* 30 (3): 579–596.

Zeller, T. (2010) *Driving Germany: The Landscape of the German Autobahn, 1930–1970*. Oxford and New York: Berghahn Books.

Ziegler, H. F. (1986) Fight Against the Empty Cradle: Nazi Pronatal Policies and the SS-Führerkorps. *Historical Social Research/Historische Sozialforschung* 38: 25–40.

Zille, H. (June 1916) Heinrich (1858–1929) The Iron Cross (Das eiserne Kreuz), plate (folio 17) from the periodical 'Der Bildermann', vol. 1, no. 8 (1916), 1916. Scala Archives-Images, www.scalarchives.com/web/dettaglio_immagine.asp?idImmagine=0162332&posizione=1&inCarrello=False&numImmagini=9&. Accessed: 08/02/2021

Zobenica, J. (2007) Rock, Death on the Installment Plan. Growing Old Gracefully the Rolling Stones Way. *American Scholar* 76 (4): 117–121.

ZS89. Fragebogen über Adolf Hitler und Beantwortung des Fragebogens über Adolf Hitler, Archiv des Instituts für Zeitgeschichte München, electronic resource, www.ifz-muenchen.de/archiv/zs/zs-0089.pdf. Accessed: 03/04/2019

Zumbro, D. S. (2006) *Battle for the Ruhr: The German Army's Final Defeat in the West*. Lawrence: University Press of Kansas.

Index

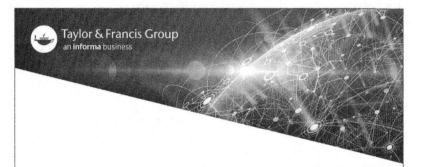

Made in the USA
Monee, IL
01 October 2023

43808211R00144